Penguin Education

Organizational Growth and Development

Edited by W. H. Starbuck

Penguin Modern Management Readings

General Editor
D. S. Pugh

Organizational Growth and Development

Selected Readings

Edited by W. H. Starbuck

Penguin Books

Penguin Books Ltd, Harmondsworth,
Middlesex, England
Penguin Books Inc., 7110 Ambassador Road,
Baltimore, Md 21207, U.S.A.
Penguin Books Australia Ltd,
Ringwood, Victoria, Australia

First published 1971
This selection copyright © W. H. Starbuck, 1971
Introduction and notes copyright © W. H. Starbuck, 1971

Made and printed in Great Britain by
Hazell Watson & Viney Ltd
Set in Monotype Times

Contents

Part One Introduction

This book discusses organizational changes over time: changes in organizational size due to explicit managerial strategies or to environmental events, and changes in organizational methods and structures due to maturation and technological evolution. Understanding such changes is essential both to students of organizational behaviour and to managers enmeshed in daily decision-making.

Students of organizations must be sensitive to the probable uniqueness of the particular organizations they study. They must attend to those variables which are most likely to indicate organizational uniqueness, and then by locating particular organizations in a spectrum of alternative forms and circumstances, project how their findings might differ in other organizations or in the same organizations at other times. The studies in this book seek to identify variables having the greatest impact on organizational development and structure and hence the variables most worthy of attention when distinguishing among organizations. The studies also provide a basis for tracing modal patterns of change. In addition, the book attempts to serve students by communicating the texture of research in progress and by presenting a range of research methodologies.

Managers must be able to predict the consequences of their policies – for example, how the desire to increase one's own salary may change the ratio of administrative to productive employees; they must anticipate what new managerial problems will confront them as results of organizational development in the future; and at least when they change jobs, they must distinguish aspects of their experience which transfer and generalize from those which do not. Most managers will take special interest in the sections of this book dealing with motives for growth, because these project long-run organizational consequences of individual preferences and managerial premises. Such consequences are not always evident to actors on the scene, and research studies like those discussed here help one to see one's own organization objectively. In addition, the sections on organizational development over time help one identify probable future changes in the way one's organization functions, and the sections on administrative structure give perspective on how technology, time, and organizational size change the way management operates.

The volume is designed to take advantage of 'Organizational growth and development' – a long survey article which was originally written for the *Handbook of Organizations*. The article organizes and summarizes nearly all of the research published before 1965, and it includes representative quotations from most of the essential writings. As a result, it affords an integrated and efficient introduction to an extensive and diverse body of literature.

The survey article defines growth and development – at least for the purposes of this volume – and suggests why organizations grow and how they change with size and age. But the article does not incorporate work completed since 1964, and it does not convey any image of how research is done. The latter is extremely important, for without it one cannot appreciate the uncertainty attending the results of individual studies, the slow pace of research progress, the dependence of conclusions upon assumptions, or the significance of methodological details. Therefore, the last two-thirds of the book is devoted to eight recent research studies and a bibliography of post-1964 publications.

The eight studies are chosen to represent the three main research methodologies – case studies, surveys and mathematical models[1] – to represent the interests of economists, political scientists, psychologists and sociologists,

1. Laboratory experiments have not, so far, dealt with organizations of relevant sizes and ages.

and to represent each of the four major subjects discussed in the survey article. Within these constraints, they are the best studies found.

The striking characteristic of the eight studies – in contrast to work done earlier – is their concern with an organization's relation to its environment. Only one of the studies describes itself as adopting an open-systems model, but only one of the studies could be said to treat an organization as a self-determining, isolated system. This pattern is not, I think, idiosyncratic to the studies chosen, but is typical of a general trend in organizational research toward perceiving an organization as a societal subsystem. Either we are tiring of traditional questions, or we are declaring that traditional questions cannot be answered within traditional frameworks.

1 W. H. Starbuck

Organizational Growth and Development

Excerpts from W. H. Starbuck, 'Organizational growth and development', *Handbook of Organizations,* Rand McNally, 1965, pp. 451–2, 453–522.

Introduction[1]

In this chapter, growth is defined as change in an organization's size when size is measured by the organization's membership or employment; development is defined as change in an organization's age. The chapter considers why and how organizations grow and develop, and examines some effects of growth and development on organizational structure and behavior.

A considerable number of words have been written about growth and development. The bibliography includes over two hundred items. The primary responsibility of the chapter is taken to be a review of this literature. In some cases it is a critical review, but it is also an optimistic review. Some of the work is interesting, imaginative, empirically based, and methodologically sound. There have been attempts to construct theories and to predict. There is even a certain amount of consistency among studies.

One reason growth and development evoke research interest is the possibility of uncovering characteristics which apply generally to organizations of various kinds. Organizational size and age can be measured in comparable units (men and years) in business firms, military units, social movements, government agencies, and hospitals. Whether a four-year-old business firm having eighty employees can be compared with a government agency of the same size and age is a moot point, but the spirit which pervades much of the research in this area is that such comparisons are valid and are likely to yield significant generalizations.

1. A. C. Cooper, C. W. Howe, J. G. March, V. L. Smith, and especially R. E. Walton have contributed helpful criticism and comment.

Certainly, if one believes that common denominators exist among large classes of organizations – and there is no point in studying organizations if one does not believe this – then comparing organizations in terms of straightforward independent variables like size and age is a sensible start. Further, as will be seen, such comparisons often produce significant correlations.

However, discovering that certain organizational characteristics correlate with size and age still leaves one a long way from being able to attribute these characteristics to size and age. The reason is that one can usually find other factors which might explain the observed differences and which correlate with size and age. Thomas's study of welfare bureaus provides an example. Thomas (1959) found that large bureaus differ from small ones, but then observed that:

Most of our results may be accounted for plausibly in terms of the population and the community setting of the county in which the welfare bureau was located. The size of the bureau itself depends largely upon the population size of a county . . . (p. 35).

The association of the workers' personal characteristics with the size of welfare bureaus probably indicates that the pool of potential employees in the counties with large populations differs from those with small populations. Available information indicates that some of the contrasts between workers in the smaller and the larger bureaus parallel those between rural residents and residents of cities (p. 30).

Unfortunately, not all researchers are as conscientious as Thomas. Correlations are often reported as if correlation were proof of causal relation; the reader is left with the problem of posing alternative hypotheses and searching for corroborative studies. It is hoped that this chapter will make the latter task less difficult, by providing a pool of information about research which has been done and by indicating areas in which further research is especially needed.

Inevitably, there will be studies which are overlooked. In particular, the author is most familiar with recent work, published in the United States and having direct relevance for business firms. Beyond those biases, three ground rules are observed in selecting studies for review:

Firstly, stress is placed on descriptive studies and theories in preference to normative ones. The author is not indifferent to the importance of being able to state how an organization *should* grow and develop, but such statements must be based on an understanding of how organizations *do* grow and develop. Current knowledge is so rudimentary that prescriptive statements seem premature.

Secondly, stress is placed on the formal aspects of organizations rather than on the informal aspects. One characteristic which distinguishes organizations from other collections of people is a commitment to achieving members' goals by means of an explicit and stable structure of task allocations, roles, and responsibilities. Mobs and informal social groups are not organizations. Social and service clubs, like Rotary and Kiwanis, are organizations only part of the time. The study of organizations should not and cannot ignore interactions and behaviors which depart from structural norms. However, so long as one is concerned with organizational behavior and not with social behavior in general, he should emphasize the modes of behavior in which organizations specialize.

Thirdly, experimental studies of small groups are ignored. These studies have produced interesting data which have potential relevance to the study of organizations. But the experimental studies concern groups of three to twelve people over short periods of time, and the concern here is with groups of 30 to 12,000 people over long periods of time. The fallacies of extrapolating from one case to the other are self-evident. One can look to the small-group studies for hypotheses, but these hypotheses must be verified independently in large, persistent organizations. In the absence of such verifying data, the results of the small-group studies are as likely to mislead as to contribute to understanding. This objection would not apply to all applications of small-group data to organizations, but, in this instance, potential differences due to group size and time span are of special significance.

The core of the chapter is divided into four parts. [. . .]

Motives for growth

Growth is not spontaneous. It is the consequence of decisions: decisions to hire or to not fire, decisions to increase output in response to demand, decisions to stimulate demand, and so forth. The relationships between specific decisions and ultimate expansion of the organization may be tenuous, but expansion is necessarily dependent upon some decisions and the actions which follow them. These decisions are, in turn, functions of the goals pursued by the members of the organization. Thus organizational growth can take place only if increased size is positively related to the achievement of the organization's goals and/or the goals of individual members of the organization (McGuire, 1963, p. 3).

This is not intended to suggest that organizations and their members are rational – making decisions which achieve optimal states. Organizational growth may work contrary to the interests of some, or even most, members of the organization. Growth may not be the best way to achieve the goals which it is intended to achieve. On occasion, growth may be a transient exploration of the organization's environment which, proving to be unrewarding, is subsequently abandoned. The point is simply that the growth of an organization is not a random event.

Increased organizational size may be a goal itself, in at least two senses. Firstly, growth may be valued as a symbol of achievement. Growth is often difficult to accomplish, both because of intraorganizational stresses which must be met and because of external forces which must be overcome. The obstacles to growth are recognized by society, and the members of an organization which has successfully expanded are awarded prestige and admiration, particularly those members who are seen as being instrumental in the expansion process. These people also receive internal rewards in the form of feelings of success and pride in their achievement (Nourse, 1944). Secondly, increased size may be an operational goal, a bench mark for progress. The size of an organization has characteristics which recommend it as an operational goal: it is easily measured and it is easy to talk about. However, the use of size as an operational goal does not necessarily mean that increases in size *per se* are valued. There is usually an implicit assumption that size is correlated with the attainment of goals which have more basic relevance to the organization's purpose or which are more immediately of interest to some sub-unit of the organizational membership.

By far the most widely accepted approach to growth has been that growth is either a means of attaining other goals or a side effect of such attainment, rather than an end in itself. Systematic empirical evidence about the goals of organizational members is not available, but a number of goals have been put forth in the literature which, with varying degrees of face validity, are related to growth. Ten of them are enumerated here.

Organizational self-realization

To quote Katona:

... the going concern is commonly viewed as a living entity of itself. Self-realization of a business concern represents, then, a topic worth further study. A corporation is not conceived by its executives simply as an organization making money, or making automobiles. It has to carry out its functions, complete the tasks taken up, and expand to justify itself. It has been recently pointed out that here may be found one of the most important explanations of the fact that our large corporations are continuously expanding in diverse fields that are often foreign to their original activity. Small investments may be made, for instance, in order to study the use of by-products or waste products. When some progress has been achieved, the task once begun is pushed toward completion. There is a drive, perhaps even a compulsion to follow through after one has begun (1951, pp. 205–6).

The round table discussion by nineteen executives which Newman and Logan (1955) have summarized came up with five reasons for growth, all of which have the same aesthetic flavor as 'self-realization'. The five reasons were:

1. Customers demand complete service, e.g. plants in all parts of the country.
2. Firms attempt to master their technologies, i.e. become vertically integrated.
3. Research laboratories develop products outside the existing product lines.
4. In order to attract retail dealers, a manufacturer must offer a complete product line, e.g. all kinds of major appliances.
5. If firms do not expand, they contract; they cannot stand still.

In his review of *Parkinson's Law,* Galbraith (1957) observed that bureaucratic expansion may be due to narrow specialization and a 'tendency to create organizations on the basis not of need but of plausibility'. One wonders if this is not Katona's 'self-realization' viewed cynically.

Adventure and risk

Organizations may grow because executives like to gamble on new activities. Gordon (1945, pp. 310–11) found that some executives are motivated by 'the urge for adventure and for "playing the game" for its own sake', and one executive whom the author has interviewed compared the desire to risk capital and effort on expansion with the compulsion which draws people to Nevada. This could explain why an entrepreneur who has reached a point of satiation with respect to wealth and power might continue to be aggressive. Within specific organizations it may be a powerful motive, but it would be surprising to find that compulsive pursuit of risk was a major factor in most organizations.

More pervasive, perhaps, than the pursuit of adventure and risk is the avoidance of boredom. Blau (1955) has reported a study of civil servants in which the boredom of personnel who had mastered their tasks favored change, and Argyris (1957) has reviewed numerous studies with similar implications.

Prestige, power and job security

In addition to the prestige which follows from the achievement of successful expansion, there is prestige attached to the supervision of a large number of people. The more people an executive supervises the greater his prestige. Ordinarily this supervisory prestige is accompanied by some degree of power over the persons supervised, autonomy, and job security – subordinates being more expendable than their superiors. Gordon (1945, pp. 305–7, 311) stated that the urge for personal power and prestige is one of the most important non-financial motives of businessmen, and Hanson (1961) found that superintendents of large hospitals have more responsibility relative to the hospital boards than superintendents of small hospitals (see also Copeland, 1955).

Parkinson is probably the best-known exponent of the prestige–power–security motive complex. He wrote: 'An official wants to multiply subordinates, not rivals, and went on to explain:

... we must picture a civil servant called A, who finds himself over-worked. Whether this overwork is real or imaginary is immaterial, but we should observe, in passing, that A's sensation, or illusion, might easily result from his own decreasing energy: a normal symptom of middle age. For this real or imagined overwork there are, broadly speaking, three possible remedies. He may resign; he may ask to halve the work with a colleague called B; he may demand the assistance of two subordinates, to be called C and D. There is probably no instance in history, however, of A choosing any but the third alternative. By resignation he would lose his pension rights. By having B appointed, on his own level in the hierarchy, he would merely bring in a rival for promotion to W's vacancy when W, at long last, retires. So A would rather have C and D, junior men, below him. They will add to his consequence and, by dividing the work into two categories, as between C and D, he will have the merit of being the only man who compre-hends them both. .... When C complains in turn of being overworked, as he certainly will, A will, with the concurrence of C, advise the appointment of two assistants to help C. But he can then avert internal friction only by advising the appointment of two more assistants to help D, whose position is much the same. With this recruitment of E, F, G and H the promotion of A is now practically certain (1957, pp. 4–5).

Executive salaries

Roberts (1956, 1959) has shown that the salary of the highest paid executive in a business firm was independent of the profit earned by the firm, and increased exponentially with the firm's sales volume. This implies that, to increase his salary, the top executive should be more interested in increasing the size of his firm than its profits. Simon then argued that Roberts's result was not adequately explained by economic variables alone. He constructed a model which yielded Roberts's empirical result on the basis of three mechanisms: '(a) economic determination, through com-petition, of the salaries at the lowest executive levels where new employees are hired from outside the organization; (b) social determination of a norm for the "steepness" of organizational hierarchies (usually called the span of control); and (c) social determination of a norm for the ratio of an executive's salary to the salaries of his immediate subordinates' (1957b, pp. 34–5). Simon pointed out that his model explained, not only the salary of the top executive, but also the numbers of executives at various salary levels throughout the hierarchy.

Williamson has taken the logical next step; he constructed a model of the firm in which management expanded itself in order to increase its salaries:

Modern organization theory treats the firm as a coalition (managers, workers, stockholders, suppliers, customers) whose members have conflicting demands that must be reconciled if the firm is to survive. In the sense that each group in the coalition is essential to the firm's continuing existence, the members of the coalition can be regarded as 'equals'. This view, however, is more useful when observing the firm in a period of crisis than when survival is not a pressing problem. Where survival is not a current concern, restoring a hierarchy among the members based on the attention they give to the firm's operations may lead to more productive insights. From this viewpoint, management emerges as the chief member of the coalition; its role as the coordinating and initiating agent as well as its preferred access to information permit it quite naturally to assume this primacy position. Thus, although in certain circumstances it may be necessary to give special attention to shifts in demands made by members of the coalition other than managers, under 'normal' conditions it may be entirely appropriate to take the demands of the other members (for wages, profits, product, and so forth) as *given* and leave to the discretion of the management the operation of the firm in some best sense. . . .

In the present model, managers are held to operate the firm so as to maximize a utility function that has as principal components (1) salaries (2) staff (3) discretionary spending for investments, and (4) management slack absorbed as cost. This utility function is maximized subject to the condition that reported profits be greater than or equal to minimum profits demanded (1963, pp. 240–1).

Williamson defined 'management slack absorbed as cost' as the difference between 'reported profits' and 'actual profits'. How he would measure this quantity is not exactly clear.

Also see Gordon (1945, pp. 271–304), McGuire, Chiu and Elbing (1962), and Patton (1961).

Profit

Profit maximization has been the catch-all motive in the traditional economic theory of the firm. Although this theory has been the center of considerable controversy, the notion that profit is a motive is not in question (Cyert and March, 1963; Penrose, 1959). As any perusal of business journals will confirm, business executives are concerned about profit and, other things being equal, prefer more profit to less.

One characteristic of the theory of the firm which was until recently controversial is the implication that profit is the *only* motive for business behavior. However, this issue seems to be nearly dead, there being no doubt that business executives pursue other motives in addition to profit. It is common now to find the theory of the firm stated in terms of utility maximization rather than profit maximization. For further discussion of business motives other than profit see Berle and Means (1932), Cyert and March (1963), Gordon (1945), Hickman and Kuhn (1956), Katona (1951), Papandreou (1952), and White (1960).

Even if nonprofit goals like prestige, security and so forth are ignored one would expect to find the firm pursuing goals other than profit as defined by the financial statements. One reason is that accounting procedures often do not tell the complete story, either because there are distortions inherent in the accounting 'conventions' or because financial statements reflect the past more than the future. Most business managers try to look beyond the financial statements when they set goals and evaluate performance and, in the process, may give functional autonomy to some of the components of profit like overhead cost or advertising expense. Cyert and March have cited six operational goals as being adequate to explain 'most price, output, and general sales strategy decisions'. They are the volume of production, the stability of production, the minimum finished inventory level, sales volume, market share, and profit (1963, pp. 40–3). Dent's (1959) study suggested a somewhat different list which is discussed below.

Profit, even if it is broadly defined as the difference between the value of services performed and the cost of these services, is not a major factor in the operation of non-profit organizations like governmental agencies, hospitals, trade associations, or labor unions. One suspects that, over long periods of time and in informal ways, the 'profit' from such organizations does get measured in the sense that organizations which cost more than they are worth disappear. Churches are a good example; they depend on voluntary contributions and fail if the 'take' is not sufficient. One theory of trade associations is that they operate on demand and cost variables outside the control of individual members, maximizing total profit to the industry. However, this may be a tautological statement. The 'revenues' of such organizations, the value of the services which they perform, are only partially measurable and not in units which can be directly compared with cost: the number of licenses issued, the number of students in school, the average score of a student body on scholastic achievement tests, the number of complaints received. So attempts to construct all-inclusive measures of net yield are not very fruitful.

Cost

The major components of profit, revenue and cost may become operational goals in their own rights. Of course, it makes no sense to minimize cost in the strictest sense. The cheapest organization is the organization which does not exist. But it may be useful to minimize cost per unit of output subject to constraints, e.g. the requirement that the organization exist.

There are at least three *a priori* reasons for believing that cost per unit decreases as the size of the organization increases, assuming that output also increases. Firstly, there is the advantage in being able to hire and fully utilize specialists. Florence called this 'The Principle of Multiples':

Specialized men and machines must . . . be used in their speciality up to capacity. But the capacity of different specialists and special machines is very different and they are indivisible; thus arises a difficult problem in 'balancing' production . . . the smaller the scale of operation (or production) and the fewer the total number of persons dividing and diffusing their labor, the less chance there is of all of them being fully made use of as specialists. . . .

Secondly, there is Florence's 'Principle of Bulk Transactions':

. . . the total monetary, physical or psychological costs of dealing in large quantities are sometimes no greater (and in any case less than proportionately greater) than the costs of dealing in small quantities; and hence the cost *per unit* becomes smaller with large quantities.

And thirdly, there is the statistical phenomenon which Florence labelled 'The Principle of Massed (or Pooled) Reserves';

. . . the greater the number of similar items involved the more likely are deviations to cancel out and leave the actual average results nearer to the expected results (1953, pp. 50–2).

That is, increasing the size of an organization increases the sample sizes of random variables and therefore decreases the variances of the means. Whitin and Peston (1954) have given representative bibliographic references on this topic; references with direct relevance to employment, are Feller (1950), Holt *et al.* (1960), and Starbuck (1966).

Increasing employment does not necessarily decrease cost. Given a level of output, the relation between cost and employment may be U-shaped. Having too few employees leads to heavy dependence on overtime and a higher per man-hour wage; having too many employees wastes manhours. Thus, an optimum level of employment, for a given level of output, may exist. Holt *et al.* (1960) have employed operations research techniques in an attempt to specify this optimum.

Suppose that the organization's level of output increases. Then the optimum level of employment will also increase (though less than proportionately, if Florence's 'Principles' are taken seriously). In this sense, output and organizational size are locked together, and cost per unit can be considered a function of size.[2] The nature of the functional relationship between cost

2. The statistical problems involved in this inference are not negligible. Steindl (1952) found that output per man increased with increasing sales volume and decreased with increasing employment. He said: 'It can easily be demonstrated that if output per worker is uncorrelated with size . . . when size is measured by output, then a negative – and spurious – correlation must obtain . . . where size is measured according to number of workers. Similarly, it can be demonstrated that if output per worker is positively correlated with size (by output), it must, under certain conditions, be negatively correlated with size (by employment)' (pp. 18–19).

and size is not clear. It is probable that *very* small firms achieve definite cost savings by expansion; several studies support this view. However, excepting that one point, the most balanced conclusion seems to be Osborn's: 'Considering all the uncertainties involved, the unsatisfactory conclusion is reached that we do not know very much about relative efficiency (as measured by cost) in relation to size' (1951, p. 92). Cost per unit may decrease uniformly as size increases, or it may decrease and then increase again as organizations get very large. For general reviews of the empirical evidence see Blair (1948), Florence (1953), Kaplan (1948), Osborn (1951), and Staehle (1942). Specific studies of interest are Bain (1954; 1956), Crum (1939), Johnston (1955–6), Melman (1956), Rostas (1948), TNEC (1941), and Woodruff and Alexander (1958).

In a sense, the actual relationship between cost per unit and size is irrelevant. The relationship which is relevant is the relationship which executives believe holds true. Eiteman and Guthrie (1952) asked business executives what they thought their products' average cost curves looked like. Their results are given in abbreviated form in Table 1.

Table 1

Cost per unit as output increases	Number of firms	Number of products
Uniform increase	0	1
Short decrease, then a long increase	1	5
Long decrease, then a short increase	130	438
Uniform decrease	203	638
Totals	334	1082

Source: Eiteman and Guthrie (1952).

The case for increasing cost in the largest organizations rests on three notions. The first is that managerial problems become inordinately complex as size increases, producing progressively higher production costs. This proposition is examined below, under the heading of administrative structure and growth. The second is that large organizations produce so much output that the demand for their products is nearly saturated, and each additional unit of output requires progressively higher selling expense. This is probably a serious consideration for some organizations and not for others. The third reason for hypothesizing a cost increase in large organizations is membership apathy. Baumgartel and Sobol (1959), Indik (1963), Revans (1958), Talacchi (1960). TAST (1953; 1957), Warner and Low (1947), and Worthy (1950a; 1950b) have concluded that morale is lower in large organizations, and Gouldner (1954) has pointed out that the use of standard operating procedures, which one associates with large bureaucracies, allows employees to perform near minimum acceptable levels. On the other hand, Newman and Logan (1955) concluded that 'size by itself is not a major determinant of morale' and Sills (1957) reported that 'the factor of size has not led to membership apathy' in an organization which was decentralized and managed participatively. In general, the research on morale has concentrated on measures of employee satisfaction without bothering to trace the consequences of satisfaction or dissatisfaction for costs, profits and productivity. March and Simon (1958) have observed that satisfaction and productivity are not perfectly correlated, and it is conceivable that low morale is a symptom of high efficiency. Further, researchers have often been sloppy about discriminating between the sizes of primary work groups and the sizes of whole organizations. The author's reading of the literature suggests that morale is more dependent on the size, structure and management of the work group than on organizational size.

When cost is considered as a function of output, output is measured as a rate of production, e.g. units of output per annum. However, cost also depends upon cumulative output, the number of units produced since production began (Alchian, 1959). This relationship between cost and cumulative output is a matter of learning. Difficulties in the production process are corrected; workers waste fewer motions; errors are made less frequently; opportunities are perceived to reduce costs and to increase productivity.

Alchian (1949), Asher (1956), Hirsch (1952), Nadler and Smith (1963), and Searle and Gody (1945) have all found that the man-hours required to produce an additional unit of product decreased significantly with each successive unit produced. This learning curve was approximated fairly well by an exponential function. Specifically, man-hours per unit equalled

$$Az^{-B}$$

where A and B are positive parameters and z is cumulative output. One interesting characteristic of these studies is that despite the variations in products studied – from cargo ships to machine tools – B was consistently close to 0·3. (The range of confidence limits was from 0·25 to 0·36.)

Cooper and Charnes (1954) have utilized learning to explain some apparently illogical data. They observed that empirical studies of total cost (C) as a function of output (Y) often yielded a negative coefficient A for the cubic function

$$C = A \cdot Y^3 + B \cdot Y^2 + D \cdot Y + E.$$

For A to be negative was illogical, because it implied that total cost would decrease for a large enough output. Cooper and Charnes argued that $A < 0$ was consistent with a model of the type

$$C = C^*(Y, T) + f(t, T) \cdot g(Y),$$

where t is time; $C^*(Y, T)$ is a long-run cost function which can be achieved at some future date T; $f(t, T)$ is a learning curve which expresses a decrease in cost as time passes; and $g(Y)$ is a perceptual function which expresses an increase in the number of opportunities to economize as output increases.

Revenue

Griffin observed that 'increased volume, to a considerable extent, is an end in itself, not merely (as it is often described) a means of increasing profit rates' (1949, p. 158). However, it is Baumol who has placed the strongest emphasis on revenue as a goal. He has taken the view that oligopolists' behavior can best be described as revenue maximization subject to a minimum profit constraint:

The evidence for my hypothesis that sales volume ranks ahead of profits as the main object of the oligopolists' concern, is again highly impressionistic; but I believe it is quite strong. Surely it is a common experience that, when one asks an executive, 'How's business?', he will answer that his *sales* have been increasing (or decreasing), and talk about his profit only as an afterthought, if at all. And I am told the requirements for acceptance to membership in the Young Presidents Organization (an honorific society) are that the applicant be under 40 years of age and president of a company whose annual volume is over a million dollars. Presumably it makes no difference if this firm is in imminent danger of bankruptcy.

Nor is this failure to emphasize profits a pure rationalization or a mere matter of careless phrasing. Almost every time I have come across a case of conflict between profits and sales the businessmen with whom I worked left little doubt as to where their hearts lay. It is not unusual to find a profitable firm, in which some segment of its sales can be shown to be highly unprofitable. For example, I have encountered several firms who were losing money on their sales in markets quite distant from the plant where local competition forced the product price down to a level which did not cover transportation costs. Another case was that of a watch distributor whose sales to small retailers in sparsely settled districts were so few and far between that the salesmen's wages were not made up by the total revenues which they brought in. When such a case is pointed out to management, it is usually quite reluctant to abandon its unprofitable markets. Businessmen may consider seriously proposals which promise to put these sales on a profitable basis. There may be some hope for the adoption of a suggestion that new plant be built nearer the market to which current transportation costs are too high, or that watch salesmen be transferred to markets with greater sales potential and a mail order selling system be substituted for direct selling in little populated regions. But a program which explicitly proposes any cut in sales volume, whatever the profit considerations, is likely to meet a cold reception. In many cases firms do finally perform the radical surgery involved in cutting out an unprofitable line or territory but this usually occurs after much heart-searching and delay (Baumol, 1959, pp. 47–8; see also Baumol, 1962).

As with cost, it is theoretically possible for very large organizations to be less well off than medium-sized organizations, for revenue to decrease as output and employment increase. The logic behind this view is: demand depends on price; in order to sell more output one must reduce price, especially if the level of output is extremely high; and therefore revenue, being the product

W. H. Starbuck 25

of output and price, may decrease when output increases (Boulding, 1953).

Price reductions and increasing sales expense both imply that organizational growth is constrained to a single market, or narrow range of markets; neither is a serious restriction on organizational size unless the specific organization chooses, or is forced, to confine itself. Most organizations can find plenty of opportunities for expansion in terms of new products and new markets, and a point of diminishing returns with respect to any single product or market is not binding. Chandler observed in his study of large corporations – particularly DuPont, General Motors, Standard Oil of New Jersey, and Sears, Roebuck – that 'As the market became more saturated and the opportunities to cut costs through more rational techniques lessened, enterprises began to search for other markets or to develop other businesses that might profitably employ some of their partially utilized resources or even make a more profitable application of those still being fully employed' (1962, p. 391).

Further, the idea that price decreases can decrease total revenue assumes that all customers buy at the same price. Many organizations which are chartered to narrow product lines, like the Community Chest and United Fund organizations, can discriminate among customers – collecting larger amounts from some and smaller amounts from others. Likert has studied the effectiveness of Leagues of Women Voters as a function of League size, defining effectiveness primarily in terms of revenue-oriented variables.[3] His data indicated that total effectiveness was a monotone increasing function of size; although effectiveness per member declined in large Leagues, there was no indication that total effectiveness ever decreased (1961, pp. 153–60). One of

3. To quote Likert: 'Each of the twenty-nine women who served as judges was asked to rate the effectiveness of each of the sample Leagues, League effectiveness was defined as the extent to which a League accomplishes its goals. The general criteria used by the League in evaluating local Leagues' strengths and weaknesses were presented to guide the raters in their evaluations: size of League in relation to the size of the community, growth of League, the quality and quantity of League materials, the level of participation of members, their interest in League activities and their knowledge about them, success in fund-raising campaigns, and effect on their community' (1961, p. 141).

Likert's interesting findings was that participation by central members (leaders) increased with League size, and participation by peripheral members decreased. It suggests that the relationships between group size and participation in small groups, obtained by Bales (1951), Coleman (1960), and Stephan and Mishler (1952), may generalize to voluntary organizations.

Monopolistic power

There has been a traditional argument that one reason for increasing organizational size is the power, as a monopolist or monopsonist, which the large organization has. This argument has less force today than it did fifty years ago so far as business organizations are concerned. In the first place, antitrust legislation and enforcement have made the exercise of monopoly power a dangerous pastime; unless the monopolist stays within fairly tight legal constraints, he gets into trouble. In the second place, empirical studies of pricing behavior suggest that monopolists probably do not take full advantage of the power which they might exercise – because they are uncertain what the limits of their power are and because they shy away from the social stigmas attached to using it (Cyert and March, 1963; Hall and Hitch, 1939). And in the third place, there are too many large firms. Monopolistic power depends more upon relative than absolute size; if a monopolist's customers and suppliers are as large as he is, he may have no power at all[4] (Galbraith, 1952).

Not that size and power are unrelated, and not that executives don't appreciate power. Increased power is unquestionably a consideration in a great many decisions to expand, but it is doubtful that Katona was right when he said: 'There are indications that the prevailing institutional set up has greatly enhanced the desire for power among American businessmen' (1951, pp. 204–5).

Large size and monopoly power can be fatal to business firms. The American economic system depends upon competition among many firms to keep prices low and efficiency high. However, beginning about 1870, many industries came to be dominated

4. But he may have compatibility. Warner and Low (1947) noted that large firms had the advantage of sizes and structures which matched the sizes and structures of their suppliers and customers.

by single firms or coalitions of firms. Among the industries so controlled were coal, gunpowder, lead, matches, meat packing, petroleum, sugar, tobacco, and whiskey. The tactics used by the monopolists to obtain their power, and the exploitation which they practiced after they obtained it, eventually led to disciplinary action by the society at large. The Sherman Act was enacted in 1890, the Clayton and Federal Trade Commission Acts in 1914, and the Robinson–Patman Act in 1936; each was more severe and explicit than the preceding ones. For a readable, if argumentative, review of the criticisms of big business, see Glover (1954). A good, technically detailed review of antitrust legislation and enforcement is Wilcox (1955).

The basic pattern of antitrust legislation and enforcement has been to penalize offensive acts and practices by monopolists, like deception, collusion, discriminatory pricing, restraint of trade, and 'unfair' competition, not to penalize monopoly itself. But it is recognized by the courts that size and power are inseparable. In his 1945 opinion in the case of the *United States v Aluminum Company of America*, Judge Learned Hand held that a distinction between latent power and exercised power is 'purely formal; it would be valid only so long as the monopoly remained wholly inert; it would disappear as soon as the monopoly began to operate; for when it did – that is, as soon as it began to sell at all – it must sell at some price and the only price at which it could sell is a price which it itself fixed. Thereafter the power and its exercise must needs coalesce' (1945, pp. 427–8, or 1948, p. 57682).

One of the most interesting facets of the Alcoa case is Hand's implication that, for a monopoly, growth itself is offensive. The company had argued that it had not actively sought a monopolistic position through merger, conspiracy, or other overt acts, but that it had simply expanded in response to demand for its products. Hand replied:

It was not inevitable that it should always anticipate increases in the demand for ingot and be prepared to supply them. Nothing compelled it to keep doubling and redoubling its capacity before others entered the field. It insists that it has never excluded competitors; but we can think of no more effective exclusion than progressively to embrace each new opportunity as it opened, and to face every newcomer with new capacity already geared into a great organization, having the advantage of experience, trade connections and the elite of personnel (1945, p. 431, or 1948, p. 57685).

There are two types of nonprofit organizations where the desire for monopolistic power is most evident as a legitimate and size-dependent motive. One is the labor union: the more members, the greater the union's bargaining power. The other is the military defense organization: the more troops, planes, and ships, the greater the retaliatory power. However, there is certainly no consensus that power increases uniformly with the size of the organization. It has frequently been argued that union bargaining power rests with specific subgroups of employees, and that once these employees have been organized, there is no advantage, and there may be disadvantages, in organizing other employees. One of the major recent changes in United States defense policy was the recognition that 'massive retaliation' was an inflexible strategy inappropriate to current problems.

Stability

It has already been pointed out that large organizations tend to face more stable environments than do small ones, the basis for this statement being that the variance of a sample mean decreases as the sample size increases. This has some obvious consequences for capacity-oriented costs like warehouse space; it has even more immediate consequences for the peace of mind of organizational members. In a large organization, the daily variations in the number of orders to be processed, the number of letters to be typed, the number of man-hours needed for production, and so forth, are proportionately less than the corresponding variations in a smaller organization. This means that work loads are more balanced and scheduling is less painful.

The desire for stability may be one of the most important considerations in choosing the direction for growth. Diversification of activity is often sought in expansion, whether by business firms or by military organizations. Katona, for one, observed that:

We engage in business in order to make money, which we desire, need, and plan to use for the sake of other more basic or more immediate satisfactions. In certain circumstances, the means may become ends, and we may strive for profits for the sake of profits themselves. More generally, however, the desire for security implies striving for continuous, regular income rather than short-period maximum profits (1951, p. 204).

Stability is one goal which has the active support of nonownership elements in the organizational coalition. Stable employment is sought by labor unions in collective bargaining, and stable usage of raw materials may be made explicit in contracts with suppliers. Of course, the desire for stability of production rates and work loads does not necessarily imply expansion, but it does tend to block contraction and to focus expansion choices on contracyclical alternatives.

That large organizations actually achieved more stable levels of income was shown by Osborn's study. He found that:

... both the rate of profit for the income corporations and the rate of loss suffered by no-income corporations vary inversely with size. Which size group is the most profitable depends to a considerable degree on the proportion of corporations of each size which falls in the no-income category. During the shift from depression to prosperity the percentage of unprofitable small firms decreases the most rapidly and the most profitable over-all size likewise declines (1951, p. 93).

In short, large corporations were the most profitable size group during a depression and the least profitable during a boom; small corporations were the most profitable size group during a boom and the least profitable during a depression.

Survival

The importance of survival to an organization cannot be overstated – at least as a logical necessity. An organization may not maximize profit or minimize cost. It may not impart prestige, power, and security to its members. It may not do many things. But one thing which it must do, if it is to be an organization at all, is survive. As Barnard pointed out:

Thus in every organization there is a quadruple economy: (1) physical energies and materials contributed by members and derived by its work upon the environment, and expended on the environment and given to its members; (2) the individual economy; (3) the social utilities related to the social environment; and (4) a complex and comprehensive economy of the organization under which both material services and social services are contributed by members and material things are secured from the environment, and material is given to the environment and material and social satisfactions to the members. The only measure of this economy is the survival of the organization. If it grows it is clearly efficient, if it is contracting it is doubtfully efficient, and it may in the end prove to have been during the period of contraction inefficient (1938, pp. 251–2).

Stigler (1950) has made a similar argument. Others who have emphasized survival goals are Drucker (1958), Maurer (1955), Ross (1947), and Rothschild (1947).

The problem with a statement like Barnard's is that it implies that survival is difficult, and hence that a relatively high level of efficiency is required. This can soon lead to a 'survival of the fittest' point of view (Alchian, 1950; Enke, 1951; Winter, 1960). The fact of the matter is that nearly all organizations, nearly all of the time, find survival easy.[5]

When survival is at stake, large size can be advantageous. It is no accident that business failures occur primarily among small firms (Steindl, 1945). An error which, though embarrassing, might be taken in stride by a large organization can wipe out the resources of a small one (Whitin and Peston, 1954). It may be that large organizations are no more profitable than small ones because they absorb potential profits as 'slack' and thus have cushions against the shock of adverse events (Williamson, 1963). One might conjecture that small firms take commensurately small risks and that the average loss incurred is proportionate to organizational size. Two points discount this. First, the average loss is not important. What does matter is a very large loss at the tail of the probability distribution – like the statistician who drowned in a creek, the average depth of which was only six inches. Second, small organizations are on the whole neither more omniscient nor more wise than large ones in choosing low risk alternatives, and may very well be less so. The author's

5. Rothschild (1947) is one who would probably disagree. He has argued that 'price wars, while tending to occur infrequently are a dominant feature of the oligopolistic situation' and therefore 'the desire for *secure* profits' is 'of a similar order of magnitude as the desire for maximum profits'.

experiences with small businessmen indicate that this is a source of concern to them.

One reason survival correlates with size is the relation between size and age. Large organizations tend to be older than small ones; they have accumulated more knowledge about the problems they are likely to encounter and they employ more experienced personnel. Woodruff and Alexander reported in their study of small firms that 'new and untried management was a worse longevity risk than management with a number of years experience behind it. The median age of the unsuccessful management was about three years, whereas the median age of successful management was about 22 years' (1958, p. 117). Crum concluded that there was 'overwhelming support for the conclusions that young corporations are more liable to suffer deficits than older corporations, and that the age structure of corporations showing a deficit is younger – more steeply J-shaped – than that of corporations showing a profit' (1953, p. 105; also see Mansfield, 1962a). Crum also found that 'the chance of death generally declines with increasing age until age reaches more than fifty-five years' (p. 135).

When an organization gets into trouble, it often needs support from outside sources. Large organizations find such support easier to obtain than do small ones. This applies in particular to capital. Small firms often find borrowing difficult even when they are profitable (Steindl, 1945; Woodruff and Alexander, 1958). When the going gets rough, the capital markets may disappear altogether (Heller, 1951). One advantage of the large organization in this case, is its age and prominence. Established relationships with financial sources tend to hold up; long-time customers may try to pay their bills quickly and even in advance; long-time suppliers may extend credit.

For further references on the abilities of small firms and large firms to survive see BBRP (1958, pp. 39–41, 67–8, 105–8).

Goals and results

Ten goals have been reviewed, the attainment of which may depend upon organizational growth or may produce growth as a by-product. Three of these goals are rooted in the self-interest of individual organizational members: the urge for adventure and risk, the desire for prestige, power and job security, and the desire for higher executive salaries. Three are rooted in the problems and aesthetics of managing an organization: the desires for a stable environment, for 'organizational self-realization', and for organizational survival. And four are rooted in organizational purpose and effectiveness: the desires for high profit and revenue, for low cost, and for monopolistic power.

It would be nice to say that some of these goals are characteristic of certain types of organizations and not of others, and that some goals are more highly correlated with growth than others. Certainly such relationships must exist. But the existing data are fragmentary, and the methodological problems to overcome are great. In particular:

1. Rarely do people speak frankly of their motives. One is more likely to get answers about mores than motives. Suppose a minister is asked why he wants his church to grow. The probability that he would say 'large churches pay more than small ones' is practically zero, whatever his personal feelings.

2. It is difficult to compare the goals of diverse organizations. Voluntary organizations often talk as if members' time is a free good, and as if the number of members is a measure of revenue. Yet these organizations decide not to undertake activities because 'they would take more time than they're worth', and leaders debate whether to appoint committees 'to get more people involved' or to do tasks themselves 'to get them done'. Do such discussions suggest that members' time has a cost? Is a profit goal implicit?

3. To distinguish cause from effect is all but impossible. The relation between goals and results is polluted by environmental effects, and people learn to pursue realistic goals. If growth is difficult, the organization will tend to pursue goals which are not growth-oriented; if growth is easy, the organization will learn to pursue goals which are growth-oriented. What one observes are the learned goals. Do these goals produce growth, or does growth produce these goals?

Dent (1959) has attempted to relate the goals of business firms to organizational size, structure, and growth rate. His study raised questions rather than answered them, but it indicated interesting relationships exist. Dent interviewed 145 chief executives, asking the question: 'What are the aims of top management in your company?' Responses were taken at face value, and there was no probing. The frequencies with which various responses occurred are tabulated in Table 2.

Table 2

| Goal | Per cent of executives mentioning goal | |
	First goal mentioned	Among first three goals mentioned
To make money or profit	36	52
To provide a good product; to provide a public service	21	39
To provide employee welfare	5	39
To grow	12	17
To run or develop the organization	9	14
To meet or stay ahead of the competition	5	13
To be efficient	4	12
To pay dividends to the stockholders	1	9
Miscellaneous	7	18

Source: Dent (1959).

The second response (to provide a good product; to provide a public service) is ambiguous. This may have been an expression of altruism. Dent seems to have interpreted it that way, and Gordon (1945) has reported that some executives have altruistic motives. However, the author suspects that it was a statement about sales strategy, about product quality as a subgoal which contributed to high revenue. For example, bankers sometimes say they are in business to provide a public service; in the author's experience, this is an injunction about the best frame of mind for dealing with customers and not a reason for being in business.

Dent correlated the goal responses with three variables: (a) total employment (b) the proportion of employment which is white-collar, professional or supervisory, and (c) the average per cent increase per annum in total employment. Significant correlations were:

1. The proportion replying 'to provide a good product, etc.' increased with total employment. (Actually, this proportion was essentially the same for all size categories greater than 100. The correlation arose because firms with less than 100 employees gave this response much less frequently than did firms with more than 100 employees.)

2. Among unionized firms, the proportion replying 'to provide employee welfare' increased with total employment.

3. Among nonunionized firms, the proportion replying 'to provide employee welfare' decreased as total employment increased.

4. The proportion replying 'to make money or profit' decreased as the per cent white-collar increased.

5. The proportion replying 'to grow' increased with the per cent white-collar. (There is a possibility that the decrease in 'to make money' responses and the increase in 'to grow' responses represented a transfer; Dent did not report the proportion giving both responses, but the sum of the proportion replying 'to make money' and the proportion replying 'to grow' was virtually constant. If the proportion giving one response or the other was constant, it would imply that the two responses were partially synonymous.)

6. The proportion replying 'to provide a good product, etc.' increased with growth rate.

7. The proportion replying 'to meet or stay ahead of the competition' increased with growth rate.

8. The proportion replying 'to run or develop the organization' decreased as the growth rate increased.

9. In an unpublished reanalysis of these data, Dent found that the proportion replying 'to make money or profit' decreased as the growth rate increased.

There are several interpretations for each of Dent's findings, but without further data, the best one can do is conjecture.

Consider for example the eighth finding: executives in organizations which were growing slowly or declining in size said they were trying to run or develop the organization; executives in organizations which were growing rapidly did not mention this problem. One possibility is that slow-growing organizations had organizational problems and the stockholders had chosen executives who were conscious of these problems. This would imply that Dent was interviewing remedial managements and reported a consequence, not a cause, of slow growth. A second possibility is that slow-growing organizations had outlived their economic usefulness and had found no new functions, and that their executives were trying to hold the organizations together as long as possible, perhaps in the hope of finding new functions. Again this would imply that the goal responses were a consequence of slow growth, but the word 'develop' would have to be taken with a grain of salt. A third possibility is that organizational development was not an effective goal to pursue from the viewpoint of growth, that when executives devoted their attention to developing the organization, they were diverting energy from the more effective goals 'to meet or stay ahead of the competition' and 'to provide a good product, etc.'. This would imply that the goal 'to run or develop the organization' was a cause of slow growth. A fourth possibility is that organization-conscious executives were poor managers, more concerned with methods than results. Woodward concluded from case studies of three firms: 'The "organization conscious" firms tended to draw on the concepts of management theory, irrespective of how appropriate they were to the technical situation.'

The most successful firms are thus likely to be the 'organization conscious' firms, in which formal organization is appropriate to the technical situation. Next would come the less 'organization conscious' firms, where informal organization mainly determines the pattern of relationships. The least successful firms are likely to be the 'organization conscious' firms, where formal organization is inappropriate and deviates from informal organization (1958, pp. 38–9).

This interpretation implies that the goal responses were correlated with a cause of slow growth.

Other conjectures can be made about the nature of Dent's

eighth finding, and the number of conjectures which can be advanced about all nine findings is enormous. One can even ask why certain relationships were *not* statistically significant. But there is no need for conjectures. What is needed is data, collected in systematic and sophisticated ways, which will untangle the basic causal relationships.[6]

Adaptation and growth

The presence of growth-oriented motives in an organization is necessary but by no means sufficient to produce expansion. For such motives to find expression in the organization's behavior strategies, they must overcome other motives which imply decreasing organizational size or maintaining the *status quo*. The behavior patterns ultimately adopted are chosen by processes of bargaining and problem-solving in which motives which tend to promote growth conflict with motives which tend to inhibit growth.

The organization's environment stages this conflict and decides its resolution. The environment supplies the human raw materials and determines their mores and aspirations, their standards for the conduct of conflict, their attitudes toward authority. Even taking the organizational personnel and their goals as given, it is the environment which determines whether these goals can best be satisfied by expansion or by contraction. For instance, the relationship between profit and employment depends on the firm's demand and cost curves, which in turn depend on the characteristics of the consuming population, the actions of competing firms, the available range of technologies, the alternative markets for raw materials, and so forth.

Clearly, environmental effects are ubiquitous. One can say

6. A mail survey conducted by McGuire (1963, pp. 93–5) vaguely supported some of Dent's findings. McGuire asked firms to rank order five goals; '. . . the ranking in order of preference was as follows: (1) profits, (2) increase sales, (3) increase or maintain market share, (4) survival, (5) growth . . .'. McGuire also endeavored to relate goal preferences to the firms' growth rates. However, he considered only the firms' first choices and, predictably, obtained uniform distributions. Since Dent's firms averaged over two responses each, one would expect firms to have difficulty describing their goals in terms of a single criterion, and hence expect a rank ordering over the first two or three goals to be unstable.

nothing about an organization without also saying something about its environment, and an organization's need for satisfactory interactive relationships with its environment is inescapable. For example, to attempt a thorough review of the effects of geographic location on organizations would require another chapter at least as long as this one. To the reader who is interested in this literature, the author suggests as starting points BBRP (1958), Blau and Scott (1962, pp. 199–206), Form and Miller (1960), and RERP (1959).

This section is concerned with some specific determinants of an organization's ability to establish effective and viable relationships with its environment, to adapt. Adaptation is an obvious precondition for survival, and survival is an obvious precondition for growth. Thus, one could legitimately discuss all the aspects of organizations which are relevant to adaptation, which means, in turn, that one could legitimately discuss everything which has been written about organizations. To keep the subject within bounds three constraints are imposed, all of which are ambiguous. First, the discussion is confined to topics which relate fairly directly to organizational size and age. Second, only long-run, gross adaptation is considered. And third, the focus is on the organization itself rather than its environment. As Dill has pointed out:

... our best strategy for analyzing the environment is probably not to try to understand it as a collection of systems and organizations external to the one we are studying. We seldom have enough data to do an adequate job of this. Instead, we can view the environment as it affects the organization which we are studying. We treat the environment as information which becomes available to the organization or to which the organization, via search activity, may get access (1962, p. 96).

The effectiveness of behavior strategies

The structure of the organization's environment determines the relative effectiveness of different behavior strategies in producing growth. Therefore, most organizations, at one time or another, attempt to manipulate their environments to make them more munificent. They advertise the advantages of new products, train new employees, and undertake research to improve manufacturing techniques (W. H. Brown, 1957). Some, like the Communist

Party in Russia, have sufficient power and longevity to begin the education of an entire nation in values that are consistent with increased organizational size and power.

Large organizations have more leverage over their environments than small organizations do. As Carter and Williams put it: 'A big firm can change or ignore its environment; a small firm depends much more on the existence of facilities provided by others' (1959, p. 69).

At least in the innovation of manufacturing techniques, one can document the leverage of large firms. Their advantage begins with their spending for research and development. They spend more per employee; they employ more scientists; they spend more per scientist; and they give each scientist more technical assistance. See NSF (Tables 5, A-28 and A-27, 1956, 1959) and for corresponding British data, DSIR (1958). A series of papers by Mansfield traced the results of this spending: the amount spent on research and development correlated with the number of innovations introduced (1962c). Hence, 'the length of time a firm waits before using a new technique tends to be inversely related to its size', and in fact, 'as a firm's size increases, the length of time it waits tends to decrease at an increasing rate' (Mansfield, 1963b, pp. 291–2; see also Phillips, 1956). Apparently, size of firm was the only organizational characteristic which did correlate with readiness to innovate; the firm's growth rate, its profitability, its liquidity, and the age of its president were not significantly correlated with innovation (Mansfield, 1963b. The profitability of the specific innovation also correlated with the firm's readiness to adopt it). A lack of correlation between innovation and growth rate only applied to the firm's growth rate *before* the innovation was introduced; although innovators had the same growth rates as noninnovators before they innovated, they grew faster than noninnovators *after* they innovated (Mansfield, 1962a). However, the relation between innovation and firm size was not consistent. No class of firms was always the innovating group (Mansfield, 1963b). There seemed to be differences among industries in the innovative leadership shown by the large firms. In particular, there would probably have been less innovation in the petroleum and bituminous coal industries if the large firms were broken up into smaller firms, but there would probably have been more innovation in the steel industry if the large firms were broken up into smaller ones (Mansfield, 1962b).

However, very few organizations can make major changes in their environments, especially in the short run. The impact of the individual organization is pretty severely limited – sometimes by law, as in the case of antitrust legislation – sometimes by the existence of powerful competing organizations, as in the case of the American political parties – sometimes by ignorance, as in the case of technological innovation – and always by the massive inertia of the existing structure, as in the case of the Russian Communist Party. This does not mean there is no advantage in taking an aggressive position toward the environment. Aggressive organizations probably gain a comparative advantage over nonaggressive organizations, as Mansfield's studies have shown, but the overriding problem of all organizations is to adjust to and to exploit resources which already exist.

In principle, an organization can expand as long as it can discover strategies which, by satisfying some needs of society, elicit additional resources. Thus, an organization which can continuously generate new, successful strategies can expand indefinitely.

That is in principle; in fact it does not happen.

For one thing, most organizations specialize. They voluntarily adhere to a limited range of behavior strategies: the production of a specific class of products, the employment of a specific type of employee, the utilization of a specific production methodology. One reason for specialization is that it provides a certain degree of insulation from the actions of competing organizations (Chamberlin, 1950). For instance, American Motors was able to survive and prosper by differentiating its product from those of General Motors and Ford and cultivating a consumer subgroup, whereas Studebaker–Packard persisted in trying to compete directly with the large firms, and failed. Another reason for specialization is that the organization is chartered with specific and limited goals, examples being the Townsend Movement and the Woman's Christian Temperance Union. These limited-charter organizations often break out of their original molds and pursue what Blau called a 'succession of organizational goals'. 'The attainment of organizational objectives generates a strain toward finding new objectives. To provide incentives for its existence, an organization has to adopt new goals as its old ones are realized' (1955, p. 195).

But it should not be assumed that all organizations which might benefit from a change in the bases for their specialization actually change. McGuire has reported:

There is considerably more product rigidity among manufacturing firms than many business scholars would expect. Respondents to the investigation into the growth patterns of 270 manufacturing firms were asked if substantial changes had been made in their products in the past (1950–59). Only 8·5 per cent indicated a major change in product line; 91·5 per cent noted that they had not made such alterations. To a certain extent, this rigidity may have been caused by investment in specialized equipment and plant, so that many firms could not change products except at a cost which they considered too exorbitant. In other instances, it seemed evident that businessmen simply lacked imagination to change and remained with their one product even though sales were declining, even when it appeared reasonable for them to change at least to similar but more profitable products (1963, p. 54).

Still another reason for specialization is the organization's desire for internal consistency as a basis for coordination and control. Communication among members requires a common language and comparable experiences; superiors must be able to understand their subordinates' problems; normal managerial succession must not alter goals and operating procedures drastically. Probably the importance of this restriction on organizational diversity becomes increasingly apparent as the organization grows. Haire (1959) has stressed the 'centrifugal' effects of large size, and Clark (1956) and Kaufman (1960) have discussed some divisive effects of geographic dispersion. One can find 'organizations' which do not display internal consistency and which do not attempt to coordinate the activities of their subunits, but the word 'organization' is misapplied in such cases.

It may be that specialization in terms of a methodology is less restrictive to growth than specialization in terms of an end product. Chandler concluded that 'the enterprises whose resources were the most transferable remained those whose men and equipment came to handle a range of technology rather than a set of end products' (1962, p. 391). And Sills stated:

In the final analysis, however, the most compelling reason for predicting that the Foundation will in the future make a successful adjustment to the achievement of its major goal is that the organization has in fact *already* been transformed, in large part by its Volunteers, into something other than a special purpose association. . . . Since the Foundation includes among its Volunteers so many who are able to conceptualize their involvement in terms of its ultimate implications (for themselves, or for society as a whole), rather than only in terms of a limited, pragmatic goal, it has already become an organization as deeply committed to its mode of operation as to its current purposes. In a word, it is an organization which is as committed to a means as it is to an end (1957, p. 270).

Nevertheless, there are serious logical problems in this proposition and it may be vacuous. First, changes in methodology are pervasive and gradual. There may be a tendency to overestimate the stability of methodologies and to classify observed changes as 'improvements'. If methodologies actually change as extensively and rapidly as products, one can hardly say that the organization specializes on either. Second, whenever an organization changes its behavior, some characteristics of its behavior do not change, and in that sense every organization specializes on something. There may be a tendency to classify the constants in behavior as methods and the variables as products, particularly when correlating the changes in behavior with environmental changes, because one thinks of products as falling on the 'boundary' between the organization and its environment and thinks of methodologies as being 'internal' to the organization.

Another constraint on an organization's ability to generate new, successful strategies is imposed by conflict among strategies. When an organization adopts one class of strategies, it automatically makes the adoption of other strategies difficult or impossible. This situation is evident in the case of political party platforms. When the Republican party espoused emancipation, its subsequent adoption of a states' rights view became something less than credible to southern voters. Another example was reported by Selznick (1949). TVA's adoption of the 'grass-roots theory' brought the support of local agencies and helped TVA achieve local success, but the policy also incurred the disaffection of the Department of Agriculture, which blocked TVA's expansion outside the Tennessee Valley.

Selznick's book stressed the importance of cooptation of the environment, including coalitions with other organizations, as a behavior strategy. Judiciously applied, cooptation can greatly strengthen an organization's power to survive and grow. Elling and Halebsky (1961) have reported that 'voluntary' hospitals, allied with their communities' social structures, increased the value of their facilities greatly, whereas the value of facilities in governmentally supported hospitals tended to remain constant. Blankenship and Elling (1962) have noted that it was important for voluntary hospitals to form alliances with powerful, upper-class members of the community rather than middle- or lower-class members; they predicted the demise of two hospitals which did not coopt their community's power structure. One reason cooptation can be helpful is that it usually constitutes one half of an exchange. The organization gives up some of its autonomy and receives in return influence in the decisions of other organizations (e.g. protection from certain kinds of competition) or access to environmental resources (e.g. financing, technical expertise). But, as Selznick's book also stressed, cooptation can be expensive. One of the hospitals in the Blankenship and Elling study, which did coopt its community's structure, nearly coopted itself out of existence. Its board decided there were too many hospitals in the community.

Gordon (1945, pp. 116–267) treated the firm as a coalition of executives, directors, stockholders, suppliers, creditors, labor unions, customers, government agencies, consultants, and competitors. Also see Cyert and March (1963, ch. 3), Levine and White (1961), Perrow (1961a), and Stocking and Mueller (1957).

Attitudes towards change

The attitudes of organizational members toward change are crucial in the growth process. They are crucial because growth is a type of organizational change, and they are crucial because a growing organization must adjust to environmental change. In fact, it can be argued that growth depends upon the organization's ability to exploit opportunities created by environmental change.

Organizational rigidity is rooted in the inducements–contributions balance of the organization. The members of an organization receive inducements in exchange for their contributions. These inducements include salaries and statuses, the pleasures of performing tasks in particular and familiar ways and of associating with particular and familiar people, and the satisfactions of contributing to the accomplishment of specific organizational goals and of molding organizational goals to personal value systems. Changes in the organization often imply new salaries, statuses, personnel, methods and goals, so the members of the organizations who stand to lose by such changes resist them. Even changes which would have insignificant long-run effects can incur opposition because of their transient effects (Coch and French, 1948).

Resistance to change can take several forms. The resisters can reduce their contributions to match the reduced inducements offered them. Not infrequently, such reactions are anticipated and viewed as desirable consequences by those who initiate the changes; more frequently, however, reduced contributions are unanticipated and/or considered undesirable. Very often, the resisters withdraw from the organization; relatively small reductions in inducements can trigger withdrawal if the affected individual perceives more favorable alternatives outside the organization. Obviously, withdrawals offer the organization opportunities to enlist new members whose value systems are more compatible with the altered organizational structure, but new members must become acclimated, learn their tasks and develop satisfactory personal relationships with other members of the organization, and the time required for this absorption delays organizational growth. Finally, the resisters may take direct action to persuade or force the organization to adhere to its existing structure. When backed by sufficient power, direct resistance can be quite effective, as 'featherbedding' on the railroads testifies.

For normative discussions of change, see Bennis (1963), Bennis, Benne and Chin (1961), Gardner and Moore (1955), Ginzberg and Reilley (1957), Likert (1961), Lippitt, Watson and Westley (1958), and Mann and Neff (1961). For discussion of the ways in which labor unions resist technological changes see Slichter, Healy and Livernash (1960, ch. 12).

Overt changes in inducements offered by the organization are not the only way that the inducements–contributions balance can be upset. Many organizational inducements derive their values from the environment, and as the environment changes, these inducements can lose their values. The obvious example is the effect of inflation on wages, but other inducements are equally susceptible. Diamond (1958) has reported the case of an organization which dissolved into a society, because intraorganizational statuses were the only inducements offered and, over a period of time, extraorganizational wealth and social mobility deprived intraorganizational statuses of their value.

Organizational rigidity can be overemphasized. In fact, gradual change may be welcomed. McClelland and his associates (1953) have postulated that small displacements from the 'adaptation level' trigger positive affect and that large displacements trigger negative affect. This suggests that an optimum rate of change may exist, that organizational members will be unhappy in an overly stable environment as well as in an overly variable one (see Fiske and Maddi, 1961, especially chs. 2, 5, 9, 13). A study by Blau was consistent with this notion. He found that the 'progressive ideology' of organizational members and boredom after mastering tasks both favored change, and he drew the conclusion that 'opposition to change in the organization, while apparently indicating perfect accommodation to existing conditions, is actually the result of insufficient adaptation to them. Newcomers, who had not yet become adapted, as well as less competent officials, felt threatened by change . . .' (1955, p. 197). Sofer (1961) has claimed that once an organization has changed, it is inclined to 'overvalue novelty' and to undervalue 'much that was functional and positive in their past'. This suggests that an organization's concept of the optimum rate of change is a function of past experience, and that acceleration of change, not velocity of change, is the central variable which evokes resistance.

Bonini has constructed a hypothetical, computerized model of the firm and examined the effects of assorted changes in the organization's structure and environment. He found that the variability of the organization's environment had very significant impacts on the organization's behavior. Firms in highly variable environments had lower costs and prices and higher sales, inventories and profits than firms in stable environments.

It is fairly easy to postulate how large amounts of variability could lead, in the real world, to a more profitable firm. Firms existing in a relatively stable environment may be sluggish in adjusting to new conditions, in taking advantage of market opportunities, and in introducing new technology. On the other hand, firms which live in a constantly fluctuating world may be quicker to sense and seize opportunities. The existence of large downswings sometimes forces the firm to seek these opportunities or perish (1963, pp. 135–6).

The proposition that young organizations are less rigid than old organizations has had wide acceptance. If frequency of repetition is evidence for its truth, it is true. Certainly the proposition sounds plausible. Young organizations are probably more accustomed to change, and the members of young organizations may not yet be enamored of specific goals, activities and social relationships. On the other hand, Cohen concluded from a series of experiments with small-group communication networks:

The most important results of the six studies viewed as a unit is that problem-solving groups selectively modify their methods of dealing with a task by calling upon their preceding experiences. Transfer of training and rationality are general concepts useful in understanding these results.

Transfer of training, though used in many contexts, refers basically to the human tendency to respond to new and separate events by placing them in classes for which attitudes and procedures already exist. Previous experience is essential: if a group knows only one way of performing a task, it tends to continue this practice without critical examination. Inexperienced groups, therefore, generally have no tradition of critical evaluation, view change as disruptive and unrewarding, find sharing the responsibility for modifying the environment difficult, lack knowledge concerning alternative methods, and have no means of perceiving some other procedure as more efficient than the one which they are using (1961, pp. 124, 128).

Systematic evidence about the relation between organizational age and flexibility is virtually nonexistent. Mansfield's studies of the relations between firm size and readiness to innovate were mentioned above. These indicated that large (old?) firms were likely to be the first to try new production techniques. However, Mansfield has published another study with different implications. Considering the speed with which firms took full advantage of innovations, he found that 'small firms, once they begin, are at least as quick to substitute new techniques for old as their larger rivals' (1963a, p. 358). Mansfield's work concerned the adoption of new production techniques. Discussions of *product* innovation have been inclined to the opinion, which Nelson (1959) summarized, that 'established firms, even progressive established firms, are usually backward about radically new inventions'. Nelson cited case studies by Bright (1949), G. Brown (1957), Maclaurin (1949; 1950), and Schlaifer and Heron (1950) as examples, and similar anecdotes were reported by Jewkes, Sawers and Stillerman (1959, pp. 189–90). However, it is not clear that small firms are less myopic than large ones when it comes to 'radically new inventions'. Carter and Williams (1959, pp. 63–5) have suggested that small firms may have advantages over large firms when it comes to unradical new inventions. Thompson and Bates (1957) and Wilson (1963) have posed hypotheses relating organizational structure and innovation.

The author suspects that one difference between young organizations and old ones is in the *kind* of change which they resist. In particular, he would hypothesize that old organizations are more flexible with respect to changes in their ultimate goals, and that young organizations are more flexible with respect to changes in their social structures. With the possible exception of young voluntary organizations, both young and old organizations tend to resist changes in their task structures.

One can distinguish three kinds of change: change in ultimate goals, change in task structure, and change in social structure. Each corresponds to a reason for organizational membership. Members may be attracted by the organization's goals; they may be attracted by the activities which they perform in the organization's task structure; or they may be attracted by the interactions experienced in the organization's social structure. A member who is strongly attracted by factor A is likely to resist changes in factor A and to resist changes in factors B and C which would devaluate factor A, but he is likely to support changes in factors

B and C which would enhance factor A. Thus, a member who is attracted by the goals of the organization will resist changes in these goals and will resist changes in the organization's task structure and social structure which he feels will impede the accomplishment of these goals, but he will support changes in the task and social structures which he feels will further these goals. Task structure is usually an intervening variable between goals and social structure. Changes in goals tend to have direct effects on task structure, but to affect social structure only indirectly. Changes in social structure tend to have direct effects on task structure, but to affect goals only indirectly. Changes in task structure tend to have direct effects on both goals and social structure.

Members of a new organization, and new members of an old organization, tend to be attracted by either goals or task structure. They tend not to be attracted by the social structure. The relative balance between interest in goals and interest in task structure varies with the type of organization. In nonvoluntary organizations like business firms, most new members are attracted by aspects of the task structure: the activities they perform, the statuses they hold, the salaries they receive. In voluntary organizations, like the National Foundation, most new members are attracted by the organization's goals (Tsouderos, 1955). To the extent that secondary commitments are relevant, one can hypothesize that new members of nonvoluntary organizations will feel secondary commitments to their organizations' goals, because of the effects of goal change on task structure, and that new members of voluntary organizations will feel secondary commitments to their organizations' task structures, both because of the effects of changes in task structure on goals and because of direct attraction by aspects of the task structures. Although the variable which determines the natures of these primary and secondary commitments is the newness of organizational membership, one associates them with young organizations because young organizations contain high proportions of new members.

As an organization ages, its members' central commitment undergoes a shift in emphasis toward the organization's social structure. There are three reasons for this shift. The first is that members become acquainted with one another: friendships spring up, social roles are stabilized and incorporated into members' expectations, and positions in the task structure become associated with the individuals who hold them.

The second reason for this shift is that organizations typically try to promote organizational loyalty among their members. They set up indoctrination programs for new employees; they publish organizational newspapers which stress the accomplishments of the organization and of individual members; they withhold responsibility from new members and reward seniority with promotions and special awards; they require members to learn organizational songs and creeds; they make intra-organizational statuses central in their inducement schemes; they put uniforms on members to distinguish them from non-members; they change members' geographic assignments so that extraorganizational loyalties are disrupted; they adopt paternalistic policies which provide for members' health, recreation, retirement, and death (Kaufman, 1960; W. H. Whyte, 1956). The net effect of most of these loyalty-inducing activities is to strengthen members' commitments to the organization's social structure and to dilute their commitments to specific goals and specific aspects of the task structure. Simon observed; 'The individual who is loyal to the *objectives* of the organization will resist modification of those objectives, and may even refuse to continue his participation if they are changed too radically. The individual who is loyal to the *organization* will support opportunistic changes in its objectives that are calculated to promote its survival and growth' (Simon, 1957a, p. 118; also see pp. 198–219, and March and Simon, 1958, pp. 73–5). Blau and Scott concluded that 'there is an inverse relationship between professional commitment and organizational loyalty' (1962, pp. 60–74).

The third reason for shifting commitments, or possibly another aspect of the second reason, is that members who are committed to the organization's social structure tend to move into central positions for policy determination. In non-voluntary organizations, this is a two-way process: the organization tends to promote members who have long tenure, who are well integrated in the social structure, and who are strongly committed to the organization *per se* and conversely, the organization concentrates its loyalty-inducing activities on central members by changing their job assignments relatively frequently, by giving special recognition to their accomplishments, and by creating a differential between the inducements it offers them and the inducements which they would receive from other organizations. Similar processes are operative in voluntary organizations, but in voluntary organizations the emphasis on social structure is increased by migration of inactive members out of the organization; active members of voluntary organizations tend to have strong commitments to social structure and weak commitments to goals and tasks. For example, several studies (Dean, 1954–5; Lipset, Trow and Coleman, 1956; Spinrad, 1960; and Tannenbaum and Kahn, 1958) have indicated that the active members of labor unions had little, if any, commitment to the labor movement in general and felt no antagonism toward their employers. As compared to inactive union members, the active members had greater seniority in their jobs, were more highly skilled, earned higher pay, and were more satisfied with their work environments. What made the active union members active was a sense of social cohesiveness: they were long-time residents of their communities and were acquainted with their co-workers; they had no desire for social mobility and escape from their class; they enjoyed social interaction. Of course, the facilitating conditions for and manifest degrees of organizational loyalty vary a great deal among cultures. Abegglen reported: 'At whatever level of organization in the Japanese factory, the worker commits himself on entrance to the company for the remainder of his working career. The company will not discharge him even temporarily except in the most extreme circumstances. He will not quit the company for industrial employment elsewhere' (1958, p. 11).

Thus, the members of old organizations, at least those members who have been around awhile, tend to focus their commitment on the organizations' social structures. This tendency is probably stronger in voluntary organizations than nonvoluntary organizations, but social structure is likely to be the primary commitment of central members in organizations of both types. Also in both types of organizations, members' secondary commitments tend to be to the task structures because of the effects of changes in task structure on social structure. Table 3 summarizes the preceding analysis.

From the above, one would expect old organizations to treat their goals opportunistically. Goal-setting becomes, as Thompson and McEwen have characterized it, the problem of 'determining a relationship of the organization to the larger society, which in

Table 3

| Type of organization | Types of change most likely to be resisted | | Type of change most likely to be supported |
	Primary	Secondary	
Young voluntary	Goals	Task structure	Social structure
Young nonvoluntary	Task structure	Goals	Social structure
Old	Social structure	Task structure	Goals

turn becomes a question of what the society (or elements within it) wants done or can be persuaded to support' (1958, p. 23). Naturally, goal flexibility is most apparent when organizational survival is threatened, and when an old *voluntary* organization (where the dominance of social structure over goals is clearest) is in danger, the changes are often dramatic. Messinger's study of the Townsend Movement is one of the best-known documentations. Originally, the movement was purely political and refused to support other groups which had more conservative aims. After the number of members and the amount of financial support dwindled, the movement began to accept compromise of its 'full program'; it undertook the merchandising of health foods and vitamins; and it emphasized social rather than business activities at meetings. Messinger summarized his findings as follows:

In the ascendant phases, when social forces press for reconstruction and changes are still in the offing, the concern of leaders and members of social movements alike is with those things that must be done to translate discontent into effective and concerted action. An evident condition of this orientation is discontent itself. In turn, this discontent must be supplied or renewed by social forces, which, it must be believed can be ameliorated by banding together. These provide the dynamic of value-oriented social movements, as well as the characteristic missions with which their organized arms become identified.

When the movements themselves lose impetus through a shift in the constellation of social forces, their organized arms are deprived of conditions necessary to sustain them in their original form. But organizations are not necessarily dissolved by the abatement of the forces initially conjoining to produce them. They may gain a certain degree of autonomy from their bases and continue to exist. We will expect, however, that the abatement of the particular constellation of social forces giving rise to the movement will have important consequences for the remaining structure. The most general of these is, perhaps, increasing lack of public concern for the organizational mission. This is reflected in the ending of public discussion of the issues which the organization represents or, perhaps, better put, with these issues in the frame of reference that they are placed by organizational representatives. Within the organization, the abatement of social forces spells dropping membership and, more serious in the long run, the end of effective recruitment. This latter may be reinforced by the development of alternative organizational structures competing for the same potential membership. The end of recruitment is quickly transformed into financial difficulty. Where the organization has been geared to financial support from its own adherents, this last consequence will be especially crucial.

The organized arms of declining social movements will tend to adapt to these changed conditions in characteristic ways. We can broadly describe this adaptation by asserting that the dominating orientation of leaders and members shifts *from the implementation of the values the organization is taken to represent* (by leaders, members and public alike), *to maintaining the organizational structure as such*, even at the loss of the organization's central mission. To this end, leaders will be constrained to direct action toward new issues or in new ways which will attenuate the organization's identification with the particular set of aims held to be central to it. In this process, the locus of issue-selection will tend to move outside the organization, to alternative leaderships who highlighted the growing irrelevance to most of the traditional central mission. Presumably, a new mission may be found. Where this is not the case, leaders will be forced to search out new means of financing as the traditional mode of appeal and reap falls on fewer and deafer ears. In this process, members, and especially potential members, will cease to be regarded as 'converts' and will come to be seen as 'customers'. Finally, membership activities initiated in a context of declining public interest to support a faltering organization, will work to turn what were once the incidental rewards of participation into its only meaning. This last, by altering the basis for whatever recruitment may take place, would seem to insure that the organization, if it continues to exist, will be changed from a value-implementing agency to a recreation facility. In sum, the organizational character will stand transformed (1955, pp. 9–10).

Sills (1957, pp. 254–64) has discussed similar findings from three other studies: Dulles (1950), Gusfield (1955) and Pence (1939). Soemardjan (1957) and Zald and Denton (1963) are also relevant.

The formalization process

The rapid and dramatic changes in the Townsend Movement during the postwar period were not, in a sense, changes in goals.[7] Accomplishment of the organization's political program was a goal at the time the organization was founded. Perhaps consensus made it the only goal. However, over the years the balance of members' commitments shifted from the political program to the organization's social structure. By the time the organization's survival was threatened, members looked upon the political program as a subgoal, as a means to organizational persistence, and not as an ultimate goal. Otherwise the postwar transition would not have been possible. Clearly it was the gradual shifting of members' commitments which constituted the basic change in the organization's goals. When commitments to the social structure began to dominate, organizational persistence became a goal beyond and apart from any specific operations to be performed.

The shifting of members' commitments began during the first few months of the organization's existence. Probably it began shortly after the initial expansion of membership but before income actually declined. It is during this early period that an organization starts to gel as an organization: statuses and roles

7. Of course, any change in the organization affects its *operational* goals, and, in that sense, the described changes were changes in the movement's goals. To quote Simon: 'When we change the organization, we change the picture that the people in it have of the concrete tasks to be done and the concrete goals to be achieved – their concept of the program. When we change the concept of the program, we change the relative emphasis that the various parts of the complex whole will receive, we alter allocations of resources and relative priorities among goals' (1953, p. 236).

are assigned; passive members begin to depart; and active members make their commitments to the organization (Simon, 1953). Tsouderos (1955) called this process 'formalization'. In his study of ten voluntary organizations, he found that the number of members was the leading variable in the over-all pattern of expansion and contraction from organizational birth to death. Income lagged membership, and administrative expense lagged income. He hypothesized that formalization begins when the number of members starts to fall, but while income and administrative expense are still rising. Other discussions of formalization have been given by Clark (1962, pp. 191–5) and Weinshall (1960–61).

Interviews conducted by McGuire supported Tsouderos' lead-lag findings; to quote McGuire:

There is a considerable time lag between the growth of numbers of production workers and the expansion in employment of other personnel. The majority of firms interviewed with sales under $100,000 added to their production work forces as sales mounted. Typically, however, they did not add to their managerial personnel or to their clerical staff below this level of sales, regardless of how rapidly sales were expanding. . . . In smaller firms, therefore, there appeared to be a much closer correlation between production workers and [sales] than between non-production workers and [sales] (1963, p. 67).

However, the author suspects that Tsouderos' hypothesis about the onset of formalization, assuming it is correct, is valid only for voluntary organizations. An initial burst of membership expansion due to newly aroused interest in the objectives of the organization is not characteristic of nonvoluntary organizations. In the latter, expansion of total employment is likely to continue for decades after formalization begins.

The formalization process continues as an organization gets older and larger, though no doubt the earliest manifestations of formalization are the most striking ones. Patterns of behavior stabilize; individuals settle into characteristic roles; standard operating procedures are established. The most significant characteristic of this development is that it represents organizational learning – the learning of a formal organizational structure expressive of the problems which must be solved and a rationale for solving them. The formal structure provides the necessary framework within which labor is divided and specialized responsibilities are delegated, routine communications are systematized, and inducements are allocated. No doubt, imitation plays a part in the creation of this structure and, to the extent that the problems of different organizations are unique, may lead to inappropriate structural elements. However, there is evidence that organizations do not imitate simply for the sake of imitation and that the consistencies to be observed among the structures of various organizations reflect legitimate similarities in the problems to be solved. For instance, after interviewing the executives of 106 small manufacturing firms, Wickesberg concluded: 'There was hesitancy ... to embark on organizational changes, such as formation of formal functional units or use of committees or outside agencies, when little or nothing was known or could be demonstrated concerning the probable net gain to the firm' (1961, p. 54).

Wickesberg obtained information about the probable sequence in which formal specialization develops in small manufacturing firms. He reported on the appearance of formal internal subunits and on the employment of outside service agencies as functions of the firm's size and age. Regrettably, he did not employ multivariate analysis, giving no basis for separating the effects of size from the effects of age, so only findings where size is assumed to be the independent variable are listed here:

1. The number of formal subunits increased with size. There was a fairly unambiguous probability preference ordering over the first four subunits to appear. The first subunit established tended to be a production department; the second tended to be a sales department; the third tended to be a purchasing department; and the fourth tended to be a quality control department. The preference ordering for the fifth and subsequent subunits was more ambiguous than that for the first four.

2. The number of outside services used also increased with size. The probability preference ordering was fairly unambiguous for the first five services used, but more ambiguous for the sixth and subsequent services. The first service used tended to be an auditing service; the second a legal service; the third a personnel

service; the fourth an advertising service; and the fifth a labor relations and negotiations service.

Baker and Davis (1954) and Weigand (1963) have also collected data on functional differentiation.

If the formalization process is permitted to continue, unhindered by environmental instability, the organization ultimately becomes a bureaucracy. Merton has described this bureaucratic extreme as follows:

A formal, rationally organized social structure involves clearly defined patterns of activity in which, ideally, every series of actions is functionally related to the purposes of the organization. In such an organization there is an integrated series of offices, of hierarchized statuses, in which inhere a number of obligations and privileges closely defined by limited and specific rules. Each of these offices contains an area of imputed competence and responsibility. Authority, the power of control which derives from an acknowledged status, inheres in the office and not in the particular person who performs the official role. Official action ordinarily occurs within the framework of pre-existing rules of the organization. The system of prescribed relations between the various offices involves a considerable degree of formality and clearly defined social distance between the occupants of these positions. Formality is manifested by means of a more or less complicated social ritual which symbolizes and supports the pecking order of the various offices. Such formality which is integrated with the distribution of authority within the system, serves to minimize friction by largely restricting (official) contact to modes which are previously defined by the rules of the organization. Ready calculability of others' behavior and a stable set of mutual expectations is thus built up. Moreover, formality facilitates the interaction of the occupants of offices despite their (possibly hostile) private attitudes toward one another. In this way, the subordinate is protected from the arbitrary action of his superior, since the actions of both are constrained by a mutually recognized set of rules. Specific procedural devices foster objectivity and restrain the 'quick passage of impulse into action'. . . .

The chief merit of bureaucracy is its technical efficiency, with a premium placed on precision, speed, expert control, continuity, discretion, and optimal returns on input. The structure is one which approaches the complete elimination of personalized relationships and nonrational considerations (hostility, anxiety, affectual involvements, etc.) (1957, pp. 195–6).

This is an overstatement, as the reviews by Argyris (1957) and March and Simon (1958) and Merton's own work (1940) have made clear, but it does capture the spirit behind bureaucracy.

Both Gouldner (1954) and Grusky (1961) have pointed out that large organizations are less liable to disruption because of managerial succession than small organizations. They attributed this relative stability to a tendency for authority to inhere 'in the office and not in the particular person'. Grusky presented data to show that 'frequency of administrative succession at the top is directly related to size of firm'; he concluded 'that succession will be rationally treated by being routinized' in large firms, and that 'because of their predispositions for stability, bureaucracies require periodic succession at the top if they are to adapt adequately to their environment' (p. 269). Grusky's hypotheses make sense, but his data could be explained by more mundane hypotheses as well. One would be that it takes longer to rise to the top of the hierarchy in a large organization, and so the people who are at the top are near retirement when they take office.

Bureaucracies can have irrational as well as rational characteristics. Selznick (1949) has shown how delegation of authority can foster the development of subunit goals which work at cross-purposes to the central goals of the organization, and eventually prevent further growth. Merton (1940) pointed out that standard operating procedures can become functionally autonomous and independent of the demands placed on the organization, and that impersonal reward systems can overlook individual achievement. Tsouderos (1955) noted that formalized communication procedures can be ineffective in voluntary associations. Stinchcombe (1959) and Udy (1959a) have suggested that rational organizations and bureaucratic organizations are different things. However, both used the term 'rational' in a highly specialized manner. Blau and Scott (1962, pp. 206-11) have provided a useful discussion of this material.

Nevertheless, such consequences fall into the 'unanticipated' category. Most organizations, when they discover undesirable consequences of their current formal structures, endeavor to correct these consequences by changing their structures. Guest inferred from his study of a large manufacturing plant that 'a point may be reached *when an organization is not capable of changing itself internally'* (1962, p. 107). The author does not know whether this proposition is true or false, but he does know that it did not follow from the case which Guest reported. First, the 'organization' was a subunit of a larger organization, one of six plants in one division of a large firm. The basic problems of the plant apparently centered in the plant manager, who was, of course, appointed by the division management. Thus, the proposition should be 'a subunit is not capable of changing aspects of its structure which are controlled by the parent organization' – a tautology. Second, the parent organization did in fact change the subunit's structure (replace the plant manager), and Guest devoted most of the book to discussing the improvements wrought by this change.

One must distinguish between structural consequences which are irrational from the viewpoint of the observer of the organization and structural consequences which are irrational from the viewpoint of the organizational members. The literature abounds with analyses of undesirable consequences by omniscient observers. Rarely do these observers recognize the possibility that their own value systems, by which they apply the term undesirable, may be quite different from the value systems of the organizational members. When such differences are recognized, the observer usually concludes that the organizational members hold the wrong values.

On the nature of adaptive processes

The formalization process is fundamentally an adaptive process. As an organization gets older, it learns more and more about coping with its environment and with its internal problems of communication and coordination. At least this is the normal pattern, and the normal organization tries to perpetuate the fruits of its learning by formalizing them. It sets up standard operating procedures; it routinizes reports on organizational performance; it appoints specialists in areas of consistent need; it discovers effective factorings of the organizational task and delegates the factored components to subunits. The organization's need for and capacity for formalization increase as it grows. Information which a small organization needs infrequently and can obtain informally must be supplied regularly and collected in a systematic manner. Task segments become large enough to occupy specialists. The necessary supervisory activity escapes the capacity of a small group of men and must be delegated.

There may be evidence of organizational adaptation in Tsouderos' study. During the period of contracting membership, administrative expense, administrative employment, and the amount of property owned all rose *cyclically*. Possibly a decline in one or more of these variables triggers adaptive changes in the behavior strategies of the organization, which in turn, renew the expansion. The author has strong reservations about this hypothesis because the variables in question are all subject to fluctuations in the economy, but it should be worth investigation. Cyclical fluctuations in the organization's expansion path are predictable from the 'fire department' model of organizational decision-making which Cyert and March have stressed:

We assume that organizations make decisions by solving a series of problems; each problem is solved as it arises: the organization then waits for another problem to appear. Where decisions within the firm do not naturally fall into such a sequence, they are modified so that they will (1963, p. 119).

The formal structure is commonly associated with the rigid and change-resistant aspects of the organization. Since one objective of the formalization process is the stabilization of behavior patterns, and since the formal structure includes the salaries, statuses, standard procedures, and goals from which members' inducements derive, some degree of association is logically necessary. However, one should not assume that formalization and resistance to change are the same thing. Resistance to change is a reaction against alteration of a familiar state of affairs. Since informality and instability can become familiar and can provide inducements, they too are associated with resistance to change. That is, organizational members are inclined to resist changes which increase formality as well as changes which decrease formality.

On the other hand, every formal structure is incompatible with – or perhaps, inadequate for – certain types of change. An organization's structure is a theory. It is a model for performance of the organizational task, and incorporates assumptions about the causal relations in the organization and the environment. This model is at best approximate. Events will occur which the model cannot anticipate, cannot comprehend, and may not perceive. Even if these unpredicted events are perceived, the model is unlikely to suggest organizational responses appropriate to them. Several studies comment on this inability of organizations to predict events and/or to generate appropriate responses. Summarizing the opinions of nineteen experienced executives, Newman and Logan wrote: 'Perhaps the most striking point made regarding the need for a change is that rarely do companies foresee this need in time to prepare for it. Instead, the common situation is for firms to outgrow their old managerial practice and find a change necessary for survival' (1955, p. 90). After interviewing executives in 106 small companies, Wickesberg concluded: 'Creation and designation of formalized units to perform major or related functions within the enterprise were, by-and-large, unplanned and perhaps not even anticipated in the earlier stages of organizational development' (1961, p. 53). And McNulty's investigation of thirty expanding firms led him to state that 'in the cases where explicit, purposeful reorganization was instituted to deal with growth in markets the results in terms of adaptation do not seem to have been clearly better than when less formal methods were used' (1962, p. 18).

Inability to foresee the future and difficulty in coping with unanticipated events are hardly unique to organizations. Doubtless some organizations have better structures than others, better in the sense that the organizations encounter unpredicted events less frequently and have less difficulty adjusting to new circumstances. But it is unreasonable to expect organizations to evolve structures which anticipate all circumstances and never confront the unforeseen. Nor is it reasonable to expect organizations to evolve structures which maximize flexibility and informality. A highly flexible and informal organization is poorly adapted to a stable set of problems, just as a highly inflexible and formal organization is poorly adapted to an unstable set of problems. The well-adapted organization is one which matches the stability of its problem set.

The stability of an organization's problem set is an increasing function of the organization's age. Young organizations have little experience in distinguishing important problems from unimportant ones, and few mechanisms for dealing with routine problems routinely. They perceive unstable problem sets and need flexible structures. Older organizations have learned to ignore unimportant problems, and have accumulated mechanisms for attending to routine problems. They perceive stable problem sets and need stable structures. The degree of stability which an organization tends finally to attain depends in part on the basic stability of the organization's environment and in part on the adequacy of the causal model imbedded in the organization's structure. The latter is usually the more serious constraint, but, from the organization's point of view, the two are indistinguishable.

Formalization is adaptive in still another way. It is formalization which stabilizes members' roles and positions and makes an organizational social structure possible, and it is formalization which places active, loyal members in central positions. Thus, formalization is a necessary (but not sufficient) condition for the shifting of members' commitments from specific goals and aspects of the task structure to aspects of the social structure. This commitment shift is adaptive. Young organizations, operating against the handicap of unstable problem sets, need a strong orientation toward efficiency and goal achievement in order to survive – particularly if their larger competitors benefit from returns to scale. Old organizations, operating with stable problem sets and possibly benefiting from returns to scale themselves do not need a strong orientation toward efficiency. Old organizations risk having their original goals rendered obsolete by changing social needs, or by their success in achieving these goals, and they need to be able to look upon their original goals as strategies which can be changed.

If formalization is a form of adaptation, it is certainly not the only kind of adaptation which an organization displays. Changes in formal structure occur gradually and cannot accommodate ubiquitous short-run fluctuations in the organization's problem set. Short-run adaptation must be handled by flexibilities within the decision structure and by informally evolved behavior patterns. Coalitions gel and dissolve. Operational goals shift.

Search procedures and attention rules are invented and discarded. Communication channels open and close (Cyert and March, 1963; Dill, 1962; Eckstein, 1958; Kaufman, 1960; March and Simon, 1958; Selznick, 1943). The formal structure is like a large log floating down a turbulent stream. The log's inertia is great enough that the log's trajectory is fairly independent of swirls and eddies in the stream itself. No doubt each obstruction which the stream passes over has effects on the log, but what effects and how are not immediately apparent. The most obvious symptoms of adaptation are found in the stream.

Models of growth

Various models of organizational growth have been proposed. They can be partitioned into four groups. *Cell-division* models and *metamorphosis* models focus on patterns in the size and structure of an organization as it expands. *Will-o'-the-wisp* models and *decision-process* models focus on the mechanisms, internal to the organization, by which growth is effected.

The sequence in which these model groups are considered corresponds, in a rough way, to the attention they pay to adaptive processes. Cell-division models tend to concentrate on effects and to ignore causes; when causes are ascribed, the connexions between cause and effect are usually vague. Metamorphosis models describe both causes and effects, but again the connexions between cause and effect are obscure. The orientation of the metamorphosis models is internal; the models describe internal problems likely to be encountered by organizations of different sizes and changes in organizational structure likely to result. Will-o'-the-wisp models are dynamic; they stress sequences of events and make time an explicit variable. Relative to the metamorphosis models, will-o'-the-wisp models generally give more attention to connexions between cause and effect and to environmental influences. Decision-process models are at the opposite end of the spectrum from cell-division models; they tend to concentrate on causes and to ignore effects. The specific processes which turn causes into effects are stated in detail, and the effects are left to emerge as outputs from these dynamic processes.

Cell-division models

Cell-division models focus on growth as a percentage change in size. The obvious example is Haire's (1959) study which made explicit use of the biological analogy. Haire fits data from eight firms to the equation

$$\frac{dN_t}{dt} = AN_t - BN_t{}^2,$$

$$\text{or} \quad \frac{N_t}{N_o} \cdot \frac{BN_o - A}{BN_t - A} = e^{At},$$

where N_t is the number of employees at time t, and A and B are parameters. A was estimated 'by observing the first (two or three) years' growth', and B was 'quite arbitrarily chosen'.

An equation like the one above is frequently employed to describe the reproduction of biological organisms. The notion is that each organism, or pair of organisms, reproduces at a fixed frequency. At time $t+\Delta$, the total number of organisms $N_{t+\Delta}$ will be N_t plus an increment proportional to N_t and to Δ:

$$N_{t+\Delta} = N_t + A\Delta N_t.$$

Stated in terms of continuous time, the equation becomes

$$\frac{dN}{dt} = AN.$$

The coefficient A nets out births and deaths – a positive A implying more births than deaths.

The second term in Haire's equation, $-BN^2$, lowers the rate of increase in N as N becomes large. N reaches a maximum at the value A/B, and decreases thereafter.[8] Haire associated this decrease in the growth rate with 'the related state of competition in the industry and the demand for the product' and also with 'the internal price paid for increase in size' (pp. 281–2).

Haire discussed two aspects of internal structure in addition

8. At this point, the assumptions behind the equation become a matter for serious consideration. An equation like the one used by Haire implies that N can ultimately go negative. At the very least one would expect $N > 0$, and in some cases it might be more reasonable to use an equation where N never decreases at all.

to the pattern of employment over time. One fanciful analysis dichotomized employees as 'internal' and 'external', and drew an analogy between these categories and the volume and surface area of a three-dimensional solid. The second analysis traced the expansion of 'staff' and 'clerical' functions. Haire reasoned: 'The two main functions of the staff are to provide information for control and coordination, and to provide expert assistance beyond the skill or training of line executives. The pressures which threaten to crack the organization as size increases must be in these areas' (p. 289). 'The clerk's job is largely concerned with information – recording, duplicating, disseminating, keeping, and finding information – to support the integrative function' (p. 298). 'As the organization grows, the force that seems likeliest to destroy it is the centrifugal force arising from the fact that the members are individuals and tend to fly off on tangents toward their own goals' (p. 302; also see Draper and Strother, 1963). However, Haire's data suggest that organizational size *per se* has little effect on either the proportion of staff employees or the proportion of clerical employees. These proportions appear to increase with organizational age during the first few years after founding, and then to remain constant. One inference would be that the early increases reflect the formalization process.

The author does not think that 'to liken a firm to an organism ... is an ill-founded procedure' (Penrose, 1952, p. 809). However, when one uses analogies as extensively as Haire, one should spell out the sense in which they are valid. Haire did not do this, a deficiency which was especially apparent in his internal–external analysis. But if the reasons for Haire's confidence in biological analogies were often obscure, Chapin's approach to growth was sheer mystique. Chapin contended that organizations develop structures and grow at rates given by the 'Fibonacci proportion'.

The Fibonacci proportion is $\frac{1}{2}(\sqrt{5}-1) \simeq 0.618$. This is the Limit $\underset{t \to \infty}{\frac{N_t}{N_{t+1}}}$ when $N_{t+1} = N_t + N_{t-1}$.

Chapin wrote: 'The Fibonacci proportion, taken as a measure of integration, harmonious balance of parts, and equilibrium of structure, suggests a mathematical model with the logarithmic spiral as the principle of growth' (1957, p. 449). The 'spiral' was obtained by graphing t as an angle and N as a radius. Otherwise, Chapin's model was nearly identical to Haire's. For large t, one has

$$\frac{N_t}{N_{t+1}} \simeq 0{\cdot}618$$

$$N_{t+1} \simeq \frac{1}{0{\cdot}618} N_t = (1{\cdot}618)N_t$$

$$N_t \simeq N_0(1{\cdot}618)^t$$

which is Haire's equation for small N and with $A = \log (1{\cdot}618)$. Haire estimated that $A = \log(1{\cdot}5)$.

Chapin's data were church memberships. At one point, he argued that the ratio of 'Church Membership' to Church Membership plus 'Sunday School Enrollment' tended to the Fibonacci proportion as the organization grew older and as 'institutional strength' increased. This is probably a correct (approximately) proposition, but not because of any magical qualities of the number $0{\cdot}618$. Church Membership is essentially the number of adult participants in the church; Sunday School Enrollment is essentially the number of children. In 1920, the proportion of people over age nineteen in the United States population was $0{\cdot}592$, and in 1930 it was $0{\cdot}612$. Further, Chapin pointed out that the ratio got larger as the church got older. Since new churches are ordinarily organized in areas which are newly settled and heavily populated by young families, this increase is expected.

Haire's study was unusual in that it used time-series data on employment in individual firms (also see Filley, 1963). Most studies use cross-section data about a number of different organizations at a given point in time. The cross-section approach generates, as Haire pointed out, 'a spurious growth curve. It is not a curve of growth representing the dynamics within an organization, but a set of static measurements arranged by size' (p. 292).

Haire's point is a valid one, but it is not an *a priori* justification for ignoring all cross-section data. The growth process involves many variables: time, number of employees, sales volume, capital investment, and so forth. Cross-section studies ignore the time dimension, particularly as it affects the initial period of adaptation and learning in young organizations. Cross-section studies also confound organizations which have stabilized at some size with organizations which are passing through that size in the course of growing or declining. In short, cross-section studies tend to focus on equilibrium states at the expense of transient states. However, in some cases it may be desirable to focus on equilibria, taking these to be a description of the 'average' organization after its initial surge of growth has passed. Whether this is a reasonable thing to do, of course, depends on whether one believes that individual organizations are eventually constrained to the pattern of the 'average' organization.

Much of the work on production functions by economists and operations research people falls into the cross-section pattern, sometimes a cross-section of firms in an industry and sometimes a time-independent cross-section of outputs from a given firm. A production function is a statement of the output which can be obtained from some combination of factors of production. In theory, the production function should state the *maximum* output from a given combination of factors, but when people get around to fitting parameters they invariably settle for an average output. A number of different functional forms have been employed. Linear functions are popular in operations research; quadratic functions are typical of theoretical economics; more complex functions have been used when techniques were available for dealing with them. One function is of particular interest, however, because a number of empirical studies have utilized it and because it is easily adaptable to exponential models of growth. It is the Cobb–Douglas function:

$$P = a.L^{\beta}.C^{1-\beta},$$

where P represents output, L represents labor, and C represents capital. When Cobb and Douglas introduced the function in 1928, they gave three reasons for their choice. When each input is multiplied by some constant, output is multiplied by the same constant, i.e. two identical plants produce twice as much as one. Secondly, if either input goes to zero, output also goes to zero. Thirdly, the function seemed to fit the data. A fourth reason can be added. If one takes logarithms of P, L and C, the parameters can be estimated by linear regression. For a fairly complete bibliography of studies done before 1944 and a worthwhile discussion of the methodological problems, see Marschak and Andrews (1944). Another worthwhile methodological discussion is provided by Phelps Brown (1957). Functions of the Cobb–Douglas type are used in the following section on administrative structure and growth.

One cross-section study is of interest because it supported the percentage-growth hypothesis, and because of its implications about the effects of competition on the size of firms. Simon and Bonini described their model as follows:

Let us assume that there is a minimum size, S_m, of firm in an industry. Let us assume that for firms above this size, unit costs are constant. Individual firms in the industry will grow (or shrink) at varying rates, depending on such factors as (a) profit, (b) dividend policy, (c) new investment, and (d) mergers. These factors, in turn, may depend on the efficiency of the individual firm, exclusive access to particular factors of production, consumer brand preference, the growth or decline of the particular industry products in which it specializes, and numerous other conditions. The operation of all these forces will generate a probability distribution for the changes in size of firms of a given size. Our first basic assumption (the law of proportionate effect) is that this probability distribution is the same for all size classes of firms that are well above S_m. Our second basic assumption is that new firms are being 'born' in the smallest-size class at a relatively constant rate (1958, p. 610).

Simon and Bonini proceeded to show: that the rate of entry of new firms as estimated by the model was close to the actual rate of entry for American firms, that the model predicted rather well the relative ingot capacities of the ten largest steel producers; and that the minimum feasible plant sizes in each of thirteen industries implied by their model were consistent with Bain's (1956) estimates.

Most important from the viewpoint of this chapter, perhaps, is the report which Simon and Bonini gave on the validity of the proportionate effect hypothesis:

Data are now available, both in Britain and the United States, that allow us to follow the changes in size of individual firms, and to construct the transition matrices from one time period to another. Hart and Prais have published such transition matrices for British business units for the periods 1885–96, 1896–1907, 1907–24, 1924–39, and

1939–50 (1956, Tables 3, 4, 5, 6, 7). From the matrices, they have been able to test directly the first assumption underlying the stochastic processes we are considering – the law of proportionate effect. They found that the frequency distributions of percentage changes in size of small, medium, and large firms, respectively, were quite similar – approximating to normal distributions with the same means and standard deviations. We found the same to be the case with the transition matrix for the 500 largest US industrial corporations from 1954 to 1955 and 1954 to 1956.

A simple, direct way to test the law of proportionate effect is to construct on a logarithmic scale the scatter diagram of firm sizes for the beginning and end of the time interval in question. If the regression line has a slope of 45 degrees and if the plot is homoscedastic, the law of proportionate effect holds and the first assumption underlying the stochastic models holds. A plot of the US data shows these conditions to be well satisfied for the 1955–56 period (Simon and Bonini, p. 612; also see Ijiri and Simon, 1964).

The author is skeptical that the law of proportionate effect is satisfied by small firms as well as large ones. The studies cited in the second section above by Crum (1953), Osborn (1951), Mansfield (1962a), and Steindl (1945) implied that small firms are more likely to fail and have more variable growth rates. McGuire (1963) concluded from his study that young firms grow faster than old ones and that large firms grow faster than small ones, but he did not use multivariate analysis, performed no statistical tests, and handled his data in ways that might have introduced bias.

Nevertheless, the hypothesis of constant (size-independent) percentage growth does seem to be approximately correct. At least, the cell-division models should be good starting points for more sophisticated models of growth.

Metamorphosis models

Metamorphosis models take the view that growth is not a smooth continuous process, but is marked by abrupt and discrete changes in the conditions for organizational persistence and in the structures appropriate to these conditions. As Sofer put it: 'The policies and procedures appropriate at one stage of an organization's history can become dramatically unsuited at another. . . . Just as different procedures are appropriate to the different phases of an organization's affairs, so are different sorts of people' (1961, pp. 163–4).

An emphasis on 'different sorts of people', particularly top management people, is characteristic of this group of models. Moore's model is typical:

The evolution of strategies in a particular business proceeds in more or less well-defined stages. The first stage is the creation of the business activity itself. . . . Someone or some small group of individuals possesses, develops or stumbles on potential assets or resources which, when combined with certain other assets, provide the conditions favourable to the development of a business. . . .

The creative strategy of a business is frequently underdeveloped and unbalanced in its initial form. It tends to emphasize the special interests, talents, possessions, behavior, and general orientation of the founding father. If the business is to survive in a competitive world, the original strategy must be consolidated. . . . If the first stage of a business requires a Promoter or Activity Generator, the next stage requires a Businessman or Consolidator. This is the stage when the business develops 'sound business practices'.

As the business grows and problems of adjustment increase, a new stage is reached – that of organization . . . the organization itself as a rationalization of means to ends becomes a strategic device for insuring an advantageous position in the socio-economic environment. This is the stage of the Manager or the Administrator (Moore, 1959, pp. 220–22).

The rough outlines of some other metamorphosis models are sketched below.

Marshall has stated that the manager of a small business must display 'energy and flexibility . . . industry and care for small details', and then as his firm grows larger, he must 'adapt . . . to his larger sphere' and display 'originality, and versatility and power of initiation . . . perseverence, tact and good luck' (1920, p. 285). This proposition that the survival of small firms depends upon 'close attention to detail and quick adjustment to uncertain circumstances' seems to be popular. For example, Florence wrote:

Many small firms survive because they give the precise and reliable service required by customers, particularly in 'jobbing' for producer-customers, with whom they keep in personal contact. They promise firm delivery dates, however unreasonable, and keep their promise; they produce the exact unstandard quality and design (usually unreasonably) required and attend to the customers' complaints, however wrong-headed. For this minute attention and adjustment to detail and circumstance, patiently building up goodwill with no place for mass production, a strong and direct incentive is required; the small entrepreneur, paid for his enterprise with profit, meets the demand (1953, pp. 64–5).

Marshall paid particular attention to the consequences of the entrepreneur's old age and death. He said that the entrepreneur's 'progress is likely to be arrested by the decay, if not of his faculties, yet of his liking for energetic work. The rise of his business may be prolonged if he can hand down his business to a successor almost as energetic as himself' (1920, p. 286). When the entrepreneur dies, his descendants will 'prefer an abundant income coming to them without effort on their part, to one which though twice as large could be earned only by incessant toil and anxiety' (p. 300). So 'after a while, the guidance of the business falls into the hands of people with less energy and less creative genius, if not with less active interest in its prosperity' (p. 316; also see Christensen, 1953).

Whyte (1948; 1961) has emphasized the shifting control problems of a restaurant manager as his business grows. Whyte identified five stages in the growth process. Stage one is the small, informal restaurant with no division of labor and direct informal relations among manager, workers and customers. Stage two involves work specialization; the manager's position is more supervisory because he must coordinate the activities of employees. Stage three is marked by the introduction of a supervisory level between the manager and the first line employees, and stage four is reached when a second level of supervision is created. The manager's relations with customers and employees are more formal in stages three and four; he has less feedback on problems encountered, and he initiates formal procedures for controlling the cost, quantity and quality of food served. His restaurant's success depends upon his ability to manage, rather than to do things himself.

When Jones was beginning, he could state his personnel problem in very simple form; How can I get the cooperation of the workers? As the organization grew, he found he had to leave that problem more and more in the hands of his supervisors. His problem was: How can I get the cooperation of my supervisors? (1961, p. 86).

Stage five is reached when the single restaurant becomes a chain. At this point, the manager must standardize recipes and service procedures because: 'From the customers' standpoint, there is little justification for a chain except in the advantage it gives them in knowing what type of food and service to expect no matter which unit they patronize' (1961, p. 87).

Fayol (1949) and Newman and Logan (1955) have viewed the organization in much the same way as Whyte. Fayol distinguished seven stages. The first is the one-man business; the second begins when employees are added; the third is marked by the introduction of a foreman to whom some supervision is delegated; in the fourth through seventh stages 'two, three, or four foremen make necessary a superintendent, two or three superintendents give rise to a departmental manager'. Newman and Logan identified three transition points – four stages. The first transition occurs when the entrepreneur becomes a manager instead of a doer; the second occurs when he delegates some of the managerial activity to subordinates; and the third, and most important, transition occurs when policy-making is decentralized.

Herbst (1957) and Starbuck (1966) have suggested that there are differences between small and large retail stores. Herbst stated that the fundamental difference between small and large stores lies in their dependence on explicit administration. Small stores are 'intrinsically regulated'; their control and coordination requirements are handled without any of the personnel explicitly assuming administrative roles. Large stores are 'extrinsically regulated'; the control and coordination functions are delegated to administrative specialists. Starbuck distinguished between 'clerking activities', which involve interaction with customers, and 'backing activities', which do not. Small stores are 'intrinsically backed' because their employees perform both clerking and backing activities; large stores are 'extrinsically backed' because some of their employees never interact with customers. Starbuck associated the transition from intrinsic to extrinsic backing with manufacturer lot purchasing and branch operations, as well as with the employment of backing specialists.

Perrow has observed that, since the late nineteenth century, 'There has been a general development among hospitals from trustee domination, based on capital and legitimization, to domination by the medical staff, based upon the increasing importance of their technical skills, and, at present, a tendency towards administrative dominance based on internal and external coordination' (Perrow, 1961b, p. 857). Perrow suggested that this same dominance cycle may be seen in the life histories of individual hospitals (ontogeny recapitulates phylogeny) and that 'As the market and technology change, this cycle could be repeated' (p. 865).

Tsouderos (1955) distinguished between the 'growth' stage of a voluntary organization, during which membership increases, and the subsequent 'formalization' stage. Filley (1963) distinguished three stages in the life of a business firm: a 'nongrowth traditional stage', a 'dynamic stage of growth', and a 'bureaucratic stage'.

The metamorphosis models clearly imply that an organization is an adaptive system capable of dealing with different problems in different ways. In fact, the metamorphosis models fit nicely into Ashby's concept of an 'ultrastable' system. Ashby was primarily concerned with biological organisms, but his analysis captured some organizational characteristics as well.

... the disturbances that come to the organism are of two widely different types (the distribution is bi-modal). One type is small, frequent, impulsive, and acts on the main variables. The other is large, infrequent, and induces a change of step-function form on the parameters to the reacting part. Included in the latter type is the major disturbance of embryogenesis, which first sends the organism into the world with a brain sufficiently disorganised to require correction (in this respect, learning and adaptation are related, for the same solution is valid for both).

To such a distribution of disturbances the appropriate regulator (to keep the essential variables within physiological limits) is one whose total feedbacks fall into a corresponding bimodal form. There will be feedbacks to give stability against the frequent impulsive disturbances to the main variables, and there will be a slower acting feedback giving changes of step-function form to give stability against the infrequent disturbances of step-function form.

Such a whole can be regarded simply as one complex regulator that is stable against a complex (bi-modal) set of disturbances. Or it can equivalently be regarded as a first-order regulator (against the small impulsive disturbances) that can reorganize itself to achieve this stability after the disturbance of embryogenesis or after a major change in its conditions has destroyed this stability (1960, p. 136).

Smelser's model of social change also stressed discrete shifts in structure, but he included only changes in which one component of the existing structure is divided into two or more new components.

When one social role or organization becomes archaic under changing historical circumstances, it differentiates by a *definite and specific sequence of events* into *two or more* roles or organizations which function more effectively in the new historical circumstances. The new social units are structurally distinct from each other, but taken together are functionally equivalent to the original unit. . . . Any sequence of differentiation is set in motion by specific disequilibrating conditions. Initially this disequilibrium gives rise to symptoms of social disturbance which must be brought into line later by mechanisms of social control. Only then do specific ideas, suggestions, and attempts emerge to produce the more differentiated social units (1959, p. 2).

In organizations the small, frequent disturbances include normal daily operating problems, turnover in noncentral personnel, and the like. The large, infrequent disturbances include major changes in consumer demand or production technology, turnover in central personnel and significant increases in organizational size. The metamorphosis models talk about structural parameters of the organization's system for adapting to routine, short-run disturbances. A specific set of parameter values constitutes a stable structure for a corresponding range of short-run disturbances. But as long-run shifts accumulate, the existing set of parameter values loses the power to provide stability and must be changed. The metamorphosis models describe probable changes in structure when the cumulative, long-run shifts are organizational growth and aging. While one might quibble over the significance of some of the structural changes which these models have described, one can hardly doubt the importance of studying structural changes which correlate with growth and age.

Will-o'-the-wisp models

Will-o'-the-wisp models explore one kind of process which might connect the motives of organizational members to increases in the size of the organization. These models make growth a process of pursuing opportunities which tend to vanish when the expansion is completed. As Penrose put it, 'there may be advantages in *moving* from one position to another quite apart from the advantages of *being* in a different position' (1959, p. 2).

Andrews has set forth a theory in which savings in unit costs provide a motive for growth. Economic theory distinguishes between short-run and long-run costs. In the long run, all costs are *variable*, meaning that all costs are affected by changes in output. In the short run, some costs are variable and some are *fixed*, meaning that they are independent of output. Andrews noted that because some costs are fixed, 'short-run costs will normally be falling even if the long-run cost curve is rising' (1949a, p. 59; see also Dixon, 1953).[9] This implies that business expansion is undertaken to obtain short-run cost savings. Further:

No business man would *expect* to be a less efficient manager at a larger scale; he will tacitly assume that he will remain as efficient as he is for any increase in scale that he is likely to make. Realized costs may, therefore, differ from the expected costs on which he plans, but that cannot affect his planning. . . .

Time is of the essence of the business man's thinking. There will be a limit to the rate at which he will be prepared to grow. He normally views a new scale as a position which once taken calls for consolidation. He will expect his costs at first to be higher than they will become when he has achieved that consolidation – in fact, for any given scale, he will expect, other things being equal, that his cost curves will fall over time, that he will always be able to make some improvements in the light of experience. The idea of an optimum size of business is outside his usual way of thinking (Andrews, p. 79; also see Alchian, 1959).

Of course, the short-run cost savings which Andrews' businessman pursues are illusory. In the long run, the long-run cost curve

9. This proposition is far from obvious at high output levels. Total short-run cost might be represented by the function $A + Bq + Cq^2$ where A, B and C are positive parameters and q is output. Cost per unit would then be $Aq^{-1} + B + Cq$, which has the derivative with respect to q: $C - A/q^2$. As q becomes large, the right hand, fixed cost, term becomes negligible. Andrews assumed that $C = 0$.

reigns. The businessman is led, by his own myopia and inability to learn from experience, to search for the nonexistent. However, this search does not continue indefinitely for: 'Even when one would consider them to be of equal efficiency on balance, business men usually differ in the interest that they take in particular aspects of their functions, and their personal predilections and abilities leave their mark on the business. This personal equation is especially important in determining the size to which a given business has been allowed to grow or towards which it is straining' (Andrews, p. 55).

Penrose (1955; 1959) has taken an approach which is in some respects similar to Andrews' and in some respects crucially different. She made growth a pursuit of 'disappearing economies' in much the same sense that Andrews did:

The growth of firms may be consistent with the most efficient use of society's resources; the result of a past growth – the size attained at any time – may have no corresponding advantages. Each successive step in its growth may be profitable to the firm and, if otherwise under-utilized resources are used, advantageous to society. But once any expansion is completed, the original justification for the expansion may fade into insignificance as new opportunities for growth develop and are acted upon. In this case, it would not follow that the large firm as a whole was any more efficient than its several parts would be if they were operating (and growing) quite independently (1959, p. 103).

Penrose rejected the notion that the long-run unit costs of a firm rise as the firm grows large. '. . . there may be an "optimum" output for each of the firm's product-lines, but not an "optimum" output for the firm as a whole. In general we have found nothing to prevent the indefinite expansion of firms as time passes. . . .' (1959, pp. 98–9). She was apparently ambivalent on the question of whether large firms suffer from management difficulties. On page 19 she said: 'Apparently what has happened as firms have grown larger is not that they become inefficient, but that with increasing size both the managerial function and the basic administrative structure have undergone fundamental changes. . . .' On page 206 she said: 'The large diversified firms, although undoubtedly wielding much power and occupying strong monopolistic positions in some areas, do not, so far as we can see, hold their position without the expenditure of extensive managerial effort.

And it is quite possible that the proportion of total managerial services required to maintain the current operations of a firm will begin to rise when it becomes large enough. . . .'

Penrose also saw growth as a means for exploiting transient advantages in goodwill and managerial and technical expertise, for increasing profit as well as for reducing cost. The primary motive for growth, she wrote, is maximization of long-run profits: 'from the point of view of investment policy, *growth and profits become equivalent as the criteria for the selection of investment programmes*. Firms will never invest in expansion for the sake of growth if the return on the investment is negative, for that would be self-defeating' (p. 30). She added: 'There is no need to deny that other "objectives" are often important – power, prestige, public approval, or the mere love of the game – it need only be recognized that the attainment of these ends more often than not is associated directly with the ability to make profits'.

The core of Penrose's theory was the supply of managerial services in the firm. Management was both the accelerator and the brake for the growth process.

Under given circumstances, therefore, the maximum amount of expansion will be determined by the relevant managerial services *available* for expansion in relation to the amount of these services *required* per dollar of expansion. . . .

If we assume that a firm is fully using its capacity to grow, the maintenance of any given rate of growth over time requires that the supply of the managerial services available for expansion increase at a rate at least equal to the rate at which the managerial services required per dollar of expansion increase; an increased rate of growth can be achieved only if the former are increasing at a rate greater than the latter; a reduced rate of growth must follow if the relevant services become available for expansion at a slower rate than the requirement for those services per dollar of expansion is increasing (1959, p. 200).

The managerial services available for expansion were a residual category, 'the difference between the total services available to the firm and those required to operate it' (p. 201). The effect of expansion on these excess services tended to be transient; 'it is clear that the creation and execution of plans for expansion absorb managerial services, and that as these services are released they become available for still further planning of expansion if they are not needed to operate the expanded concern' (p. 50). In fact: 'If there is not scope for the full use of the capacity of individuals in the firm to perform administrative services, to plan and execute production programs, to sell the firm's products, to test new ideas, a pressure to expand will be exerted on the firm' (p. 54). So the excess services created opportunities for their own employment.

The supply of excess managerial services increased with time, other things being equal, because 'when men have become used to working in a particular group of other men, they become individually and as a group more valuable to the firm in that the services they can render are enhanced by their knowledge of their fellow-workers, of the methods of the firm, and of the best way of doing things in the particular set of circumstances in which they are working' (p. 52). The rate of adjustment increased with the work load. 'If a group is to gain experience in working together, it must have work to do. The total amount of work to be done at any time in a firm depends on the size of the firm's operations . . .' (pp. 46–7). On the other hand, the addition of new managerial personnel disrupted the existing managerial structure and forced the firm to pause for acclimation; 'if a firm deliberately or inadvertently expands its organization more rapidly than the individuals in the expanding organization can obtain the experience with each other and with the firm that is necessary for the effective operation of the group, the efficiency of the firm will suffer, even if optimum adjustments are made in the administrative structure . . .' (p. 47).

Bits and pieces of Penrose's theory have been supported by others. Heller has quoted an executive he interviewed as follows:

Perfecting a layout involves a minimum amount of managerial and technical work that you can't escape. You have to handle expansion projects in a series, because you simply don't have the necessary number of men of the required caliber around to keep up a doubled-up pace. If we had gone ahead too fast, we would not have been able to get either proper supervision or the technical brains required to get the bugs out. Also, we have to keep production up during the change-overs . . . or we will be losing part of our market. So it's the scarcity and costliness of brains that slow down our rate of investment (1951, p 102).

March and Simon's discussion of innovation supported the idea that expansion depends upon managerial resources which are, in some sense, excess (1958, pp. 185-8), Cyert and March have suggested that the planning undertaken by firms is primarily of the short-run variety (1963, pp. 110-12, 120-22, 285-6). Andrews has pointed out that pressure to expand is sometimes due to 'the young up-and-coming men, pressing for promotion and looking for ways in which to achieve it' (1949b, p. 282). Whyte has stressed the importance of 'fitting-in' as a precondition for managerial authority (1961, pp. 571-4). Weiss made this observation:

It seems that an integration slowly develops of the expectations of the new person and those of the staff members already a part of the group; a mutual confidence in who can be relied on to do what. The new staff member learns what the co-workers expect of him, and what he can in turn expect of them. The older staff members learn to think about their units as including the new person, and to take his contributions as a matter of course, as they do the contributions of the other members of the unit.

Until the new staff member is fully accepted there is a certain hesitancy in interaction involving him. Everyone is very careful. Things are to be made as explicit as possible. There may be a tendency to exclude him from group tasks requiring close co-ordination, and to count on him more than is necessary for routine work (1956, p. 23).

Other pieces of evidence have been cited above, including Blau's (1955) observation that task-mastery produces pressure for change, McNulty's (1962) finding that planning changes in organization structure is not advantageous, and numerous reports of learning effects.

Although the dynamics of Penrose's theory stressed factors inside the firm, she did devote attention to environmental influences like market conditions, the availability of financing, the nature of competitive relationships, and the kinds of opportunities presented. She looked upon the internal processes as determinants of a hypothetical maximum rate of expansion, and treated environmental factors as constraints on the firm's ability to actually achieve this maximum growth rate. Of course, which factors constrain which factors is a chicken-or-egg question.

What is important is that she tried to take both internal and external factors into account.

The appendix to this chapter presents a mathematical treatment of Penrose's theory. Only the internal dynamics are considered, and they are greatly simplified, but the mathematical model does lead one to question Penrose's statement that 'we have found nothing to prevent the indefinite expansion of firms as time passes'. In particular, her theory appears to imply that the expansion path of any given firm could fall into either of two patterns, depending on such things as the productivity of managerial employees, the gross margins obtainable on products, and the 'manager-intensiveness' of the production process. One pattern corresponds to expansion into the indefinite future, as she suggested. The other pattern corresponds to expansion followed by contraction. Thus, Penrose's theory ended up where Haire's began.

Decision-process models

Decision-process models attempt to reproduce the fabric of organizational decisions. These models are potentially the most fruitful approach to organizational growth but they are expensive. The model-builder must try to specify, by direct observation of individual organizations, all of the major decision rules used by the organizations and then test his model against detailed data on actual behavior. Because little is known about decision processes at present, and because the processes are complex, armchair theorizing tends to be unrewarding.

The current body of knowledge on decision-process models is due almost completely to Cyert and March and their associates. 'Our conception of the task we face is that of constructing a theory that takes (1) the firm as its basic unit, (2) the prediction of firm behavior with respect to such decisions as price, output, and resource allocation as its objective, and (3) an explicit emphasis on the actual process of organizational decision making as its basic research commitment' (1963, p. 19).

Cyert, Feigenbaum and March developed a duopoly model which, although it has less direct empirical basis than one might like, illustrates the application of a decision-process model to growth. The authors considered a market, formerly monopolized by one firm, in which the monopolist has been forced to permit the establishment of a smaller 'splinter' firm. Their interest was the relative profitabilities and sales volumes of the two firms.

The theory we have used differs from conventional [economic] theory in six important respects: (1) The models are built on a description of the decision-making process. That is, they specify organizations that evaluate competitors, costs, and demand in the light of their own objectives and (if necessary) re-examine each of these to arrive at a decision. (2) The models depend on a theory of search as well as a theory of choice. They specify under what conditions search will be intensified (e.g. when a satisfactory alternative is not available). They also specify the direction in which search is undertaken. In general, we predict that a firm will look first for new alternatives or new information in the area it views as most under its control. Thus, in the present models we have made the specific prediction that cost estimates will be re-examined first, demand estimates second, and organizational objectives third. (3) The models describe organizations in which objectives change over time as a result of experience. Goals are not taken as given initially and fixed thereafter. They change as the organization observes its success (or lack of it) in the market. In these models the profit objective at a given time is an average of achieved profit over a number of past periods. The number of past periods considered by the firm varies from firm to firm. (4) Similarly, the models describe organizations that adjust forecasts on the basis of experience. Organizational learning occurs as a result of observations of actual competitors' behavior, actual market demand, and actual costs. Each of the organizations we have used readjusts its perceptions on the basis of such learning. The learning rules used are quite simple. This is both because simple rules are easier to handle than complex rules and because we expect the true rules to be susceptible to close approximation by simple ones. (5) The models introduce organizational biases in making estimates. For a variety of reasons we expect some organizations to be more conservative with respect to cost estimates than other organizations, some organizations to be more optimistic with respect to demand than others, some organizations to be more attentive to and perceptive of changes in competitors' plans than others. As we develop more detailed submodels of the estimation process, these factors will be increasingly obvious. In the present models we have not attempted to develop such submodels but have simply predicted the outcome of the estimation process in different firms. (6) The models all introduce features of 'organizational slack'. That is, we expect that over a period of time during which an organization is achieving its goals a certain amount of the resources of the organization are funneled into the satisfaction of individual and subgroup objectives. This slack then becomes a reservoir of potential economies when satisfactory plans are more difficult to develop.

In order to deal with these revisions, the models have been written explicitly as computer programs. Such treatment has two major values. First, simulation permits the introduction of process variables. The language of the computer is such that many of the phenomena of business behavior that do not fit into classical models can be considered without excessive artificiality. Entering naturally into the model are cost and demand perceptions within the firm in relation to such factors as age of firm, organizational structure, background of executives, and phase of the business cycle; information handling within the firm and its relation to the communication structure, training, and reward system in the organization; and the effects of organizational success and failure on organizational goals and organizational slack.

Secondly, simulation easily generates data on the time path of outputs, prices, etc. For that large class of economic problems in which equilibrium theory is either irrelevant or relatively uninteresting, computer methodology provides a major alternative to the mathematics of comparative statics (1959, pp. 93–4).

In the model which Cyert, Feigenbaum and March developed, each firm followed a decision sequence involving five basic steps: (a) forecast competitor's behavior, (b) forecast demand, (c) estimate costs, (d) specify a profit goal, and (e) determine whether any level of output will satisfy the profit goal. If (e) implied that a satisfactory profit could be obtained, the firm chose an output level. If (e) implied that no output level would yield a satisfactory profit, the firm (f) revised its estimate of costs, or (g) revised its forecast of demand, or, as a last resort, (h) revised its profit goal. The ex-monopolist and the splinter firm were assumed to display crucial differences. The ex-monopolist was more heavily influenced by past performance, and the splinter by recent performance, when forecasting their competitor's behavior and when setting their profit goals. The ex-monopolist made a pessimistic forecast of demand and was less willing than the splinter to revise this estimate; the splinter made an optimistic forecast of demand. The ex-monopolist started out with a higher unit cost than did the splinter.

The authors compared this model with actual data on 'the

competition between American Can Company and its splinter competitor, Continental Can Company, over the period from 1913 to 1956', and obtained results which they felt were 'rather surprisingly good' (pp. 90–93). As they pointed out, there are serious problems in fitting this type of model to data. The number of parameters in the model was so large that, if one could find a practical computation scheme, an exact fit might have been possible, But the model was so complex, and the relations among parameters so obscure, that no such computation scheme existed. As a result, *a priori* parameter estimates were as much a part of the hypothesis tested as the structure of the decision process.

Since 1959, Cyert and March have constructed more elaborate models based on case studies of actual decisions. These models differed from the duopoly model in including several, independent and partially conflicting goals instead of the single profit goal. But they resembled the duopoly model in emphasizing adaptation, learning, search, and dynamic interactions between the organization and its environment. One of these models was 'a summary of our understanding of the key microprocesses in price and output determination by a modern firm' (Cyert and March, 1963, ch 8). However, this model was too complex to discuss here, and it has not been applied to a situation of immediate relevance for growth.

One problem with most models of organizational growth is that they imply a degree of autonomy and predestination which is difficult to reconcile with one's direct observation. The decision-process models take the organization's concern with immediate and unique problems as their central theme, letting long-run patterns emerge as by-products of short-run decisions. This is a realistic and promising approach. But before decision-process models can start to make major contributions to the understanding of organizational growth, a great deal more work will have to be invested in them. For one thing, little is known at present about long-run learning. The studies to date have tried to capture the organizational decision structure at one point in time. Virtually no evidence has been gathered about the way this decision structure evolves – how it came to be and by what mechanisms it changes. For another thing, methods must be discovered for handling decision-process models methodologically. The stronger the empirical base of these models, the more complex they become; and the more complex the models become, the harder it is to understand why they do what they do. For instance, Bonini has said of his hypothetical model:

The majority of this chapter has been devoted to discussing specific mechanisms which influenced the major results. It is important, however, not to overemphasize the importance of these mechanisms in causing the results. They certainly have contributed, but there are many interactions and interconnections in the model. It is the whole system which produced the result, and we must be cautious in attaching undue importance to any specific part (1963, p. 144).

We cannot explain completely the reasons why the firm behaves in a specific fashion. Our model of the firm is highly complex and it is not possible to trace out the behavior pattern throughout the firm. ... Therefore, we cannot pinpoint the explicit causal mechanism in the model (p. 136).

Administrative structure and growth

Structural correlates of size and age are popular topics for debate and speculation. Regrettably, many more people have speculated about them than have collected and analyzed data about them. But there is some empirical evidence, and this section exploits it unmercifully.

As a focal question around which to arrange the discussion, it is asked: do old, large organizations suffer from declining administrative efficiency? This is an issue in the will-o'-the-wisp and cell-division models of growth, in the formalization process, and in such goals as cost, profit, executive salaries, and prestige–power–security. However, the central interest is in what actually happens to administrative structure as organizational size and age increase, not in what should be done to make an organization efficient. Normative commentaries are cited only because, if organizations try to organize themselves efficiently, normative statements may turn out to be descriptive statements. Moreover, since administrative efficiency is not the only concern, the discussion ranges over subjects which have little direct bearing on this question. In particular, the final sections are devoted to data on managerial employment.

The question of administrative efficiency

There is a proposition, accepted primarily among economists, that 'the difficulties of internal organization usually check the growth of individual enterprises well short of complete monopoly' (Warner and Low, 1947, p. 113).

Economists have adopted this proposition opportunistically. As Andrews observed:

Economists have found that the application to the real world of the abstract theory of pure competition requires that long-run costs should rise with increased scale. This has made it easy for the supposition to be accepted in economics that long-run costs do, in fact, rise, and, in the absence of any other plausible explanation as to why they should rise, economists have tended to call in increasing managerial inefficiency as a fairly plausible hypothesis which could not easily be refuted (1949b, p. 128).

Ross (1952–3, p. 148) has made a similar statement.

The theory of pure competition assumes no market limitation on the sales of any single firm. A firm produces whatever quantity will maximize the firm's total profit, and has no difficulty disposing of the chosen quantity at the given market price. Suppose that the market price is p and that the firm's total cost curve is given by

$$c_0 + c_1 q + c_2 q^2,$$

where q represents output and c_0, c_1 and c_2 are non-negative. The firm's profit is

$$pq - [c_0 + c_1 q + c_2 q^2],$$

and profit would be maximized when

$$q = \frac{p - c_1}{2c_2}.$$

The importance of c_2 is evident. Only if c_2 is positive will the optimum q be finite; if c_2 is zero, the firm will produce an infinite output. Economic theorists have made managerial costs the basis for a positive c_2. The 'logical' argument, stripped to essentials, has been: (a) a firm has a finite size; (b) therefore c_2 must be positive; (c) but technology implies that c_1 is small and c_2 zero (e.g. specialization of labor, quantity discounts on raw materials, stochastic returns to scale); (d) 'increasing managerial inefficiency' could make c_2 positive, and it is 'a fairly plausible hypothesis which could not easily be refuted'.

Robinson is usually credited with the managerial inefficiency hypothesis.

... an optimum firm with an upper limit imposed by the difficulties and costs of co-ordination is both logically satisfactory and a necessary hypothesis to explain the existing facts (1934, p. 256)

Robinson argued that managerial efficiency depended primarily on the skills of the entrepreneur at the peak of the managerial hierarchy. As the firm grew larger, the talents of this one man were spread more and more thinly across the range of operations, and decreasing efficiency ensued. Chamberlin took issue with Robinson, pointing out that management was not a 'fixed factor'. Others besides the entrepreneur could display managerial skill, and the organization's total managerial resources could be expanded by adding managers to the structure. Nevertheless, like Robinson, Chamberlin was bound to the logical necessity of a positive c_2. He attributed this to managerial inefficiency, specifically, 'the greater complexity of the producing unit as it grows in size, leading to increased difficulties of coordination and management'. Chamberlin was frank about the motivation for his assumption:

It is sometimes argued that a policy of decentralization may be adopted beyond the minimum point, reproducing the conditions there found in substantially independent units, and thus eliminating, almost by definition, the problems of complexity. ... In so far as decentralization is an effective means of combating the diseconomies of size, far from being denied, it is, of course, included by definition in the envelope curve at all points ... and its effect may often be to postpone net diseconomies far beyond the scales of production to be found in reality. It is contended only that the curve does turn up somewhere (1948, p. 250).

Discussions by organization theorists have partially paralleled those by economists – contrasting, on the one hand, the returns to scale from specialization and, on the other hand, the problems of coordinating divided labor. For example, Fordham (1957–8) suggested that the efficiency of an individual member of the organization was the product of two functions. One was an increasing function of the span of control, implying that as the span of control increased, each subordinate became more of a specialist and developed more expertise. The other was a decreasing function of the span of control, implying that as the span of control increased, each subordinate had to spend more and more time communicating with other members of the organization.

However, the organization theorists' interest in the complexity assumption appears to have derived less from theoretical opportunism than from wide-eyed absorption in the binomial expansion. Among those who have used the complexity assumption are Bossard (1945), Caplow (1957), Davis (1951), Dubin (1959), Entwisle and Walton (1961), Haire (1959), Herbst (1957), Kephart (1950), and Urwick (1956). Most of the complexity arguments by organization theorists and sociologists have paid homage to Graicunas (1933). Graicunas observed that a group composed of persons A, B and C might behave differently from a group composed of A, B and D. From this he concluded that the 'complexity' of a group composed of n people was proportional to the total number of distinct dyads, triads and so forth which could be formed from the group. That is, complexity was proportional to[10]

$$\sum_{k=2}^{n} C_k^n = 2^n - n - 1.$$

However, few of Graicunas's disciples have adopted this formula in its full glory. They have emphasized only the number of dyads in the group:

$$C_2^n = \frac{n(n-1)}{2}.$$

10. This is not the formula given by Graicunas. He used n to represent the number of subordinates; here n represents the subordinates plus their supervisor. Further, Graicunas's formulation has been corrected. He counted some dyads twice, including them under 'direct single' relationships and 'cross' relationships and also under 'direct group' relationships. The formula given is the correct one for the number of relationships 'computed on minimum basis', that is, equating the dyads AB and BA.

Herbst's discussion is indicative:

Let us suppose that the components of a system are independent of one another or very nearly so, then the amount of work required for control would be proportional to the number of components (n) of the system, so that the

amount of control work $= b_1 n.$

If the component parts are interconnected, then the amount of work required additionally for the coordination of components may be taken to be a function of the number of interconnections between components. The maximum number of interdependence links between n components is $n(n-1)/2$ so that in the simplest case

maximum coordination work $\simeq b_2 n^2.$

If we compare the amount of work in the form of control and integration in the case where there is complete interdependence between component parts with that where there is complete linkage between components, we find that this is a function of n (the number of components) in one case and of n^2 in the other. The size of the integrating unit may then be taken to be a function of the size of the system raised to the power $1 + a$ where a may be taken as a measure of the degree of complexity of the system in terms of the degree of connectedness between its components (1957, p. 341).

The idea that complexity varies with 'the degree of connectedness between its components' has been a standard part of the complexity discussions. Urwick (1956) was careful to restrict his discussion of complexity to subordinates *'whose work interlocks'*, and Graicunas observed that 'this factor will operate with much less force where the work done by each of various subordinates does not come into contact with that done by others'.

Herbst was, however, one of the few organization theorists who have made complexity the basis for declining efficiency in the organization as a whole. Among most, there has been a consensus of confidence in an organization's ability to factor its tasks among work groups without producing serious coordination problems. The purpose for which Graicunas created his formula, and the purpose to which complexity arguments have typically been put, is the justification of small work groups within the organization, i.e. the justification of a small span of control. Graicunas argued that the span of control should be such that the number of relations supervised approximately equaled the maximum 'span of attention' of one supervisor. As a matter of fact, the specific functional form of the complexity function was irrelevant to Graicunas's argument. He used only one arbitrary point of the function and any increasing function of n would have been equally satisfactory.

The optimum span of control was supposed to be smaller near the top of the management hierarchy than near the bottom, because there was greater need for coordination near the top. Hamilton (1921) said the span of control should be approximately three near the top, increasing to six at the bottom. Several other theorists have agreed with him. Caplow (1957) justified spans between three and six on a different basis. He argued that this was the natural size range for 'groups of intimates', and he cited James's (1951; 1953) data on the size distribution of 'free-forming' small groups as evidence for his position. For statistical discussions of James's data, see Coleman and James (1961), Simon (1955), and H. White (1962). Trist and Bamforth (1951) also have stressed the importance of organizing around 'primary groups'.

There has by no means been a consensus that spans between three and six were optimal. Likert wrote: 'The optimum size of units in local Leagues has been found from experience to be about fifteen to twenty persons. This is also true of boards. Similarly, the optimum size of resource committees is usually not more than about fifteen to twenty persons.' He conceded that even below this size 'there is some decrease in effectiveness per member', but 'as the groups exceed about twenty, the decrease in effectiveness becomes more marked' (Likert, 1961, p. 159). Suojanen said, 'the institutionalization of the organization and the development of primary relationships among the members of the executive group together provide such a high degree of control that the area of effective supervision of the chief executive is much wider than that predicted by the span of control principle' (1955, p. 13). Argyris objected that small spans 'increase the subordinates' feelings of dependence, submissiveness, passivity, and the like' (1957, p. 66).

One argument against small spans of control pointed out that, holding the size of the organization constant, small spans implied many hierarchical levels. According to Simon:

> The dilemma is this: in a large organization with interrelations between members, a restricted span of control inevitably produces excessive red tape, for each contact between organization members must be carried upward until a common superior is found. . . .
> The alternative is to increase the number of persons who are under the command of each officer, so that the pyramid will come more rapidly to a peak, with fewer intervening levels. But this, too, leads to a difficulty, for if an officer is required to supervise too many employees, his control over them is weakened.
> Granted then, that both the increase and the decrease in span of control have some undesirable consequences, what is the optimum point? (1957a, p. 28).

Dubin noted that 'the greater the number of links in the system, the greater will be the probability of "noise" in functional connections among organization units' (1959, p. 229). Richardson and Walker (1948) and Worthy (1950a; 1950b) have reported situations where reductions in the number of hierarchical levels were correlated with heightened morale (also see Blau and Scott, 1962, ch. 5).

Most theories of organization have taken the position that – provided the span of control, the number of hierarchical levels, and other variables were properly manipulated – organizational size had little effect on managerial efficiency. The self-confidence of Mooney and Reiley was atypical, but their fundamental attitude was not:

> If the principles of organization we have asserted are real and not imaginary, then their correct application must contain the solvent of all such problems. Given this application, it is impossible to conceive of any human organization too vast for organized efficiency (1931, pp. 504–5).

One consequence of this attitude has been that organization theorists have searched for solutions to the organizational problem – effective factorings of the organization into departments – and have not worried about the possibility that such solutions might be less efficient for large organizations than for small ones.[11] For example, March and Simon said:

The problem of departmentalization that emerges out of this section and the previous one centers on two variables: self-containment (or alternatively, coordination requirements), and skill specialization. Its central proposition is that the forms of departmentalization that are advantageous in terms of one of these outcomes are often costly in terms of the other: process departmentalization generally takes greater advantage of the potentialities for economy through specialization than does purpose departmentalization; purpose departmentalization leads to greater self-containment and lower coordination costs than does process departmentalization. As size of organization increases, the marginal advantages accruing to process organization from the first source become smaller, while the coordination costs become larger. Hence, the balance of net efficiency shifts from process to purpose organization as the size of organization increases (1958, p. 29; also see Miller, 1959).

Empirical studies of administrative structure

There has been a tendency, stronger among early organization theorists than among recent ones, to view the administrative structure as a pyramidal hierarchy. One man comprises the top level in this hierarchy; he has s subordinates who comprise the second level; each of these has s subordinates, giving s^2 people in the third level; and so forth. Of course, s is the span of control and the total number of administrative employees in a hierarchy with λ levels is

$$A = 1+s+s^2+s^3+\ldots+s^{\lambda-1}$$

$$= \frac{s^{\lambda}-1}{s-1}.$$

Taking σ to be the number of production workers per foreman, there are

$$P = \sigma.s^{\lambda-1}$$

11. The author does not mean to exaggerate the difference between economists and organization theorists. Ross (1952–3) and Andrews (1949a; 1949b) seem to have agreed with Mooney and Reiley. Conversely, Davis (1951) and Warner and Low (1947) were convinced that efficiency declined as size increased.

production workers and

$$T = A + P = \frac{s^\lambda - 1}{s - 1} + \sigma \cdot s^{\lambda - 1}$$

total employees (Beckmann, 1960). Only three of the four variables s, σ, λ and T are free. In particular,

$$\lambda = \frac{1}{\log s} \cdot \left[\log\{1 + T(s-1)\} - \log\left\{1 + \sigma\left(1 - \frac{1}{s}\right)\right\} \right].$$

Administrative efficiency can be measured by the ratio of administrative employees to production employees. The pyramidal model implies that the ratio A/P increases very slightly as T increases. For virtually any organization of interest,

$$\frac{A}{P} > \frac{1}{\sigma}$$

and in the limit as T goes to infinity,

$$\frac{A}{P} \to \frac{1}{\sigma} \cdot \frac{s}{s-1}.$$

Figure 1 shows the A/P ratio as a function of T, for $s = 6$ and for two values of σ. Note that the abscissa is logarithmic.

The possibility that s is smaller at the top of the hierarchy than at the bottom can be ignored. For example, if the chief executive had a span of 3, his subordinates had spans of $3 + \alpha$, their subordinates had spans of $3 + 2\alpha$, and so forth, and if α were chosen so that the average span for all administrative employees were 6, then the A/P ratio would graph exactly as shown in Figure 1. The number of hierarchical levels would not be the same, however, λ being larger in this second case.

At first glance, the pyramid is a horribly oversimplified model of organizational structure. Nevertheless, this model, or a variant of it, is consistent with the available data on administrative employment. Studies of administrative structure can be separated into three categories: studies taking *size* as the independent variable, studies taking *technology* as the independent variable, and studies taking *time* or age as the independent variable. Each category is considered in turn.

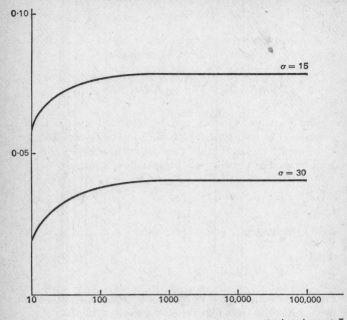

total employment, T

Figure 1 A/P as a function of T for $s = 6$

Studies of structure as a function of size. Healey surveyed 620 plants having more than 100 employees. He concluded that 'in practice, the span of control closely adheres to that usually advocated in theory' (1956, p. 116). The chief executives in the surveyed plants reported spans of control as shown in Table 4. Although some executives reported spans greater than five, 'no executive mentioned more than five subordinates in the group of preferred policy formulators' (p. 108). Thus, the span-of-control principle has some descriptive value. One reason for this may be that businessmen believe in the 'principles of management' (Newman and Logan, 1955, pp. 20–21).

Healey also reported that the span for executives in branch plants was greater than the span for executives in main plants. Taking a branch plant executive to be lower in the organizational hierarchy than a main plant executive, he interpreted this as evidence that spans were smaller near the top of the hierarchy.

Table 4

| Size of span | Per cent reporting span | |
	445 Main plants	175 Branch plants
1	12·0	10·3
2	11·7	13·3
3 to 8	70·0	60·6
>8	6·3	15·8

Source: Healey (1956).

Without the original data one cannot be certain, but a rough check suggests that the mean spans for the two groups and the two frequency distributions are significantly different. The problem, of course, is that this might have been a plant-size effect. On the same theme, Blau and Scott have reported that 'in the two welfare agencies the top managers had fewer subordinates . . . while the first-line supervisors had more. . . .' (1962, p. 169).

However, the model of Figure 1 may be inappropriate as it stands. s may increase with T. Healey wrote, 'as the size of the establishment increases, the span used by the chief executive also increases' (p. 108). Woodward reported that 'in the large-batch and mass-production group . . . the span of control of both the chief executive and the first line supervisor . . . tended to increase with size' (1958, p. 20). Two surveys of the span for chief executives have given numerical data. Entwisle and Walton (1961) found that colleges and business firms in the size range 100–700 had a median span of 5. Dale (1952) found that business firms in the size range 500–5000 had a median span of 6·5, and that firms larger than 5000 had a median span of 8·5.

Doing some wild guessing on the basis of the Entwisle and Walton and Dale reports, one can estimate:[12]

$$s \simeq 2.\log_{10} T.$$

This makes what may be a significant change in the behavior of A/P as a function of T. The relationship is graphed in Figure 2. Note that the ratio rises rapidly to a maximum and then decreases monotonically. Although A/P is still relatively constant, the rate of change is greater than, and of opposite sign to, the situation shown, in Figure 1. In the limit as T goes to infinity,

$$\frac{A}{P} \to \frac{1}{\sigma}.$$

Evidence about the behavior of σ as a function of T is even more sketchy than the evidence about s. What evidence there is suggests that σ increases with T. Woodward's finding was quoted above, and Haire said: 'The ratio of supervisors to supervised does not go up as the company grows. On the contrary, as the line increased, each supervisor was responsible for more men' (1959, p. 296).

12. The organizations studied by Entwisle and Walton had a mean size of 225, and the range 100–700 implies a geometric mean of 265. Dale's group in the range 500–5000 has a geometric mean of 1580, so one estimates the mean size of the organizations to have been

$$1580.\frac{225}{265} = 1340.$$

Now, the ratios of the mean size to the lower bound are $\frac{225}{100}$ and $\frac{1340}{500}$. Fitting these ratios to the logs one can estimate that the mean size of the over-5000 organizations was

$$5000.(3\cdot29) = 16,450.$$

To summarize:

Estimated mean size (T)	Median span of chief executive (s)
225	5·0
1340	6·5
16,450	8·5

A straight line through these points would be $s = 0\cdot6 + 1\cdot9.\log_{10} T$.

It is equally hard to uncover data on the A/P ratio as a function of T. Terrien and Mills surveyed California school districts and concluded: 'The relationship between the size of an administrative component and the total size of its containing organization

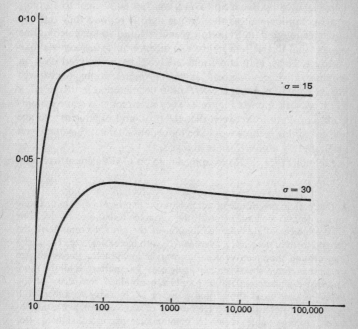

Figure 2 A/P as a function of T for $s = 2 \cdot \log_{10} T$

is such that the larger the size of the containing organization the greater will be the proportion given over to its administrative component' (1955, p. 11). Their data appear to have been consistent with Figure 1 where $\sigma = s$ and where the span is 7 for elementary schools, 5 for high schools, and 6 for unified systems. It seems logical that the span for high schools would be smaller than the span for elementary schools, and also that the span for unified systems would be the average of the spans for high schools and elementary schools. Baker and Davis (1954) have reported data on direct and indirect employment in 211 Ohio manufacturing firms. They drew a number of graphs, but did no statistical analyses and treated the data in a way that gave great weight to three very large firms. The indirect-employment category used by Baker and Davis was not equivalent to administrative employment as the term is used here, and they did not publish enough data to permit reanalysis, but rough calculations suggest that the ratio of indirect to direct employees behaved like Figure 1. Haas, Hall and Johnson (1963) have analyzed data on administrative employment in thirty organizations of various kinds. They found that the A/P ratio decreased as T increased, a result which supports Figure 2. They also reported some insignificant correlations between the A/P ratio and organizational age and technology; these would be more convincing if they had been generated by a multivariate analysis.

Melman (1951, 1958) examined data on 1741 business firms and decided:

Differences in magnitude of administrative overhead [A/P] at one time appear to be independent of all the variables tested, except size. For all the indices of size the distribution of the plotted points took the general form of decreasing average A/P with increasing size. The variation around the mean values, however, is greatest for the small size units, then diminishes with increasing size. This pattern is all the more impressive since comparable results are obtained regardless of the index of size used. (For firms grouped by industry: number of P personnel; total assets; average number of wage-earners per establishment; average value added by manufacture per establishment. For individual firms: net sales; total assets.) The apparent similarity of the distribution relating A/P with degree of mechanization (average horsepower per wage-earner) is consistent with these findings, for mechanization has generally correlated with size difference, larger plants using, on the average, more machinery per wage-earner. . . .

The magnitude of administrative overhead does not appear to be systematically related to the following factors: corporate organizations; multi-plant firms; concentration; profitability; pricing practices; selling effort; age of firm; employment of technicians; product type (1951, p. 75).

Regrettably Melman did not make statistical tests or use multiple regression. He wrote: 'Through graphic presentation we attempt to establish the presence or absence of presumed relationships.' Consequently, his findings must be taken with a large grain of salt. His graphs suggest that regression of A/P against the various measures of size would probably have yielded negative slopes, as he said, but also that these slopes would not have been significantly different from zero. The most reasonable conclusion is that Melman found no significant correlations. A related, and more serious, problem arises from his treating all manufacturing firms as one homogeneous class of organization. With the exception of one figure his data points represented industry averages, not individual firms, and his graphs were plotted *mutatis mutandis*. As a result, there is a real question what his independent variables were.

Another study of administration as a function of size was by McNulty (1956–7). He related administrative cost to plant size. However, his data concerned A and not P, so there was no basis for inference about their ratio.

Studies of structure as a function of technology. Harbison and Myers (1959) have stated some hypotheses about the relations between administrative structure and technology.

Anderson and Warkov (1961) obtained data on general and TB hospitals and found that the A/P ratio decreased as size increased. Their paper presented little data, but their results appear to have been consistent with Figure 2 *provided* that one assumes that σ increased with T. The rate of decrease implied by their data is greater than the rate of decrease implied by Figure 2 with σ constant. Rough calculations imply

$\sigma = 3 \cdot 8 \cdot \log_{10} T$, for TB hospitals
$\sigma = 3 \cdot 1 \cdot \log_{10} T$, for general hospitals,

where it is assumed that $s = 2 \cdot \log_{10} T$. The resultant behavior of A/P as a function of T is graphed in Figure 3.

Anderson and Warkov recognized the apparent conflict between their findings and those of Terrien and Mills, and explained this difference on technological grounds. They hypothesized three relations: (a) *A/P decreased* as the number of personnel performing identical tasks in the same place increased; (b)

A/P increased as the number of different tasks performed in the same place increased; (c) *A/P increased* as the number of different places – geographic locations – increased. They argued that

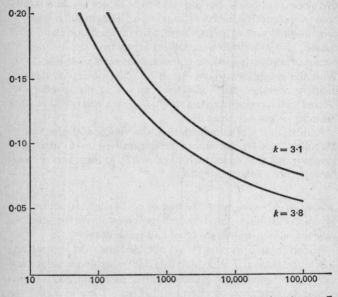

Figure 3 *A/P* as a function of *T* for $s = 2 \cdot \log_{10} T$ and $\sigma = k \log_{10} T$

general hospitals had higher *A/P* ratios than TB hospitals of the same size because TB hospitals were more specialized – relations (a) and (b) – and that Terrien and Mills obtained an increasing *A/P* ratio because each school system included several schools in distinct geographic locations – relation (c).

The consistency Anderson and Warkov perceived between their data and the Terrien and Mills data is not self-evident, but one way it might work is this: suppose that each organization is composed of *N* 'departments', each representing a distinct location and task, and that these departments are joined by an administrative superstructure. *N*, the number of departments, is essentially the product of the number of locations and the number of tasks. The A/P ratio for the whole organization is

$$\frac{A_s}{N.P_d} + \frac{A_d}{P_d},$$

where A_s is the number of administrators in the superstructure, A_d is the number of administrators in one department, and P_d is the number of production workers in one department. Now, suppose that growth is a matter of adding new departments and not of expanding existing departments. This kind of growth would leave the average size of a department, $A_d + P_d$, constant, and the term A_d/P_d would be independent of the size of the whole organization. The other term, A_s/N, would increase with the size of the organization. For the superstructure, N is equivalent to the P in Figures 1 and 2, so A_s/N should behave like A/P in those figures. Because P_d is constant, it can be ignored. In school systems, $A_s + N$ is nearly always less than 100, and therefore A_s/N would be an increasing function of organizational size under either Figure 1 or Figure 2. If $A_s + N$ is greater than 100, A_s/N would be an increasing function of organizational size only if Figure 1 obtains.

Another technologically oriented study of the A/P ratio was Woodward's survey of 100 manufacturing firms having more than 100 employees. Woodward classified the firms in three groups which she took to represent successive stages of 'technical complexity'. (It is not really accurate to call the technological variable 'complexity', since this complexity seems to correspond to the *smoothness* of production, but this was Woodward's term.) Group I represented small batch and *unit* production; group II represented large batch and *mass* production; and group III represented continuous-flow or *process* production. Only eighty of the 100 firms were actually placed in one of the three categories; the other twenty had ambiguous technologies. The frequency distribution of the eighty was rather uniform. Twenty-four firms were classified as 'unit'; thirty-one firms were classified as 'mass'; twenty-five firms were classified as 'process'.

The case studies confirmed that variations in organizational requirements between firms are nearly always linked with differences in their techniques of production. For example, differences in two large-batch-production firms of approximately equal size were traced to the fact that one of them, although mainly producing large batches, also made a few articles to customers' individual requirements.

Thus it was possible to trace a 'cause and effect' relationship between a system of production and its associated organizational pattern and, as a result to predict what the organizational requirements of a firm are likely to be, given its production system. For example, the following features can be traced to the technology of each system of production: a coordination of functions and centralization of authority in unit production; an extensive specialization and delegation of authority in mass production; and in process industry a specialization between development, marketing and production, combined with integration within each function and the co-operative character of decision-making.

The background survey showed that the successful firms approximated to the medians of the group in which they had been placed. This indicates that the medians for each group represented a pattern of organization appropriate to the technology of that group (Woodward, 1958, p. 37; also see p. 21).

Woodward's data on the A/P ratio suggest that there was no correlation between A/P and size, but that there was a significant correlation between A/P and 'technological complexity'. A least-squares fit to the equation

$$A/P = C_0 + C_1 . [\text{complexity coefficient}] + C_2 . \log_{10} T$$

gives $C_0 = 0 \cdot 04$
$C_1 = 0 \cdot 1$
$C_2 = -0 \cdot 001,$

where the following complexity coefficients are assigned: 0 for unit firms, $0 \cdot 23$ for mass firms, and 1 for process firms. The complexity coefficient for mass-production firms, $0 \cdot 23$, was estimated as a parameter in the least-squares fit. Woodward reported that similar data were obtained on the ratio of indirect to direct labor and the ratio of administrative and clerical staff to hourly paid workers. Thus, Woodward's findings generally supported Figures 1 and 2, since the firms were all large enough to be on the flat portions of both curves.

Woodward found that 'the number of levels of authority in the management hierarchy increased with technical complexity' and 'the span of control of the chief executive widened considerably with technical advance' (pp. 16–17; Figure 2, p. 14). Apparently these were technological effects, not size effects, because in Woodward's sample 'no significant relationship was revealed between the size of the firm and the system of production' (p. 20; Table II, p. 20).

Udy (1959b) has also attempted to relate the number of hierarchical levels to technology. He defined the 'required span of attention' of an organization to be the sum of the total number of tasks performed by the organization, the maximum number of specialized operations performed at one time, and a binary variable which was one if combined effort was ever present and zero if combined effort was always absent. Applying this *ad hoc* measure to 82 nonindustrial production organizations, Udy obtained a significant positive relationship between the 'required span of attention' and the number of hierarchical levels in the organization.

One of Woodward's most interesting findings was that σ was a $\cap$-shaped (concave) function of complexity. 'The span of control of the first-line supervisor . . . reached its peak in mass production and then decreased' (p. 16; Figure 3; p. 15). This finding has been corroborated, in a sense, by Blau (1957), Faunce (1958), Harbison *et al.* (1955), and Simpson (1959). Blau and Simpson reported that mechanization increased σ; Faunce and Harbison and associates reported that mechanization decreased σ. Simpson suggested that these results were consistent. Mechanization in the sense of transition from unit to mass production reduced the need for vertical communication and coordination because the machines did part of the work scheduling (Walker and Guest, 1952). Mechanization in the sense of transition from mass to process production increased the need for technical expertise.

Chowdhry and Pal (1957) have reported the effects of a technological difference similar to Woodward's complexity. They compared two weaving mills of approximately the same size. In Mill A, product characteristics were changed frequently in response to shifts in demand (unit production). In Mill B, product characteristics were changed infrequently, the emphasis being on high quality staples (mass production). Mill A made its product changes during the day shift. Mill A had a higher A/P ratio during the day than at night; Mill B had the same A/P ratio on both shifts. Mill A's day shift seems to have had a smaller σ than either its night shift or Mill B. Depending on how one counts, Mill B might have had more levels in its managerial hierarchy. Thus, Chowdhry and Pal's results were consistent with Woodward's except that A/P *decreased* with 'complexity' in the weaving mills. The significance of this difference depends a great deal, of course, on the luck Chowdhry and Pal had in choosing their sample of two.

Harbison and associates (1955) have pointed out some cultural variations in structure. For one thing, German top and middle managers tended to become involved in the technical details of problems whereas American managers tended to 'supervise'. For another thing, σ was much higher in German mills than in American mills. They attributed this to the higher skill of German workers and to the greater mechanization of American plants.

Studies of structure as a function of time. Bendix (1956), Chester (1961), and Melman (1951, 1958) have suggested that the A/P ratio increases with time. Melman summarized his findings:

2. The A/P ratio has been increasing in all countries where the business process is the dominant form of decision-making in industrial production.

3. The growth of administrative overhead has been traceable to the elaboration of administrative functions. The development has been toward enlarging the scope of decision-making by management, as well as its intensity.

4. The growth in the A/P ratio has occurred as a net result, taking into account the increase in productivity in both administration and production occupations.

5. Both the growth of administrative overhead over time, and variations in levels of administrative overhead at single times, have been found to be independent of variation in the productivity of the production work force. [In his 1951 paper, Melman implied that the increase in A/P was partially due to 'the steady increase in the productivity of directly productional manhours'.]. . .

7. The growth of administrative overhead has been substantially homogeneous among firms and industries, though displaying variation at given times and over short periods (1958, pp. 121–2).

And Chester, who reported an international study of chemical and metal-goods firms, wrote:

The phenomenon recently described in the United States for industry to show a relatively greater increase in non-manual workers was fully confirmed by this study. Indeed, it seems to have been greatest in the chemical firms, generally more acclaimed as perhaps the most efficient symbol of modern times – Parkinson's Law put on its head! (1961, p. 62).

So far as can be judged from the current investigation increases in size of establishment and scale of operations appear to have a greater impact on organizational change than technological innovation (p. 48).

It has already been pointed out that Melman's conclusions were drawn without benefit of formal statistical analyses. The same was true of Chester's conclusions. However, Chester's study had two virtues: his data applied to specific individual firms, and he published his data. Consequently, further analyzing can be done here.

Four hypotheses can be posed: administrative employment increases with production output;[13] administrative employment increases with total employment; administrative employment increases with time; and administrative employment increases with technological complexity.

The first hypothesis implies that administrative work is primarily a matter of processing customers' orders, ordering raw materials, and scheduling production. The second implies that administrative work is primarily a matter of coordinating the activities of people. The third implies that the nature of administrative work changes over time; Melman, for example, said:

The explanation of the rather homogeneous increase in the administrative type of overhead will be found, we suggest, in the growing variety

13. This hypothesis was implicit in Chester's statement that the increasing A/P ratio was attributable, in part, to the increasing productivity of production workers. Since

$$\frac{A}{P} = \frac{A}{Q} \cdot \pi,$$

where π is productivity and Q is output, an increasing A/P means that A is more or less proportional to Q. Also see point 5 in Melman's summary above.

of business activities which are being subjected to controls, both private and public. As administrators have sought to lessen the uncertainty of their prospects, by controlling more of the factors which determine the advantage of their plants and firms, they have attempted to control, in ever greater detail, production costs, intensity of work, market demands for products, and other aspects of firm operation (1951, p. 92).

Since Chester's data included metal-goods and chemical firms, the fourth hypothesis amounts to saying that administrative employment should be different in these two classes of firms. On the premise that Woodward would probably classify most metal-goods firms as 'mass' and most chemical firms as 'process', one would expect administrative employment to be higher in the chemical firms.

These four hypotheses are virtually impossible to disentangle empirically because, in typical data, the variables are all correlated with one another. Using Q to represent output, t to represent time, and I to represent the type of firm, the four hypotheses might be written

$$A = \alpha Q \qquad\qquad 1$$
$$A = \beta T \qquad\qquad 2$$
$$A = \gamma t \qquad\qquad 3$$
$$A = \delta I. \qquad\qquad 4$$

Relations between Q, T, t and I can be assumed. By definition

$$A = T - P; \qquad\qquad 5$$

the number of production employees depends on output,

$$P = \eta Q; \qquad\qquad 6$$

for most firms output increases with time,

$$Q = \varepsilon t; \qquad\qquad 7$$

and output is probably higher in one industry than the other,

$$Q = \zeta I. \qquad\qquad 8$$

These hypothetical relations greatly oversimplify, but they capture the basic spirit of the problem. The result is that A can be stated as a function of any variable, whatever the hypothesis, as shown in Table 5.

Table 5

Hypothesis	A as a function of Q	A as a function of T	A as a function of t	A as a function of I
$A = \alpha Q$	$A = \alpha Q$	$A = \dfrac{\alpha}{\alpha+\eta}T$	$A = \alpha\varepsilon t$	$A = \alpha\zeta I$
$A = \beta T$	$A = \dfrac{\beta\eta}{1-\beta}Q$	$A = \beta T$	$A = \dfrac{\beta\varepsilon\eta}{1-\beta}t$	$A = \dfrac{\beta\zeta\eta}{1-\beta}I$
$A = \gamma t$	$A = \dfrac{\gamma}{\varepsilon}Q$	$A = \dfrac{\gamma}{\gamma+\varepsilon\eta}T$	$A = \gamma t$	$A = \dfrac{\gamma\zeta}{\varepsilon}I$
$A = \delta I$	$A = \dfrac{\delta}{\zeta}Q$	$A = \dfrac{\delta}{\delta+\zeta\eta}T$	$A = \dfrac{\delta\varepsilon}{\zeta}t$	$A = \delta I$

The confusion is compounded when the hypotheses are more complex. α depends upon the productivity of production employees. It is generally agreed that productivity increases with time (t); productivity certainly depends on the type of industry (I); and it may be that productivity increases with plant size (P, T or Q). β is probably not constant either. At least the possibility that A/P is a function of T has just been discussed, and the second hypothesis implies

$$\frac{A}{P} = \frac{\beta}{1-\beta}.$$

One of the most serious problems with a system like this one is bias in the regression coefficients. Consider the second hypothesis. Even if it were complex enough to capture the basic relations, one would not expect the equation $A = \beta T$ to hold exactly. Certainly one would not run a regression unless he thought that random deviations from the basic relation were possible. Consequently, the relation should be written

$$A = \beta T + \mu,$$

where μ is a random deviation. By definition $A = T - P$, so one can perform the indicated substitutions and obtain

$$A = \frac{\beta}{1-\beta}P + \frac{1}{1-\beta}\mu$$

$$T = \frac{1}{1-\beta}P + \frac{1}{1-\beta}\mu.$$

Suppose that in order to 'test' the hypothesized relation, one uses the regression equation

$$A = \hat{\beta}_0 + \hat{\beta}_1 T$$

and expects to estimate

$$\hat{\beta}_0 \simeq 0$$
$$\hat{\beta}_1 \simeq \beta.$$

The actual estimates would be

$$\hat{\beta}_0 = -(1-\beta).\{\bar{P}[\mathrm{var}(\mu)+\mathrm{cov}(\mu P] - \bar{\mu}[\mathrm{var}(P)+\mathrm{cov}(\mu P)]\} \div$$
$$\div \{\mathrm{var}(P)+\mathrm{var}(\mu)+2\mathrm{cov}(\mu P)\}$$

$$\hat{\beta}_1 = \frac{\beta.\mathrm{var}(P)+\mathrm{var}(\mu)+(1+\beta).\mathrm{cov}(\mu P)}{\mathrm{var}(P)+\mathrm{var}(\mu)+2.\mathrm{cov}(\mu P)};$$

which would be quite different from the expected values in most cases. One is very likely to reject a hypothesis which is nearly correct . . . or to accept one which is incorrect.

Chester's data cover one metal-goods firm and one chemical firm in each of seven European countries.[14] For each firm the ratios A_2/A_1, T_2/T_1, and Q_2/Q_1 are available, where the subscript 2 indicates 1956 and the subscript 1 indicates a base year. In ten of the fourteen cases the base year is 1947; in the other four cases it varies from 1948 to 1952. Administrative employment is taken to be Chester's category 'nonmanual' employment. He did not say what measure of production output was used.

14. Appendix 2 of Chester's report included data, usable for present purposes, on 18 metal-goods firms and on 17 chemical firms, but because there may have been national differences in the classification of data, the sample is restricted to one firm from each country. The seven countries were Austria, Belgium, West Germany, the Netherlands, Norway, Sweden and the United Kingdom.

Two series of regressions have been run using the equation

$$\log_{10}(Y_2/Y_1) = C_1 \cdot \log_{10}(Q_2/Q_1) + C_2 \cdot \log_{10}(T_2/T_1) + (C_3 + C_4 I) \cdot (t_2 - t_1),$$

where I is a binary variable taking the value one for chemical firms and taking the value zero for metal-goods firms. In one series of calculations $Y = A$ and in the other series $Y = A/P$. This equation has little theoretical rationale; it implies that A can be greater than T. However, the values of all variables, except $(t_2 - t_1)$, are close to zero. The smallest is $-0 \cdot 12$ and the largest is $0 \cdot 65$. As a result, the rationale behind the equation is not really brought into question. The regression coefficients represent partial derivatives rather than structural parameters.

This equation does have three important advantages. First, the variables are ratios. This minimizes differences between firms in the ways employees are classified, in the manner in which output is measured, and in technological vagaries. Second, A_2/A_1 seems to have a lognormal distribution about the regression line. Third, the regression coefficients should be relatively unbiased. One thing which tends to keep bias in the regression coefficients small is the relative constancy of $(t_2 - t_1)$. This means that $(t_2 - t_1)$ is not highly correlated with $\log(Q_2/Q_1)$, $\log(T_2/T_1)$, or perturbations of the regression equations. Regresssions with $\log(Q_2/Q_1)$ and $\log(T_2/T_1)$ appearing simultaneously should have more bias than regressions with only one of these variables, because the two variables are correlated. Rough calculations suggest that when both variables appear, one can expect to underestimate C_1 and to overestimate C_2 and C_3.

The regression coefficients are given in Table 6. The probability appearing with each coefficient is the probability that a greater (absolute value) estimate might be obtained by chance when the true value of the coefficient is zero.

Two functions describe the data well:

$$A = \alpha(t) \cdot \sqrt{Q} \text{ and } A = \beta(t) \cdot T,$$

where $\alpha(t)$ and $\beta(t)$ are increasing functions of t. The relation between A and T is tighter than the relation between A and Q. One is inclined to say that the number of administrative employees depends on total employment and is comparatively independent

Table 6

Independent variables		Q		T		t		It		Multiple correlation coefficient, R
Dependent variable, Y	Degrees of freedom	Coefficient C_1	Probability $C_1 = 0$	Coefficient C_2	Probability $C_2 = 0$	Coefficient C_3	Probability $C_3 = 0$	Coefficient C_4	Probability $C_4 = 0$	
A	10	0·10	0·61	0·92	0·01	0·0088	0·23	0·0072	0·32	0·952
A	11	—	—	1·00	0·00	0·0112	0·05	0·0076	0·28	0·950
A	12	—	—	1·09	0·00	0·0141	0·00	—	—	0·945
A	11	0·42	0·07	—	—	0·0056	0·55	0·0117	0·23	0·900
A	12	0·49	0·04	—	—	0·0091	0·33	—	—	0·883
A/P	10	0·17	0·46	−0·13	0·71	0·0100	0·25	0·0088	0·31	0·855
A/P	11	—	—	0·02	0·95	0·0142	0·04	0·0095	0·26	0·846
A/P	12	—	—	0·12	0·66	0·0178	0·00	—	—	0·825
A/P	11	0·12	0·49	—	—	0·0104	0·21	0·0083	0·31	0·853
A/P	12	0·17	0·33	—	—	0·0128	0·11	—	—	0·835

Source: Chester (1961).

of output. Considering the fact that these are short-run data and none of the variables changes drastically, the proposition sounds sensible. On the other hand, the regression coefficients are probably biased, and T and Q are logically connected. The riddle is not likely to be untangled until firms are discovered which vary their outputs and employments independently.[15] (In the version of this paper published in the *Handbook of Organizations*, the preceding hypotheses and conclusions were supported by a lengthy appendix which has been omitted here.)

There are differences between the metal-goods firms and chemical firms. These are not overwhelming, but neither are they negligible. (Since C_4 was predicted to be positive, a better measure of significance is obtained by halving the probabilities: 0·16, 0·14, and 0·12. The same principle applies to the other probabilities as well.) On the whole, Chester's data fall into the same pattern as Woodward's: regression of A/P against T and I produces insignificant size effects.

There is little question that A and A/P increase with time. Since the firms studied are all large ($420 < T < 5500$), one can infer that this is a long-run trend and not a transient characteristic of new enterprises. Haire's (1959) data implied that the A/P ratio was less stable in young organizations than in old ones.

Summary. The author draws the following conclusions from the studies of administrative structure:

1. The available evidence is sketchy, and he has low confidence in his ability to draw sensible conclusions at all.

2. The administrative span of control, s, probably increases with organizational size. Studies consistent with this increase are Dale (1952), Entwisle and Walton (1961), Haas, Hall and Johnson (1963), Healey (1956), Melman (1951; 1958), Terrien and

15. Ford (1963) may have uncovered such data. He collected financial and employment data on Purdue University over a period of years and found: financial support was independent of the number of students in the short run; the financial allocation to administrative activities – as contrasted to instruction and research activities – increased with time and was independent of the number of students; and the number of administrative employees depended primarily on the amount of money available.

Mills (1955), Woodward (1958), and the regression with Chester's data.

3. The administrative span of control, s, may also increase with 'technological complexity', but Woodward (1958) is the only study to note such an effect.

4. The number of production workers per foreman, σ, may increase with organizational size. Studies consistent with this increase are Anderson and Warkov (1961), Haire (1959), Terrien and Mills (1955), and Woodward (1958).

5. The number of production workers per foreman, σ, is probably a concave function of 'technological complexity'. Studies consistent with this view are Anderson and Warkov (1961), Blau (1957), Faunce (1958), Harbison et al. (1955), Simpson (1959), Woodward (1958), and the regression with Chester's data.

6. For organizations with more than 100 employees, the A/P ratio is essentially independent of organizational size. The only study not consistent with this conclusion is Anderson and Warkov (1961).

This means that the effects described in (2) and (4) above are not likely to occur simultaneously, or if they do, that neither is very pronounced. It also means that the A/P ratio tends to be dominated by technological effects. A/P is probably an increasing function of 'technological complexity'. Woodward's (1958) study and the regressions with Chester's data are consistent with this increase.

7. There are virtually no data on the A/P ratio in organizations with less than 100 employees, but Figures 1 and 2 suggest that A/P is an increasing function of T in this range. One expects the A/P ratio to be highly variable in small firms; the studies by Haire (1959) and Melman (1951; 1958) indicate as much. Although Woodward (1958) found no correlation between firm size and 'technological complexity' in large firms, one would expect to find a correlation in small firms.

8. The A/P ratio is probably an increasing function of time. This may be due to increasing 'technological complexity'; it may be a consequence of changing definitions of 'administrative'

work; or it may be the result of new requirements imposed on and new activities undertaken by the firm.

Empirical studies of managerial employment

So far, no distinction has been made between managers and other administrative employees. Secretaries, file clerks and telephone operators have been grouped with their bosses. The reason for this aggregation is that the activities of managerial and nonmanagerial employees are highly substitutable. The manager of a small organization spends a good part of his time on activities which would be performed by nonmanagerial employees in a large organization; he writes his own letters, maintains his own files, and answers his own phone. In large organizations, nonmanagerial employees are often promoted to the managerial group without replacements being hired to fill their previous jobs.

However, managers are unlike non-managerial employees in at least one respect: they are called managers. This is not a trivial distinction, and this section considers some of its implications.

A first look is provided by Chester's (1961) data. He reported the increases in managerial employment for most of the firms in his study, and these figures can be compared with the data on administrative employment. The regression equation is analogous to the one used previously:

$$\log_{10}(Y_2/Y_1) = C_1 . \log_{10}(Q_2/Q_1) + C_2 . \log_{10}(T_2/T_1) + \\ + C_3 . \log_{10}(A_2/A_1) + (C_4 + C_5 I) . (t_2 - t_1),$$

but in this instance Y is either M or $M/(T-M)$, where M is the number of managers. The regression coefficients are given in Table 7; they should contain less bias than the regression coefficients for administrative employment.

The correlation between M and Q is much higher than the correlation between A and Q. Correspondingly, the correlation between M and T is not as high as the correlation between A and T. At least two hypotheses are consistent with this. Changes in Q correlate with changes in profitability, and more profitable firms have more managers. Changes in Q correlate with changes in technology, and technological change requires more managers.

Table 7

Dependent variable, Y:	Sample size	Degrees of freedom	Q Coefficient C_1	Probability $C_1 = 0$	T Coefficient C_2	Probability $C_2 = 0$	A Coefficient C_3	Probability $C_3 = 0$	I Coefficient C_4	Probability $C_4 = 0$	It Coefficient C_5	Probability $C_5 = 0$	Multiple correlation coefficient, R
M	13	9	0·29	0·07	0·05	0·84	—	—	0·0076	0·17	0·0127	0·05	0·964
M	13	9	0·22	0·17	—	—	0·13	0·52	0·0066	0·27	0·0095	0·17	0·957
M	13	10	0·30	0·03	—	—	—	—	0·0075	0·20	0·0129	0·04	0·955
M	13	10	—	—	—	—	0·35	0·06	0·0104	0·07	0·0093	0·17	0·949
M	13	10	—	—	0·33	0·19	—	—	0·0147	0·01	0·0125	0·10	0·938
M/T−M	10	6	0·26	0·30	−0·95	0·03	—	—	0·0104	0·26	0·0148	0·19	0·883
M/T−M	10	7	—	—	−0·74	0·04	—	—	0·0172	0·02	0·0173	0·13	0·856
M/T−M	10	7	−0·08	0·80	—	—	—	—	0·0153	0·29	0·0080	0·63	0·564

Source: Chester (1961).

Both hypotheses are consistent with the finding that chemical firms have significantly more managers than metal-goods firms.

M is more highly correlated with A than with T, but this is to be expected. M is a major component of A and not of T, and A and T are highly correlated. The ratio M/A ranges from $\frac{1}{6}$ to over $\frac{2}{3}$, and in most firms, is between $\frac{1}{4}$ and $\frac{1}{3}$. The ratio M/T goes as high as $\frac{2}{7}$, and in most firms, is approximately $\frac{1}{20}$.

One of Chester's conclusions was that the greatest increases in M 'took place at the top and middle management levels'. He was only partially correct. Table 8 tests the proposition $\Delta = 0$; where $\Delta = \log(Y_2/Y_1) - \log(X_2/X_1)$. The sample size is 12, and the probability includes two tails. The data actually show that the number of middle managers increased significantly more than either the number of top managers or the number of junior managers. There is no significant difference between the increases in top and junior managers. The author is not certain what this finding means, if anything. Chester interpreted it to say that 'the development was not merely a proliferation of junior supervisors, but an increased representation of men of calibre and responsibility' (1961, p. 46). However, the greater increases in middle management may simply be a characteristic of Chester's classification scheme; he wrote: 'Top managers were supposed to be those managers who were making decisions affecting the firm as a whole, lower managers were supposed to be the foremen and managers of equivalent status. Everybody in between was to be allocated to middle management' (p. 27).

Table 8

Y: \ X:	Junior		Top	
	Δ	Probability $\Delta = 0$	Δ	Probability $\Delta = 0$
Top	0·01	0·89	—	—
Middle	0·12	0·09	0·11	0·03

Source: Chester (1961).

Another of Chester's conclusions concerned the functional areas in which the greatest increases took place. He placed managers in five groups – production, service, research, accounting, and other – and decided that the increases 'were more pronounced in production, service, and research departments than elsewhere'. He was again partially supported by his data. Table 9 tests the proposition $\Delta = 0$ as before. Unfortunately, the sample size is only four. The increases in the service and research categories are significantly greater than the increase in the production category, but none of the other differences are statistically significant.

Table 9

X: Y:	Research		Accounting		Other		Production	
	Δ	Probability $\Delta = 0$	Δ	Probability $\Delta = 0$	Δ	Probability $\Delta = 0$	Δ	Probability $\Delta = 0$
Service	0·119	0·42	0·174	0·27	0·224	0·19	0·322	0·07
Research	—	—	0·055	0·74	0·105	0·36	0·203	0·03
Accounting	—	—	—	—	0·050	0·74	0·148	0·40
Other	—	—	—	—	—	—	0·098	0·25

Source: Chester (1961).

Hypotheses about managerial employment. Chester's data are sufficient to convince one that the number of managers in a firm is not simply proportional to either the number of administrative employees or total employment. Conveniently, Haire has gathered some rather detailed data on employment in ten firms over a period of years, and he has made these data available for analysis here. Before plunging into his numbers, however, consider four characteristics of the title 'manager'.

First, a manager has status. He is set apart from nonmanagerial employees, and he is accepted in the managerial class. He stops eating lunch with nonmanagerial associates and starts eating lunch with other managers, often in a private dining room. Many of his nonmanagerial friendships dissolve and are replaced by friendships within the managerial group. He is admitted to membership in social clubs which were formerly closed to him, by convention if not by fiat. He is invited to be an officer in charitable and professional organizations.

Most organizations use managerial status as a formal reward. They tie status to other rewards, like salary, and they reinforce the distinction between managerial and non-managerial employees. Managers are given expense accounts, private secretaries, and access to the company plane. The organization may pay its managers' dues in private social clubs or establish a country club especially for managers. Of course, 'A title on the door rates a Bigelow on the floor'.

Second, a manager has job security. He is less likely to be fired than a nonmanagerial employee. In fact, it is not a great exaggeration to say that the number of managers is a nondecreasing function of time, irrespective of other events. Chester's data included two firms which had lower outputs in 1956 than in the base year. The data are given in Table 10.

Table 10

Firm:	A	B
Q_2/Q_1	0·22	0·95
T_2/T_1	0·26	1·00
M_2/M_1	0·95	1·19

Source: Chester (1961).

A second example, taken from Haire's data, is given in Table 11. In this case, the observations cover seven consecutive years. Still another example was described by Weber (1959).

Table 11

i	1	2	3	4	5	6	7
P_i/P_1	1·00	1·17	1·33	0·98	0·82	0·79	0·69
T_i/T_1	1·00	1·14	1·15	0·94	0·85	0·85	0·79
M_i/M_1	1·00	1·04	1·07	1·07	1·11	1·26	1·30

Source: Haire (1959).

Faltermayer (1961) has reported some of the steps firms take to avoid firing managers. Some firms cut salaries. Others ask men near retirement age to retire early. In large organizations, the number of managers can be reduced by simply not hiring replacements for men who resign or retire. However, the most popular alternatives appear to be those which reduce the fringe benefits of managerial status. The company stops paying club dues. Fewer long distance calls are made. Trips are cancelled or made tourist class instead of first class. Secretaries are fired. And one firm required its executives to eat in the cafeteria with the rest of the employees.

Third, a manager has delegated responsibility. Most managers have charge of distinct segments of the organizational task. In this sense, they are specialists. Most organizations endeavor to assign managerial jobs in a way that minimizes coordination problems and maximizes the autonomy of individual managers. Obviously, the managers are not the only people in an organization who have responsibility, nor are they the only specialists. But there is a relationship between an organization's task factorings and its managerial job assignments.

Fourth and finally, a manager manages. Nearly all managers supervise nonmanagerial employees. This means that an organization is unlikely to create a managerial position unless the task segment associated with the position is large enough to occupy more than one person.

These four characteristics imply that the number of managers, M, increases with: the size of the organization, T, the age of the organization, t, and the cumulative experience of organizational members, E.

The relation between M and T is straightforward. In large organizations, the volume of work in a particular activity is large enough to occupy several employees, including a manager. In small organizations, the volume of work in the same activity may not occupy even one person. Thus, large organizations have more managers than small organizations. Chester noted this in his study:

New managers were also brought in to supervise the operation of many functions not undertaken in the firm before. For example, personnel management, quality control, cost control and research, to name but a few, all required extra managers.

In some firms these functions were performed before the survey period but the scale of operations was smaller, the person concerned often had other duties, and not being specialized the job required no manager. As the scale of the firms increased it became worthwhile appointing managers as specialization became possible, and in some firms staff performing the same function, but scattered over a number of departments, were united into a newly-created department to carry out the function on a centralised basis, and of course managers were needed to control its operation (1961, p. 45; also see Wickesberg, 1961).

Total employment is not necessarily the best measure of the organization's size or scale of operations as this variable affects the number of managers. In fact, the regressions run on Chester's data imply that sales volume or some other index of output is a better measure of size than total employment. However, in the case of Haire's data, sales volume figures are available for only six of the ten firms, and for those firms the data are fragmentary. Being confined to employment data, three possible measures of size were considered: total employment, production employment and sales employment.[16] The correlation between M and T was higher than the correlation between M and P in all ten firms, and in one firm the correlation between M and P was very small. The correlation between M and T was higher than the correlation between M and sales employment in seven firms, and in one firm (not the same one), the correlation between M and sales employment was negative.

The relation between M and t is partially the result of the formalization process. New organizations tend to have vague definitions of their tasks. They are not sure which task segments are important or necessary, and they are not sure how the overall tasks should be factored. Consequently, they tend to operate with a relatively small number of managers whose responsibilities overlap. As time passes and the organization grows older, the over-all tasks are more clearly defined. Important task segments are distinguished from unimportant ones, and effective task factorings are discovered. Standard operating procedures are developed, reducing the need for coordination between subunits

16. Total employment was divided into five categories: *control* which included activities like accounting, production scheduling, and quality control; *research; service* which included secretaries, clerks, personnel and labor relations people, janitors, and so forth; *sales* which included salesmen, advertising and public relations personnel, and delivery personnel when appropriate; and *production* which included first line production personnel and foremen.

and increasing the proportion of coordinating activity performed routinely by nonmanagerial employees. All of these changes create opportunities for factoring tasks into finer segments, and for appointing managers to take responsibility for the segments. Thus, one expects to find an association between M and t due to formalization primarily in older organizations.

Managerial job security is another factor relating M and t. When employment in nonmanagerial categories falls, managerial employment falls less than proportionately, and may rise. When employment in nonmanagerial categories rises, managerial employment again rises less than proportionately. Such fluctuations clearly reduce the correlation between M and T, and to the extent that M increases *mutatis mutandis*, they increase the correlation between M and t.

In view of these considerations, one can predict that M is more closely associated with T than with t in young firms which have stable scales of operation. M is more closely associated with t than with T in older firms which have unstable or fluctuating scales of operation.

The cumulative experience variable, E, combines the characteristics of T and t. Cumulative experience is defined here as the total number of man-years invested in the organization since its founding. For T measured annually,

$$E = \sum_{\tau=0}^{t} T(\tau).$$

E increases monotonically with t, but less rapidly when T is small than when T is large. Therefore, one can predict that M will be more closely associated with E than with either T or t in young firms which have unstable scales of operation and in older firms which have stable scales of operation.

The association between M and T, t or E may also reflect the standards established for promotion. An organization which adheres to the organization theorists' precepts concerning span of control, without a great deal of regard for the skills and talents of promoted personnel, would tend to have M associated with T. At least among young organizations, an organization which promotes primarily on the basis of seniority would tend to have M associated with t. An organization which promotes on the basis of 'merit', considering both the employee's native ability and his experience with the organization, would tend to have M associated with E. The author is, however, very skeptical that the effects of promotion policies will be large enough to show up in data.

One might also hypothesize that firms which expand rapidly have a more difficult learning problem and thus tend to have M associated with T. The trouble is another proposition counters that one: firms which learn rapidly, expand rapidly.

Analysis of Haire's data. Haire's data are time series on equivalent full-time employment in ten firms. The time series terminate in the late 1950s and proceed backward, in annual or semi-annual intervals, as far as the companies' records permitted. In eight cases, the series extend to the year of founding. The basic data sources were the companies' payroll records, and data collection was a rather Herculean task because it was often necessary to trace the activities of individual employees. Very large firms were excluded by the size of the collection problem, so all ten firms are medium-sized – having from 177 to 2653 employees at the end of the sample period. This restriction of the sample to medium-sized firms means that old firms were slow growers and new firms were fast growers. Consequently, interfirm comparisons to obtain correlates of rapid growth are biased.

Several firms expressed concern that their anonymity be protected – for reasons not apparent. Within that constraint, the ten firms are described in Table 12.

The regressions present interesting methodological problems. An equation like the ones above was used,

$$\log_e M = C_0 + C_1 . \log_e T + C_2 . \log_e E + C_3 . \log_e t,$$

but in this instance the distribution is homoscedastic only for old, large firms. Deviations are much greater for young, small firms. (The variable t was considered as a substitute for log t. t gave a better fit in the case of two firms, Beata and Janet, but the improvement was negligible.)

Heteroscedasticity is predictable *a priori*. First, young firms experiment and misallocate more than old firms. This produces a variance component which decreases as the firm grows older. Second, managers are nearly always full-time employees; if three-fourths of a man is needed, one man is hired. This produces a variance component which decreases on a percentage basis as the number of managers increases. Third, the data collectors

Table 12

Code name	Activity	Market area	Firm Age on First data date	Firm Age on Last data date	Total employment on First data date	Total employment on Last data date	Sample interval
Addie	Manufacturers of staple food products	National	30	69	30	240	Annual
Beata	Printers and publishers	Regional	17	59	55	178	Annual
Carla	Manufacturers of prepared food products	Regional	1	45	1	395	Annual with 7 omissions
Daisy	Fabricators of capital goods for industrial customers	National	1	38	3	177	Annual
Edith	Manufacturers of building materials	National	0·5	31·5	8	217	Annual with 4 omissions
Faith	Manufacturers of women's clothing	Regional	1	19	14	963	Annual with 2 exceptions
Gilda	Manufacturers of electronic equipment	National	1	15	20	2653	Semi-annual with 2 exceptions
Hazel	Manufacturers of aircraft	National	1	14·5	18	1000·5	Annual with 1 exception
Irene	Manufacturers of electric building materials	National	0·5	13	8	288	8 annual and 9 semi-annual
Janet	Fabricators of metal and plastic products with structural uses	National	1	12	4	383	6 annual and 10 semi-annual

Source: Haire (1959).

rounded to the nearest one-half man. This produces a bias in the regression curve and a variance component, both of which decrease rapidly as the number of managers increases, but both of which can be significant when M is small.

As a result, the author first estimated the variance about the regression line and then used weighted regression to estimate the coefficients (David and Neyman, 1938; Starbuck, 1965). This procedure weights observations having small variances more heavily than observations having large variances and, assuming that the *a priori* variance estimate is correct, produces best, unbiased, linear, maximum-likelihood coefficient estimates. The estimates are unbiased in the Markoff sense. The correlation between T, E and t is still a problem. The estimates are given in Table 13. In interpreting the multiple correlation coefficient, one should bear in mind that small deviations are counted more heavily than large deviations.

Table 13

Independent variables Firm	T Coefficient C_0	Coefficient C_1	E Coefficient C_2	t Coefficient C_3	Multiple correlation Coefficient R
Addie	−0·10	0·67	1·64	−3·36	0·985
Beata	−0·26	0·38	−0·73	1·85	0·840
Carla	−1·38	−0·06	0·19	0·95	0·986
Daisy	−0·83	0·55	−0·20	0·77	0·977
Edith	−2·62	0·39	1·17	−1·58	0·962
Faith	−0·49	0·81	−0·40	0·86	0·968
Gilda	−2·55	0·33	0·78	−0·17	0·991
Hazel	−0·73	0·68	−0·26	1·19	0·993
Irene	1·29	0·42	−0·42	0·91	0·975
Janet	−2·99	0·23	2·41	−5·22	0·979

Source: Haire (1959).

The independent variables in these regressions are highly intercorrelated. As a consequence, the coefficient estimates are biased and have large standard deviations. Rather than depend upon individual coefficient estimates consider them in combination. Suppose that the number of managers is actually a function of total employment,

$$M = A_1 . T^{B_1}.$$

But total employment increases with time,

$$T = A_0 . t^{B_0},$$

and so $E = \int_0^t T . dt = \dfrac{A_0}{B_0 + 1} . t^{B_0 + 1}.$

The regression implies:

$$M = A_1 . T^{B_1} = A_1 . A_0^{B_1} . t^{B_1 B_0}$$
$$= C_0 . T^{C_1} . E^{C_2} . t^{C_3}$$
$$= C_0 . (A_0 . t^{B_0})^{C_1} . \left(\frac{A_0}{B_0 + 1} . t^{B_0 + 1} \right)^{C_2} . t^{C_3},$$

or $t^{\Delta_T} = $ constant, where

$$\Delta_T = C_1 B_0 + C_2 (B_0 + 1) + C_3 - B_1 B_0.$$

If $M = A_1 T^{B_1}$ is actually the case, as hypothesized, then one should find that $\Delta_T = 0$. When one starts with the hypothesis $M = A_2 E^{B_2}$, he deduces that $\Delta_E = 0$, where

$$\Delta_E = C_1 B_0 + C_2 (B_0 + 1) + C_3 - B_2 (B_0 + 1).$$

And when one starts with the hypothesis $M = A_3 t^{B_3}$, he deduces that $\Delta_t = 0$, where

$$\Delta_t = C_1 B_0 + C_2 (B_0 + 1) + C_3 - B_3.$$

This triplet of numbers – Δ_T, Δ_E, and Δ_t – can be used to characterize the firms. If Δ_T has the smallest absolute value, the corresponding firm can be described as scale-oriented. If Δ_E has the smallest absolute value, the firm can be described as experience-oriented. If Δ_t has the smallest absolute value, the firm can be described as age-oriented. Such classifications are given in Table 14.

The preceding discussion of T, E and t argued that young, stable firms are scale-oriented; old, unstable firms are age-oriented; young, unstable firms and old, stable firms are experience-oriented. This collection of hypotheses can be tested. Define a variable Z which assumes the value zero if the firm is age-oriented, and assumes the value one if the firm is scale-oriented. Since E combines the characteristics of T and t, Z assumes the value one-half if the firm is experience-oriented. As a measure of age, take the mean value of log t, and as a measure of stability, take the 'correlation' between log t and log T. (The mean of log t and the 'correlation' between log t and log T were computed by the regression program and therefore were subject to the

Table 14

Firm	B_0	B_1	B_2	B_3	Δ_T	Δ_E	Δ_t	Orientation
Addie	2·30	1·22	1·02	2·94	0·792	0·212	0·650	Experience
Beata	0·94	0·71	0·34	0·71	0·128	0·125	0·083	Age
Carla	1·51	0·83	0·49	1·39	0·078	0·107	−0·053	Age
Daisy	1·24	0·82	0·55	1·06	−0·017	−0·229	−0·061	Scale
Edith	0·98	0·84	0·49	0·81	0·301	0·146	0·310	Experience
Faith	0·76	0·78	0·37	0·69	0·179	0·121	0·078	Age
Gilda	2·97	1·01	1·06	3·08	0·907	−0·321	0·818	Experience
Hazel	1·69	0·94	0·66	1·68	0·049	−0·122	−0·038	Age
Irene	1·40	0·39	0·26	0·58	−0·071	−0·147	−0·103	Scale
Janet	1·85	0·80	0·58	1·50	0·588	0·403	0·566	Experience

Source: Haire (1959).

weighting procedure. The word 'correlation' is in quotation marks because it is not clear what the term means in the context of heteroscedastic distributions.) These hypotheses imply that in the regression

$$Z = D_0 + D_1 . (\text{Age}) + D_2 . (\text{Stability})$$

one should find

$$D_1 < 0$$
$$D_2 > 0.$$

At this point a choice must be made. One alternative is to weight all firms equally. However, the minimum value of Δ is much smaller for age-oriented and scale-oriented firms than for

Table 15

			Equal weights		Unequal weights	
Coefficient	Hypothesis	Null hypothesis	Coefficient	Probability tail	Coefficient	Probability tail
D_1	$D_1 < 0$	$D_1 = 0$	−0·10	0·31	−0·32	0·14
D_2	$D_2 > 0$	$D_2 = 0$	2·07	0·18	3·38	0·09

experience-oriented firms, and the choice of $Z = 0.5$ for experience-oriented firms is arbitrary. Consequently, it might be sensible to weight the scale-oriented and age-oriented firms more heavily than the experience-oriented firms. Table 15 presents coefficient estimates for both approaches; the probability represents one tail because the hypotheses are inequalities.[17]

The hypotheses are not rejected, since the coefficients have the predicted signs, but the sizes of the probability tails are hardly an overwhelming vote of confidence.

Summary. Managers are unlike other employees in at least one respect: they are called managers. As a result, managerial employment differs from administrative employment as a function of size, time and technology.

Four characteristics of the title 'manager' are noted. A manager has status. A manager has job security. A manager has delegated responsibility. A manager manages. These characteristics suggest that in young firms having stable scales of operation, managerial employment is scale-oriented, i.e. closely associated with the firm's size. In old firms having unstable or fluctuating scales of operation, managerial employment is age-oriented, i.e. closely associated with the firm's age. In young firms having unstable scales of operation and in old firms having stable scales of operation, managerial employment is experience-oriented. The 'cumulative experience' variable combines the characteristics of size and age.

17. The age- and scale-oriented firms are weighted 18·5 times as heavily as the experience-oriented firms, because

$$\frac{\text{mean: (smallest value of } \Delta)^2 \text{ for experience}}{\text{mean: (smallest value of } \Delta)^2 \text{ for age and scale}} = 18 \cdot 5.$$

The estimated values of Z are:

		Estimated value of Z	
Firm	Z	Equal weights	Unequal weights
Addie	0·50	0·19	0·00
Beata	0·00	0·27	0·17
Carla	0·00	0·31	0·29
Daisy	1·00	0·33	0·38
Edith	0·50	0·30	0·34
Faith	0·00	0·01	0·06
Gilda	0·50	0·33	0·50
Hazel	0·00	0·38	0·57
Irene	1·00	0·44	0·68
Janet	0·50	0·49	0·77

Empirical data from ten firms suggest that it is easy to find variables which correlate highly with managerial employment, but that the behavior of managerial employment differs among firms. The hypotheses concerning the orientations of various firms are given weak confirmation.

Concluding remarks

Most studies of organizational growth and development are typical examples of social science research, and as such, are subject to faults common in social science research. In particular:

1. A tendency to substitute theorizing for data collection.
2. A tendency simply to present data without formal analyses.
3. A tendency to base formal analyses on naive assumptions.

However, this is not to suggest that any of the work which has been published should not have been. No study is perfect, and bad studies often provoke better ones. Considering the bibliography as a whole, an impressive amount of useful work has been done. Few, if any, questions have been answered completely and convincingly, but many questions have been explored in a tentative way, and researchers are in a good position to start making real strides toward a predictive understanding of growth and development.

At this point, what is needed more than anything else is data – data on goals, data on behavior strategies, data on structural variables, data on patterns of development, data on nearly every aspect of organizational growth and development. Some areas of social science research suffer from a lack of theory, there being well-established facts and no theories adequate to explain them. The subject of organizational growth is not such an area. Indeed, it seems that the theories outnumber the facts. In few instances can one point to systematic bodies of data and analysis concerning interrelated phenomena, as one can, for example, point to Mansfield's studies of technological innovation. There are many instances wherein one can point to a collection of theoretical formulations based on single case studies or on the theorists' personal experiences. Extrapolations from samples of size one have a place in science. So do introspective insights. However, the worth of such contributions depends greatly on the specific theorist's genius, and an entire area of research can hardly be founded on the premise that the average researcher is a genius. Further, personalized schemas are most valuable in bringing light to dark areas where little or no knowledge exists. The subject of organizational growth has progressed beyond abysmal darkness. It is ready for – and badly needs – solid, systematic empirical research directed toward explicit hypotheses and utilizing sophisticated statistical methods.

The kind of data likely to be most useful is time-series data on individual organizations. The researcher should obtain at least two observations of each organization studied, and preferably several. This is desirable because one current deficiency is the lack of effective classification schemes for organizations such that two organizations in the same class can be validly compared as if they were two observations of the same organization. Until such classification schemes are created, cross-section studies will be inefficient. At best, they require very large samples to establish statistical significance, and at worst, they produce spurious correlations due to systematic but unobserved differences among organizations. Moreover, the author doubts that effective classification schemes will be developed in the immediate future (see Blau and Scott, 1962, pp. 40–57). Their creation must follow the establishment of an empirically based consensus as to which organizational characteristics are most critical in determining the course of behavior, and the field is a long way from that. In the interim, the best approach is to work with multiple observations of each organization, taking maximum advantage of opportunities to compare each organization with itself rather than with other organizations. This approach does not obviate any major theoretical tasks, but it does minimize the number of assumptions about similarity which are implicit in a given comparison.

In other words, the subject of organizational growth and development needs work toward a general theory, not work on a general theory. At present, it is a mistake to bet heavily on the ability to classify and group different organizations. Granting this, however, the subject appears ripe for some major advances. If a few people will commit themselves to build formal models, to collect detailed time-series data on individual organizations over several years, and to confront models with data in a rigorous way, a lot of progress can be made in a short time. Before long, the beginnings of a general theory will appear. As Cyert and March have said:

What we tend to forget is that uniqueness . . . is not an attribute of the organization alone; it is an attribute of the organization and our theory of organizations. An organization is unique when we have failed to develop a theory that will make it nonunique. Thus, uniqueness is less a bar to future theoretical success than a confession of past theoretical failure (1963, p. 287).

Appendix

A mathematical treatment of Penrose's model

Penrose's model of growth (1959) contains a number of logical circularities which are difficult to disentangle when the model is stated verbally. In such a circumstance, an algebraic model can be very helpful. Define:

$X(T) = $ the number of managers at time T,

$Z(T) = $ the firm's output at time T,

$V(T, \Theta) = $ the cumulative experience at time T of a manager hired at time Θ,

$Y(T, \Theta) = $ the 'managerial resources' at time T provided by one manager hired at time Θ,

$U(T) = $ the total managerial resources at time T, and

$W(T) = $ the excess managerial resources at time T available for expansion.

Considering Penrose's statement that experience is a function of work load, assume:

$$V(T, \Theta) = \int_{\Theta}^{T} \frac{Z(t)}{X(t)} . dt \qquad\qquad 1$$

and then, because nearly all studies of learning are consistent with an exponential representation, assume:

$$Y(T, \Theta) = \alpha - \beta . \mathrm{Exp}\{-\gamma . V(T, \Theta)\} \qquad\qquad 2$$

where α, β and γ are all positive and $\beta > \alpha$. By definition:

$$U(T) = \int_{0}^{T} Y(T, \Theta) . X'(\Theta) . d\Theta, \qquad\qquad 3$$

where X' indicates the derivative.

Penrose hypothesized some effects of size and age on the demand for managerial services for operations (1959, ch. 9). However, in the interest of simplicity, assume that the managerial services needed for operations are proportional to output:

$$W(T) = U(T) - \delta . Z(T), \delta > 0. \tag{4}$$

Similarly, assume that the rates of expansion of output and managerial employment are both proportional to excess managerial resources:

$$X'(T) = \varepsilon . W(T), \varepsilon > 0 \tag{5}$$

$$Z'(T) = \zeta . W(T), \zeta > 0. \tag{6}$$

Note that, once employed, a manager never retires. Because a time lag must be introduced to deal with retirement, allowing for it greatly complicates the model without commensurately increasing realism.

A. Relations 5 and 6 imply:

$$Z(T) = Z(0) + \frac{\zeta}{\varepsilon}\{X(T) - X(0)\}. \tag{7}$$

B. Relations 4, 5 and 7 imply:

$$X'(T) = \varepsilon . U(T) - \varepsilon \delta . Z(0) - \zeta \delta . \{X(T) - X(0)\}. \tag{8}$$

C. Relations 2 and 3 imply:

$$U(T) = a . \{X(T) - X(0)\} - \beta . I \tag{9}$$

where $I = \int_0^T X'(\Theta) . \text{Exp}\{-\gamma . V(T, \Theta)\} . d\Theta.$

D. Relations 8 and 9 imply:

$$X'(T) = (a\varepsilon - \zeta\delta) . \{X(T) - X(0)\} - \varepsilon\delta . Z(0) - \beta\varepsilon . I. \tag{10}$$

E. Relation 1 and the definition of I imply:

$$\frac{\partial I}{\partial T} = X'(T) - I \left[\frac{\gamma\zeta}{\varepsilon} + \frac{\gamma}{X(T)} . \left\{ Z(0) - \frac{\zeta}{\varepsilon} . X(0) \right\} \right]. \tag{11}$$

F. Relation **11** and the derivative of **10** imply:

$$X''(T) = (a\varepsilon - \zeta\delta - \beta\varepsilon) \cdot X'(T) +$$

$$+ I \cdot \left[\beta\gamma\zeta + \frac{\beta\gamma}{X(T)} \cdot \{\varepsilon \cdot Z(0) - \zeta \cdot X(0)\} \right]. \qquad 12$$

G. Relations **10** and **12** imply:

$$X''(T) + \left[\zeta\delta + \beta\varepsilon - a\varepsilon + \frac{\gamma\zeta}{\varepsilon} \right] \cdot X'(T) + \frac{\gamma\zeta}{\varepsilon} \cdot [\zeta\delta - a\varepsilon] \cdot X(T)$$

$$= -a\gamma\zeta \cdot X(0) - \left[Z(0) - \frac{\zeta}{\varepsilon} \cdot X(0) \right]$$

$$\gamma \left[\frac{X'(T)}{X(T)} + 2\zeta\delta - a\varepsilon + \frac{1}{X(T)} \cdot \{\varepsilon\delta \cdot Z(0) - (\zeta\delta - a\varepsilon) \cdot X(0)\} \right]. \qquad 13$$

H. On the premise that the concern is not with starting transients, assume

$$X(0) = \frac{\varepsilon}{\zeta} Z(0). \quad \text{Relation } \textbf{13} \text{ becomes simply:}$$

$$X''(T) + 2A \cdot X'(T) + B^2 \cdot X(T) = -a\gamma\zeta \cdot X(0), \qquad 14$$

where $A = \frac{1}{2}\left[\zeta\delta - a\varepsilon + \beta\varepsilon + \frac{\gamma\zeta}{\varepsilon} \right] > 0$ and $B^2 = \frac{\gamma\zeta}{\varepsilon}(\zeta\delta - a\varepsilon)$.

I. Relation **14** has the solution

$$X(T) = C_1 \cdot \text{Exp}[(-A + \sqrt{A^2 - B^2})T] +$$

$$+ C_2 \cdot \text{Exp}[(-A - \sqrt{A^2 - B^2})T] - \frac{a\varepsilon}{\zeta\delta - a\varepsilon} \cdot X(0), \qquad 15$$

where $C_1 + C_2 = \frac{\zeta\delta}{\zeta\delta - a\varepsilon} \cdot X(0)$.

J. When $X(0) = 0$, relation **15** becomes:

$$X(T) = C_0 \cdot e^{-AT} \cdot \text{Sinh}(T \cdot \sqrt{A^2 - B^2}). \qquad 16$$

Relation **16** implies that $X(T)$ and $Z(T)$ display one of three modes of behavior:

1. When $B^2 < 0$, $X(T)$ and $Z(T)$ will grow indefinitely. $X'(T)$ and $Z'(T)$ are positive for all T. The condition $B^2 < 0$ says

$$\frac{\left[\begin{array}{c} \text{Total managerial} \\ \text{services needed} \\ \text{for production} \end{array}\right]}{\text{Total managers}} < \left[\begin{array}{c} \text{Maximum managerial} \\ \text{services available} \\ \text{from one manager} \end{array}\right].$$

This requirement can always be satisfied by employing more managers, if there are no financial constraints. But, of course, there always are.

2. When $0 < B^2 < A^2$, $X(T)$ and $Z(T)$ will grow and then decay. There is a T^* such that $X'(T)$ and $Z'(T)$ will be non-negative for $T \leq T^*$, and then will be non-positive for $T \geq T^*$.

3. When $B^2 > A^2$, $X(T)$ will oscillate. $X'(T)$ and $Z'(T)$ will be alternately positive and negative. However, given the assumptions that all coefficients are positive, this condition can never be realized. $B^2 > A^2$ implies

$$A^2 - B^2 = \frac{1}{4} \cdot \left[\varepsilon(\beta - \alpha) + \zeta\left(\delta - \frac{\gamma}{\varepsilon}\right) \right]^2 + \gamma\zeta\beta < 0;$$

the squared term is positive for all real coefficient values, and the other term is positive by assumption. A negative β implies that the longer a manager is in the organization, the less productive he becomes. A negative ζ implies that excess managerial resources decrease the organization's output.

Thus, the system has only two modes of behavior. $B^2 < 0$ corresponds to continuous growth; $B^2 > 0$ corresponds to growth and then decay. The secret to maintaining growth would be keeping B^2 negative.

References

ABEGGLEN, J. C. (1958), *The Japanese Factory*, Free Press.

ALCHIAN, A. A. (1949), *An airframe production function*, paper P–108, Rand Corp.

ALCHIAN, A. A. (1950), 'Uncertainty, evolution and economic theory', *J. pol. Econ.*, vol. 58, pp. 211–21.

ALCHIAN, A. A. (1959), 'Costs and outputs', in M. Abramovitz *et al.*, *The Allocation of Economic Resources*, Stanford University Press, pp. 23–40.

ANDERSON, T. R., and WARKOV, S. (1961), 'Organizational size and functional complexity: study of administration in hospitals', *Amer. sociol. Rev.*, vol. 26, pp. 23–8.

ANDREWS, P. W. S. (1949a), 'A reconsideration of the theory of the individual business', *Oxford econ. Papers*, vol. 1, pp. 54–89.

ANDREWS, P. W. S. (1949b), *Manufacturing Business*, Macmillan.

ARGYRIS, C. (1957), *Personality and Organization*, Harper.

ASHBY, W. R. (1960), *Design for a Brain*, 2nd edn., Wiley.

ASHER, H. (1956), 'Cost-quantity relationships in the airframe industry', report R–291, *Rand Corp.*

BAIN, J. S. (1954), 'Economies of scale, concentration, and the condition of entry in twenty manufacturing industries', *Amer. econ. Rev.*, vol. 44, pp. 15–39.

BAIN, J. S. (1956), *Barriers to New Competition*, Harvard University Press.

BAKER, A. W., and DAVIS, R. C. (1954), 'Ratios of staff to line employees and stages of differentiation of staff functions', *Res. Monog.*, no. 72, Bureau of Business Research, Ohio State University.

BALES, R. F. (1951), *Interaction Process Analysis*, Addison-Wesley.

BARNARD, C. I. (1938), *The Functions of the Executive*, Harvard University Press.

BAUMGARTEL, H., and SOBOL, R. (1959), 'Background and organizational factors in absenteeism', *Personnel Psychol.*, vol. 12, pp. 431–43.

BAUMOL, W. J. (1959), *Business Behaviour, Value and Growth*, Macmillan.

BAUMOL, W. J. (1962), 'On the theory of expansion of the firm', *Amer. econ. Rev.*, vol. 52, pp. 1078–87.

BBRP (1958), *Small Business Bibliography*, Bureau of Business Research, University of Pittsburgh.

BECKMANN, M. J. (1960), 'Some aspects of returns to scale in business administration', *Q. J. Econs*, vol. 74, pp. 464–71.

BENDIX, R. (1956), *Work and Authority in Industry*, Wiley.

BENNIS, W. G. (1963), 'A new role for the behavioural sciences: effecting organizational change', *Admin. Sci. Q.*, vol. 8, pp. 125–65.

BENNIS, W. G., BENNE, K. D., and CHIN, R. (1961), *The Planning of Change*, Holt, Rinehart & Winston.

BERLE, A. A., and MEANS, G. C. (1932), *The Modern Corporation and Private Property*, Macmillan.

BLAIR, J. M. (1948), 'Technology and size', *Amer. econ. Rev.*, vol. 38, no. 2, pp. 121–52.

BLANKENSHIP, L. V., and ELLING, R. H. (1962), 'Organizational support and community power structure: the hospital', *J. Health hum. Behav.*, vol. 3, pp. 257–69.

BLAU, P. M. (1955), *The Dynamics of Bureaucracy*, University of Chicago Press.

BLAU, P. M. (1957), 'Formal organization: dimensions of analysis', *Amer. J. Sociol.*, vol. 63, pp. 58–69.

BLAU, P. M., and SCOTT, W. R. (1962), *Formal Organizations*, Chandler.

BONINI, C. P. (1963), *Simulation of Information and Decision Systems in the Firm*, Prentice-Hall.

BOSSARD, J. H. S. (1945), 'The law of family interaction', *Amer. J. Sociol.*, vol. 50, pp. 292–4.

BOULDING, K. E. (1953), *The Organizational Revolution*, Harper.

BRIGHT, A. A. (1949), *The Electric-Lamp Industry*, Macmillan.

BROWN, G. (1957), 'Characteristics of new enterprises', *New Eng. bus. Rev.*, June, pp. 1–4; July, pp. 5–7.

BROWN, W. H. (1957), 'Innovation in the machine-tool industry', *Q. J. Econs*, vol. 71, pp. 406–25.

CAPLOW, T. (1957), 'Organizational size', *Admin. Sci. Q.*, vol. 1, pp. 484–505.

CARTER, C. F., and WILLIAMS, B. R. (1959), *Science in Industry*, Oxford University Press.

CHAMBERLIN, E. H. (1948), 'Proportionality, divisibility and economies of scale', *Q. J. Econs*, vol. 62, pp. 229–62; reprinted as 'The cost curve of the individual producer', in Chamberlin (1950), pp. 230–59.

CHAMBERLIN, E. H. (1950), *The Theory of Monopolistic Competition*, 6th edn, Harvard University Press.

CHANDLER, A. D., Jr (1962), *Strategy and Structure*, MIT Press.

CHAPIN, F. S. (1957), 'The optimum size of institutions: a theory of the large group', *Amer. J. Sociol.*, vol. 62, pp. 449–60.

CHESTER, T. E. (1961), *A Study of Post-War Growth in Management Organizations,* Project 347, European Productivity Agency, OEEC.

CHOWDHRY, K., and PAL, A. K. (1957), 'Production planning and organizational morale', *Hum. Organ.*, vol. 15, no. 4, pp. 11–16.

CHRISTENSEN, C. R. (1953), *Management Succession in Small and Growing Enterprises*, Harvard Business School.

CLARK, B. R. (1956), *Adult Education in Transition*, University of California Press.

CLARK, B. R. (1962), *Educating the Expert Society*, Chandler.

COBB, C. W., and DOUGLAS, P. H. (1928), 'A theory of production', *Amer. econ. Rev.*, vol. 18 (supplement), pp. 139–65.

COCH, L., and FRENCH, J. R. P., Jr (1948), 'Overcoming resistance to change', *Hum. Rel.*, vol. 1, pp. 512–32.

COHEN, A. M. (1961), 'Changing small group communication networks', *J. Commun.*, vol. 11, pp. 116–24, 128.

COLEMAN, J. S. (1960), 'The mathematical study of small groups', in H. Solomon (ed.), *Mathematical Thinking in the Measurement of Behaviour*, Free Press.

COLEMAN, J. S., and JAMES, J. (1961), 'The equilibrium size distribution of freely-forming groups', *Sociometrics*, vol. 24, pp. 36–45.

COOPER, W. W., and CHARNES, A. (1954), 'Silhouette functions of short-run cost behaviour', *Q. J. Econs*, vol. 68, pp. 131–50.

COPELAND, M. T. (1955), *The Executive at Work*, Harvard University Press.

CRUM, W. L. (1939), *Corporate Size and Earning Power*, Harvard University Press.

CRUM, W. L. (1953), *The Age Structure of the Corporate System*, University of California Press.

CYERT, R. M., FEIGENBAUM, E. A., and MARCH, J. G. (1959), 'Models in a behavioural theory of the firm', *Behav. Sci.*, vol. 4, pp. 81–95; the central model is reprinted in Cyert and March (1963), pp. 84–98.

CYERT, R. M., and MARCH, J. G. (eds), (1963), *A Behavioral Theory of the Firm*, Prentice-Hall.

DALE, E. (1952), *Planning and Developing the Company Organization Structure*, res. rep. no. 20, Amer. Manag. Assoc., particularly pp. 66–82.

DAVID, F. N., and NEYMAN, J. (1938), 'Extension of the Markoff theorem on least squares', *Statist. Res. Mem.*, vol. 2, pp. 105–16.

DAVIS, R. C. (1951), *The Fundamentals of Top Management*, Harper.

DEAN, L. R. (1954–5), 'Social integration, attitudes and union activity', *Indust. lab. relat. Rev.*, vol. 8, pp. 48–58.

DENT, J. K. (1959), 'Organizational correlates of the goals of business managements', *Personn. Psychol.*, vol. 12, pp. 365–93.

DIAMOND, S. (1958), 'From organization to society: Virginia in the seventeenth century', *Amer. J. Sociol.*, vol. 63, pp. 457–75.

DILL, W. R. (1962), 'The impact of environment on organizational development', in S. Mailick and E. H. Van Ness (eds.), *Concepts and Issues in Administrative Behavior*, Prentice-Hall, pp. 94–109.

DIXON, R. L. (1953), 'Creep', *J. Account.*, vol. 96, pp. 48–55.

DRAPER, J., and STROTHER, G. B. (1963), 'Testing a model for organizational growth', *Hum. Organ.*, vol. 22, pp. 180–94.

DRUCKER, P. F. (1958), 'Business objectives and survival needs: notes on a discipline of business enterprise', *J. Bus.*, vol. 31, pp. 81–99.

DEPARTMENT OF SCIENTIFIC AND INDUSTRIAL RESEARCH (1958), *Estimates of Resources Devoted to Scientific and Engineering Research and Development in British Manufacturing Industry, 1955*, DSIR.

DUBIN, R. (1959), 'Stability of human organizations', in M. Haire (ed.), *Modern Organization Theory*, Wiley, pp. 218–53.

DULLES, F. R. (1950), *The American Red Cross: A History*, Harper.

ECKSTEIN, H. (1958), *The English Health Service*, Harvard University Press.

EITEMAN, W. J., and GUTHRIE, G. E. (1952), 'The shape of the average cost curve', *Amer. econ. Rev.*, vol. 42, pp. 832–8.

ELLING, R. H., and HALEBSKY, S. (1961), 'Organizational differentiation and support: a conceptual framework', *Admin. Sci. Q.*, vol. 6, pp. 185–209.

ENKE, S. (1951), 'On maximizing profits: a distinction between Chamberlin and Robinson', *Amer. econ. Rev.*, vol. 41, pp. 566–78.

ENTWISLE, D. R., and WALTON, J. (1961), 'Observations on the span of control', *Admin. Sci. Q.*, vol. 5, pp. 522–33.

FALTERMAYER, E. K. (1961), 'Executive austerity', *Wall St J.*, 26 Jan., pp. 1, 4.

FAUNCE, W. A. (1958), 'Automation in the automobile industry: some consequences for in-plant social structure', *Amer. sociol. Rev.*, vol. 23, pp. 401–7.

FAYOL, H. (1949), *General and Industrial Management*, Pitman.

FELLER, W. (1950), *An Introduction to Probability Theory and its Applications*, vol. 1, Wiley, pp. 379–83.

FILLEY, A. C. (1963), 'A theory of business growth', unpublished manuscript, School of Commerce, University of Wisconsin.

FISKE, D. W., and MADDI, S. R. (1961), *Functions of Varied Experience*, Dorsey.

FLORENCE, P. S. (1953), *The Logic of British and American Industry*, University of North Carolina Press.

FORD, F. R. (1963), 'The growth of supporting operations within a university organization: a historical study', unpublished doctoral dissertation, Purdue University.

FORDHAM, S. (1957–8), 'Organization efficiency', *J. indust. Econs*, vol. 6, pp. 209–15.

FORM, W. H., and MILLER, D. C. (1960), *Industry, Labor and Community*, Harper.

GALBRAITH, J. K. (1952), *American Capitalism*, Houghton Mifflin.

GALBRAITH, J. K. (1957), 'Many hands make heavy work', *Reporter*, vol. 17, no. 6, pp. 46–7.

GARDNER, B. B., and MOORE, D. G. (1955), *Human Relations in Industry*, 3rd edn, Irwin.

GINZBERG, E., and REILLEY, E. W. (1957), *Effecting Change in Large Organizations*, Columbia University Press.

GLOVER, J. D. (1954), *The Attack on Big Business*, Harvard Business School.

GORDON, R. A. (1945), *Business Leadership in the Large Corporation*, Brookings.

GOULDNER, A. W. (1954), *Patterns of Industrial Bureaucracy*, Free Press.

GRAICUNAS, V. A. (1933), 'Relationship in organization', *Bull. int. Manag. Inst.*, vol. 7, pp. 39–42; reprinted in Gulick and Urwick (1937), pp. 183–7.

GRIFFIN, C. E. (1949), *Enterprise in a Free Society*, Irwin.

GRUSKY, O. (1961), 'Corporate size, bureaucratization and managerial succession', *Amer. J. Sociol.*, vol. 67, pp. 261–9.

GUEST, R. H. (1962), *Organizational Change*, Dorsey.

GULICK, L., and URWICK, L. (eds.) (1937), *Papers on the Science of Administration*, Inst. Pub. Admin., Columbia University.

GUSFIELD, J. R. (1955), 'Social structure and moral reform: a study of the Woman's Christian Temperance Union', *Amer. J. Sociol.*, vol. 61, pp. 221–32.

HAAS, E., HALL, R. H., and JOHNSON, N. J. (1963), 'The size of the supportive component in organizations: a multi-organizational analysis', *Soc. Forces*, vol. 42, pp. 9–17.

HAIRE, M. (1959), 'Biological models and empirical histories of the growth of organizations', in M. Haire (ed.), *Modern Organization Theory*, Wiley, pp. 272–306.

HALL, R. L., and HITCH, C. J. (1939), 'Price theory and business behaviour', *Oxford econ. Papers*, no. 2, pp. 12–45.

HAMILTON, I. (1921), *The Soul and Body of an Army*, Arnold.

HAND, L. (1945), *Opinion in United States v Aluminum Company of America, et al.*, United States Circuit Court of Appeals for the Second District, vol. 144; reprinted in *Trade Cases 1944–1945* (1948), case 57342, Commerce Clearing House, pp. 57676–700.

HANSON, R. C. (1961), 'Administrator responsibility in large and small hospitals in a metropolitan community', *J. Hlth hum. Behav.*, vol. 2, pp. 199–204.

HARBISON, F. H., KOCHLING, E., CASSELL, F. H., and RUEBMANN, H. C. (1955), 'Steel management on two continents', *Manag. Sci.*, vol. 2, pp. 31–9.

HARBISON, F. H., and MYERS, C. A. (1959), *Management in the Industrial World*, McGraw-Hill.

HART, P. E., and PRAIS, S. J. (1956), 'The analysis of business concentration', *J. Roy. Stat. Soc.*, series A, vol. 119, no. 2, pp. 150–90.

HEALEY, J. H. (1956), 'Coordination and control of executive functions', *Personnel*, vol. 33, pp. 106–17.

HELLER, W. W. (1951), 'The anatomy of investment decisions', *Harv. bus. Rev.*, vol. 29, no. 2, pp. 95–103.

HERBST, P. G. (1957), 'Measurement of behaviour structures by means of input-output data', *Hum. Rel.*, vol. 10, pp. 335–46.

HICKMAN, C. A., and KUHN, M. H. (1956), *Individuals, Groups and Economic Behavior*, Dryden.

HIRSCH, W. Z. (1952), 'Manufacturing progress functions', *Rev. Econs. Stats.*, vol. 34, pp. 143–55.

HOLT, C. C., MODIGLIANI, F., MUTH, J. F., and SIMON, H. A. (1960), *Planning Production, Inventories and Work Force*, Prentice-Hall, esp. chs. 2, 3, 8.

IJIRI, Y., and SIMON, H. A. (1964), 'Business firm growth and size', *Amer. econ. Rev.*, vol. 54, pp. 77–89.

INDIK, B. P. (1963), 'Some effects of organization size on member attitudes and behavior', *Hum. Rel.*, vol. 16, pp. 369–84.

JAMES, J. (1951), 'A preliminary study of the size determinant in small group interaction', *Amer. sociol. Rev.*, vol. 16, pp. 474–7.

JAMES, J. (1953), 'The distribution of free-forming small group size', *Amer. sociol. Rev.*, vol. 18, pp. 569–70.

JEWKES, J., SAWERS, D., and STILLERMAN, R. (1959), *The Sources of Invention*, St Martin's Press.

JOHNSTON, J. (1955–6), 'Scale, costs and profitability in road passenger transport', *J. indust. Econ.*, vol. 4, pp. 207–23.

KAPLAN, A. D. H. (1948), *Small Business: Its Place and Problems*, McGraw-Hill.

KATONA, G. (1951), *Psychological Analysis of Economic Behavior*, McGraw-Hill.

KAUFMAN, H. (1960), *The Forest Ranger*, Johns Hopkins Press.

KEPHART, W. M. (1950), 'A quantitative analysis of intragroup relationships', *Amer. J. Sociol.*, vol. 55, pp. 544–9.

LEVINE, S., and WHITE, P. E. (1961), 'Exchange as a conceptual framework for the study of inter-organizational relationships', *Admin. Sci. Q.*, vol. 5, pp. 583–601.

LIKERT, R. (1961), *New Patterns of Management*, McGraw-Hill.

LIPPITT, R., WATSON, J., and WESTLEY, B. (1958), *The Dynamics of Planned Change*, Harcourt, Brace.

LIPSET, S. M., TROW, M. A., and COLEMAN, J. S. (1956), *Union Democracy*, Free Press.

McCLELLAND, D. C., ATKINSON, J. W., CLARK, R. A., and LOWELL, E. L. (1953), *The Achievement Motive*, Appleton-Century-Crofts.

McGUIRE, J. W. (1963), *Factors Affecting the Growth of Manufacturing Firms*, Bureau of Bus. Res., University of Washington.

McGUIRE, J. W., CHIU, J. S. Y., and ELBING, A. O. (1962), 'Executive incomes, sales and profits', *Amer. econ. Rev.*, vol. 52, pp. 753–61.

MACLAURIN, W. R. (1949), *Invention and Innovation in the Radio Industry*, Macmillan.

MACLAURIN, W. R. (1950), 'The process of technological innovation: the launching of a new scientific industry', *Amer. econ. Rev.*, vol. 40, pp. 90–112.

McNULTY, J. E. (1956–7), 'Administrative costs and scale of operations in the US electrical power industry – a statistical study', *J. indust. Econs*, vol. 5, pp. 30–43.

McNULTY, J. E. (1962), 'Organizational change in growing enterprises', *Admin. Sci. Q.*, vol. 7, pp. 1–21.

MANN, F. C., and NEFF, F. W. (1961), *Managing Major Change in Organizations*, Foundation for Research on Human Behavior.

MANSFIELD, E. (1962a), 'Entry, Gibrat's law, innovation, and the growth of firms', *Amer. econ. Rev.*, vol. 52, pp. 1023–51.

MANSFIELD, E. (1962b), *Size of Firm, Market Structure, and Innovation*, Cowles Foundation Discussion Paper no. 137, Yale University.

MANSFIELD, E. (1962c), *The Expenditures of the Firm on Research and Development*, Cowles Foundation Discussion Paper no. 136, Yale University.

MANSFIELD, E. (1963a), 'Intrafirm rates of diffusion of an innovation', *Rev. Econs Stats.*, vol. 45, pp. 348–59.

MANSFIELD, E. (1963b), 'The speed of response of firms to new techniques', *Q. J. Econs*, vol. 77, pp. 290–311.

MARCH, J. G., and SIMON, H. A. (1958), *Organizations*, Wiley.

MARSCHAK, J., and ANDREWS, W. H., Jr (1944), 'Random simultaneous equations and the theory of production', *Econom.*, vol. 12, pp. 143–205.

MARSHALL, A. (1920), *Principles of Economics*, 8th edn, Macmillan.

MAURER, H. (1955), *Great Enterprise, Growth and Behavior of the Big Corporation*, Macmillan.

MELMAN, S. (1951), 'The rise of administrative overhead in the manufacturing industries of the United States, 1899–1947', *Oxford econ. Papers*, vol. 3, pp. 62–112.

MELMAN, S. (1956), *Dynamic Factors in Industrial Productivity*, Wiley; especially pp. 159–62.

MELMAN, S. (1958), *Decision-Making and Productivity*, Wiley.

MERTON, R. K. (1940), 'Bureaucratic structure and personality', *Soc. Forces*, vol. 18, pp. 560–68.

MERTON, R. K. (1957). *Social Theory and Social Structure*, rev. edn., Free Press.

MESSINGER, S. L. (1955), 'Organizational transformation: a case study of a declining social movement', *Amer. sociol. Rev.*, vol. 20, pp. 3–10.

MILLER, E. J. (1959), 'Technology, territory, and time', *Hum. Rels.*, vol. 12, pp. 243–72.

MOONEY, J. D., and REILEY, A. C. (1931), *Onward Industry!*, Harper.

MOORE, D. G. (1959), 'Managerial strategies', in W. L. Warner and N. H. Martin (eds.), *Industrial Man*, Harper, pp. 219–26.

NADLER, G., and SMITH, W. D. (1963), 'Manufacturing progress functions for types of processes', *Int. J. prod. Res.*, vol. 2, pp. 115–35.

NELSON, R. R. (1959), 'The economics of invention: a survey of the literature', *J. Bus.*, vol. 32, pp. 101–127.

NEWMAN, W. H., and LOGAN, J. P. (1955), *Management of Expanding Enterprises*, Columbia University Press.

NOURSE, E. G. (1944), *Price Making in a Democracy*, Brookings.

NATIONAL SCIENCE FOUNDATION (1956), *Science and Engineering in American Industry*, NSF.

NATIONAL SCIENCE FOUNDATION (1959), *Funds for Research and Development in Industry*, NSF.

OSBORN, R. C. (1951), 'Efficiency and profitability in relation to size', *Harv. bus. Rev.*, vol. 29, no. 2, pp. 82–94.

PAPANDREOU, A. G. (1952), 'Some basic problems in the theory of the firm', in B. F. Haley (ed.), *A Survey of Contemporary Economics*, Irwin, pp. 183–219.

PARKINSON, C. N. (1957), *Parkinson's Law*, Houghton Mifflin, pp. 2–13.

PATTON, A. (1961), *Men, Money and Motivation*, McGraw-Hill.

PENCE, O. E. (1939), *The YMCA and Social Need*, Association Press.

PENROSE, E. T. (1952), 'Biological analogies in the theory of the firm', *Amer. econ. Rev.*, vol. 42, pp. 804–19.

PENROSE, E. T. (1955), 'Limits to the growth and size of firms', *Amer. econ. Rev.*, vol. 45, no. 2, pp. 531–43. [See also the discussion by W. W. Cooper, pp. 559–63 of the same journal.]

PENROSE, E. T. (1959), *The Theory of the Growth of the Firm*, Wiley.

PERROW, C. (1961a), 'Organizational prestige: some functions and dysfunctions', *Amer. J. Sociol.*, vol. 66, pp. 335–41.

PERROW, C. (1961b), 'The analysis of goals in complex organizations', *Amer. sociol. Rev.*, vol. 26, pp. 854–66.

PHELPS BROWN, E. H. (1957), 'The meaning of the fitted Cobb-Douglas function', *Q. J. Econs*, vol. 71, pp. 546–60.

PHILLIPS, A. (1956), 'Concentration, scale and technological change in selected manufacturing industries, 1899–1939', *J. indust. Econs*, vol. 4, pp. 179–93.

REAL ESTATE RESEARCH PROGRAM (1959), *Industrial Location Bibliography*, Grad. Sch. Bus. Admin., University of California, RERP.

REVANS, R. W. (1958), 'Human relations, management and size', in E. M. Hugh-Jones (ed.), *Human Relations and Modern Management*, North-Holland, pp. 177–220.

RICHARDSON, F. L. W., Jr, and WALKER, C. R. (1948), *Human Relations in an Expanding Company*, Labor and Management Center, Yale University.

ROBERTS, D. R. (1956), 'A general theory of executive compensation based on statistically tested propositions', *Q. J. Econs*, vol. 20, pp. 270–94.

ROBERTS, D. R. (1959), *Executive Compensation*, Free Press.

ROBINSON, E. A. G. (1934), 'The problem of management and the size of firms', *Econs J.*, vol. 44, pp. 242–57.

ROSS, A. M. (1947), 'The trade union as a wage-fixing institution', *Amer. econ. Rev.*, vol. 37, pp. 566–88.

ROSS, N. S. (1952–3), 'Management and the size of the firm', *Rev. econ. Stud.*, vol. 19, no. 3, pp. 148–54.

ROSTAS, L. (1948), *Comparative Productivity in British and American Industry*, Cambridge University Press.

ROTHSCHILD, K. W. (1947), 'Price theory and oligopoly', *Econ. J.*, vol. 57, pp. 299–320.

SCHLAIFER, R., and HERON, S. D. (1950), *The Development of Aircraft Engines and Fuels*, Harvard Business School.

SEARLE, A. D., and GODY, C. S. (1945), 'Productivity changes in selected wartime shipbuilding programs', *Month. lab. Rev.*, vol. 61, pp. 1132–47.

SELZNICK, P. (1943), 'An approach to a theory of bureaucracy', *Amer. sociol. Rev.*, vol. 8, pp. 47–54.

SELZNICK, P. (1949), *TVA and the Grass Roots*, University of California Press.

SILLS, D. L. (1957), *The Volunteers*, Glencoe Free Press.

SIMON, H. A. (1953), 'Birth of an organization: the Economic Cooperation Administration', *Pub. Admin. Rev.*, vol. 13, pp. 227–36.

SIMON, H. A. (1955), 'On a class of skew distribution functions', *Biometrica*, vol. 42, pp. 425–40.

SIMON, H. A. (1957a), *Administrative Behavior*, 2nd edn, Macmillan.

SIMON, H. A. (1957b), 'The compensation of executives', *Sociom.*, vol. 20, pp. 32–5.

SIMON, H. A., and BONINI, C. P. (1958), 'The size distribution of business firms', *Amer. econ. Rev.*, vol. 48, pp. 607–17.

SIMPSON, R. L. (1959), 'Vertical and horizontal communication in formal organizations', *Admin. Sci. Q.*, vol. 4, pp. 188–96.

SLICHTER, S. H., HEALY, J. J., and LIVERNASH, E. R. (1960), *The Impact of Collective Bargaining on Management*, Brookings.

SMELSER, N. J. (1959), *Social Change in the Industrial Revolution*, University of Chicago Press.

SOEMARDJAN, S. (1957), 'Bureaucratic organization in a time of revolution', *Admin. Sci. Q.*, vol. 2, pp. 182–99.

SOFER, C.(1961), *The Organization from Within*, Tavistock.

SPINRAD, W. (1960), 'Correlates of trade union participation: a summary of the literature', *Amer. sociol. Rev.*, vol. 25, pp. 237–44.

STAEHLE, H. (1942), 'The measurement of statistical cost functions: an appraisal of some recent contributions', *Amer. econ. Rev.*, vol. 32, pp. 321–33.

STARBUCK, W. H. (1965), *The Heteroscedastic Normal*, paper no. 106, Institute of Quantitive Research in Economics and Management, Purdue University.

STARBUCK, W. H. (1966), 'The efficiency of British and American retail employees', *Admin. Sci. Q.*, vol. 11, pp. 345–85. [See Reading 2 of this selection.]

STEINDL, J. (1945), *Small and Big Business*, Blackwell.

STEINDL, J. (1952), *Maturity and Stagnation in American Capitalism*, Blackwell.

STEPHAN, F., and MISHLER, E. G. (1952), 'The distribution of participation in small groups: an exponential approximation', *Amer. sociol Rev.*, vol. 17, pp. 598–608.

STIGLER, G. J. (1950), 'Monopoly and oligopoly by merger', *Amer. econ. Rev.*, vol. 40, pp. 23–34 (proceedings).

STINCHCOMBE, A. L. (1959), 'Bureaucratic and craft administration of production', *Admin. sci. Q.*, vol. 4, pp. 168–87.

STOCKING, G. W., and MUELLER, W. F. (1957), 'Business reciprocity and the size of firms', *J. Bus.*, vol. 30, pp. 73–95.

SUOJANEN, W. W. (1955), 'The span of control – fact or fable?', *Advanced Manag.*, vol. 20, no. 11, pp. 5–13.

TALACCHI, S. (1960), 'Organization size, individual attitudes and behavior: an empirical study.' *Admin. Sci. Q.*, vol. 5, pp. 398–420.

TANNENBAUM, A. S., and KAHN, R. L. (1958), *Participation in Union Locals*, Row, Peterson.

TAST (1953), *Size and Morale*, pt 1, Action Society Trust.

TAST (1957), *Size and Morale*, pt 2, Acton Society Trust.

TERRIEN, F. W., and MILLS, D. L. (1955), 'The effect of changing size upon the internal structure of organizations', *Amer. sociol. Rev.*, vol. 20, pp. 11–13.

THOMAS, E. J. (1959), 'Role conceptions and organizational size', *Amer. sociol. Rev.*, vol. 24, pp. 30–37.

THOMPSON, J. D., and BATES, F. L. (1957), 'Technology, organization and administration', *Admin. Sci. Q.*, vol. 2, pp. 325–43.

THOMPSON, J. D., and McEWEN, W. J. (1958), 'Organizational goals and environment: goal-setting as an interaction process', *Amer. sociol. Rev.*, vol. 23, pp. 23–31.

TNEC (1941), *Relative Efficiency of Large, Medium-Sized and Small Business*, Monogr. no. 13, Temporary National Economic Committee.

TRIST, E. L., and BAMFORTH, K. W. (1951), 'Social and psychological consequences of the longwall method of coal-getting', *Hum. Rel.*, vol. 4, pp. 3–38.

TSOUDEROS, J. E. (1955), 'Organizational change in terms of a series of selected variables', *Amer. sociol. Rev.*, vol. 20, pp. 206–10.

UDY, S. H., Jr (1959a), '"Bureaucracy" and "rationality" in Weber's organization theory: an empirical study', *Amer. sociol. Rev.*, vol. 24, pp. 791–5.

UDY, S. H., Jr (1959b), 'The structure of authority in non-industrial production organizations', *Amer. J. Sociol.*, vol. 64, pp. 582–4.

URWICK, L. F. (1956), 'The manager's span of control', *Harvard Bus. Rev.*, vol. 34, no. 3, pp. 39–47.

WALKER, C. R., and GUEST, R. H. (1952), 'The man on the assembly line', *Harvard Bus. Rev.*, vol. 30, no. 3, pp. 71–83.

WARNER, W. L., and LOW, J. O. (1947), *The Social System of the Modern Factory*, Yale University Press.

WEBER, C. E. (1959), 'Change in managerial manpower with mechanization of data-processing', *J. Bus.*, vol. 32, pp. 151–63.

WEIGAND, R. E. (1963), 'The marketing organization, channels, and firm size', *J. Bus.*, vol. 36, pp. 228–36.

WEINSHALL, T. D. (1960–61), 'Problems of change in organizational structure in growing enterprises', unpublished doctoral dissertation, Grad. Sch. Bus. Admin., Harvard University.

WEISS, R. S. (1956), *Processes of Organization*, Survey Research Center, University of Michigan.

WHITE, C. M. (1960), 'Multiple goals in the theory of the firm', in K. E. Boulding and W. A. Spivey (eds.), *Linear Programming and the Theory of the Firm*, Macmillan, pp. 181–201.

WHITE, H. (1962), 'Chance models of systems of casual groups', *Sociom.*, vol. 25, pp. 153–72.

WHITIN, T. M., and PESTON, M. H. (1954), 'Random variations, risk, and returns to scale', *Q. J. Econs*, vol. 68, pp. 603–12.

WHYTE, W. F. (1948), *Human Relations in the Restaurant Industry*, McGraw-Hill.

WHYTE, W. F. (1961), *Men At Work*, Dorsey Press.

WHYTE, W. H., Jr (1956), *The Organization Man*, Simon & Schuster.

WICKESBERG, A. K. (1961), *Organizational Relationships in the Growing Small Manufacturing Firm*, University of Minnesota.

WILCOX, C. (1955), *Public Policies Toward Business*, Irwin.

WILLIAMSON, O. E. (1963), 'A model of rational managerial behavior', in R. M. Cyert and J. G. March, *A Behavioral Theory of the Firm*, Prentice-Hall, pp. 237–52.

WILSON, J. Q. (1963), 'Innovation in organization: notes toward a theory', paper read at Amer. Pol. Sci. Assoc.

WINTER, S. G., Jr. (1960), *Economic Natural Selection and the Theory of the Firm*, paper P–2167, Rand Corp.

WOODRUFF, A. M., and ALEXANDER, T. G. (1958), *Success and Failure in Small Manufacturing*, University of Pittsburgh Press.

WOODWARD, J. (1958), *Management and Technology*, HMSO.

WORTHY, J. C. (1950a), 'Factors influencing employee morale', *Harvard Bus. Rev.*, vol. 28, no. 1, pp. 61–73.

WORTHY, J. C. (1950b), 'Organizational structure and employee morale', *Amer. sociol. Rev.*, vol. 15, pp. 169–79.

ZALD, M. N., and DENTON, P. (1963), 'From evangelism to general service: the transformation of the YMCA', *Admin. Sci. Q.*, vol. 8, pp. 214–34.

Part Two Motives for Growth

Organization theorists have traditionally and continually been interested in the interaction between task assignments and worker productivity, the interaction between worker productivity and organizational performance, and the interaction between the performance of individual organizations and the social system in which they operate. 'The efficiency of British and American retail employees' analyses these three interactions as a mutually-reinforcing system – in this instance, a system determining the relation between sales volume per employee and the size of retail stores. The analysis suggests that specialization and division of labour make British clerks less productive than American clerks; that maximum profit to a store rarely implies maximum sales volume per employee; and that the allocation of tasks within stores and the price structure of the economy jointly constrain the size distribution of stores and the extent of cooperative relations among stores.

A major recent trend in organization theory has been the surge of interest in open-systems models. These models emphasize the transactions between an organization and its environment, and the transactions between interest groups within an organization, and consequently, they force one to look upon the assessment of organizational performance as a multi-dimensional process. 'Components of effectiveness in small organizations' analyses data from small businesses and concludes that employee fulfilment, owner fulfilment and societal fulfilment vary almost independently of one another, and that firms find it quite difficult to satisfy all clienteles simultaneously. Larger firms are more successful than smaller firms in fulfilling the needs of communities, owners and customers, but less successful in fulfilling the needs of employees.

Were there space to include another article in this section, it would be Stanley Seashore and Ephraim Yuchtman's 'Factorial analysis of organizational performance'. It also derives from the open-systems viewpoint, being an attempt to identify the independent dimensions comprising effectiveness by insurance sales agencies. However, Seashore and Yuchtman begin with the assumption that one can infer the 'penultimate goals' for behavior from observations of the behavior itself, and they end with the conclusion that organizations 'are not purposive'. Both the assumption and the conclusion seem extreme.

2 W. H. Starbuck

The Efficiency of British and American Retail Employees

William H. Starbuck, 'The efficiency of British and
American retail employees', *Administrative Science Quarterly*, vol. 11,
no. 3, 1966, pp. 345–85.

Organization theorists have devoted considerable attention to
differences between large organizations and small ones – to
differences in the goals they pursue in the behavioral strategies
they adopt, and in the resources they command (Starbuck, 1965).
This paper examines one kind of difference between large organizations and small ones, the organizations being retail stores.[1]

When stores of various sizes are compared, sales volume per
employee varies in a characteristic way.[2] As store size increases,
from one-employee stores to stores with several employees, sales
volume per employee increases; the increase is especially rapid
among stores having less than two employees. At some point, as
stores get larger, sales volume per employee begins to decrease, so
that the largest stores have lower sales per employee than stores of
medium size. These regularities are qualitatively independent of
the commodity or service sold and independent, at least for the
United States and Great Britain, of the nation in which the stores
are located. Scatter diagrams for the two countries are shown in
Figure 1.

This paper develops a mathematical theory to explain the
behavior of the sales-per-employee curve, and then applies the
theory to American and British data to analyse the cross-cultural
differences in retail organizations.[3] The theory is framed on a

1. This paper has benefited by the comments of J. M. Dutton. J. R. T.
Hughes and N. Rosenberg contributed helpful observations on British
retail practices.
2. The term 'employees' refers to anyone working in the store. Later, a
distinction is made between proprietors and paid employees.
3. For another model of these phenomena and discussions of them, see
Herbst (1957) and Starbuck and Herbst (1963).

societal scale. It describes the gross characteristics of all retail organizations, or all retail organizations in a commodity group, but does not purport to describe any single store as it changes

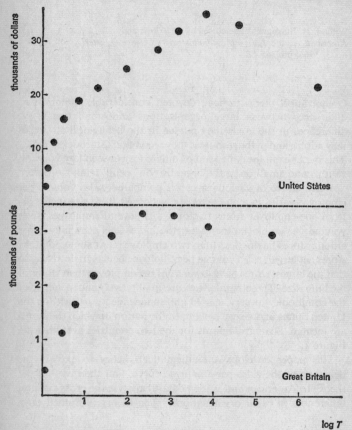

Figure 1 Sales volume per employee, S/T

size. The assumptions understate the complexity of task interactions within a single organization, and oversimplifications of heroic magnitudes are made to avoid having more parameters than observations.

Symbol dictionary

Symbol	Use
a and b	Two coefficients controlling the rate of increase in the number of different commodities sold in a store as the store's total (dollar) sales volume increases.
c	The smallest (dollar) quantity of a commodity which is eligible for manufacturer-lot quantity discounts.
f	A short-hand symbol representing a complicated function of N.
k	The number of customers in a store.
K	The expected number of customers in a store.
n	The number of clerks in a store.
N	The optimum number of clerks in a store.
P	The number of proprietors in a store.
R	A short-hand symbol representing a complicated function of N and P.
S	The (dollar) sales volume per unit time period of a store.
S_0	The sales volume at which extrinsic backing becomes necessary.
t	Time.
T	The total number of employees in a store.
a	The probability that a customer will arrive at a store during an infinitesimal time period.
β_0	The (dollar) amount sold by a clerk per unit time period; also the amount purchased by a customer per unit time period.
β_1	Variable cost per (dollar) unit of sales.
β_2	Variable cost per clerk.
β_3	Costs that do not vary linearly with S or n.
β_4	The monetary contribution from manufacturer-lot purchasing per (dollar) unit of central store sales.
β_5	Variable cost per backer.
γ	A short-hand symbol representing a complicated function of β_0, β_1 and β_2.
γ_P	The value that γ takes in (very small) stores which have no paid employees.

γ_0	The value that γ takes in (medium-sized, intrinsically backed) stores which have more paid employees than proprietors.
δ	A coefficient controlling the rate at which γ shifts from γ_P to γ_0 as the ratio of paid employees to proprietors increases.
θ	The ratio of the sales volume of a central store plus its branches to the sales volume of the central store itself.
θ_0	The value that θ takes in very, very large stores.
λ	The probability, per customer in the store, that a customer will leave during an infinitesimal time period.
μ	The man-hours of retailer backing required per unit of time and per customer.
ν	The man-hours of wholesaler backing per unit time and per central store customer.
π	Profit per unit of time.
ρ	The proportion of goods purchasable in manufacturer-lot quantities; also the rate at which central stores expand their branch operations.
τ	The length of time a customer stays in a store.
Ψ	A coefficient controlling the rate at which ρ increases as S increases.

The model

Our basic analytic approach is to characterize all retail organizations as having one uniform goal: to maximize their profits. Of course, this is unrealistic. Organizations pursue a multiplicity of goals, and organizations of different sizes tend to have different goals. However, profit-maximization is not an undefensibly narrow assumption in the present instance. First, all of the organizations considered are business organizations. Although they may not all be equally committed to profit-making, they are likely to be strongly concerned with profit and economic efficiency. Second, because the focus is on the hypothetical average store, how stores of the same size differ is not important. Some goal differences related to store size will be taken into account, particularly in the case of very small stores. Third, profit-maximization is adopted as a heuristic rather than a complete description. Only qualitative relations between variables are sought, and at no point is it assumed that actual profits have been, or could be, measured.[4]

The effects of employment policy on profit obviously depend upon how employees are utilized. In particular, we distinguish between two classes of activities that retail store employees perform. Activities that involve direct interaction with customers are called *clerking activities*. Activities which do not involve direct interaction with customers are called *backing activities*.

A store's supply of clerking services has immediate impact on that store's sales volume. Any given store has a potential customer load determined by its selection of merchandise, its pricing policy, its advertising, the number and natures of competing stores, and similar factors. The supply of clerking services determines whether the store actually realizes the sales volume which its potential customer load represents. The reason for this is that, other things being equal, customers would rather not wait to be served. If customers must wait consistently, they will tend to migrate to other stores. On the other hand, the store's supply of backing activities does not affect sales volume directly, because backing activities do not contribute directly to customer satisfaction. Thus, the employment problem amounts to trying to balance the incremental sales accruing from additional clerking services against the incremental cost of these services.

In small and medium-sized stores, backing activities are usually performed during lulls in the customer load by the same employees who perform clerking activities. All, or nearly all, employees can earn their salaries by the clerking activities that they perform during peaks in the customer load. Backing services can be regarded as costless, a free good. Since there is no clear division of labor between clerking and backing activities, some criterion must be established for classifying the employees. The criterion adopted here is that an employee is a *clerk* if he *ever* performs clerking activities; he is a *backer* if he *never* performs clerking activities. It is argued that small and medium-sized stores employ only clerks and are characterized by *intrinsic backing*, and that

4. Thus, this could be called a utility maximization model. For further discussion of the philosophical issues involved, see Starbuck (1965, pp. 336–46).

large stores employ both clerks and backers and are characterized by *extrinsic backing*. One consequence of extrinsic backing is that large stores establish branches in an effort to offset the cost of employing backers.

Sales volume with intrinsic backing

When backing is intrinsic, it is a free good and can be left out of a profit-oriented model. Hence, the intrinsically backed store is the simplest place to begin analysis. Later, the conditions are developed under which intrinsic backing fails, and the model is modified to incorporate extrinsic backing.

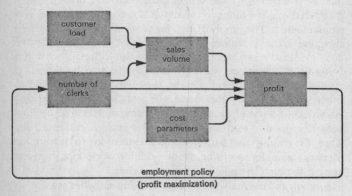

Figure 2 Assumed causal structure

We characterize the customer load on a store by a probabilistic arrival-and-departure process. Given this customer load, the sales volume of a store can be stated as a function of the number of clerks in the store. Then we solve for the number of clerks that will maximize a linear profit function. This process is illustrated in Figure 2. Since the optimum number of clerks depends upon the customer load, the approximate customer load can be inferred from the number of clerks. This leads to a statement of the relationship between sales volume and the number of clerks, as shown in Figure 3.

First, assume that nonrandom fluctuations in customer load are predicted and that employment schedules are varied accordingly. Second, assume that customers never wait to be served by a clerk; customers only enter a store if clerks are available to serve them. Neither of these assumptions is empirically valid, but they simplify the initial analysis and both are modified as the analysis proceeds.

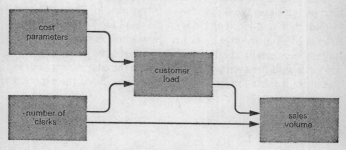

Figure 3 Inferred structural relations

The symbols k and n represent the number of customers and clerks, respectively, in a given store. The probability that exactly one customer arrives at the store during a short time interval is taken to be α times the length of the time interval. An arriving customer enters the store if $k < n$, and does not enter if $k \geqslant n$. The probability that exactly one customer leaves the store during a short time interval is taken to be λ times k times the length of the time interval, so that the probability of a departure is twice as large when six customers are in the store as when three are. Finally, because employment schedules are matched to fluctuations in customer load and because our interest is in cross-section data rather than time-series data, it is assumed that the stochastic arrival-and-departure process has stabilized; the probability of finding k customers in a store with n clerks is constant over time.

The preceding assumptions imply[5] that the probability of finding k customers in a store with n clerks is

$$\Pr(k) = \frac{1}{k!}\left(\frac{\alpha}{\lambda}\right)^k\left\{\sum_{k=0}^n \frac{1}{k!}\left(\frac{\alpha}{\lambda}\right)^k\right\}^{-1}, \qquad \mathbf{1}$$

5. Details of the mathematical development are given in Appendix A.

and that the probability any one customer remains in a store for a total time τ is

$$\Pr(\tau) = \lambda e^{-\lambda \tau}. \qquad \qquad 2$$

Sales volume per time period is the number of transactions per time period times the dollar sales per transaction. Data collected by Galbraith and Holton (1955) on the retail food trade in Puerto Rico show that average sales per transaction is much higher in large stores than in small ones. Assume that sales per transaction increases with the average amount of time the customer spends in the store; it takes longer to buy more things. Since the expected value of τ is

$$\lambda \int_0^\infty \tau e^{-\lambda \tau} \, d\tau = 1/\lambda, \qquad \qquad 3$$

sales per transaction is taken to be β_0/λ. β_0 represents the amount purchased by an average customer per unit time period of shopping, or alternatively, the amount sold by an average clerk per unit time period of clerking.

Over long time intervals, the number of transactions per unit time period will be approximately the average number of customers in the store divided by the average amount of time each customer stays: the expected value of k divided by the expected value of τ. The expected value of k is denoted K, and equation 1 implies that

$$K = \left(\frac{a}{\lambda}\right) \left\{ \sum_{k=0}^{n-1} \frac{1}{k!} \left(\frac{a}{\lambda}\right)^k \right\} \bigg/ \left\{ \sum_{k=0}^{n} \frac{1}{k!} \left(\frac{a}{\lambda}\right)^k \right\}. \qquad 4$$

Since the expected value of τ is $1/\lambda$, the number of transac ions per time period is λK, and sales volume per time period is

$$S = \beta_0 K.$$

At this point, we have stated sales volume in terms of K, where K represents a complicated function of a, λ and n. Now consider the consequences of profit maximization. We characterize profit by a linear function,

$$S - \beta_1 S - \beta_2 n - \beta_3 = (1 - \beta_1)\beta_0 K - \beta_2 n - \beta_3. \qquad 5$$

This function recognizes two kinds of variable cost: $\beta_1 S$ is a cost that increases with sales volume, and $\beta_2 n$ is a cost that increases with employment. β_3 represents all other costs which the store might encounter, but which do not vary linearly with S or n. Profit maximization means that n is set equal to an optimum value N.

In principle, both n and its profit-maximizing value N are discrete (noncontinuous) variables taking only integer (whole number) values. This is certainly true for a single store at a given time; it can employ one clerk or two clerks, but not 1·4 clerks. Thus, in principle, N equals zero whenever the customer load is too small. The smallest feasible store is one with a single employee; a one-employee store has

$$K = \left(\frac{a}{\lambda}\right) \bigg/ \left(1 + \frac{a}{\lambda}\right)$$

and a profit equal to

$$\left\{ \left(\frac{a}{\lambda}\right)(1-\beta_1)\beta_0 \bigg/ \left(1+\frac{a}{\lambda}\right) \right\} - \beta_2 - \beta_3.$$

If this profit were negative, the store would go out of business. For a store to exist at all, the customer load and cost coefficients must be such that

$$\frac{a}{\lambda} > \frac{\beta_2+\beta_3}{\beta_0(1-\beta_1)-\beta_2-\beta_3}. \qquad\qquad 6$$

However, to impose this reasoning on our hypothetical 'average' store is to go too far. The 'average' store can have 1·4 employees, or 1·4639. Consequently, we convert to a continuous approximation in which N can take any value. In the process of finding this approximation, we firstly compute the profit-maximizing relationship between N and K and secondly, make the transition from Figure 2 to Figure 3, so that N becomes a basis for inferring K. The best approximation seems to be[6]

$$K \simeq N(1-e^{-f}), \qquad\qquad 7$$

where: $f = e^{1-2\gamma}(N^{0.4\gamma})$

6. The nature of the approximation is discussed in Appendix B. The basic characteristics of the function can be seen in the two solid lines of Figure 4, which graphs $S/N = \beta_0(K/N)$ for two values of γ.

and $\quad \gamma = \log\left(1 - \log\dfrac{\beta_2}{\beta_0(1-\beta_1)}\right).$

This approximation modifies the earlier assumption about customers waiting to be served. In general, the approximation understates optimum employment, making customers more tolerant of small imbalances in the number of clerks. Customers will enter a store even though all clerks are involved with other customers.

The very small store

Initially, it was assumed that employment schedules could be varied to match predictable fluctuations in customer load. It is obvious, however, that the number of clerks cannot be varied when the store has only one employee. A very small store may be able to add part-time help during major peaks in customer load, e.g. Christmas, but it cannot reduce employment during major troughs. Because of this relative inflexibility in employment scheduling, one can make four predictions:

1. The very small store will appear to be economically irrational by objective criteria. These stores have essentially no effect upon the input factor markets; they tend to be proprietorships financed from personal capital and having no paid employees. The bases for objective criteria of profitability are controlled by larger stores which have no handicap in transactions per clerk-hour. The objective minimum store size will correspond to a store with average employment greater than one. There is much anecdotal evidence in the managerial accounting literature to substantiate this point.

2. Relative to the commodity-group distributions of larger stores, very small stores will be concentrated in commodity groups with high gross margins. Since absolute profits are as crucial to survival as relative profits, low gross margins will have a much more direct relation to the failure of very small stores than to the failure of larger stores. In the context of the model, very small stores will be characterized by a smaller β_1 than is typical of larger stores.

3. Because very small stores make comparatively extravagant expenditures of labor per transaction, one major aspect of their

irrationality will be low monetary valuation of labor. In the context of the model, very small stores will be characterized by a smaller β_2 than is typical of larger stores. This effect is amplified by the use of unpaid family workers during peaks in customer load.

4. The tendency of very small stores to appear economically irrational will disappear rapidly as the ratio of paid employees to proprietors increases. First, paid employees are, no doubt, less ascetic than their employers. If labor is to be valued cheaply, it is the employer, not the employee, who must bear the brunt of it. Second, the proprietor's own asceticism probably disappears when he begins to hire other people. Third, and possibly most important, paid employees introduce flexibility into the employment schedule. We have no data from which to estimate the range of predictable variation in customer load, but it seems likely that the effects of inflexible employment will only appear in stores where the ratio of proprietors to paid employees exceeds one.

Tendencies to undervalue labor (small β_2) and to sell commodities with high gross margins (small β_1) will have similar effects on γ. The γ for very small stores should be larger than the γ for large and medium-sized stores. We contend that γ depends upon the relation between the number of proprietors, P, and the total number of clerks, N. A store with no paid employees ($N = P$) might be characterized by γ_P, whereas larger stores with several paid employees ($N >> P$) might be characterized by γ_0, $\gamma_0 < \gamma_P$. We choose the function

$$\gamma = R\gamma_P + (1-R)\gamma_0, \qquad\qquad 8$$

where $R = \exp\{-\delta(N-P)/P\}$. $(N-P)/P$ is the ratio of paid employees to proprietors. We predict that $\gamma \simeq \gamma_0$ when $N-P > P$, or that $(\gamma_P - \gamma_0)e^{-\delta} \simeq 0$.

Figure 4 illustrates the correction for very small stores. The solid lines show sales volume per clerk for $\gamma = 1$ and $\gamma = 2$. The dashed line shows the transition[7] from $\gamma = \gamma_P = 2$ to $\gamma = \gamma_0 = 1$.

7. The dotted line is calculated on the basis of $\delta = 5$ and $P = 1$ where P is independent of N.

Breakdown of intrinsic backing

The total amount of backing activity that must be performed should be roughly proportional to K. Activities like purchasing, handling inventories, customer billing, and delivery of goods should all increase in proportion to the number of items sold or

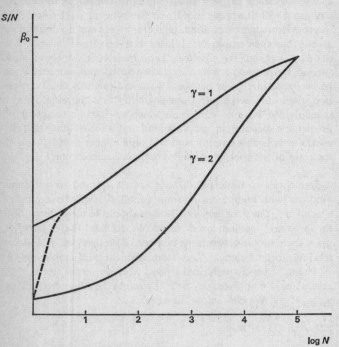

Figure 4 Sales volume per clerk, S/N

the number of customers passing through the store, both of which are proportional to K. Assume, therefore, that an intrinsically backed store must devote μK man-hours to backing.[8]

The man-hours devoted to clerking average K, so

$$N-K \simeq Ne^{-f}$$

8. The proper measure of backing activity is man-hours per hour or man-years per year. We use man-hours as an abbreviation.

man-hours are available for backing. When $Ne^{-f} > \mu K$, the clerks can perform all of the backing, but when $Ne^{-f} < \mu K$, there is more backing to be done than the clerks can do. Backers must be hired – backing becomes extrinsic – at the point where $e^{-f} = \mu/(1+\mu)$. It will be convenient to refer to this breakdown point by its corresponding sales volume, S_0. Sales volume per clerk will be $\beta_0/(1+\mu)$ at S_0.

Figure 5 illustrates the breakdown in intrinsic backing. The demand for backing activity, $\mu N(1 - e^{-f})$, is nearly zero in very small stores and increases very rapidly. The average number of clerks available to do backing work, Ne^{-f}, will be nearly one in very small stores, but increases less rapidly than the backing requirement. Intrinsic backing breaks down at the intersection of the two curves.[9]

Manufacturer-lot purchasing and branch operations

At least two other technological changes should correlate with extrinsic backing: first, large stores can purchase goods at discount in manufacturer-lot quantities; second, large tores tend to be central stores which operate branches.

Clearly a store with large sales volume can purchase a higher proportion of its goods in manufacturing-lot quantities than can a store with small sales volume. Casual observation suggests that large stores sell many more commodities than small ones, but that this increase in the number of commodities handled is not proportional to the increase in sales volume. If the number of different commodities is taken to be $(1/a)S^{1-b}$, then sales volume per commodity will average aS^b, where $0 < b < 1$. The combination of storage and handling costs and manufacturer terms of sale implies a minimum sales volume for purchasing in manufacturer-lot quantities. As sales volume per commodity increases, an increasing proportion of the commodities handled exceeds this minimum volume for discount purchasing.

The probability that a given customer purchases a given commodity should be inversely proportional to the price of the commodity and to the number of different commodities sold. Hence,

9. These curves are based on the same parameters as Figure 4: $\gamma_P = 2$, $\gamma_0 = 1$, $\delta = 5$, $P = 1$; in addition, $\mu = 0\cdot4$. It follows that $e^{-f} = 0\cdot286$ at S_0 and $S_0 = 15\cdot285\,\beta_0$.

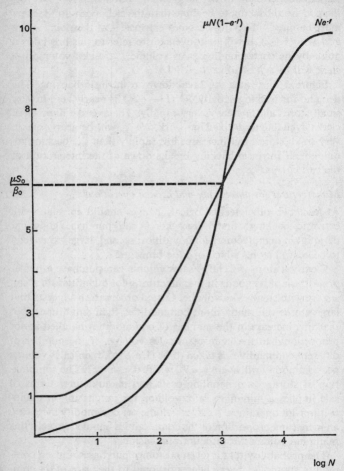

Figure 5 The breakdown of intrinsic backing

when the number of commodities is large, total sales volume should be distributed among commodities by a Poisson distribution. Both the mean and variance of this distribution would be aS^b, and the proportion of goods purchasable in manufacturer lots would be the upper tail of the distribution. The symbol ρ represents the proportion of goods purchasable in manufacturer lots. The reasoning above suggests that

$$\rho_1 = \sum_{x=c}^{\infty} \frac{aS^{bx}\exp(-aS^b)}{x!}, \qquad\qquad 9$$

where c is the minimum sales volume for buying in manufacturer-lot quantities. A curve of the type indicated is shown by the line labelled $\theta = 1$ in Figure 6.

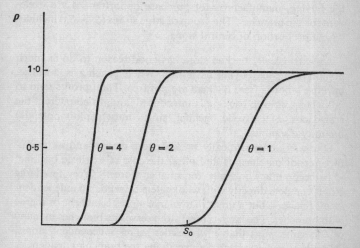

sales volume

Figure 6 Proportion of goods purchasable in manufacturer-lot quantities, ρ

S_0 should fall somewhere near the point indicated in Figure 6. Stores with $S < S_0$ do little manufacturer-lot buying, but as S increases above S_0, ρ increases rapidly. There are three reasons for associating S_0 with the point where ρ begins to increase.

1. A store with S slightly below S_0 tends to ignore its opportunities to buy in manufacturer-lot quantities. The clerks are working essentially all the time. Additional demands on their time, created by departures from standard sources of supply, cannot not be satisfied.

2. Clerks are customer oriented; their attention is focused on the customer. Consequently, an organization which includes only clerks will tend to overlook supply alternatives. Backers, on the other hand, can be supply oriented. An organization which includes backers tends to recognize, and even invent, supply alternatives.

3. The group of medium-sized stores $(0 < < S < S_0)$ includes a high proportion of stores that are branches of chains. Since the central stores and central warehouses of the chains do the buying, manufacturer-lot purchase opportunities are irrelevant for the branches. The group of large stores $(S > S_0)$ includes a high proportion of central stores.

An extrinsically backed store has good reason to do as much manufacturer-lot buying as it can. When backing is intrinsic, backing labor is free. Backers are not free. Total profits tend to fall when extrinsic backing is introduced, and, to counteract the added cost of extrinsic backing, stores must exploit potential quantity discounts.

One way an extrinsically backed store can expand its manufacturer-lot purchasing, and offset the cost of extrinsic backing, is to become a wholesaler for smaller stores.[10] Very few large stores compete directly with wholesalers by servicing independent small retailers, but a great many large stores establish, or merge with branches. The large central store serves its branches in many of the same ways that a wholesaler serves independent stores. There is no *a priori* basis for specifying the branching tendencies of large stores, but the expansion should be qualitatively similar to ρ_1. Intrinsically backed stores should do virtually no wholesaling; extrinsically backed stores should expand their branch operations rapidly.

10. The author is indebted to E. Ames for calling the wholesaling activities of central stores to his attention.

We assume that the total volume of goods handled by backers is θS, where θ is a coefficient that increases from 1 to θ_0 as the store adds branches. As long as $S < S_0$, the store's sales volume for backing is the same as its sales volume for clerking. When S increases above S_0, the store adds branches with sales volume $(\theta_0 - 1)S\rho_1$, so that $\theta = 1 + (\theta_0 - 1)\rho_1$. The very large store (for which $\rho_1 = 1$) will have a branch sales volume of $(\theta_0 - 1)S$ and a total sales volume for backing of $\theta_0 S$.

Of course, the expansion into branch operations accelerates the increase in ρ. When the sales volume for backing is θS,

$$\rho = \sum_{x=c}^{\infty} \frac{a(\theta S)^{bx}.\exp\{-a(\theta S)^b\}}{x!}. \qquad 10$$

Figure 6 shows ρ for three values of θ. When θ increases from 1 to θ_0, ρ comes to look very much like a step function at S_0. ρ remains near zero for $S < S_0$, and then increases very rapidly to unity when S exceeds S_0. The total volume of goods purchasable in manufacturer-lot quantities is $\rho\theta S$. This function remains near zero for $S < S_0$ because ρ is nearly zero; when S exceeds S_0, $\rho\theta S$ approaches $\theta_0 S$ very rapidly, because both ρ and θ are increasing. Figure 7 shows the behavior of $\rho\theta S$.[11]

The preceding derivation sets forth our understanding of the basic relationships affecting sales volume per employee in large stores. But the model includes too many parameters: a, b, c and θ_0. The qualitative behavior of $\rho\theta$ suggests the approximation:

$$\rho\theta \simeq 0 \qquad \text{for} \quad S < S_0$$
$$\rho\theta \simeq \theta_0\rho \qquad \text{for} \quad S > S_0, \qquad 11$$

where $\rho = 1 - \exp\{-\Psi(S-S_0)/S_0\}$. Whether this is a good approximation for the a, b and c that characterize the data is an open question.

Sales volume per employee with extrinsic backing

The backing activity in an extrinsically backed store is qualitatively different from the backing activity in an intrinsically backed store. The retailing and wholesaling aspects can be

11. The graphs in Figures 6 and 7 were calculated on the basis of $a = 25$, $b = 0.25$, and $c = 1000$. In Figure 7, $\theta_0 = 3$.

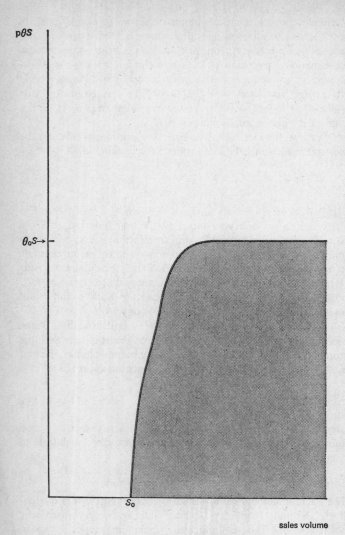

Figure 7 Sales volume purchased in manufacturer-lot quantities, $\rho\theta S$

separated. Backing activity of the type found in an intrinsically backed store should still require μK man-hours. The wholesaler functions demand an additional $(v/\beta_0 \theta_0)\theta_0 \rho S$ man-hours. Since clerks can contribute $N-K$ man-hours, the number of backers is $\mu K + v\rho K - (N-K)$. Total employment, T, is $K(1+\mu+v\rho)$, and sales volume per employee is

$$\frac{S}{T} = \frac{\beta_0}{1+\mu+v\rho}. \qquad\qquad 12$$

Sales per employee is maximized at S_0, and decreases toward $\beta_0/(1+\mu+v)$ as S becomes very large.[12]

Summary of the model

When $S < S_0$, all employees of the store are clerks, and sales volume per employee is

$$\frac{S}{T} = \frac{S}{N} = \beta_0(1-e^{-f}), \qquad\qquad 13$$

where: $f = e^{1-2\gamma}(N^{0.4\gamma})$
$\gamma = R\gamma_P + (1-R)\gamma_0$
$R = \exp\{-\delta(N-P)/P\}$.

Sales volume per employee reaches a maximum at $S = S_0$; at this point

$$\frac{S}{T} = \frac{S}{N} = \frac{\beta_0}{1+\mu}. \qquad\qquad 14$$

When $S > S_0$, the store employs backers as well as clerks, and sales volume per employee is

$$\frac{S}{T} = \frac{\beta_0}{1+\mu+v\rho}, \qquad\qquad 12$$

where: $\rho = 1-\exp\{-\Psi(S-S_0)/S_0\}$.

The model involves seven parameters: γ_P, γ_0, δ, Ψ, v, and two of β_0, μ and S_0. Figure 8 shows the hypothesized behavior of sales volume per employee[13] for both $S < S_0$ and $S > S_0$.

12. Appendix C explores the behavior of N in large stores.
13. Figure 8 uses the same parameter values as Figure 5, plus $v = 0.6$ and $\Psi = 0.5$.

We now turn to data on retail stores in the United States and Great Britain. These data are not introduced as a test of the model. Rather, the model provides a framework for contrasting American and British organizational structures. That is why our *a priori* logic has been stated in detail.

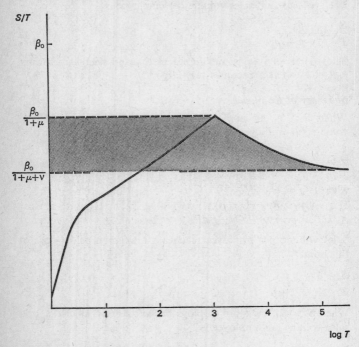

Figure 8 Sales volume per employee, S/T

The data

All retail and services trades are treated as a single, homogeneous activity. The data represent averages for total retail trade as defined by Great Britain's *Census of Distribution* (Board of Trade, 1954), and total retail trade, less eating and drinking places, as defined by the United States' *Census of Business* (Bureau of the Census, 1957).

An aggregative approach does not do justice to the wealth of available data, but some cross-cultural differences are pervasive.[14] Data on individual commodity groups display substantially the same characteristics as the aggregate data. Hall, Knapp and Winsten (1961), tabulated sales per employee as a function of store size for 'each of the trades given by a fairly fine division in the United States census'. The results conform nicely to our model: 'It will be seen that in every case except one (drug stores) there is a fairly sharp increase in sales per person between the smallest and the middle size. Even for the drug stores the figure is constant and does not drop. ... As the size of shop increases [to ten or more employees], sales per person dropped again slightly in rather over half of the trades.'(p. 67.)[15]

The census tabulations

Sales and employment data are available in two forms: with the establishment's sales volume as the independent variable, and with the establishment's employment as the independent variable. The figures used are taken from the sales-size classifications. Although the model states sales volume as a function of employment, this was not the assumed causal relationship. Both sales volume and employment were causally dependent variables in the model of intrinsically backed stores; the independent variable was the customer load coefficient α/λ. Neither the sales-size nor the employment-size tables are ideally suited to our purposes, but sales volume is tied more closely to customer load than employment is. Sales volume became an independent variable in the model of extrinsically backed stores, making the sales-size tables even more appropriate.

The two censuses are not directly comparable. One problem is a lack of information on work weeks. We reduce the employment data to equivalent full-time employees, but the relative significance of a 'full-time' employee may be different in the two

14. See Hall, Knapp and Winsten (1961), especially chs 2, 5, 7 and 11. Chapter 7 considers the same problem we do. Further discussion of British retailing can be found in ch. 3 of Jeffery (1954). Retail trade in the United States is surveyed in Barger (1955).

15. The trade breakdowns are shown in their Table 35.

countries. Hall, Knapp and Winsten marshalled the available evidence and concluded that the work weeks are roughly the same length in both countries but 'probably slightly longer in Britain' (p. 52). Certainly there is too little data for an assumption that the work weeks are not equal.

Another problem is created by unpaid workers or proprietors. The United States' census does not distinguish between part-time and full-time proprietors; the data represent the number of unpaid workers who devote *most* of their time to the store. Since proprietors typically work longer hours than paid employees, we treat all American proprietors as full-time employees. The sales-size tables of Great Britain's census do not distinguish between paid and unpaid employees, but do classify unpaid workers under the appropriate full-time or part-time headings.

The United States census gives annual payroll and the full-time payroll and employment for the census sample week. Hence, the average number of paid employees per establishment is estimated by

$$\frac{(\text{annual payroll}) \times (\text{full-time employment for sample week})}{(52 \text{ weeks}) \times (\text{number of establishments}) \times} \\ \times (\text{full-time payroll for sample week})$$

Total employment per establishment is then taken as the number of paid employees per establishment plus the number of proprietors per establishment. The United States' data are given in Table 1.

The sales-size tables of Great Britain's census do not give payroll data, and part-time employees must be reduced to equivalent full-time employees on another basis. The usual assumption that part-time employees work half time seems unnecessarily crude. Firstly, the census data imply that paid part-time employees average about 36 per cent of a week in the United States. Secondly, part-time employees work longer hours as the ratio of part-time to full-time employees increases.

The last statement deserves elaboration, because this phenomenon is used to translate the British part-time data. Suppose that the fluctuations in customer load are known, and the optimum number of employees for any moment is calculated. It would then be possible to state the number of people needed as a function of the fraction of the work week that they work. Full-time employees satisfy the store's demand for people who work a large fraction of the work week, and part-time employees satisfy the store's demand for people who work a small fraction of the work week. Now suppose that, other things being equal, the number of full-time employees is increased and the number of part-time employees is decreased. The additional full-time employees will absorb jobs previously held by part-time employees who worked large fractions of the work week; the average fraction of the week worked by the remaining part-time employees will decrease. When nearly all of the store's employees work full time, the few remaining part-time employees will work very small fractions of the work week.

Table 1 United States: Sales Volume per Employee, 1954

Data point	Annual sales volume (1000s of dollars)	Average number of proprietors per establishment, P	Average total employment per establishment, T	Average annual sales volume per establishment, S (in dollars)	Average annual sales volume per employee S/T (in dollars)
1	Under 5	1·005	1·035	3399	3284
2	5–9	1·015	1·097	6927	6315
3	10–19	1·010	1·264	14,285	11,301
4	20–29	1·016	1·523	23,971	15,739
5	30–49	1·004	2·069	38,790	18,748
6	50–99	0·978	3·303	71,139	21,538
7	100–299	0·865	6·496	162,280	25,065
8	300–499	0·628	13·342	382,480	28,667
9	500–999	0·440	21·557	690,440	32,029
10	1000–1999	0·254	38·866	1,371,700	35,293
11	2000–4999	0·149	84·913	2,883,500	33,958
12	Over 4999	0·082	546·20	11,890,000	21,769

Source: Bureau of the Census (1957), Table 2A.

Figure 9 shows the scatter diagram for the part-time work week in the United States as a function of the ratio of part-time to full-time employees. The figure is based on the census sample week data for paid employees. The regression line through the origin is

$$\frac{\text{average part-time work week}}{\text{full-time work week}} = (1·39)\frac{\text{part-time employees}}{\text{full-time employees}}.$$

Blatantly assuming that the same coefficient applies in Great Britain, we convert the British part-time employees to equivalent full-time employees. The resulting data are given in Table 2. The British ratio of part-time to full-time employees is more variable than the American ratio, probably because proprietors are included in the British data.[16] The estimates imply that the

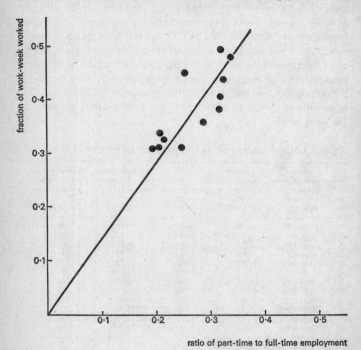

Figure 9 The part-time work week in the United States

average British part-time employee works about 47 per cent of a full-time week. Scatter diagrams of the British and American data are shown in Figure 1 (on page 146).

One difference in the two censuses cannot be allowed for. The United States' census distinguishes between businesses that

16. The estimated part-time work week is over 60 per cent in stores with sales volumes under £1000 and less than 13 per cent in stores with sales volumes between £50,000 and £100,000.

operate essentially all year and (seasonal) businesses which do not; the data used here refer to full-year businesses. The British census does not distinguish between seasonal and full-year businesses. The effects of this difference will be noticeable primarily in the data on small stores.

Table 2 Great Britain: Sales Volume per Employee, 1950

Data point	Annual sales volume (1000s of pounds)	Average total employment per establishment, T	Average annual sales volume per establishment, S (in pounds)	Average annual sales volume per employee, S/T (in pounds)
1	Under 1	1·035	488·6	472·1
2	1 –2·5	1·521	1735·7	1141·2
3	2·5–5	2·193	3674·3	1675·5
4	5 –10	3·203	7103·1	2217·6
5	10 –25	5·191	15,005	2890·6
6	25 –50	10·253	33,844	3300·9
7	50 –100	20·796	67,888	3264·5
8	100 –250	48·026	146,570	3051·9
9	Over 250	212·72	619,040	2910·1

Source: Board of Trade (1954), Table 5.

Table 3 Estimates of Coefficients

Coefficient	United States		Great Britain
β_0	$43,280		£17,440
γ_0	0·9142		1·9846
γ_P	1·9011		2·3749
δ	5·743		4·865
Asymptotic S/T	$18,000*	$21,000*	£2908
S_0	$2,105,000	$2,362,000	£21,000
$\beta_0/(1+\mu)$	$36,910	$37,360	£3409
T at S_0	57·03	63·23	6·162
ν	1·2318	0·9026	0·8809
μ	0·1726	0·1584	4·1164
ψ	0·2334	0·6242	0·1866

* Assumed.

Fitting the data

The number of free parameters is large compared to the number of data points, and the functional forms make maximum-likelihood computations impractical. Therefore, no attempt was made to obtain confidence limits for the coefficients. Instead, the data were transformed to make the model linear, and then least-squares fits were computed. Coefficient estimates are given in Table 3, and the fitted functions are graphed in Figures 10 and 11.

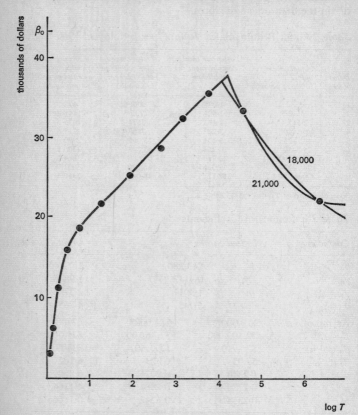

Figure 10 Sales volume per employee for the United States

First, β_0 and γ_0 were estimated from British data points 2–5 and from American data points 5–10. Then γ_P and δ were estimated from British data points 1 and 2 and from American data points 1–5. The British estimates of γ_P and δ assume that the average number of proprietors per establishment is exactly one. The large-store coefficients (S_0, v and Ψ) were estimated from American data points 11 and 12 and from British data points 6–9.

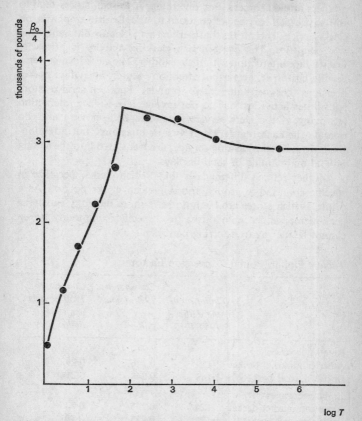

Figure 11 Sales volume per employee for Great Britain

Because there are only two American data points and hree parameters to fit, the asymptotic value of S/T as $T \to \infty$ is unknown. Estimates are given for two assumptions about the asymptotic S/T.

W. H. Starbuck 171

Discussion of results

There are striking differences between British and American retailers and customers. For one thing, American stores tend to emphasize self-service in contrast to the British emphasis on clerk-service. This means that clerking activities are different in the two countries. The clerk-service clerking activity is primarily face-to-face interaction with the customer. The clerk locates items for the customer, acts as an attention focuser, and often makes decisions between alternative brands. The self-service store substitutes activities that do not involve face-to-face interaction for many of the clerk-service functions. Self-service clerks do operate the cash registers and answer questions, but attention-focusing and item-locating services are translated into the setting up and maintaining of shelf displays.

Another related difference is that British clerks specialize in specific commodity groups and American clerks do not. As a result, British stores are likely to have more difficulty satisfying peak demands, because peaks in a specific commodity group cannot be met by transferring personnel.

Table 4 Dollar–Pound Conversion Factors .

	Inflation of the dollar 1954/1950	Conversion: 1950 pounds per 1950 dollar	Conversion: 1950 pounds per 1954 dollar
Retail purchases			
American market basket	1·119	0·346	0·292
British market basket	1·163	0·248	0·214
Employee wages			
American market basket	1·124	0·265	0·236
British market basket	1·125	0·215	0·191

These differences imply that British retailing expends more labor in selling a given market basket than American retailing does. Using Gilbert's (1958) data and components of the American consumer price index, we have estimated dollar–pound conversion factors for retail purchases. The factors[17] are shown in Table 4. Hereafter, figures converted on the basis of the American market basket are identified by AMB, and figures converted on the basis of the British market basket are identified by BMB.

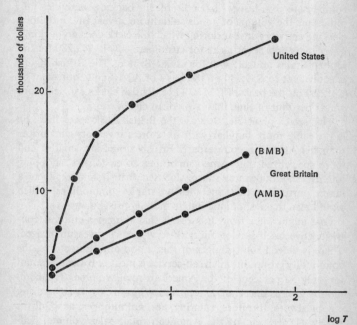

Figure 12 Sales volume per employee in 1954 dollars

Sales per employee are graphed in Figure 12. Only the smaller stores are shown. Intrinsic backing breaks down in British stores when $Log\ T \simeq 1{\cdot}8$, and extrinsically backed stores should not be

17. The retail purchase factors include foods, alcoholic beverages, tobacco, clothing and textiles, household goods, household and personal services, transport, equipment, recreation, health, and miscellaneous purchases. The wage factors include clothing and health at their raw weights; food, housing, and utilities at double their raw weights; and all other consumption items at one-half their raw weights.

compared directly. The graph suggests that there are about two BMB or three AMB British clerks for each American clerk.[18]

The contrast in labor usage is clarified by the model parameter estimates. British stores actually expend fewer man-years on clerking activities than American stores do, but more than compensate by heavy expenditure in backing activities. β_0 represents the volume of goods sold during a year of continuous clerking activity – a year during which the clerk does no backing, never loafs and never lacks for customers – β_0 is \$43,280 for the United States and £17,440 for Great Britain. The British figure is equivalent to \$59,730 on the basis of AMB and equivalent to \$81,500 on the basis of BMB. Thus, British clerks can sell more goods per unit of time than American clerks can.

This seems plausible. Because the British clerk specializes, he is probably more familiar with his store's inventory and prices than his American counterpart. British stores are smaller and more specialized than American stores, so customers' shopping interests should be more sharply focused. British shoppers spend a larger portion of their incomes on staple commodities, which would also make shopping habits more consistent.

One might infer from this result that the cross-cultural contrast between self-service and clerk-service can be overemphasized. There is indeed some danger of this. Food and drug stores, the commodity groups in which self-service is most prevalent, account for only 30 per cent of the American retail volume. The commodity groups that Hall, Knapp and Winsten classify as luxuries, e.g. hardware, furniture, catering, and automobiles, account for nearly 41 per cent of the American retail sales volume. Self-service is less important in luxury sales.[19]

The parameter μ estimates the amount of backing activity per customer. American backing requirements are about one employee for six customers in the store; British backing requirements are about four employees for each customer in the store. In terms

18. One *cannot* infer from Figure 12 that British stores are more efficient at selling the things that the British buy. Only a commodity-by-commodity study would answer that question.

19. For a contrast in shopping habits: British food and drug stores account for over 39 per cent of sales and the British luxury groups account for less than 34 per cent.

of the volume of goods handled, British backing requirements look somewhat better, but they are still enormous. β_0/μ is sales volume per man-year of backing. This figure is \$251,000 for the United States if S/T is assumed asymptotic to \$18,000, and it is \$273,000 if S/T is assumed asymptotic to \$21,000. The British value of β_0/μ is £4237; which is \$14,500 on the basis of AMB and \$19,800 on the basis of BMB. The conclusion seems inescapable that the high expenditure of labor in British stores is not in clerking activities but in backing activities.

The large amount of backing activity in British stores probably represents some increase in real services to customers over the American service pattern. For example, home delivery is more prevalent in Great Britain. However, we suspect that most of the difference is due to what Americans would call inefficiency. The most significant factor making British stores less efficient than American stores is probably the relative specialization of British clerks. An inability to transfer personnel among various segments of a store's operation means that large and medium-sized stores have little advantage over small stores. A ten-man store would have the same efficiency characteristics as five two-man stores.

Table 5 Man-Years of Part-Time Employment per Man-Year of Full-Time Employment

United States		Great Britain	
Establishment sales-size (1000s of dollars)	*Percentage utilization of part-time employees (paid employees only)*	*Establishment sales-size (1000s of pounds)*	*Percentage utilization of part-time employees (all employees)*
Under 5	0·6	Under 1	26·2
5–9	1·2	1 –2·5	18·6
10–19	2·8	2·5–5	20·9
20–29	4·1	5 –10	17·5
30–49	6·0	10 –25	8·9
50–99	6·9	25 –50	2·0
100–299	6·0	50 –100	1·2
300–499	5·7	100 –250	1·6
500–999	6·2	250 or more	1·7
1000–1999	7·7		
2000–4999	7·0		
5000 or more	11·2		

Also, there is evidence that British stores place greater emphasis on full-time employment than American stores do. Table 5 gives estimates of the use of part-time labor in the two countries. The small store ratios should be distorted by the assumption that the American proprietors are all full-time employees and by the inclusion of seasonal businesses in the British data. In large stores, however, where nearly all employees are paid and nearly all businesses operate all year, the ratios imply that American stores make more extensive use of part-time labor. This contrast is reinforced by the observation that American part-time employees work a smaller fraction of a full work week than British part-time employees do. Finally, the model makes no explicit provision for loafing. If clerks refuse to work more than a given portion of the time, or work slowly, the lost man-hours are attributed to backing.

Naturally, wage rates are consistent with the higher labor intensity of British retailing. Table 6 gives annual wages per equivalent full-time employee. Since £294 is a pittance, it would be misleading to convert it to dollars on the basis of average spending habits. The conversion factors for employee wages in Table 4 have been constructed for this purpose; they weight food and housing heavily and luxuries lightly (see footnote 17).

Table 6 Relative Wage-Rates and the Relative Importance of Size-Variable Costs for the US and Great Britain

	United States	Great Britain		
	1954 dollars	*1950 pounds*	*1954 dollars AMB*	*1954 dollars BMB*
Average annual wage	3130	294	1240	1540
$\beta_2/(1-\beta_1)$	9710	32·8	112	153

The parameter γ reflects this wage differential; γ is higher for British stores, suggesting that labor-variable costs per employee are lower. However, the difference in the γ's is not wholly attributable to the wage rates. The fraction $(1-\beta_1)$ is the margin of revenue over sales-variable costs per dollar of sales volume; β_2 is the labor-variable cost per employee. Hence, the ratio $\beta_2/(1-\beta_1)$ is an index of the relative importance of size-variable costs in store operation. If the ratio is high, labour-variable and/or sales-variable costs are high, and vice-versa. Estimates of $\beta_2/(1-\beta_1)$, made on the basis of γ_0, are given in Table 6. It is obvious that the wage-rate difference alone cannot explain the difference in $\beta_2/(1-\beta_1)$. Moreover, relative costs of merchandise operate in the opposite direction. The average British gross margin is about 20 per cent and the average American gross margin is about 28 per cent.[20] Consequently other size-variable costs, including profit, must be higher in the United States. The inference seems reasonab'e, since American advertising expenses and rents are known to be very much higher than British advertising and rents.

The difference $(\gamma_P-\gamma_0)$ is smaller for British stores than for American stores, indicating that there is a smaller increment in efficiency between very small and medium-sized stores in Great Britain. No doubt, this is partially due to the relative inefficiency of British medium-sized stores. It is probably also due to differences between the British and American data. The British census includes seasonal businesses; the British proprietors are treated like paid employees, although proprietors typically work longer hours than paid employees; and the average work week may be longer in Great Britain. All of these factors tend to make British small stores look more efficient *vis-à-vis* British medium-sized stores and American small stores.

The prediction that small-store effects disappear by the time $N-P = P$ seems to be confirmed. The primary evidence is the fact that stores of this size conform to the pattern of larger stores. With reference to the prediction that $(\gamma_P-\gamma_0)e^{-\delta} \simeq 0$, it is found that:

	United States	Great Britain
$\gamma_P-\gamma_0$	0·9869	0·3903
$(\gamma_P-\gamma_0)\varepsilon^{-\delta}$	0·0032	0·0030

Little can be said about the declines in sales volume per employee in very larg2 stores. The parameter v, which represents

20. These estimates are based on Tables 11 and 17 in Hall, Knapp and Winsten (1961).

'wholesale' backers per central store customer, is roughly the same for both countries. If the extent of the central store, branch store type of organization is the same in both countries, the differences in β_0 would suggest that the British wholesale backers are more efficient. On the other hand, central store operations are probably more extensive in the United States if only because there are many more, very large American stores. We have no data which would shed light on this issue.

Hall, Knapp and Winsten provided some indirect support for the hypotheses about manufacturer-lot buying:

A study of the two-dimensional frequency-curves for a variety of trades shows one surprising and persistent feature. Suppose one looks at the upper boundary of the surface where the shops with highest sales per person in their respective persons-size group or sales-size group lie. Then as one runs along this boundary from the smallest to the largest establishments (however measured) sales per person tend quite noticeably to fall in contrast to the regression line. This appears to go against the idea that the technically possible savings will be exploited by just such shops and that these must inevitably show economies of scale (1961, p. 70).

In short, sales volume per employee drops fastest in the most efficient stores. The phenomenon should not be surprising: the most efficient stores should be most dependent upon extrinsic backing and most aggressive in discovering and exploiting supply opportunities. Because these stores are extrinsically backed, sales volume per employee is not a meaningful indicator of their economies of scale.

Many stores belong to chains that are not organized on the central store, branch store pattern. These chains operate warehouse and administrative units that are distinct from any of the stores. The personnel at these central units are not included in the census establishment tables, so from our point of view the stores in these chains should behave like stores that buy from independent wholesalers. Nevertheless, chain affiliation does offer an alternative for stores which are too small to participate alone in manufacturer-lot purchasing, but which are forced into extrinsic backing by a high μ. Since the British μ is very high, relatively small stores must support backers. In order to offset the resulting pressure on costs, these small stores can be expected to seek quantity discounts through chain membership. The American μ is very low and extrinsic backing occurs only in very large stores. Therefore, one would expect to find chain operations less pervasive in the United States and concentrated in fairly large stores. In fact, 18 per cent of the British stores belong to chains and cooperatives, and these stores account for 37 per cent of all retail sales; only 7 per cent of American stores belong to chains, and these account for 24 per cent of all retail sales.[21] On a per-store basis, the share of retail sales held by American chain members is about half again the share held by British chain members. One implication of this reasoning is that high μ is an important factor in the existence of the ubiquitous British cooperative societies.

Summary

A model is presented relating the number of employees in a store to the store's sales volume. The first part of the model, which applies to small and medium-sized stores, derives from the necessity of matching the clerking services in a store to the store's potential customer load. Profit maximization implies that sales volume per clerk increases with store size until, in large stores, the ratio of customers to clerks becomes so high that backers must be hired. Extrinsic backing is associated with manufacturer-lot purchasing and the establishment of branch operations by central stores. Consequently, declining sales volume per employee in large stores is a plausible result of efforts to increase profits, not evidence of diseconomies of scale.

Applied to data on retail trade in the United States and Great Britain, the model yields some interesting conclusions:

1. Relative specialization of British clerks enables them to sell more goods per unit of time than American clerks can, suggesting that contrasts between British clerk-service and American self-service are oversimplifications.

2. Specialization restricts transfers of personnel within a store and greatly increases backing time. The net result is that British

21. See Hall, Knapp and Winsten (1961), Table 13. According to their Table 12, the average American store sales is between two and three times the average British store sales.

retailing organizations expend two or three times as much labor selling an average market basket of goods as American organizations expend.

3. The inefficiency of British organizational structures forces wage rates to a very low level. These low wages reinforce the persistence of existing organizational practices, but a change in the wage level would not by itself greatly alter the relative pattern of employee utilization because other size-variable costs are also low. The converse holds in the United States. Both the American organizations and the British organizations are bound to their present structural characteristics by overall patterns of profit-related forces.

4. In both countries, small stores lose their economically irrational appearance rapidly as the ratio of paid to unpaid employees approaches unity. We attribute this shift primarily to the increased flexibility in work schedules that paid employees make possible.

5. It is probable that the comparative inefficiency of British organizational structures is the reason for chain membership being more prevalent in Great Britain than in the United States. Thus, the structural characteristics of the organizations which make up an industry may have dictated structural characteristics of the industry as a whole.

Appendix A

Assume the probability that exactly one customer arrives during the infinitesimal time period $(t, t+\Delta)$ is $a\Delta$; the probability that exactly one customer leaves during $(t, t+\Delta)$ is $\lambda k\Delta$; the probabilities of more than one arrival or departure during $(t, t+\Delta)$ are negligible. Then the following difference equations describe $Pr(k, t)$, the probability of having exactly k customers in the store at time t:

$$\Pr(0, t+\Delta) = (1-a\Delta).\Pr(0, t)+(1-a\Delta)\lambda\Delta.\Pr(1, t),$$

$$\Pr(k, t+\Delta)=(1-a\Delta)(1-k\lambda\Delta).\Pr(k, t)+ka\lambda\Delta^2.\Pr(k, t)+ \\ +\{1-(k-1)\lambda\Delta\}a\Delta.\Pr(k-1, t)+ \\ +(1-a\Delta)(k+1)\lambda\Delta.\Pr(k+1, t)$$

for $1 \leqslant k \leqslant n-1$,

$$\Pr(n, t+\Delta) = (1-n\lambda\Delta).\Pr(n, t) +$$
$$+ \{1-(n-1)\lambda\Delta\}a\Delta.\Pr(n-1, t). \quad \textbf{A1}$$

In the limit as Δ goes to zero,

$$\frac{\partial}{\partial t}\Pr(0, t) = -a.\Pr(0, t) + \lambda.\Pr(1, t),$$

$$\frac{\partial}{\partial t}\Pr(k. t) = -(a+k\lambda).\Pr(k, t) + a.\Pr(k-1, t) +$$
$$+ (k+1)\lambda.\Pr(k+1, t)$$

for $1 \leqslant k \leqslant n-1$,

$$\frac{\partial}{\partial t}\Pr(n, t) = -n\lambda.\Pr(n, t) + a.\Pr(n-1, t). \qquad \textbf{A2}$$

This is a Poisson birth-and-death process. The stochastic steady-state $\left(\dfrac{\partial}{\partial t}\Pr(k, t) = 0\right)$ implies

$$\Pr(k) = \frac{1}{k!}\left(\frac{a}{\lambda}\right)^{k}\left[\sum_{k=0}^{n}\frac{1}{k!}\left(\frac{a}{\lambda}\right)^{k}\right]^{-1}. \qquad \textbf{1}$$

Since any given customer has probability $\lambda\Delta$ of leaving during $(t, t+\Delta)$, the probability that a given customer stays a total time τ is described by $\Pr(\tau+\Delta) = (1-\lambda\Delta).\Pr(\tau)$. In the limit at Δ goes to zero,

$$\frac{d}{d\tau}\Pr(\tau) = -\lambda.\Pr(\tau), \qquad \textbf{A3}$$

and since $\int_{0}^{\infty}\Pr(\tau).d\tau = 1$, then

$$\Pr(\tau) = \lambda e^{-\lambda\tau}. \qquad \textbf{2}$$

Appendix B

The parameters a, λ, β_0, β_1, β_2 and β_3 condense into two aggregate parameters: a/λ and $\beta_2/\{\beta_0(1-\beta_1)\}$. The ratio a/λ arises naturally in the solution of the birth-and-death process as an aggregate customer load parameter, no information being lost if one writes

$$K = K\left(\frac{\alpha}{\lambda}, n\right) \tag{B1a}$$

$$S = \beta_0 . K\left(\frac{\alpha}{\lambda}, n\right). \tag{B1b}$$

The other ratio occurs in a similar fashion. Profit, π, can be written

$$\pi = (1-\beta_1)\beta_0 . K\left(\frac{\alpha}{\lambda}, n\right) - \beta_2 n - \beta_3. \tag{B2}$$

Profit maximization with respect to n implies

$$\pi(N) > \pi(N+1), \tag{B3a}$$
$$\pi(N) > \pi(N-1). \tag{B3b}$$

Conditions **B3** are equivalent to

$$K\left(\frac{\alpha}{\lambda}, N\right) > K\left(\frac{\alpha}{\lambda}, N-1\right) + \frac{\beta_2}{\beta_0(1-\beta_1)} \tag{B4a}$$

$$K\left(\frac{\alpha}{\lambda}, N\right) > K\left(\frac{\alpha}{\lambda}, N+1\right) - \frac{\beta_2}{\beta_0(1-\beta_1)}. \tag{B4b}$$

β_3 does not appear and β_0, β_1 and β_2 appear only as the ratio.

Solution of the inequalities **B4** would enable one to state N as a function of the two composite parameters α/λ and $\beta_2/\{\beta_0(1-\beta_1)\}$,

$$N = N\left(\frac{\alpha}{\lambda}, \frac{\beta_2}{\beta_0(1-\beta_1)}\right). \tag{B5}$$

There are two problems with this statement. First, N is a discrete variable, and a continuous variable is desired. Second, we need a relation in which K depends on N, whereas application of formula **B5** would produce a relation in which K depends on the two composite parameters,

$$K = K\left\{\frac{\alpha}{\lambda}, N\left(\frac{\alpha}{\lambda}, \frac{\beta_2}{\beta_0(1-\beta_1)}\right)\right\} = K\left(\frac{\alpha}{\lambda}, \frac{\beta_2}{\beta_0(1-\beta_1)}\right). \tag{B6}$$

We would prefer to have a statement of the form,

$$\frac{\alpha}{\lambda} = \alpha\left(N, \frac{\beta_2}{\beta_0(1-\beta_1)}\right) \qquad \text{B7}$$

and make the substitution

$$K = K\left\{\alpha\left(N, \frac{\beta_2}{\beta_0(1-\beta_1)}\right), N\right\} = K\left(N, \frac{\beta_2}{\beta_0(1-\beta_1)}\right). \qquad \text{B8}$$

Both problems were solved simultaneously. The relation between K and N was converted to a continuous single-valued function by choosing arbitrary values of α/λ and $\beta_2/\{\beta_0(1-\beta_1)\}$, and numerically maximizing profit. This gives a crude, and highly subjective, relation between K and N. Figure 13 indicates the nature of the fit, showing the function $\log\log(N/(N-K))$ graphed against $\log N$. The points were calculated by setting α/λ equal to 1/2, 1, 2, 4, 10 and 11. The solid lines represent

$$\frac{\beta_2}{\beta_0(1-\beta_1)} = 0\cdot002, 0\cdot010, 0\cdot040, 0\cdot200, 0\cdot400, 0\cdot900.$$

The dashed lines represent

$$\frac{\beta_2}{\beta_0(1-\beta_1)} = 0\cdot004, 0\cdot020 \text{ and } 0\cdot100.$$

Corresponding approximations are shown by the straight lines.

The approximation, as would any linear approximation, implies a logical fallacy. Suppose that β_2 is smaller for store A than for store B ($\gamma_A > \gamma_B$). All else being equal, store A will employ at least as many clerks as store B. $N_A \geqslant N_B$, and

$$\frac{N_A}{N_A-K} \leqslant \frac{N_B}{N_B-K}. \qquad \text{B9}$$

However, the approximation lines all converge at $\log\log(N/N-K), = 1$, $\log N = 5$. For $\log N > 5$, the approximation implies

$$\frac{N_A}{N_A-K} > \frac{N_B}{N_B-K}. \qquad \text{B10}$$

We do not correct for this fallacy, because extrinsic backing occurs when $\log N < 5$.

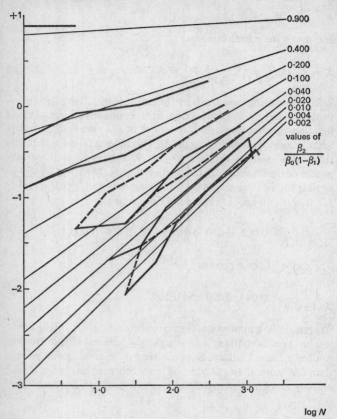

Figure 13 Log log $[N/(N-K)]$

Appendix C

The data do not permit distinctions between clerks and backers, but a comment on the behavior of N for $S > S_0$ is appropriate. Buying in manufacturer-lot quantities, the store receives discounts on its goods. Suppose that these discounts provide β_4/θ_0

per monetary unit of goods in excess of any storage costs. The extrinsically backed store then has $\beta_4 \rho S$ of incremental contribution to offset the additional cost of backers. Suppose that backers receive β_5 each, so the marginal profit of an extrinsically backed store is

$$\beta_0 \beta_4 \rho K - \beta_5 \mu K - \beta_5 \nu \rho K + \beta_5 N - \beta_5 K$$
$$= (\beta_0 \beta_4 - \beta_5 \nu) \rho K + \beta_5 \{N - (1+\mu)K\}. \quad \text{C1}$$

The existence of wholesalers implies $\beta_0 \beta_4 - \beta_5 \nu > 0$. However, $N - (1+\mu)K < 0$ for $S > S_0$, this being the definition of S_0.

The marginal profit implies that an extrinsically backed store gains by increasing the ratio of clerks to customers. Other things being equal, it would like to make $N - (1+\mu)K$ positive. When the retailing and wholesaling profits are combined, this tendency to increase N becomes clearer. Ignoring fixed costs, the profit of an extrinsically backed store is

$$\{\beta_0(1-\beta_1) - \beta_5(1+\mu)\}K + (\beta_0 \beta_4 - \beta_5 \nu)\rho K - (\beta_2 - \beta_5)N. \quad \text{C2}$$

The marginal cost of a clerk has decreased from β_2 to $\beta_2 - \beta_5$. (There is an implicit assumption here that backers work for lower wages than clerks do.) Saying that an intrinsically backed store can exist implies that

$$K > \beta_2 N / (\beta_0(1-\beta_1)) \quad \text{when} \quad K < (1+\mu)N. \quad \text{It follows that}$$

$$\frac{\beta_2}{\beta_0(1-\beta_1)} > \frac{\beta_2 - \beta_5}{\beta_0(1-\beta_1) - \beta_5(1+\mu)}. \quad \text{C3}$$

At S_0, there will be a jump in the value of γ from

$$\gamma = \log\left(1 - \log\frac{\beta_2}{\beta_0(1-\beta_1)}\right)$$

to a higher value,

$$\gamma = \log\left(1 - \log\frac{\beta_2 - \beta_5}{\beta_0(1-\beta_1) - \beta_5(1+\mu)}\right). \quad \text{C4}$$

The increase in γ means the ratio of clerks to customers is increased. A further increase in γ follows from the increasing ρ; as ρ approaches unity, γ will approach

$$\gamma = \log\left(1 - \log\frac{\beta_2 - \beta_5}{\beta_0(1-\beta_1) - \beta_5(1+\mu) + (\beta_0 \beta_4 - \beta_5 \nu)}\right). \quad \text{C5}$$

Actually, the above analysis probably exaggerates the increase in clerks per customer, because clerks and backers are assumed to be perfect substitutes. Even if perfect substitution is reasonable for the μ (retail) component of backing labor, clerks are not likely to be perfect substitutes for the ν (wholesale) component. Nevertheless, the qualitative characteristics of N seem clear.

References

BARGER, H. (1955), *Distribution's Place in the American Economy since 1869*, Princeton University Press.

BOARD of TRADE (1954), *Census of Distribution and Other Services, 1950*, vol. II: *Retail and Service Trades, General Tables*, HMSO.

BUREAU OF THE CENSUS (1957), *Census of Business, 1954*, vol. 1: *Retail Trade, Summary Statistics*, US Government Printing Office.

GALBRAITH, J. K., and HOLTON, R. H. (1955), *Marketing Efficiency in Puerto Rico*, Harvard University Press.

GILBERT, M., *et al.* (1958), *Comparative National Products and Price Levels*, OEEC.

HALL, M., KNAPP, J., and WINSTEN, O. (1961), *Distribution in Great Britain and North America*, Oxford University Press.

HERBST, P. G. (1957), 'Measurement of behaviour structures by means of input-output data', *Hum. Rel.*, vol. 10, pp. 335–46.

JEFFERY, J. B. (1954), *Retail Trading in Britain, 1850–1950*, Cambridge University Press.

STARBUCK, W. H. (1965), 'Organizational growth and development', in J. G. March (ed.), *Handbook of Organizations*, Rand McNally, pp. 451–533.

STARBUCK, W. H., and HERBST, P. G. (1963), 'A discussion of "Measurement of behaviour structures by means of input-output data"', *Hum. Rel.*, vol. 16, pp. 385–9.

3 F. Friedlander and H. Pickle

Components of Effectiveness in Small Organizations

F. Friedlander and H. Pickle, 'Components of effectiveness in small organizations', *Administrative Science Quarterly*, vol. 13, no. 2, 1968, pp. 289– 304.

If it is to become effective in terms of survival and growth, an organization must fulfill the needs and demands of its employees, its owners, and the relevant members of the society with which it transacts – its community, its governments, its customers, its suppliers, and its creditors. In this study, ninety-seven small-business organizations and their relevant societal components were surveyed in order to explore the extent to which the organization fulfilled the needs of these components. Data indicate relatively few significant relationships among various types of employee fulfillment, owner fulfillment, and societal fulfillment, and these few relationships are of a rather low magnitude. The feasibility of an organization concurrently fulfilling the variety of demands made upon it is discussed. The organization is viewed as an open system of interdependent components with energy transfer within the organization as well as between the organization and the societal components.

A primary focus for those interested in understanding or changing organizations has been upon the internal dynamics of the organization. This focus has led to emphasis on methods of enhancing the worth of the employee – to himself or to the organization – through selection, training, group participation, job restructuring, etc.; and consequently to criteria of effectiveness that are limited to the internal dynamics of the organization. The criteria have typically been of two kinds: those dealing with individual human resources such as motivation, mental health, cohesiveness, satisfaction, etc., and those concerned with individual performance, such as amount produced, quality of output, error rate, etc. The generally low relationship between these two sets of criteria has been disturbing for the researcher and has resulted in numerous dilemmas for the practitioner (Seashore, 1964). Since the two criteria have for the most part been uncorrelated, it appears useless to attempt to maximize them both. On the other hand, favoring one over the other produces either inefficiency for the organization or dissatisfaction for the individual. This dilemma has spurred some researchers to expand the scope of their analyses to encompass situational determinants of the satisfaction–performance relationship (see Katzell, Barrett and Parker, 1961). Others have, in one way or another, explicitly recognized the inescapable tension between the individual and the organizational goals and have concentrated upon the reduction of these tensions (see Levinson, 1959; Argyris, 1962; Shepard, 1965).

For the most part, theories and research concerned with individual performance, employee satisfaction and reduction of tension between individual and organizational goals are dealing only with internal aspects of the events, relationships and structures that make up the total organizational system. If the organization is viewed as an open-energy system, however, it is apparent that it is dependent for survival and growth upon a variety of energy transfer not only within the organization, but also between the organization and its external environment (Katz and Kahn, 1966). It is obvious then, that the internal and external dynamics of the organization are complementary and interdependent. Modifications in one of these structures have an impact upon the other. This perspective of the organization is similar to the model proposed by Parsons, in which four fundamental processes are specified for every social system: adaptation, goal achievement, integration, and latency (Parsons, Shils, Naegle and Pitts, 1961). These functions provide a structural framework within which internal and external relationships may be explored.

A perspective that includes the organization's societal relationships can account for the full cycle of energy, since it incorporates both the importation of energy from this societal environment and the output of energy into that environment. The relationship between organization and environment is recognized by several research workers. For example, Bennis (1964) claims that bureaucracy is least likely to cope and survive if unable to adapt to a rapidly changing, turbulent environment. Emery and Trist (1959) stress that the primary task of managing an enterprise as a whole is to relate the total organizational system to its environment, and not just internal regulation. If the organization is to survive and grow, it must control its boundary conditions – the forms of exchange between the enterprise and the environment. Strother (1963) reverses the direction of this influence process by claiming that one must allow for control of the organization by an outside and changing environment. Pepinsky, Weick, and Riner (1965) observe that the organization must adapt to regulatory control by the environment. Typical models of organization behavior, however, treat the organization as a closed system and concentrate upon principles of internal functioning as if these problems were independent of the external environments (Katz and Kahn, 1966).

System effectiveness

Parallel to the need to understand the total organization system as interdependent with its environment is the establishment of criteria of organizational effectiveness that reflect these interdependencies. Such criteria include those with some element of the organization's contribution *to society*, and those that describe effectiveness in terms of maximization of return *from society* to the organization. Bass (1952), for example, suggests that an organization be evaluated in terms of its worth to the individual worker and the value of the worker and the organization to society. Similar criteria suggested by Davis (1940) include broad social values, economic values and the personal values. The emphasis is in a reversed direction for Katz and Kahn (1966), who describe organizational effectiveness as referring to the maximization of return to the organization by all means – technological, political, market control, personnel policies, federal subsidies, etc.

Most behavioral scientists have come to realize that organizational effectiveness is not a unitary concept. Guion (1961), for example, points out that 'the fallacy of the single criterion lies in its assumption that everything that is to be predicted is related to everything else to be predicted – that there is a general factor in all criteria accounting for virtually all of the important variance in behavior at work and its various consequences of value'.

The assumption of unitary criteria of organizational effectiveness has its counterpart in the concept of utility maximization, in which utility is defined as the value to an individual of all things he can possibly enjoy or possess. All of the nonmonetary components are assumed to be translatable into a single utility scale, which allows trade-offs between the nonmonetary and monetary components. The behavioral theory of the firm, by contrast, is rooted in the 'satisficing' concept of individuals searching until a satisfactory – not an optimal – solution is found (Simon, 1957). Individuals are not likely to combine their various sources of satisfaction into a single function and certainly are not likely to maximize such a function. They are likely to seek satisfactory solutions in the several areas of their activities, with few trade-offs.

These differences in assumptions parallel those of organizational behavior, not only in terms of the internal dynamics of the organization, but also in terms of the criteria of organizational effectiveness. In the behavioral theory of organizations, it is assumed that goals are formulated for organizational activity in several areas. The rational-man assumptions of economics for the individual become profit maximization for the organization. If organizational goals are extended beyond profit maximization, the organizational utility function must incorporate effectiveness in these other areas (Charnes and Stedry, 1965). If satisficing in these several activities rather than profit maximization is an organization goal, relative independence in their attainment might be expected.

Although the degree-of-fulfillment terminology is used in this article, fulfillment is probably more accurately represented in terms of the degree to which the organizational or environmental component is satisfied. Furthermore, it is probable that the expectations which a component holds of the organization in general, and the specific organization with which it transacts affect the degree to which that component is satisfied with the organization.

Clearly, effectiveness criteria must take into account the profitability of the organization, the degree to which it satisfices its members, and the degree to which it is of value to the larger society of which it is a part. These three perspectives include system maintenance and growth, subsystem fulfillment, and environmental fulfillment. Each is obviously composed of several related components, and each component is hypothetically related to the other. The degree to which these several components of organizational effectiveness are interrelated is a primary focus of this paper.

The purpose of this study, then, was to explore the concept of total organizational effectiveness by studying the relationships between internal and external system effectiveness. Internal system components were those within the formal boundaries of the organization. Societal components with which the organization transacts by exporting and importing energy were considered part of the larger environment in which the organization is located. Effectiveness was viewed as the degree to which the needs of components were fulfilled – or satisfied – in their transactions with the organization. The specific interest was in the degree of interdependence in the satisfaction of components.

The particular subsystem components chosen for study do not exhaust the variety of components, but were selected to include seven of primary importance for the maintenance and growth of the organization in its society: the owner, the employees, and five societal components – the customers, the suppliers, the creditors, the community, and the government.[1]

Data
Sample

Small organizations were preferred as sample units in the study because it was felt that whatever relationships exist among components might be explored more adequately, since the links among these components are presumably shorter and less numerous. The

1. While customers, suppliers, creditors, communities and governments were grouped in the general category of the organization's societal environment, other models are obvious. In accord with Parson's A G I L model (adaptation, goal attainment, integration, latency), for example, owners and customers are crucial to goal attainment of product exchange; creditors, communities, governments and suppliers provide necessary resources and support for the organization and are thus instrumental in the organization's adaptation to its environment; and employees perform integrative functions within the organizational system (Parsons, Shils, Naegle and Pitts, 1961, pp. 38–41).

sample included ninety-seven small businesses, each with only one level of management, and each employing from four to about forty employees.

A random stratified technique was used. The distribution of types of small businesses in the United States was determined from various census data and this distribution was approximated in a random selection of small businesses within the state of Texas. Since responses from two of the initial ninety-seven business organizations were suspect, two additional organizations were substituted for these. The final sample of ninety-seven small businesses was composed of fifty-four retail establishments, twenty-six service establishments, eight wholesale establishments, six manufacturers, and three mineral extraction firms.

Societal components

The data for measuring the degree of fulfillment for each of the five societal components for each of the ninety-seven organizations were gathered by questionnaires and interviews. All data were collected in quantified form, either in a Likert-type, multiple-choice format, or in specific dollar amounts or frequency information.

Initially, satisfaction for each of the five societal components was measured by from five to thirty-seven items. Correlation coefficients were then computed among all items within each of the five components. Items within each of the five components which correlated highly with each other were then selected to represent that component, so as to maximize its internal consistency or cohesion. The items so selected were then given equal weight and averaged to form mean scores for each of the components. As a final check on this process and on the internal consistency of each component scale, reliability coefficients for internal consistency[2]

2. The internal consistency of each total societal component scale was computed using Kuder–Richardson's formula 20:

$$r_{tt} = \left(\frac{n}{n-1}\right)\left(\frac{\sigma T^2 - \sum pq}{\sigma_T^2}\right).$$

Essentially, this formula measures the proportion of the total scale variance (σ_T^2), which comprises the sum of the inter-item covariances $(r_{12}\sigma_1\sigma_2)$. This formula was not applied to the creditor scale, since data were gathered from different types of statistical and financial records and were, therefore, not comparable.

were computed for each scale with the following results: customers, 0·96; suppliers, 0·77; owners, 0·92; communities, 0·65; and governments, 0·60. This method of scale construction, based upon maximizing the internal consistency of items within each scale, yielded improved results over some of our earlier procedures which did not utilize this method.

The data gathered and the methods used follow:

Community. Community fulfillment was measured in the general areas of membership and leadership in local and nonlocal organizations, the number of committees and drives that managers participated in during the past two years, and their attendance at community affairs such as fund-raising dinners, bazaars, etc. These data were obtained through a questionnaire survey administered to the managers in directed interviews.

Government. Relations with the federal, state and local government were measured through the administration of a questionnaire to managers. Items concerned questioning by officials of the Internal Revenue Service on income tax returns, penalties paid on local, state or federal taxes, or reprimands or censures by tax officials. In general, these items reflected the degree to which the organization carried out its explicit and implicit responsibilities with governmental agencies.

Customers. Customers were surveyed by the use of a questionnaire administered in an interview. The sample size for each organization was proportional to its total number of customers within a framework of a minimum of fifteen and a maximum of twenty-five customers per organization. Customers rated the respective business on a five-point scale on each of the following features: quality of goods or services; quantity of goods or services available; neatness, cleanliness, and uniformity of appearance of product; management's knowledge of product or service; speed of service; dependability of business; rank of this business in relation to others in its field; helpfulness, friendliness and appearance of employees.

Suppliers. Supplier fulfillment was measured in the following areas: promptness of payment of accounts, fairness in transactions, receptiveness to suggestions, and overall evaluation as a customer. Of 403 survey questionnaires mailed, 208 were completed and returned, representing a return of approximately 52 per cent.

Creditors. Levels of creditor fulfillment with each organization were obtained from statistical data gathered during interviews with banks, retail merchant associations, and Dun and Bradstreet.

Owner components

The degree of satisfaction for the owner of each organization was primarily financial. The score was composed of equal weights of the average yearly profit for the owner for the last ten years and the average yearly profit as a function of the hours per week that the owner worked for the organization. Since the correlation between these two measures was 0·95, the component was essentially a measure of owner financial profit.

Employee component

The SRA Employee Inventory, a measure of employee satisfaction, was administered to all employees of each organization having ten or fewer employees. For organizations having more than ten employees, ten were randomly selected to represent the organization. A total of 513 inventories were completed, representing an average of 5·29 employees per organization.

Five types of employee fulfillment were measured within each organization. These types of fulfillment had been previously derived from a factor analysis of the SRA Employee Inventory (Dabas, 1958). Types of fulfillment included the following:

1. *Satisfaction with working conditions:* nine items related to adequacy of working conditions, effects of these conditions on work efficiency, adequacy of equipment, reasonable hours of work, and absence of physical and mental pressures.

2. *Satisfaction with financial reward:* seven items related to adequacy of pay, effectiveness of personnel policies with respect to pay, and benefit programs and pay in comparison with other companies.

3. *Confidence in management*: nineteen items related to management's organizing ability, its handling of employee benefit policies, its adequacy in two-way communication, and its interest in employees.

4. *Opinion about immediate supervisor*: twelve items related to how well the supervisor organized his work, knowledge of the job, ability to get things done on time, supplying adequate equipment, letting employees know what was expected, emphasizing proper training, making employees work together, treating employees fairly, keeping his promises, giving encouragement, and interest in employee welfare.

5. *Satisfaction with self-development*: five items related to employee's feeling of belongingness, of participation, of pride in the company, of doing something worth while, and of growth on the job.

Results

Correlation coefficients were computed in order to explore the relationships among the components.[3] The relationships between external and internal criteria of organizational effectiveness were considered first. External criteria were those related to fulfillment of the needs of the five components of the societal system; internal criteria were those related to the five needs of the employees.

In a moderate number of instances, organizations were able to satisfice both societal needs and employee needs simultaneously, as indicated in Table 1. In almost all cases where significant relationships do exist, however, these are of a relatively low magnitude. Thus, while some mutual satisficing of employees and societal components does occur, the degree of this concurrent satisficing is rather low. Of the five societal components, only community and customer satisfaction seem to vary consistently (and positively) with the several types of employee satisfaction. In the case of community fulfillment, this finding is understandable.

3. To check for curvilinear relationships between variables, scatter plot outputs from computer runs were examined visually. In those cases where some curvilinearity was suggested, tests of curvilinearity were made. In no case was the appropriate coefficient (n) significant.

Organizations that recognize community needs and fulfill them are likely to be effective in providing similarly for their employees.

Table 1 Relationships among Societal Fulfillment, Owner Fulfillment, Organizational Size and Employee Fulfillment

Components fulfilled	Employee fulfillment				
	Working conditions	Financial rewards	Confidence in management	Immediate supervisor	Self-development
Societal components					
Community	0·33*	0·06	0·28*	0·23†	0·24†
Government	−0·09	0·00	−0·06	−0·03	−0·12
Customer	0·11	0·20†	0·21†	0·23†	0·32*
Supplier	0·10	0·12	0·16	0·05	0·10
Creditor	0·09	−0·03	0·09	0·15	0·16
Owner					
Financial profit	0·12	0·07	0·20†	0·22†	0·23†
Organizational size (size of work force)	−0·03	−0·21	−0·10	−0·03	0·01

* $p < 0.01$.
† $p < 0.05$.
$N = 97$.

Furthermore, in smaller communities, the membership of community and employee groups may overlap to a considerable degree. The reasons for the employee–customer satisfaction relationship are perhaps similar to those of the finding on the employee–community satisfaction relationship. Furthermore, in retail and service organizations, close contact between customers and employees may serve as a mechanism of contagion of satisfaction. Customer satisfaction may fulfill employee service needs, thereby causing employee satisfaction which, in turn, is sensed by customers. Finally both the community and customer components represent more personal and less organized entities within the society. A management which takes action to increase employee fulfillment might thus tend also to focus upon increased customer and community satisfaction.

In the association between employee satisfaction and owner fulfillment, several significant relationships were found. Financially successful organizations were also those in which employees had confidence in management, held higher opinions of the supervisor, and sensed opportunities for self-development. Although these correlations were not of a high magnitude, they do point to the tempting conclusion that satisfied employees contribute toward (or are a product of) an organization profitable for the owner. The relationship is highest between owner fulfillment and employee self-development, a finding that seems understandable since the self-development measure reflects the employee's feelings of belongingness, participation, and pride in the company – a sense of 'psychological ownership' in the organization. Previous findings in this area are ambiguous, however. Bass, McGhee, and Vaughan (1965) found that satisfaction with one's particular job in the company did not seem particularly related to financial performance of the company. Katzell, Barrett, and Parker (1961), however, reported that about three-fourths of their attitude items correlated positively with organizational performance and no items correlated negatively with performance. They also reported consistently negative relationships between job satisfaction and size of work force, a finding validated to some extent in this study. Table 1 reveals consistent (but generally not significant) negative relationships between organizational size, as measured by size of work force, and employee fulfillment. The single significant relationship indicates that employees are less satisfied with pay policies in organizations composed of larger work forces.

Since the relationships between internal and external criteria of organizational effectiveness were relatively weak, the relationships among the several external criteria were of interest, as well as those between external criteria and owner fulfillment and organizational size.

The relationships among the external components of the organizational system show no definite pattern, as indicated in Table 2. Only five of the fifteen relationships are significant. Customer satisfaction is correlated positively with supplier and owner fulfillment, which is understandable, since both are societal units with which the organization exchanges services directly for financial remuneration. This is also the case for exchanges with the employee components of the organization.

There was a negative relation between government and customer fulfillment, which was unexpected. It appears that organizations that focus upon goal achievement through customer interactions are less concerned with the adaptive functions of fulfilling governmental obligations. However, the adaptive function of fulfilling community needs does appear to be related to the goal of achieving organizational profitability; organizations whose managers are actively involved in community affairs are also those that are most profitable for the owner.

Table 2 Relationships among Societal Fulfillment, Owner Fulfillment and Organizational Size

Components fulfilled	Fulfillment of needs of					Organ. size
	Government	Customer	Supplier	Creditor	Owner	
Societal components						
Community	0·00	−0·04	0·03	0·03	0·32*	0·29*
Government		−0·25†	−0·11	0·20†	−0·11	−0·07
Customer			0·20†	0·10	0·21†	0·20†
Supplier				0·09	0·08	0·13
Creditor					−0·02	0·10
Owner						0·28*

* p < 0·01.
† p < 0·05.
N = 97.

Perhaps one of the most direct exchanges leading to goal attainment is that between the owner and the customer of the organization. Table 2 indicates that organizations in which owner needs are fulfilled are also those in which customer fulfillment is high. The tempting conclusion is that the successful organization (for the owner) is one which satisfices customer needs also.

As might be predicted, government and creditor fulfillment were moderately correlated. The needs of both of these components can be viewed more as financial obligations of the organization. These needs are fulfilled as they are continually reduced to a minimum.

Organizational size is also related to the ability of the organization to fulfill the needs of the societal component. The larger the organization (in number of employees), the more likely it is to fulfill the needs of its community, its owner, and its customers. Organizations with larger human and financial resources can be expected to provide greater support for the community in which they exist; they are able to offer a wider variety of products and services to customers, and thus greater psychological and financial satisfaction for the owner. Two notes of caution should be mentioned in connexion with these inferences. First, one cannot be sure as to the causal direction of these relationships. It is possible that because an organization provides fulfillment for its community, owner, and customers, it has grown larger. It is more probable that causality changes its direction over time: at one time the organization grows because it fulfills societal needs; subsequently, society's needs are fulfilled to a greater extent because the organization is larger and offers greater resources. Second, organizational size in this study was limited to organizations of less than forty employees. In organizations with many more than forty employees, it is probable that the size-fulfillment relationship becomes asymptotic; similar increments in size may produce decreasing gains in societal fulfillment.

Discussion

In this study we have attempted to avoid the dichotomy of satisfaction versus productivity, by which organizational effectiveness is traditionally gauged. This dichotomy has left both organizational researchers and practitioners with discomforting dilemmas, and resulted in a focus on internal criteria to the exclusion of the demands of the organization's environment. Instead, the organization has been conceived as interdependent components or subsystems through which energy is transferred; and energy exchange occurs both within the organization and also between it and its environment. In this light, organizational effectiveness is the extent to which all forms of energic return to the organization are maximized.

The five societal components upon which the organization is dependent for its survival and growth include the community, government, customers, suppliers and creditors. The organization is also dependent upon maximizing energy transformation within the firm, a process in which its employees play a major role. A third component important in the survival and growth of the organization is its owner. The focus of the study was on the degree to which fulfillment of the needs of the organization's environmental components was related to fulfillment of the needs of the organization's internal subsystem components, and whether organizational size was related to these.

Findings of this study indicate that there are only a moderate number of relationships between the degree to which the organization concurrently fulfills the needs of its internal subsystem components (its employees), its owner, and the components of its larger society. Concurrent fulfillment of the needs of the five societal components is also of a rather low magnitude.

Evidently, organizations find it difficult to fulfill simultaneously the variety of demands made upon them. Whether the organization *can* concurrently fulfill all or even a major share of the divergent demands made upon it is a provocative and hypothetical question. It is probable that organizations do not strive to maximize fulfillment of any one system component, but operate in accordance with a policy of satisficing several system components. A no-layoff policy, for example, may partially fulfill employee needs, but might do so at the cost of diminishing fulfillment of other societal components. Fulfillment of needs of the various organizational components must, therefore, be treated as separate and, apparently independent. Components in the organization's system are linked together more by the flow of energic activities than by common goal attainment.

From a broader vantage, then, the manager's task is not only to coordinate functions within the organization, but to relate these internal functions to the organization's societal environment. Lack of concurrent maximization of the organization's components calls for greater focus upon the role of the manager as a systems balancer as well as a mediator of the boundaries of the organization (Davis and Blomstrom, 1966; Bass, 1965).

The inability of the organization to fulfill concurrently the needs of its societal components, its owners, and its employees presents dilemmas for theorists in organizational behavior as well as for practitioners in industrial organizations. If prophesies and predictions (Bennis, 1964) are correct, the tasks and goals of organizations will become far more complex in the future and will require greater adaptive and innovative capabilities. These increasing organizational complexities will demand the articulation and development of meta-goals that shape and provide the foundation for the goal structure. For example, one meta-goal might be the creation of a system for detecting new and changing goals of the organization or methods for deciding priorities among goals.

Finally, as Bennis predicts, there will be an increase in goal conflict, more and more divergency and contradictoriness between and among effectiveness criteria. While at this date the different effectiveness criteria among the variety of organizational functions appear unrelated and divergent, lethargy by management may allow these relationships to become negatively related to each other. Management's awareness of these relationships and of how they may change with differing goal structures seems a first step toward maximizing future organizational effectiveness.

References

ARGYRIS, C. (1962), *Interpersonal Competence and Organizational Effectiveness*, Dorsey Press.

BASS, B. M. (1952), 'Ultimate criteria of organizational worth', *Personn. Psychol.*, vol. 5, pp. 157–73.

BASS, B. M. (1965), *Organizational Psychology*, Allyn & Bacon.

BASS, B. M., MCGHEE, W. P., and VAUGHAN, J. A. (1965), 'Three levels of analysis of cost-effectiveness associated with personnel attitudes and attributes', prepared for the *Proceedings of the Logistics Research Conference*, Department of Defense, May.

BENNIS, W. G. (1964), 'Organizational developments and the fate of bureaucracy', paper presented at the meetings of the American Psychological Association, September.

CHARNES, A., and STEDRY, A. C. (1965), 'Quasi-rational models of behavior in organization research; *Manag. Sci. Res. Report*, no. 31, Grad. Sch. Indust. Admin., Carnegie-Mellon University.

DABAS, Z. S. (1958), 'The dimensions of morale; an item factorization of the SRA employee inventory', *Personn. Psychol.*, vol. 11, pp. 217–34.

DAVIS, K., and BLOMSTROM, R. L. (1966), *Business and Its Environment*, McGraw-Hill.

DAVIS, R. C. (1940), *Industrial Organization and Management*, Harper.

EMERY, F. E., and TRIST, E. L. (1959), 'Socio-technical systems', paper presented at 6th annual internat. meeting of *Instit. Manag. Sci.*, September.

GUION, R. M. (1961), 'Criterion measurement and personal judgements', *Personn. Psychol.*, vol. 14, pp. 141–9, esp. p. 145.

KATZ, D., and KAHN, R. L. (1966), *The Social Psychology of Organizations*, Wiley.

KATZELL, R., BARRETT, R. S., and PARKER, T. C. (1961), 'Job satisfaction, job performance and situational characteristics', *J. appl. Psychol.*, vol. 45, pp. 65–72.

LEVINSON, H. (1959), 'Role, personality and social structure in the organizational setting', *J. abnorm. soc. Psychol.*, vol. 58, pp. 170–80.

PARSONS, T., SHILS, E., NAEGLE, K., and PITTS, J. (1961), *Theories of Society*, Free Press, pp. 38–41.

PEPINSKY, H. B., WEICK, K. E., and RINER, J. W. (1965), *Primer for Productivity*, Research Foundation, Ohio State University.

SEASHORE, S. (1964), *Assessing Organization Performance with Behavioral Measurements*, Foundation for Research on Human Behaviour.

SHEPARD, H. A. (1965), 'Changing interpersonal and intergroup relationships in organizations', in J. G. March (ed.), *Handbook of Organizations*, Rand McNally, pp. 1115–43.

SIMON, H. A. (1957), *Models of Man*, Wiley.

STROTHER, G. B. (1963), 'Problems in the development of social science of organization', in H. J. Leavitt (ed.), *The Social Science of Organizations*, Prentice-Hall, pp. 3–37.

Part Three **Adaptation and Growth**

Each year, it seems, more and more organization theorists express their dissatisfaction with the case-study methodology. The objectors feel that case studies are too liable to spurious explanations, too dependent on nonobjective standards of explanatory power, informationally inefficient in their ratios of irrelevant to relevant data, and noncontributory to the field's pool of generalized findings. (The editor's own opinions on these issues are presented in Starbuck, 1968.) However, most research studies contain about the same number of observations, so that as the number of sequential observations increases, the number of organizations studied tends to decrease. The greatest part of what we think we know about organizational development over time is based upon case studies of single organizations, and no anthology of organizational research would be representative if it did not include a case study.

'On spitting against the wind' affords the reader an opportunity to form some methodological opinions of his own. It is one of the rare studies of organizational failure, and it is a study which is especially relevant to contemporary student radical movements.

'Determinants of innovation in organizations' is an exceptionally well-executed survey study of public health departments. It begins by carefully defining a domain of inquiry and a conceptual framework within which to organize observations. It systematically cites concurring and dissenting findings from parallel studies. It recognizes plausible alternative explanations for its findings and attempts to assess their validities. It balances a knowledge of the unique institutional characteristics of health departments against the need for findings which generalize to other organizational contexts.

The reader may wish to examine three other articles which were seriously considered for inclusion in this section. 'Organizational interdependence and intra-organizational structure' by Michael Aiken and Jerald Hage is a study of health and welfare organizations which partially parallels Mohr's study; trying to identify and explain the differences in the findings of the two studies is an interesting exercise. Aiken and Hage focus upon the associations between inter-organizational relations and intra-organizational structure; 'Organizational structure and the multinational strategy' by Lawrence Fouraker and John Stopford focuses upon the associations between international expansion and intra-organizational structure. Again, a contrast between the findings of Hage and Aiken and those of Fouraker and Stopford can be interesting.

Finally, Elmer Burack's 'Industrial management in advanced production systems' traces the effects of technological changes on organization structures in four manufacturing firms.

Reference

STARBUCK, W. H. (1968), 'Some comments, observations and objections stimulated by "Design of proof in organizational research"', *Admin. Sci. Q.*, vol. 13, no. 1, pp. 135–61.

4 N. J. Demerath III and V. Thiessen

On Spitting against the Wind[1]

N. J. Demerath III and Victor Thiessen, 'On spitting against the wind: organizational precariousness and American irreligion', *American Journal of Sociology*, vol. 71, no. 6, 1966, pp. 674–87.

This paper offers a belated diagnosis of an organization that is currently in its death trance. The analysis follows the development and demise of a small-town Wisconsin free-thought movement or *Freie Gemeinde* which began in 1852, reached its zenith in the 1880s, and then began to atrophy with the pursuit of legitimacy. The study is intended as both a perverse chapter in the sociology of religion and a paragraph in the theory of organizational change. It has two primary justifications.

First, in focusing on irreligion it directs attention to a neglected phenomenon on the American religious scene. Although the sociology of religion has been born again, the sociology of irreligion remains in the womb[2] despite the current talk of secularization and the steady flow of theological amendments to nineteenth-century orthodoxy and despite the predictions of Weber (1958, 1961), Marx (1964) and Durkheim (1958, 1961) that the twentieth century would witness the decline of the religious establishment.[3] Certainly irreligion has failed to replace the

1. This is an expanded version of a paper delivered at the American Sociological Association meetings in Chicago, 1 September 1965. We are indebted to the Danforth Study of Campus Ministries and to Dr Kenneth Underwood for research support. We are grateful to the members of the Sauk City *Freie Gemeinde* for their patience, their candor, and their hospitality. Finally, we have profited from the suggestions of a number of colleagues, including Kenneth Lutterman, Roberta Goldstone, Gerald Marwell, Philip Hammond and Berenice Cooper.

2. Organizational studies of irreligion are non-existent, although there have been several surveys that tap irreligion in wider populations. See, e.g., Middleton and Putney (1962), and Putney and Middleton (1962).

3. Although all of these predictions are refuted in that the church remains strong, they are partially confirmed in the preconditions of that strength. Thus, the church has staved off irreligion by becoming increasingly secular and allowing room for potential irreligionists within its own ranks. The establishment may not have passed, but it certainly has changed.

churches. At the same time, studies of irreligion may provide insight into its difficulties and a new comparative basis for analysis of the churches themselves.

A second justification is more abstract. Irreligious groups are precarious by dint of their dissidence and their illegitimacy. Examination of this precariousness may inform the study of organizational dynamics generally. Most organizational analysis follows in the wake of Weber's concern with the bureaucratic monolith. While the topic of organizational growth is common, studies of organizational demise are rare. While the conservative organization has been compelling, the deviant organization is frequently ignored and often shunted to the less attended realm of collective behavior. There is, of course, a range of studies on religious sects[4] as well as the literature on political extremism[5] and social movements.[6] And yet the freethinkers have features that distinguish them from each of these.

Unlike religious sects, the free-thought movement lacks any crystallized doctrine and falls beyond the pale of American religious tolerance. Unlike political movements, the freethinkers have no sharply defined organizational goals, and pressures against them are more informal than the sanctions of the electorate or the courts. Finally, unlike the Townsend movement, the Women's Christian Temperance Union, or an educational reform group, irreligion has neither a natural population from which to recruit nor a set of values which are in any way consistent with the normative mainstream.

Because the *Freie Gemeinde* is peculiar in these and other

4. For the classic statement on the religious sect, see Troeltsch (1960) Several recent treatments include Wilson (1959), Johnson (1963), and McNall (1963), See also Festinger, Riecken and Schachter (1956) for a more psychological analysis of a precarious religious cult.

5. Much of the literature on political extremism is more polemical than academic. Some of the better works include Bell (ed.) (1963), Howe and Coser (1962), Selznick (1960), Nahirney (1962), Bittner (1963) and Smelser (1963).

6. The term 'social movement' is, of course, a catchall. Several broad theoretical treatments include the divergent perspectives of Smelser (1963) and Cantril (1941). Case studies include Clark (1956), Gusfield (1955), Messinger (1955) and Lincoln (1961). Finally, for related treatments of delinquency and lower-class culture see Yinger (1960) and Yablonsky (1959).

respects it points to considerations that are largely mute in previous work. These include community structure and differentiation as they relate to expressed hostility; the effect of social class on the response to hostility; the difficulties of nurturing charisma as well as its importance in sustaining an illegitimate group; the problems of rallying commitment around a nihilistic doctrine and a goalless program; and the conflict between commitment and recruitment as organizational imperatives. Precisely because irreligion taxes previous frameworks without falling wholly outside of them, it should provide important additions to our current knowledge. Still, the study has no illusions of definitiveness. Since both irreligion and organizational precariousness have been little explored, our errors may be as instructive as our insights.

The paper comprises five sections. The first describes the study's methodology. The second offers a brief historical account of the group at issue. Third, we shall discuss some general characteristics of organizational precariousness and the range of adaptations to it. Fourth, we shall show how adaptation is influenced by external community factors. Fifth and finally, we shall discuss adaptation to dissidence and precariousness in the light of internal organizational characteristics.

Methodology

The study invokes three methodological strategies: observation, historical records, and lengthy personal interviews. Although we intend more rigorous research in the future, this first study is undeniably 'soft'. Accordingly, we shall heed the advice of Howard S. Becker (1958) and present a chronology of the investigation as one slim basis for evaluation.

As is frequently the case in exploratory research, the analytic problem which finally emerged was not the one that launched the study. Our first information on the *Freie Gemeinde* included only its location in the small, predominantly Catholic community of Sauk City and its shrinking size. This suggested conflict between the group and its context, a conflict which was to be the focus of the research.

It took only a few visits to teach us otherwise. We soon discovered that actual conflict had seldom occurred and that even past hostility had evanesced as the group began to camouflage its principles and seek survival instead of reform. Thus, the study quickly shifted from static to dynamic. Rather than focus on the contemporary scene, we were led to the historical problem of a changing organization and its changing community relations.

This was the result of the research's first stage, involving lengthy conversations with strategic members of the organization. A second stage quickly followed and persisted. This involved 'quasi-participant observation'[7] in the society's affairs, ranging from Sunday afternoon meetings held twice monthly to more informal gatherings. Third, we took advantage of the group's unique but dusty library to read and translate historical documents on nineteenth-century free thought. Fourth, we interviewed members of the movement more systematically. By this time we were aware of most of the key issues in the group's development. We had formed a number of hypotheses around which to probe for information.

Because the current membership is less than fifty, we decided to interview the entire population. But many members are no longer in the community, and others are so old as to be non-communicating. We completed interviews with twenty. Although these span all significant viewpoints within the group, there is no way of accurately assessing their representativeness. This together with the small number precludes statistical analysis and confines the yield to qualitative insights and illustration. In addition, we also interviewed apostates and non-affiliates in the community to gain a wider perspective. There was no formal community survey for fear of artificially reviving rancor and friction.

Finally, after the study was completed, we submitted drafts to several respondents for their comments. This revealed a few minor errors of fact, but all agreed that the basic theoretical points were sound, even those based on our own deductions rather than any direct mention in the interviews. Of course, acceptance

7. Participant observation is not quite apt since we were conspicuous as outsiders and made no attempt to hide our research objectives. At the same time, we were graciously received, invited to every meeting, and witnessed no inhibitions. It is a commentary on the group itself, however, that it no longer discusses issues about which inhibitions might arise.

of this sort may raise as many issues as it settles. It may be that our critics are too kind, especially to two outsiders who were giving them rare attention. It also may be that we suffered the analytic seduction that lurks for any observer. Nevertheless, these evaluations do confer one small stamp of validity, and validity is a precious commodity in a study of this sort.

The *Freie Gemeinde* in historical review

As the analysis shifted from current conflict to organizational dynamics, history became a crucial ingredient. American irreligion has enjoyed more historical than sociological attention,[8] but even so, work on ethnic irreligion in the tradition of the *Freie Gemeinde* is sparse.[9] This brief chronology draws heavily upon personal recollections and untranslated documents. Some of the details await the theoretical discussion to follow.

The *Freie Gemeinde* emerged out of the religious and social unrest in Germany and Eastern Europe of the 1840s. Upon the excommunication of one Johannes Ronge for doubting the sacramental validity of a 'holy robe' in Trier, a number of Catholics severed their ties with Rome and founded Free Christian or German-Catholic churches. The movement was neither united nor homogeneous. Ronge himself was anti-institutional rather than anti-doctrinal. Yet some were more radical than others, and upon persecution, many fled the country. The emigration was accelerated by the German Revolution of 1848; hence the term 'forty-eighters' to refer to this first major wave of German settlers.

The first *Freie Gemeinde* in the United States began in St Louis in 1850. Other communities formed in Pennsylvania, California, Washington, D.C., New York, Illinois and Wisconsin.

8. Most of this historical attention has been devoted to early American deists such as Jefferson, Franklin and Paine, together with the East Coast offspring of Unitarianism, including the ethical-culture movement. See, e.g. Persons (1947), Warren (1943), and Marty (1961).

9. Most of the literature here was locally published in limited editions and in German. For the European background of the free-thought movement, see Schuenemann-Pott (1861), Ronge (1849). For historical materials on the Wisconsin movement, see Heinzen (1879), Hempel (1877), Schuenemann-Pott (ed.) (1855–71), Schlichter (1944, 1945), Freidenker Convention zu Milwaukee (1872). A good recent summary is provided in Cooper (1964).

In Wisconsin there were some thirty groups by 1852 ranging from Milwaukee and Madison to Polktown and Koshkonong. The Sauk City group in question organized on 24 October 1852. Its declared purpose occurs in its articles of incorporation:

The United German Free Congregation is our name for our organization, for we wish to unite the enemies of clericalism, official hypocrisy and bigotry, the friends of truth, uprightness and honesty to be found scattered among all religions, creeds, churches and sects.

By means of such united strength we intend to erect a strong fortification against the pernicious power of the churches, sects and clericalism.

The foundation of this organization is *reason*, which is defamed by the priests of all 'revealed' religions, and the book of nature and world history, feared and repudiated by clericals, but loved and honored by the wise of all nations and all times.

Obviously we do not recognize as 'godless' those so called on account of their views (theoretical atheists) but rather the godless in fact – practical atheists, who behave as though there were no universal law to which they are obliged to submit, and no moral cosmic law to which they must conform. We dictate neither belief nor disbelief in God or immortality (Rung, 1940).[10]

Despite its stridency, the early *Freie Gemeinde* was a strong and cautiously respected element in the local community throughout the nineteenth century. Not only did they help to guide secular affairs, but they were often called in to mediate disputes within the churches themselves. The freethinkers were also an important

10. Note that the statement is bitingly opposed to the church but somewhat ambiguous concerning doctrine. This Kierkegaardian syndrome was characteristic of early free thought, but two things are worth noting about its subsequent development in the Sauk City group. First, there is an ever widening gap between the statements of the organization and the beliefs of the individual members – perhaps an operationalization of both precariousness and bureaucracy. Confining ourselves to the former, the organization was forced to become more publicly accepting of both church and doctrine while its members increased their opposition to doctrine in particular. This leads to a second point. Over time the Kierkegaardian position has been reversed: the members' original hostility toward the church has ebbed, but their atheism has become more *pro*nounced if less *an*nounced. This tendency to accept the church while rejecting its doctrine has, of course, cut a swath through the religious establishment as well, accounting for the concomitant rise of both secularization and church participation.

cultural force. Their activities emphasized music, drama, poetry, ethics and philosophy. Their periodic festivals drew capacity crowds and guest lectures from all over the country.

All of this reached its zenith under the guidance of one leader in particular, Eduard Schroeter. He had received theological training in Germany but was later forced out of the country to the United States. From 1853 to his death in 1888, he was the rallying point for Wisconsin free thought. Not only was he the leader of the Sauk City group, but he also started the Milwaukee *Freie Gemeinde* and made yearly visits to many of the other free congregations.

At the time of Schroeter's death, the Sauk City organization had an active membership of over one hundred. Its militancy was pronounced. For example, one prominent freethinker bequeathed land for use as a cemetery and stipulated only that priests and ministers were never to set foot on the plot. A current member describes his grandfather this way: 'He wasn't too tactful a person. He was a Bible scholar; he knew as much about religion as any preacher, and he'd just walk up to the preacher and argue with him about it. . . . I've seen some of the letters to the editor my grandfather wrote. I don't know of anyone now who would write things like that.'

Indeed, with Schroeter's death and the turnover from first to second generation members, the *Freie Gemeinde* began to lose its momentum. Gradually, its membership decreased, its activities grew less frequent, and its militancy subsided. The *Freie Gemeinde* began to co-operate more and condemn less. Its members began to attend the services of the orthodox churches whose own members were increasingly present at the Free Congregation's meetings. Some freethinkers began contributions to the Catholic church, and intermarriage increased. All of this is reflected in the group's changing constitution. Gradually it became less vindictive. The constitution drafted in 1917 lacks any polemic against the church, and a 1951 revision drops all reference to atheism. While nineteen of our twenty respondents are admitted atheists, organizational imperatives demand a less stigmatizing public stand.

Finally, consider the Sauk City group in contrast to its Milwaukee counterpart. Both were founded by the same man, at the same time, and with the same purpose. Yet the two are now estranged. The Milwaukee *Freie Gemeinde* has cleaved more closely to its original ideals and is more aggressive in pursuing them. To this end, it has joined the American Rationalist Federation (ARF): a lower-class, militant association that embraces Madalyn Murray and *The Realist*,[11] together with rationalist societies in St Louis, Philadelphia, New York, Baltimore, Cleveland, Chicago, and elsewhere. The ARF has repeatedly invited the Sauk City group to join. The invitations have never been answered. Instead Sauk City has chosen a different alliance. In order to legitimate itself and boost its recruitment potential, it became a member of the Unitarian–Universalist Fellowship in 1955. The move has had none of the salutary consequences expected and has even led to an unintended disruption. Recruitment and activities have remained at the same low ebb. The affiliation provoked sharp opposition from some members who felt betrayed and bolted to form a smaller but less compromising circle of their own. Hence this predominantly Catholic community of some 4000 now hosts *two* irreligious groups. Although one is moribund and the other militant, the latter may very well follow the path of its predecessor. Free thought is neither big business nor aggressive associationalism.

Organizational precariousness and adaptive strategies

In a society in which a leading liberal politician can assert, 'I don't care what a man's religion is as long as he believes in God', it is no surprise to consider the *Freie Gemeinde* a precarious organization. The term 'precarious' is appropriate for any organization that confronts the prospect of its own demise. The confrontation need be neither intentional nor acknowledged. The important criterion is a threatened disruption of the organization such that achievement of its goals and the maintenance of its

11. Madalyn Murray is an outspoken and formidably aggressive atheist who has used her legal background to push for wider separation of church and state through the courts. Her recent moves from Baltimore to Hawaii and to Texas have left behind a cloud of legal proceedings and embittered former colleagues. *The Realist* is a magazine of free-thought satire that covers issues from homosexuality to foreign policy in the unflinching manner of a literary Lenny Bruce.

values are so obstructed as to bring on a loss of identity through deathly quiescence, merger, or actual disbandment.

There is no single source of precariousness. It may arise out of structural weaknesses concerning leadership, communication, compliance, or role differentiation. It may emerge from poor recruitment or from low commitment. It may stem from abrasive relations with a hostile environment, even relations that fall short of blatant conflict. The last is plainly the most conspicuous source for the precariousness of the dissident *Freie Gemeinde*. It is also a central factor in Burton Clark's (1956) insightful analysis of 'precarious values'. Clark argues that a value may be precarious because it is undefined, because its functionaries are illegitimate, or because the value itself is 'unacceptable to a "host" population'. All three of these conditions apply to the *Freie Gemeinde* at one time or another. And yet Clark's suggestion that groups with precarious value are led into strenuous social service in the search for acceptance is less apt. There are other forms of adaptations and other factors that govern the pressure to adapt in the first place.

In general the possible responses to a hostile environment may be ranged along a continuum. The alternatives move in two directions. On the one hand, the group may follow Clark's scheme and pursue legitimation by changing or camouflaging its values, switching its functionaries and public spokesmen, or performing redeeming services for the community. Many groups attain stability in precisely this fashion. But for others the path may lead to organizational death. This is especially likely in groups like the *Freie Gemeinde* for whom dissidence itself was an original *raison d'être*.

On the other hand, a second adaptation involves increased militancy. Selznick, Nahirney and Bittner have all pointed to the organizational gains that may be had by widening the gulf between the group and its context.[12] If membership commitment is a concern, one way to bolster it is to make commitment irrevocable by burning the members' bridges behind them and precluding competing allegiances to more legitimate organizations. Thus, a radical group's effectiveness may be judged by its

12. See also the general literature on the sociology of conflict, including Coser (1956), Boulding (1962).

ability to turn external hostility to an internal advantage. As we shall see, however, this ability is difficult to come by.

But is it necessary to adapt drastically in either direction? Certainly some organizations are able to compensate for hostility without radical shifts in either tactics or character. Some have no design on their context, and its hostility is therefore less urgent. Organizational structure and commitment may provide an imperviousness to opposition. Finally, the hostility itself may be poorly communicated, non-consensual, or effectively blunted. In short, there are really two issues involved in the adaptation to a hostile environment: is a major adaptation necessary and, if so, in which direction? To explore these questions further, let us return to the *Freie Gemeinde* in theoretical rather than historical relief. The problem is to account for the Sauk City group's adaptation in the direction of legitimacy. Possible solutions lie in two artificially distinguished clusters, one having to do with the community itself, the other relating to the group in particular.[13]

Differentiation and the community context

There is perhaps no concept more central to community analysis than that of 'differentiation'. Yet there are at least two dimensions to this concept, both of which are important to the changing position of the *Freie Gemeinde*. First, one can speak of *vertical* differentiation, referring to social class and the ability to sustain class distinctions and elites. Second, there is *horizontal* or 'structural' differentiation,[14] referring to the degree of auto-

13. At this point it is instructive to compare the approach to follow with Smelser's landmark, *Theory of Collective Behavior*. Although the *Freie Gemeinde* fits into Smelser's category of the 'value oriented movement', it cannot be understood in Smelser's terms. Because of his emphasis on political revolutionism, Smelser puts a great deal of stress on repressive control by formally constituted authorities. He gives little attention to either informal control from the wider context or to 'self-control' through internal organizational characteristics. Both of these are crucial to the free-thought movement, and this is one of a number of ways in which irreligion departs from previous cases and previous theories.

14. The theoretical literature on structural differentiation is burgeoning. For a critical exchange on its applicability to social change, see Parsons (1964) and Eisenstadt (1964). For two discussions of its applicability to religion in particular, see Bellah (1964) and Peterson and Demerath (1965).

nomy between various institutional spheres, including economics, politics, education, religion and, indeed, irreligion.[15]

The relevance of vertical differentiation is discernible in two propositions. One is that strong elites may thwart the sentiments of the wider community by resisting or rechanneling their expression. Another is that a small town like Sauk City is unlikely to retain effective elites under the encroachments of the current 'mass society'.[16] In all of this, the contrast between the Sauk City group of 1865 and 1965 provides an illustration. Recalling the diatribe against the church in the *Freie Gemeinde*'s original statement of principles, one might have expected countermeasures from the local Catholics. And yet the reciprocity was frustrated by an aristocratic class allegiance between the freethinkers and the most influential Catholics. Sauk City Catholics were originally polarized into two groups occupying the same church. The 'old' Bavarian Catholics – wealthy, prominent and educated – knelt in sharp contrast to the 'new' Prussian Catholics who were lower rather than upper class and had migrated for economic rather than political reasons. One member of the Catholic church had this to say about the situation:

There was more in common between the 'Old Catholics' and the *Freie Gemeinde* than between the 'Old Catholics' and the lower-class Catholics. . . . The freethinkers were a powerful force in the community. For many years they provided a cultural leadership. . . . The 'Old Catholics' are contemptuous of many of the young priests who come in here who are ignorant, who have no real grasp of theology for all the preaching they do. So although the Catholics grew till they represented 70 per cent of the population of this community, they were never in a position to challenge the *Freie Gemeinde*. The bond between the 'Old Catholics' and the *Freie Gemeinde* was too great.

Although the lower-class Catholics commonly had the priest as ally in their intended war against the freethinkers, the upper-

15. Note that differentiation can be seen *within* each of these spheres as well as *between* them. This is even the case for irreligion itself. Thus, St Louis hosts both a strong Ethical Culture Society (middle class and church-like) and the headquarters of the A R F (lower class and more sectlike). The groups seldom communicate, and there is virtually no overlap in membership.

16. For a discussion of the role of elites in the contemporary small town, see Vidich and Bensman (1960).

class Catholics had the church coffers as a weapon in their opposition. As long as the elite retained its distinctive power in the church and community, the *Freie Gemeinde* was protected. By the turn of the century, however, this protective kinship had decreased. With acculturation and both upward and downward mobility, the Catholic church grew more homogeneous. Later we will note the downward mobility of the *Freie Gemeinde* itself. As both Catholics and freethinkers lost their upper-class character, pressure intensified and made an adaptive strategy necessary for the *Freie Gemeinde*.

But why a strategy of legitimation rather than increased militancy? Here the horizontal dimension of differentiation offers insight and Milwaukee offers a comparison. As a structurally differentiated urban center,[17] it affords its dissident groups both autonomy and a structured irrelevance. We would expect the Milwaukee *Freie Gemeinde* to choose the adaptive tack of militancy for several reasons. It not only must if it is to be heard, but it is allowed to since few are listening. Despite its bluster and intent, its disruptiveness is more threatened than real. Its militance is generally ignored because its activities do not impinge upon other community sectors or even upon the Milwaukee churches. But the less differentiated small town of Sauk City poses a different situation for its freethinkers. Because Sauk City forces an interpenetration of the activities of the *Freie Gemeinde* and every other institution, hostility increases and legitimation becomes a more likely response. In a small town, an irreligious group that occupies a prominent building on a large lot in the center of the community is more visible, more stigmatizing and more consequential. Where this group is a dwindling minority, legitimation is the only recourse in the struggle for survival.

In all of this, there is a paradox and two tainted alternatives. In a differentiated community, the dissident group may be militant precisely because its militance goes unnoticed or ignored. In an undifferentiated community, the dissident group is much more noticed and, therefore, must put a damper on its pronouncements. Thus, one may have militancy at the cost of neglect or one

17. For an account of the role of structural differentiation in urban centres, see Miller (1958), Dahl (1961), Schultze (1958) and Freeman (1963).

may have attention at the price of legitimation. Of course, after a point, militancy may stimulate attention and legitimacy may bring on neglect. The latter is a major tactic of the Sauk City group. We mentioned earlier that the *Freie Gemeinde* joined the Unitarian–Universalist Fellowship to facilitate its recruitment by increasing its legitimacy. Even so, the group has qualms about risking a cultivated anonymity by launching a membership campaign of any sort. One member puts its this way: 'If we ever battled for a member with one of the churches, then we might antagonize them. Our methods of obtaining members are far from the hard-sell type so that we don't antagonize any other group by trying to take members away from them.' Of course, the churches have confronted the same problem among themselves. In many cases, they have evolved a complex set of recruitment boundaries to insure that every church has access to potential members without encroaching upon each other. The *Freie Gemeinde* is hardly eligible for the arrangement.

Organizational characteristics and the pursuit of legitimacy

Other things being equal, a dissident group in an undifferentiated context will move toward legitimacy. But, of course, other things are seldom equal. Another set of factors that may mediate the influence of the community concerns internal characteristics of the dissident organization itself. Although we can assume that most groups would like to remain true to their original goals and values, we cannot assume that every group is up to the task.

Consider first the *social status of the membership*. In general, the higher the status of the members, the more militant a dissident group can be. This is so for several reasons. For one, the aura of prestige confers a certain license in itself. For another, high status often implies a crucial role in the community that redeems one's illegitimacy. For a third, high status makes the person more eligible for the support and tolerance of the community's wider elite. The early members of the Free Church had unequivocally high status in the community. In addition, they had power as editors of the local press, members of the community council, leaders of the local clubs, representatives on the village planning commission, and officers of the school board. We have already seen how these early freethinkers won the succor of the aristocratic Catholics. They also had leverage on the community as a whole, despite its hostility. A quote from Martin Marty's analysis of nineteenth-century Deism makes the point well for another irreligionist in another community; 'Judge Driscoll could be a free thinker and still hold his place in society because he was the person of most consequence in the community, and therefore could venture to go his own way and follow his own notions' (1961, p. 76).

But, paradoxically, although the upper classes *can* be more militant they frequently opt not to be. Lacking the mutual reinforcement of the ethnic freethinkers, they may be concerned about overreaching the tolerance threshold and they may be coopted by conservative elements in the community. On the other hand, the lower classes are more militant in spite of the greater likelihood of arousing hostility. They have less to lose, and continued frustration may lead them to spurn rather than eat the pie in the sky. In all of this, it is the middle class that is most constrained. Here, occupations depend on the good will of the community. Insurance agents, small businessmen, barbers and others in personal services cannot afford to antagonize their customers. One member of the *Freie Gemeinde* explained, 'In a small town, a tradesman can't afford to be anti-anything'. As this suggests, the Sauk City freethinkers are now more middle than upper class and this has been a factor in their increased pursuit of legitimacy. Of course, none of this is new or surprising. Homans (1961) comments on the license of high status; middle-class constraint has become a sociological cliché; and Gusfield (1955) corroborates the relationship between dissidence and low status.

Now, however, we turn to a more theoretically provocative area, that of *leadership*. Leadership is obviously crucial in a dissident group.[18] It is here that Weber makes some of his most

18. Yet there is a tentative qualification here concerning the relation between leadership and ideology. This is based on comparative observations of other irreligious groups, including the ethical movement and the A R F, together with the senior author's current analysis of civil rights organizations and their student volunteers. Where leadership is absent a strong ideology may fill the void by becoming doubly rigid and compelling. Where leadership and efficient organization occur, the ideology need be less compulsory and may be more flexible. The first case characterizes both the

important contributions to theories of social change. For Weber (1947), charisma was a key factor in producing innovations and 'breakthroughs' in the social order.[19] It was only by rallying around the magical that the membership could escape the mundane. And yet once the breakthrough had occurred, it was important to consolidate the gains. At this point, Weber discusses the shift from charismatic to non-charismatic authority as a way of stabilizing the movement and insuring its orderly march into future generations.

As apt as this theory may be for other groups, it must be amended for the *Freie Gemeinde*. Unlike the religious sect, irreligion provides poor soil for the nurturance of charisma. Weber puts strong emphasis on charisma's magical component, but freethinkers are vehemently oriented to science and rationality. Weber also stresses the importance of sacramental trappings for routinized charisma, yet freethinkers explicitly repudiate all ceremony let alone any doctrine resembling apostolic succession. This is a first instance of the way in which irreligious organizations are betrayed by irreligious tenets. Charisma is crucial to any dissident group's success, but free thought frustrates its development. Note, however, that the *Freie Gemeinde* did have an early approximation. Schroeter was charismatic in most respects save the magical. Indeed, his case points to several additional elaborations of Weberian theory.

It is important to recall that German immigrants had organized Wisconsin free thought *before* the emergence or arrival of a charismatic leader. This suggests that charisma is not always necessary for the inception of social movements. While charisma may be crucial in launching movements among an *indigenous* and rooted population, it may be less important for movements occurring among uprooted transplants or those who are sufficiently alien to band together without having to be rallied. Further, charisma may be more important in sustaining a militant movement than in starting it. Although a shift away from charisma

---

ARF and the Student Non-Violent Coordinating Committee. The second describes the ethical movement and the Southern Christian Leadership Conference.

19. See also the critical piece based upon new evidence by Berger (1963).

may be salutary once a group has been *accepted* by its context, it may be fatal if the group remains stigmatized. Certainly Schroeter's primary contribution was to persistence rather than inception. With his death in 1888, the group began its slow demise. Although the current leader is responsible and efficient, he makes no pretense of serving charismatic functions. Unlike Schroeter, he lacks the glamor of previous persecution, and his work as an insurance salesman brands him as all too ordinary. He has no prophetic role and even avoids ethical or intellectual leadership. Here then is one more reason why the group has opted for legitimacy rather than militancy.

But note that once legitimation is pursued, the pursuit itself has further consequences for the leader. Under conditions of militancy and consequent duress, the leader's power is centralized and maximized. Under conditions of legitimation, he faces increasing difficulty in maintaining his authority since his decisions and programs are less urgent. Sensing the compromise of legitimation, the group is apt to hark back to the time when its original ideals were being forged and defended militantly. It may then idealize past rather than present leadership and confer a wishful 'charisma *in absentia*' upon one long gone. This cultivation of the past has the best of both worlds. It reminds the group of its militant strain but locates this militancy safely in a bygone age where it can provoke no contemporary disruptions. In this regard it is important to note that although Schroeter was crucial to the *Freie Gemeinde* in both Milwaukee and Sauk City, he is given much less attention in the former. Milwaukee's militance has more nearly obviated such wistful glances into the heroic past.

A third organizational variable concerns values and goals or, more properly, their absence. As Clark has suggested, undefined values are one condition of precariousness. Unattainable or unrealistic goals may be another. Certainly conventional religious groups suffer on both counts since salvation is neither clear cut nor easily achieved. For this reason churches have long suffered from goal displacement or what could be termed the 'means–ends inversion' in which means such as recruitment replace goals such as salvation. All of this underscores the importance of charisma; it may serve as an antidote by providing an alternative source of meaning and a more immediate rallying point. It is hardly surprising that religious groups have long outdistanced more pragmatic organizations in their production of charismatic types.[20]

But if undefined and unattainable goals are a vulnerability of the churches, they are doubly so for the freethinkers. Here the problems escalate since values tend to be wholly relativistic and goals are rarely stipulated at all. The freethinker's high regard for individual autonomy makes an organizational creed anathema. The following quotations illustrate the members' amorphous conception of the *Freie Gemeinde*'s purpose:

Well, I think we're looking for something we can believe in.

We try to educate people in cultural things, in anything that's above and beyond the average humdrum existence. When I talk about 'above and beyond', I mean above and beyond our lives, the way we live now, where we came from and where we're going. . . . I think we all look for meanings; if there are any we hope to find them. We don't presuppose that there are meanings, however, that there are always answers. There may not be.

We are a group of seekers rather than a body of believers. We think that through advancements of science the truth will change. We are prepared to accept this, and we can change our beliefs very easily, because if it follows the truth, then we believe we are right in changing it in contrast to other religions.

With such vague goals, passion dissipates. There are no concrete actions, no gauges by which to measure progress. There is little worth suffering for, and legitimacy is seductive to those who are dissident for no compelling reasons and with no measurable end in view.

Like the churches, then, the *Freie Gemeinde* has indeed witnessed an inversion of means and ends. Many respondents confessed that their participation was motivated more by social reasons than anything else. The combination of 'mighty fine

20. Note the reference here to the 'production of charisma'. This is intended to suggest that charisma is often more imputed than claimed and that it relates more to group needs than to the psychology of leadership. In this interpretation, Weber is hardly an advocate of the 'great man theory of history'. For an analysis in this vein, see Festinger *et al.* (1956) and their implicit treatment of charisma as a response to collective dissonance.

food' and German 'egg coffee' has supplanted the reformist zeal of overturning the churches and emancipating their parishioners. Insofar as substantive issues occur, one member comments upon their deliberation as follows:

In our meetings we never talk about the *Freie Gemeinde* as such, or try in any way to belittle the beliefs of others. We don't do anything except maybe we have a meditation or reading with the idea that they're not too strongly worded so that they won't cause any friction or hard feelings. Some ideas appeal to us more than others, but we don't use them because we don't want people to feel that we are trying to ram our ideas down their throats.

Part of this is due to the natural legacy of free thought; part of it is a redounding effect of legitimation. For whatever reason, irreligion has been replaced by areligion, and an organization has become a collectivity.

All of this leads in turn to the further factor of *commitment*. Obviously, membership commitment is another pre-condition to organizational militancy.[21] The commitment of most Sauk City members has flagged to the point where increased militancy would tax it beyond its breaking point. Nor does the decreasing strength of the organization bother them. One member shrugged and commented as follows:

If the Free Church does disintegrate, fine, let it go; I've had it for fifty years, it's given me a lot of personal happiness. Let's make it pleasant for ourselves. I wouldn't want any people to join with very vehement feelings. . . . We had two or three who did that and everyone felt rather uncomfortable. It's a lot more pleasant just to let it go and not worry about it.

Certainly commitment is affected by the unattainability of goals above, but there are other factors as well. One is the generation of membership. Despite their differences, the *Freie Gemeinde*

21. The emphasis here is on the consequences of undercommitment for the pursuit of legitimation. And yet *overcommitment* is a pathology that may disrupt the militant group. Its symptoms are a penchant for the spectacular rather than the efficient and a tendency to grapple with the first task at hand instead of considering other tasks with more delayed but more important effects. Over-commitment is visible not only in the ARF as the most militant irreligious group but in civil rights organizations as well.

and the religious sect are similar in that second- and third-generation members are generally less sensitive to the original ideals and less militant in maintaining them.[22] One elderly free-thinker recalled the change this way:

The Freie Gemeinde was more antichurch at that time because the people had come from Europe and were more opposed to it and were more eager to further their education. . . . Our forebears, when they first came, were getting away from something . . . there was something to fight for, there was much more. These things were fresh in their minds and now there is an entirely different attitude.

Yet the members of later generations must not be confused with the convert. There is a difference between those whose membership is a family legacy and those who join out of independent conviction. Those respondents whose parents had *not* been members of the group were much more disgruntled with the current complacency. Most of them favored a more militant and more active program. However, as outsiders to a familistic organization, they lacked the influence to effect a change.

Finally, it is important to consider commitment alongside recruitment. One can relate the two hypothetically. Thus a militant group maximizes the commitment of its existing members but jeopardizes the recruitment of new adherents; a legitimizing group maximizes recruitment opportunities but minimizes commitment. In short, a dissident group cannot maximize commitment and recruitment at the same time. In order to secure commitment the group must adhere strongly to its dissident values, thereby alienating a flock of potential recruits who are not prepared to go so far. In order to enhance recruitment, the group must widen its appeal by reducing its dissidence, thereby betraying the allegiances of many of its original members.

The *Freie Gemeinde* offers a partial illustration. It is true that

22. Clearly ethnic acculturation has taken its toll in this connexion. Originally the *Freie Gemeinde* served an ancillary function in providing an island of old-world identity in the new-world sea. As ethnic lines blurred, the movement lost this role. Since then it has had to 'make it' on the basis of irreligion alone. But, while this is an undeniable factor in the organization's decline, it is hardly a sufficient cause. Other ethnic free-thought movements in Milwaukee, St Louis, and Philadelphia have maintained their militancy and conserved their strength in spite of acculturation.

the group failed to take advantage of the recruitment opportunities afforded by their affiliation with the Unitarian–Universalist Fellowship. And yet merely securing the advantage at all had the predicted consequence of decreased commitment. Two lifelong members expressed their reactions as follows:

I didn't like it very well, and I know that our forefathers wouldn't have agreed to it at all. I would rather that the group were like the way our forefathers had it.

The Free Church now is a negative force – even in my youth it was still a positive force culturally . . . they are not a free church anymore; they are now a segment of the Unitarian church.

The dissension's denouement was a splinter movement that followed the classic path of the religious sect except that it moved to the radical left instead of the fundamentalist right. While the new group has only a dozen members, it is both more active and more militant. It also elicits envious reactions from older members of the parent *Freie Gemeinde* who did not make the jump but could understand it.

One of the reasons they don't come anymore is that the *Freie Gemeinde* isn't as outspoken as it used to be. The group wasn't active enough to suit them. They became discouraged and therefore started a more active discussion group. . . . When Madalyn Murray was here last year, she was not invited to speak to the Free Church. She spoke to the other discussion group though, and many of us would have liked to talk to her.

Summary

The preceding section isolated four distinct intra-organizational factors which inform adaptation to dissidence and precariousness: social status, leadership and charisma, organizational goals and values, and commitment and recruitment.[23] At this point it is

23. What is the basis of four factors, only four factors, and these four factors? They are not random choices, and they are recommended by two considerations. First, of course, they resonate in the interviews and documents that provide the data. Second, they articulate with broader theoretical schemes. E.g. there is a contrived but provocative parallel between status, leadership, commitment, and values, on the one hand, and A-G-I-L, on the other. Certainly Parsons's model can be employed in the analysis of precariousness and dissidence, as Smelser has indicated. Yet our present intention is more to elucidate a single case than to engage in high-order systematics.

worth considering their mutual relations. Although the four are intimately associated, this is not to say that they will always be consistent in leaning toward militancy or legitimation, growth or decline. Some organizations will maximize the conditions for growth in all four respects; some will maximize conditions in one factor but fall short on others; finally, there will be organizations like the Sauk City group that come a cropper on each. The Sauk City *Freie Gemeinde*'s entire history reveals a succession of disasters as it systematically loses first one and then another factor in its favor. In its early phase it had an upperclass membership, a quasi-charismatic leader, a compelling goal in the revolt against the churches, and the high commitment of first-generation membership. Gradually each of these advantages fell away.

Nor has the community been of recent help, as was seen in the section on differentiation and the external context. The early alliance between the *Freie Gemeinde* and the aristocratic Catholics has dissipated and there is no longer a defending elite. Sauk City has never had the structural differentiation of Milwaukee, and therefore the freethinkers have always had to contend with a hostile community sensitive to their actions and declarations. In all of this, it is no surprise that the *Freie Gemeinde* is on the verge of disbanding. It may have a fling at immortality in the continued existence of its splinter movement. But even this may soon follow the path of its forerunner and convert current militancy into proximate legitimacy and ultimate demise.

References

BECKER, H. S. (1958), 'Problems of inference and proof in participation observation', *Amer. sociol. Rev.*, vol. 23, December, pp. 652–60.

BELL, D. (ed.) (1963), *The Radical Right*, Doubleday.

BELLAH, R. (1964), Religious evolution', *Amer. sociol. Rev.*, vol. 29, pp. 358–74.

BERGER, P. L. (1963), 'Charisma and religious innovation: the social location of Israelite prophecy', *Amer. sociol. Rev.*, vol. 28, December, pp. 940–50.

BITTNER, E. (1963), 'Radicalism and radical movements', *Amer. sociol. Rev.*, vol. 28, December, pp. 928–40.

BOULDING, K. E. (1962), *Conflict and Defense: A General Theory*, Harper & Row, esp. pp. 162–4.

CANTRIL, H. (1941), *The Psychology of Social Movements*, Chapman & Hall.

CLARK, B. R. (1956), 'Organizational adaptation and precarious values: a case study', *Amer. sociol. Rev.*, vol. 21, June, pp. 327–36.

COOPER, B. (1964), 'Die Freien Gemeinden in Wisconsin', *Wisconsin Academy of Science, Arts and Letters*, vol. 53, pp. 53–65.

COSER, L. (1956), *The Functions of Social Conflict*, Free Press, pp. 87–194.

DAHL, R. A. (1961), *Who Governs*, Yale University Press.

DURKHEIM, E. (1958), *Professional Ethics and Civic Morals*, Free Press, esp. pp. 55–6.

DURKHEIM, E. (1961), *The Elementary Forms of the Religious Life*, Collier Books, pp. 427–9.

EISENSTADT, S. N. (1964), 'Social change, differentiation and evolution', *Amer. sociol. Rev.*, vol. 29, pp. 375–85.

FESTINGER, L., RIECKEN, H. W., and SCHACHTER, S. (1956), *When Prophecy Fails*, Minnesota University Press.

FREEMAN, L., *et al.* (1963), 'Locating leaders in local communities', *Amer. sociol. Rev.*, vol. 28, October, p. 796.

Freidenker Convention zu Milwaukee (1872), *Blitzstrahlen der Wahrheit*, Milwaukee Freidenker.

GUSFIELD, J. R. (1955), 'Social structure and moral reform: a study of the Women's Christian Temperance Union', *Amer. J. Sociol.*, vol. 61, November, pp. 221–32.

HEINZEN, K. (1879), *Deutscher Radikalismus in Amerika*, Verein zur Verbreitung radikaler Prinzipien.

HEMPEL, M. (1877), *Was Sind die Freien Gemeinden von Nord-Amerika*, Philadelphia.

HOMANS, G. C. (1961), *Social Behavior: Its Elementary Forms*, Harcourt, Brace & World, pp. 349–55.

HOWE, I., and COSER, L. (1962), *The American Communist Party: A Critical History*, Praeger.

JOHNSON, B. (1963), 'On church and sect', *Amer. sociol. Rev.*, vol. 28, August, pp. 539–49.

LINCOLN, C. E. (1961), *The Black Muslims in America*, Beacon Press.

MCNALL, S. G. (1963), 'The sect movement', *Pacific sociol. Rev.*, vol. 6, Autumn, pp. 60–64.

MARTY, M. (1961), *The Infidel*, Living Age Books.

MARX, K. (1964), 'Anti-church movement – demonstration in Hyde Park', in *Marx and Engels on Religion*, Schocken Books, pp. 127–34.

MESSINGER, S. L. (1955), 'Organizational transformation: a case study of a declining social movement', *Amer. sociol. Rev.*, vol. 24, February, pp. 3–10.

MIDDLETON, R., and PUTNEY, S. (1962), 'Religion, normative standards and behavior', *Sociometrics*, vol. 25, pp. 141–52.

MILLER, D. C. (1958), 'Decision-making cliques in community power structures: a comparative study of an American and English city', *Amer. J. Sociol.*, vol. 64, November, pp. 299–310.

NAHIRNEY, V. C. (1962), 'Some observations on ideological groups', *Amer. J. Sociol.*, vol. 67, January, pp. 397–405.

PARSONS, T. (1964), 'Evolutionary universals in society', *Amer. sociol. Rev.*, vol. 29, pp. 339–57.

PERSONS, S. (1947), *Free Religion: An American Faith*, Yale University Press.

PETERSON, R. A., and DEMERATH, N. J., III (1965), 'Introduction to Liston Pope', in *Millhands and Preachers*, Yale University Press, 5th edn, pp. 25–32.

PUTNEY, S., and MIDDLETON, R. (1962), 'Ethical relativism and anomia', *Amer. J. Sociol.*, vol. 68, pp. 430–38.

RONGE, J. (1849), *Rede Gehalten beim Ersten Gottesdienste der Freien Christlichen Gemeinden zu Schweinfurt am Palm Sonntag*, Schweinfurt.

RUNG, C. (1940), 'The Free Congregation of Sauk City', unpublished manuscript, p. 11.

SCHLICHTER, J. J. (1944, 1945), 'Eduard Schroeter the humanist', *Wisconsin Magazine of History*, December, March.

SCHUENEMANN-POTT, F. (ed.) (1855–71), *Blaetter fuer Freies Religioeses Leben*, Wisconsin, vols. 1–16.

SCHUENEMANN-POTT, F. (1861), *Die Freie Gemeinde*, B. Stephen Publishers.

SCHULTZE, R. O. (1958), 'The role of economic dominants in community power structure', *Amer. sociol. Rev.*, vol. 23, February, pp. 3–9.

SELZNICK, P. (1960), *The Organizational Weapon*, Free Press.

SMELSER, N. J. (1963), *Theory of Collective Behavior*, Free Press, pp. 270–382.

TROELTSCH, E. (1960), *The Social Teachings of the Christian Churches*, Harper & Bros., vol. 1, pp. 328–54.

VIDICH, A. J., and BENSMAN, J. (1960), *Small Town in Mass Society*, Doubleday, esp. pp. 114–39, 287–9.

WARREN, S. (1943), *American Freethought: 1860–1914*, Columbia University Press.

WEBER, M. (1947), *The Theory of Social and Economic Organization*, Free Press, pp. 358–92.

WEBER, M. (1958), *The Protestant Ethic and the Spirit of Capitalism*, Scribner's, pp. 181–3.

WEBER, M. (1961), *General Economic History*, Collier Books, p. 270.

WILSON, B. R. (1959), 'An analysis of sect development', *Amer. sociol. Rev.*, vol. 24, February.

YABLONSKY, L. (1959), 'The delinquent gang as a near-group', *Soc. Probs*, vol. 7, Autumn, pp. 108–17.

YINGER, J. M. (1960), 'Contraculture and subculture', *Amer. sociol. Rev.*, vol. 25, October, pp. 625–45.

5 L. B. Mohr

Determinants of Innovation in Organizations[1]

L. B. Mohr, 'Determinants of innovation in organizations',
American Political Science Review, vol. 63, no. 1, 1969, pp. 111–26.

The present study is an attempt to identify the determinants of innovation in public agencies, i.e. the degree to which they adopt and emphasize programs that depart from traditional concerns. Innovation is suggested to be the function of an interaction among the motivation to innovate, the strength of obstacles against innovation and the availability of resources for overcoming such obstacles.

The significance of the research can be viewed in terms of Hyneman's (1950) observation nearly twenty years ago that bureaucratic agencies '. . . may fail to take the initiative and supply the leadership that is required of them in view of their relation to particular sectors of public affairs . . .'. His concern was the responsiveness of the public sector not only to expressed wants but to public wants that may go unexpressed, or be only weakly expressed, and whose utility is much more easily recognized by the informed bureaucratic official than by the ordinary citizen.[2]

While the results and conclusions to be reported appear to be

1. I wish to express my gratitude for valuable advice and comments from Robert Friedman, Irwin Rosenstock, Philip Converse, Ferrel Heady, M. Kent Jennings, Robert Northrop, and John Romani. Many of the ideas were sharpened and elaborated in discussions during the preparation of 'Innovation in state and local bureaucracies', by R. S. Friedman, L. B. Mohr and R. M. Northrop, a paper presented at the annual meeting of the American Political Science Association, New York, 1966. The research reported here was supported by the Public Health Service, Research Grant no. CH 00044 from the Division of Community Health Services.

2. For a much more recent treatment of bureaucratic innovation and public responsiveness, see Simon (1967). 'The "power" to innovate,' says Simon (p. 106), '. . . is probably the principal power of the bureaucracy in the realm of policy and value.'

largely valid for organizations in general, the empirical focus will be local departments of public health which, as a class, have had a rather dramatic succession of opportunities to respond to new public problems over the past twenty-five years. A brief introductory paragraph will orient the reader to the applied setting.

By the early 1940s – the end of the 'traditional' period in public health programming from the viewpoint of this study – the American Public Health Association had defined the task of the local health department essentially in terms of a basic set of six services: vital statistics, basic sanitation, communicable disease control, laboratory services, maternal and child health services, and health education (see Emerson, 1945). Since the middle 1940s, infectious diseases (which these services were designed to combat) have declined radically as a health problem. In the last two decades, the professional leadership has increasingly called upon local health departments to turn their attention to the control of chronic diseases, the prevention of accidents, the provision of mental health services, the control of the quality of water and air, to dental health needs and to a host of additional non-traditional concerns. Many local public health organizations have responded to these newer concerns as advancing technology has provided ways of meeting them. However, it appears that while some departments have indeed reacted innovatively, a great many others continue to pursue the traditional objectives, if not exclusively, then certainly with primary emphasis.

The study group for the present research included all full-time local health departments in Illinois, Michigan, New York, Ohio and Ontario, serving a jurisdiction no greater than 600,000 in population, whose chief executive – the local health officer – had occupied his current position during the entire period of 1960–64. This group comprised ninety-four agencies. Since one health officer refused to participate in the study, ninety-three elements were provided for analysis. The data were collected primarily by interviews with the local health officers during the summer of 1965.

The concept of innovation

Because the term innovation has been employed so widely and ambiguously, it is essential to specify at the outset how the concept will be used and how it is related to other usages. Innovation will be defined here as *the successful introduction into an applied situation of means or ends that are new to that situation.* Alternative and generally more inclusive definitions have been offered in the past (see Thompson, 1965; Rogers, 1962; Wilson, 1966; and Barnett, 1953). For example, there has been a frequent tendency to combine the idea of adoption or adaptiveness with the idea of invention; occasionally, the term 'innovative' has been assigned to mean exclusively what is more generally called 'inventive' or 'creative'.

It seems important at the present stage of research and theory to separate the idea of invention from the idea of innovation. Invention implies bringing something new into being; innovation implies bringing something new into use.[3] In the organizational world this distinction is particularly important, for we are interested at times in whether an organization can create something new for its own use or for exploitation by others, and at other times in whether an organization can successfully adopt goals or processes or policies that are new in the sense of being departures from its own tradition.

There appears to be a good deal of agreement now on some of the factors that most enhance inventiveness or creativity in organizations, including the availability of individuals capable of producing new ideas (see Steiner, 1965) and the development of an organizational pattern that maximizes flexibility and opens lines of communication (see Guetzkow, 1965; Burns and Stalker, 1961; Thompson, 1965). Unfortunately, less unanimity can be reported on the correlates of organizational innovation. There has been much more empirical research in this area, but it consists of scattered projects representing different disciplines, motivated by different considerations, and employing a strikingly heterogeneous selection of independent variables.

If any one group of variables may be said to stand out among all others as empirically determined correlates of innovation, it is the group of interrelated factors indicating size, wealth, or the availability of resources. Mansfield (1963), Mytinger (1965), Hage and Aiken (1967), Eisenstadt (1963), and Rogers (1962,

3. The same general distinction has been made by others, cf. Rogers (1962, pp. 195–6), and Simon (1967, p. 107).

pp. 40, 285–92) all conclude that organizational size and wealth are among the strongest predictors of innovation in the sense of readiness to adopt new patterns of behavior. Other organizational characteristics have also been identified as predictors of innovation in this sense, including informality, complexity, and decentralization in organizational structure (Hage and Aiken, 1967, pp. 503–19), breadth of organizational goals, and absence of dominance by a single professional ideology (Zald and Denton, 1963).

In addition to the organization itself, the environment of the organization appears to be extremely important in two ways. An organization may be more likely to innovate when its environment is rapidly changing than when it is steady. In this sense, 'environment' includes such factors as market conditions, technological changes, clientele needs and demands, and the labor market. Burns and Stalker (1961, p. 96) count this variable heavily as determining whether or not the firms they studied adopted new, more organic management techniques. In addition, innovation should also be more likely when the *social* environment to which an organization (or an individual) belongs has norms that favor change than when its norms do not favor change. In this regard, Rogers (1962, pp. 285–92) reports research in which fairly strong correlations were found between innovation and the norms of the relevant community, placed on a dimension from 'traditional' to 'modern'.

Each of the foregoing correlates of innovation must be viewed as an attribute of a collectivity – an organization. To complete the list, numerous variables measured at the individual level have also been found to relate to the type of innovative change of interest to us here. It would appear from a review of the literature that chief among these are the attitudes of an individual toward change, or any ideology he may have that would influence a specific type of innovation. Such factors were found to be important by Blau (1963, p. 246), Fliegel (1956), Rogers (1962, pp. 285–92) and Eisenstadt (1963). In addition, the 'cosmopoliteness' (Merton, 1949, 1957, pp. 387–420; Gouldner, 1957, 1958, pp. 281–306, and pp. 444–80) of an individual is reported to be a significant correlate of innovation by Mytinger (1965, pp. 212, 195) and by Rogers (1962, pp. 285–92). Blau (1963,

p. 296) found both the competence of an individual and his material and status interests to be associated with innovation. A positive professional orientation was found by Rogers to be associated with innovation, as was opinion leadership status within a relevant communications network.

It seems fairly clear, then, that the determinants of invention and the determinants of innovation in organizations are not identical. Inventiveness seems to be affected most by individual creativity and by the degree of hierarchical informality in organizational structure. Innovation, on the other hand, has been linked to size, wealth. environment, ideology, motivation, competence, professionalism, non-professionalism, decentralization, opinion leadership, and still other variables. Because of this difference, it appears highly desirable to distinguish innovation from invention in research.

If the preceding discussion is considered in light of the definition of innovation offered above, it is clear that we have been elaborating upon the word 'introduction' and upon the sense of the phrase 'new to that situation'. We have, in other words, emphasized that innovation is meant to exclude creativity *per se* and to include the notion of adopting something non-traditional whether it was invented within or outside of the organization concerned.

The term 'successful', like 'introduction', has important implications for the measurement of innovation. The successful introduction of some new method or goal implies its acceptance by the individual or group that constitutes the human element in a pertinent applied situation. If a health department tentatively introduces a new program, action of the department to increase emphasis on the program over time continues to be innovative behavior until the change has been completely accepted by organizational personnel, the public or other relevant groups. Such action is no longer innovative, of course, when the idea has become part of the organization's tradition.

The same point has been made in connexion with innovation by individuals, but it is especially significant in organizational behavior, where we have long recognized and been concerned with the phenomenon of resistance to change (see Leavitt, 1965, for a valuable summary and critique). It is important to note that both organizations and individuals may adopt a practice and then discontinue it for one reason or another or maintain it only on a token level. Rogers (1962, pp. 88–93) reports some studies in which discontinuance rates were found to be quite high. It may help us to gain insight into innovation, therefore, if we do not restrict ourselves to its usual operational definition, the simple adoption of new practices, but include also a definition that allows for increased emphasis upon non-traditional programs recently introduced.[4] For this reason and others to be noted subsequently, two basic working measures of innovation will be employed in the analysis. One is the total number of non-traditional services adopted by the department. The other is the total number of personnel units (measured in man-years or the equivalent in dollars) that were added in all non-traditional program areas during the five-year period 1960–64. This latter view of innovation will be labeled 'progressive programming'.

The term 'new' appears almost invariably and as a matter of course in definitions of innovation, but it has an implication that should not be taken for granted. Innovation is difficult because it involves doing something new. The introduction of innovative practices into a social setting implies actions that entail a certain amount of uncertainty, risk or hazard. This, then, suggests one significant factor that may help to explain innovation, i.e. there are certain obstacles or deterrents to innovation that may be more or less operative in any given case.[5] These are, first, the cost of such things as materials, time, or skills, and second, the power of human forces and fears, individual and social, that may be arrayed against the introduction of new means or ends. The latter category may include the power of tradition and social values, the power of individuals and groups who may be threatened by an innovation, and the power of one's concern for his own safety, security and self-esteem, as well as the security of people who are important to him. The more staunchly these

4. See the introductory paragraphs, above, for examples of traditional and non-traditional programs. The primary sources for determining the precise composition of the two lists were 'An official declaration of attitude of the American Public Health Association on desirable standard minimum functions and suitable organization of health activities', (1940), and Mustard (1945, pp. 128, 146–82).

5. cf. Mytinger's (1967) discussion of 'barriers' to innovation.

forces are arrayed against a particular innovation, the more difficult will it be for that innovation to take place, other things being equal. Furthermore, when one thinks of 'newness' in these terms, it is not the absolute or objective sense of the word that counts, but rather the relative newness of an idea to a given role or set of roles, for it is in that context that obstacles to innovation will frequently arise. Thus, the innovations we will consider here are not necessarily new to the professional leadership in the field of public health, but they are indeed innovations for the local community, the organization, or the small clique of fellow health officers or local physicians.

Although obstacles may generally be expected to inhibit innovation, previous studies indicate that other factors may stimulate or enhance it. One individual or organization will usually have greater motivation than another to adopt a new idea. In addition, one may have greater resources than another, including not only the money and skills to overcome obstacles of expense, but also resources such as a position of authority, a charismatic effect, the support of prestigious individuals and self-confidence to overcome obstacles presented in terms of human forces.

On the basis of the foregoing considerations, the following three-dimensional hypothesis is specified: *Innovation is directly related to the motivation to innovate, inversely related to the strength of obstacles to innovation, and directly related to the availability of resources for overcoming such obstacles.*

It is thus possible to specify in more general terms why some of the many independent variables covered by previous studies were related to innovation; each indicated either a relative absence of obstacles or a relative presence of motivation or resources. Environmetal changes and demands, for example, frequently constitute an important source of motivation, as do material and status interests and certain relevant ideologies. 'Traditional' community norms, personal attitudes generally unfavorable to change, worker resistance to change, narrow organizational goals, lack of information, mechanistic decision structures – all of these are examples of obstacles to innovation. Competence and wealth are significant resources for innovation.

Having defined innovation and presented a theoretical framework in which to consider it, let us turn now to the findings of the research and an examination of the specific determinants considered. We shall have a two-fold purpose: to explain a substantial proportion of the innovation studied, and to arrive at a better understanding of the nature of the explanatory model itself.

Motivation

Before constructing the interview schedules, four exploratory interviews were conducted with highly placed public health professionals. These interviews disclosed a consensus on the importance of attitudes of the health officer for the innovativeness of local health departments. Specifically, the health officer's public health ideology and his inclination toward activism were considered to be the best indicators of the likelihood that his organization would introduce and emphasize non-traditional programs. Ideologically, a 'conservatism–liberalism' dimension concerning the proper breadth of local public health programming was considered important. In addition, a health officer was considered more likely to innovate if he was a 'go-getter', 'aggressive', 'ambitious', 'interested in accomplishment', and 'willing to stick his neck out'. These opinions expressed in the exploratory interviews were supported by prior research, which both relates innovation to similar attitudes conducive to change and emphasizes the substantial importance of leadership motivation and behavior. Thus, the 'activism' and the 'ideology' of the health officer, taken together, were selected to indicate motivation to innovate.

Activism is more precisely defined as the health officer's perception of the extent to which the role of local health officer requires interaction with others, especially outside the health department, to obtain ideas, support, approval, and resources for departmental programs. The attitude was measured by a twenty-three-item Likert-type instrument that was completed by the respondent in the presence of an interviewer. The individual items were designed to measure opinions regarding the desirability of four different kinds of role activity: a) attempts to influence the health power structure in the community, i.e. higher administrative and legislative officials, the local medical society, and influential community leaders; (b) attempts to obtain support, such as grant support, beyond local appropriations, (c) relative emphasis to be placed upon interagency and public-related affairs as opposed to intra-agency activities; and (d) attempts to seek out community problems as opposed to waiting for them to be pointed out by others. It should be repeated that 'activism' as measured is an attitude or perception rather than a demonstrated behavior.

Public health ideology is more precisely defined as the health officer's opinion regarding the scope of services that should properly be offered by the local public health agency (as distinguished from local private and voluntary enterprise) in nontraditional public health program areas. The great majority of full-time local health officers in the area covered by this research are physicians, most of whom have had years of experience in private practice. These individuals are highly likely to feel conflicting ideological pulls from their dual identification with the medical profession and the profession of public health, the one allocating to the private sphere all medical care except those programs specifically or traditionally relinquished to government by organized medicine, and the other allocating to the public sector all unmet health needs. Not surprisingly, many of the programs considered innovative in public health today, such as screening for chronic diseases, for example, are addressed toward meeting unmet health needs traditionally allocated to private medicine. The public health ideology instrument was therefore designed to determine how far the health officer leaned toward either of these poles by asking his opinion of the proper locus of control for twenty-six kinds of medical and health care. The form and method of administration of this instrument were essentially the same as that of the activism scale.

Turning now to the findings concerning attitudes of leaders, our first concern is with the relationship between activism and ideology themselves. If it could be shown that each measure was correlated with innovation, but not highly intercorrelated, then they could profitably be combined. Their joint explanatory power would be greater than either attitude alone. Our day-to-day experience indicates that the liberal is not necessarily energetic in pursuing his views, nor is the conservative necessarily a passive reactor to events. There was good reason to predict that activism and ideology would not be strongly related and that indeed proved to be true with this group of local health officers. The correlation between the two variables is $r = 0.27$, a statistically significant relationship in a group this size ($p < 0.005$), but certainly not a strong one.[6] For further analyses, the single variable 'activism-ideology' was constructed, which represents the simple sum of the two attitude scores for each health officer.[7]

The finding of central interest in this section, the correlation between the activism–ideology, of the health officer and progressive programming, is $r = 0.36$. However, to interpret that finding it is necessary to rule out the effects of community size, since progressive programming is an expression of the absolute amount of resources added in non-traditional program areas during 1960–64, and large communities will naturally be served by greater numbers of personnel than small ones. When the control is introduced, the resulting partial correlation becomes $r = 0.40$,[8] indicating that the size of communities makes essentially no difference for the relationship between activism–ideology and progressive programming in these agencies.[9]

The relationships just reported do not hold uniformly for the

6. A significance level does not have the usual meaning here, since the group studied is a population rather than a probability sample. However, the test does provide some additional information about the strength of the reported relationship. It tells us the probability that a relationship this strong would appear if the group were divided into categories at random rather than according to actual scores on the independent variable. In light of these considerations, I have elected not to sprinkle significance levels throughout the report but to provide some bench marks that may be used as a guide by the interested reader. For $N = 93$, using a one-tailed test and the 0.05 level, the correlation $r = 0.18$ is significant; the comparable coefficients for other sample sizes in which we will be interested are $r = 0.21$ (for $N = 69$), $r = 0.24$ (for $N = 49$), and $r = 0.30$ (for $N = 33$).

7. Since the standard deviation of the ideology scores is greater than that of the activism scores (10.9 to 7.8), ideology contributes slightly more than activism to the summed index.

8. Separately, the correlation between activism and innovation, controlling for community size, is partial $r = 0.32$; for ideology and innovation, controlling for size, partial $r = 0.29$.

9. It will be of interest to note here how much innovation actually took place. Progressive programming ranged in these agencies from zero to 25.5 man-years with a mean of 3.5 and a standard deviation of 4.9. Adoption, which will be considered in a moment, ranged from 2 programs to 27, with a mean of 11.7 and a standard deviation of 6.1.

entire group of health officers studied. In Ontario, apparently owing to cultural differences in attitude toward the role of government and the station of private medicine, the relationship between ideology and innovation was slightly negative.[10] The data do not provide a direct explanation of this finding, but it became quite evident during the interviews that many Ontario health officers conduct a number of innovative programs in earnest while at the same time believing that this type of activity is, in general, more properly the responsibility of private medicine. From responses to open-ended questions, it appears that Ontario health officers generally feel even more strongly than those in the four American states that personal health matters are the province of private practice, but they also feel it quite proper for the government to step in when this responsibility is not being fully met. The orientation is a peculiar but understandable mixture of British socialism on one hand and small town American capitalism on the other. Because of such differences, ideology as measured here was not a good indicator in Ontario of the motivation to innovate, nor was it in any other way a good predictor of innovation in the Ontario departments. With this understood, the findings reported below will at times be given both for the group as a whole and also for the four American states considered separately ($N = 69$). In the American states alone, for example, the correlation between progressive programming and the activism–ideology of the health officer is $r = 0.40$, and when community size is controlled the partial correlation becomes $r = 0.44$.

It is desirable to show how activism–ideology is related to the total number of non-traditional programs adopted as well as to progressive programming; only then may we really compare these results with the results of other studies, most of which have defined innovation as the simple adoption of new ideas. However, the total group of organizations cannot be used in this analysis; many programs might have been adopted before the incumbency of the current health officer, making his attitudes largely irrelevant.[11] We must use a subgroup of organizations in which all

10. $r = -0.17$, a non-significant correlation.
11. Nor would it have been feasible to consider only post-1960 adoptions: such a procedure would have penalized the early adopters, many of whose innovations were made prior to 1960.

adoption of non-traditional services can reasonably be attributed to the health officer who was interviewed. Specifically, the subgroup includes all health officers who had held the post in that organization for at least fifteen years, i.e. since 1950, plus each health officer whose annual rate of adoption during 1960–64, when multiplied by his total years of tenure, yields a product that is equal to or greater than the total number of innovative programs adopted by the department.[12] This group contains thirty-three US organizations and, including Ontario, forty-nine departments in all. The subgroup is small but quite well representative of the entire study population on key indicators.[13] We find that in this subgroup the correlations between activism–ideology and adoption are essentially the same as those reported above, when progressive programming was the dependent variable. In the thirty-three US departments in the subgroup, for example, the uncontrolled correlation between activism–ideology and the number of programs adopted is $r = 0.38$. When community size is controlled, the partial correlation becomes $r = 0.43$. In the entire subgroup of forty-nine organizations, the corresponding product–moment correlations are $r = 0.38$ and $r = 0.40$. (To make comparisons among groups and subgroups convenient for the reader, separate intercorrelation matrices among the major variables in the study are provided in Tables 1 and 2.)

Thus, we have good reason to conclude that the motivation of the health officer, as measured, is indeed related to the innovation of the department, whether this be defined as number of

12. For example, one health officer had adopted one non-traditional program per year during 1960–64 and had been in the job for ten years. One might, therefore, reasonably estimate that ten of the department's non-traditional programs are associated with his incumbency. Since this department had a total of fourteen non-traditional programs it was not included in the subgroup. If its total had been ten or less, it would have been included. If the health officer had been there for fifteen years, the department would have been included regardless of total number of adoptions, for almost none of these programs had been introduced in local health departments before 1950.

13. The means for the whole group and for the subgroup, respectively, are: number of programs adopted, 11·7 and 11·2; population of jurisdiction, 110,000 and 109,000; 1959 expenditures, $188,000 and $165,000; activism–ideology, 119·9 and 120·1.

programs adopted or as increments in resources devoted to those programs.

On the other hand, it is noteworthy that behavior in this study is only *moderately* predictable from attitudes, and especially from

Table 1 Correlations among the Primary Variables for all Health Departments Studied*

	B	1	2	3	4	5
A. Adoption	0·70	NA	0·40	0·67	0·64	NA
	0·70	NA	0·46	0·65	0·63	NA
B. Progressive programming		0·40	0·33	0·60	0·60	0·49
		0·36	0·41	0·60	0·61	0·33
1. Health officer activism–ideology			−0·04	0·10	0·08	0·24
			0·01	0·12	0·10	0·15
2. % of the population in white collar occupations				0·41	0·41	0·28
				0·42	0·45	0·11
3. Health department expenditures, 1959					0·88	0·35
					0·88	0·26
4. Population of the health jurisdiction, 1959						0·38
						0·26
5. Extent of public health training of key employees						

* Correlations in italics apply to the US health departments studied, only. NA: Not applicable, since some adoptions may have predated the incumbency of the health officer and key employees.

ideology. Furthermore, the zero order correlation between ideology and innovation observed here ($r = 0.24$, $N = 93$) is not substantially different from that obtained in similar studies. In the research of Fliegel and of Rogers cited above, the comparable relationships were $r = 0.42$ and $r = 0.26$, respectively. In the study by Hage and Aiken, the comparable measure was slightly negative ($r = -0.15$). Blau and Mytinger concluded that ideology was important for change, but their results were not obtained through systematic measurement of the ideology of respondents and subsequent statistical analysis of all cases.

While it is possible that ideologies are so difficult to measure that their true effects cannot often be captured two alternative explanations seem more compelling. Both begin with the inference, drawn from the empirical results discussed above, that ideology *in itself* is indeed *not* an important predictor of innovation. The first alternative is that a mere willingness to innovate, as reflected by ideology, is an attitude of secondary importance to the *determination* to innovate. The second alternative is that an attitude such as ideology may lead to predicted behavior only

Table 2 Correlations among the Primary Variables for Health Departments in Which Adoption is Associated with the Health Officer Interviewed*

	1	2	3	4
A. Adoption	0·38	0·30	0·70	0·64
	0·38	0·36	0·63	0·63
1. Health officer activism–ideology		−0·21	0·10	0·08
		−0·14	0·12	0·10
2. % of the population in white collar occupations			0·27	0·23
			0·30	0·30
3. Health department expenditures, 1959				0·83
				0·83
4. Population of the health jurisdiction, 1959				

* Correlations in italics apply to the US health departments studied, only.

when *other* important conditions are also favorable. These possibilities suggest two research strategies. One is to measure the intensity with which an ideology is held in addition to measuring its mere existence, for in that way one may well capture the difference between those who are merely willing to behave consistently with an ideology and those strongly impelled to do so. Secondly, there should be an attempt to measure other conditions that may determine whether or not an ideology will be expressed in behavior in a given situation and to analyse the relationship between attitudes and behavior in the light of such conditions. In the present study, for example, it is quite possible that health officer attitudes resulted in innovative behavior only when other conditions, such as the balance between obstacles and resources, were also favorable. This possibility will be explored after other relevant findings have been presented.

Obstacles

Two sources of obstacles were thought to be important in explaining differences in innovation among local health departments: the extent to which (a) the community and (b) the organization itself are prepared to accept or resist such departures from established practice.

Community obstacles to innovation

Since no direct measure of community readiness to innovate was available, an attempt was made to study it indirectly by ascertaining social class levels, as measured by education (per cent of the population twenty-five years old and older who have completed high school) and occupation (per cent of the labor force in white collar occupations). The rationale for using these data as measures of readiness is derived from other research. It has been shown that the social class of an individual is correlated with his beliefs and behavior regarding the efficacy of preventive health actions (see Haefner *et al.*, 1967); by extension to the aggregate level public acceptance of the efficacy of preventive health measures may render a community favorable to action by its local health department. Another type of evidence indicates that the higher social classes tend to vote in favor of measures (such as bond issues) perceived as benefitting the general public, even to the extent of voting against their own apparent self-interest. Wilson and Banfield (1964) refer to this attitude as 'public-regardingness'.

Our finding is that education level, as measured, is only weakly related to innovation (the correlation with progressive programming is $r = 0.23$; with adoption, $r = 0.24$). When controlled for community size, the partial correlation of education level with progressive programming is only $r = 0.03$, and with adoption, $r = 0.04$.[14] Occupation level, on the other hand, was strongly enough related to innovation to retain at least some independent explanatory power. The extent of white collar employment is related to the number of programs adopted at the level $r = 0.46$ and to progressive programming at the level $r = 0.41$. When community size is controlled the relationships drop to $r = 0.25$

14. The per cent who completed two or more years of college may well have been a better measure for our purpose. Unfortunately, such information is not available from the normal central sources, such as the *County and City Data Book* published by the US Bureau of the Census. It should definitely not be concluded on the basis of these correlations that aggregate education level has little or nothing to do with resistance to change in communities.

and $r = 0.19$, respectively, so that occupation level does not provide a great deal of additional explanatory power once the size of the community is considered. We will keep in mind, however, that if extent of innovation seems to be determined by community size the reason may lie partly in a relationship between size and social class characteristics. At some level of probability, for example, the larger the health jurisdiction, the greater the per cent white collar, and therefore the greater the readiness to accept innovations in public programs.

Organizational obstacles to innovation

Within the organization, the readiness to accept innovations was measured by the extent of public health training of key lower echelon employees – their capacity to handle the supervisory aspects of the new programs.[15] Some of these supervisors hold advanced degrees in public health, some have had undergraduate programs with substantial public health content, and some have participated in special courses administered by state and federal health agencies and by nearby universities. Some, on the other hand, have had little or no specific public health training; their supervisory capacity is based largely on years of work experience with traditional programs.

A correlation of $r = 0.33$ was obtained between the public health training of supervisors and progressive programming in the department. When controlled for community size, the partial correlation becomes $r = 0.22$. It is of interest to note that the lack of training of supervisors is an obstacle primarily when the *health officer* is motivated to innovate. Dividing the organizations into two approximately equal groups according to the activism–ideology of the health officer, we find that when motivation to innovate (as measured) is low, the correlation between progressive programming and the training of supervisors is only $r = 0.15$, but when motivation is high, this

15. Extent of public health training was measured on a ten-point scale. The data were obtained through a self-administered questionnaire left with the supervisors at the time of the health-officer interview. It would have been far better to have obtained this information on all professional employees in the department, but turnover is such that very few in each department had been there from 1960 through 1964.

relationship is just under $r = 0.40$. Thus, when the health officer appears ready to innovate, lack of training at the supervisory echelon can apparently constitute one further obstacle to organizational innovation.

The interview data, supported by impressions obtained during the field work, suggest that continuing education of staff nurses and sanitarians through short courses dealing with the more novel program areas is effective in winning their cooperation and enthusiasm. When asked whether the department operated a specific program, many health officers complained that the unwillingness of lower echelon employees had proven to be an insurmountable obstruction to desired innovation. This seemed to apply particularly to nurses quite advanced in age, a fairly common personnel characteristic of local health departments. On the other hand, new programs such as mental health nursing were frequently established or substantially expanded in some departments after most or all of the employees to be involved had taken the opportunity to receive special training for these new duties. There was no evidence of an employee's refusing or even resisting such training. Thus, if they are not already doing so, it is suggested that leaders who would like to put more emphasis on non-traditional services should devote serious attention to the matter of employee training.

Resources, size and innovation

It was expected on the basis of prior research that a great deal of the variance in program innovation among local health departments might be explained by the amount of money available to the health department for innovation. The primary operational definition of resources, therefore, was simply the level of expenditures of the health department in 1959 (the last year prior to the period over which progressive programming was measured). Clearly, expenditures do not precisely indicate resources available for innovation since funds might possibly be inextricably bound to ongoing, traditional activities. It was tentatively assumed, however, that greater absolute income would generally imply greater discretion in the commitment of resources, not only in local health departments but also in organizations in general. For example, the health department with ten nurses might send one nurse at a time to a training course in mental health, but the health department with only one or two nurses might have great difficulty in doing so.

The finding is that there is indeed a strong relationship between expenditures and innovation in these organizations – stronger than that between innovation and either the activism–ideology of the health officer or obstacles presented by community and organizational factors. The correlation between expenditures and progressive programming is $r = 0.60$, and that between expenditures and the number of non-traditional programs adopted is $r = 0.65$. We must ask, however, whether 'expenditures' is really an indicator of resources or, perhaps, an indicator of the motivation to innovate. Is there a strong relationship because larger *communities* need or demand more programs, or because the greater resources accompanying *organizational* size *enable* more extensive innovation in some departments?

One excellent way to attack this question is to carry out a three-variable causal analysis using partial correlation and regression.

Unfortunately, extreme multicollinearity would seem to render current methodology for the evaluation of causal models unreliable in this case.[16] Despite this problem, and especially considering that there is no attempt here to make inferences to a sampled universe, the analysis was undertaken for the insights and cues to further analysis it might provide.

The partial correlation between expenditures and adoption, controlled for community size, is $r = 0.27$. In terms of causal interpretation, this result is ambiguous. The relationship is depicted by model c in Figure 1, but one wonders whether it actually looks *more* like model a or model b, both of which are contained in model c. Since essentially the same coefficient is expected in both cases, the partial correlation does not enable us to ascertain whether this is *primarily* a relation of spuriousness (expenditures and adoption are related mainly by the coincidence that community size caused them both to vary) or a develop-

16. The correlation between community size and health department expenditures is $r = 0.88$; between expenditures and adoptions, $r = 0.65$; between size and adoption, $r = 0.63$.

mental sequence, community size caused expenditures to vary and expenditures, in turn, caused adoption to vary. However, the partial slope of adoption on expenditures, controlling for community size, does suggest a particular causal interpretation.

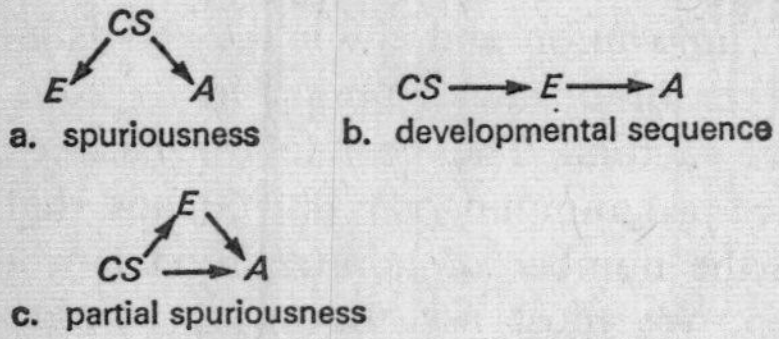

a. spuriousness   b. developmental sequence

c. partial spuriousness

Figure 1 Possible causal relationships among health department expenditures, E, the adoption of innovative programs, A, and community size, CS

If the true causal relationship were developmental (model b), a control for community size would leave the partial regression coefficient essentially unchanged – the slope should not be affected by controlling for a prior cause – whereas if complete spuriousness were involved (model a), the partial regression coefficient would be reduced to zero (see Blalock, 1961). Analysis shows that in this case, the slope is in fact reduced, but not substantially, when controlled for community size. The zero-order slope of adoption on expenditures is $b = 0.017$, and when controlled for size the partial slope becomes $b = 0.011$. The inference to be drawn is that a partially spurious relationship exists, but one that includes a substantial direct effect of expenditures on innovation. Community size causes organizations to be large (while at the same time motivating them to be innovative in some small degree) and the size of the organization then makes possible the variety of programming that constitutes the dependent variable.

Let us now examine some additional factors in order to place size in even sharper perspective. In preceding analyses, it was observed that many variables associated with innovation were also associated with community size, suggesting that the effects of size might not be so pronounced if these other specific variables were not involved. These include the activism of the health officer, the training of key employees, and, most importantly, the expenditure level of the health department. Although the correlation between community size and the number of innovative programs adopted is $r = 0.63$, when it is controlled for health department expenditures, the relationship is reduced to partial $r = 0.15$. When additional controls are introduced for health officer activism and per cent white collar, the relationship is reduced further to partial $r = 0.09$. This 'partialling out' of the effects of community size implies that, for these data, how community size acted upon innovation in the health department may be almost completely understood in terms of the other variables just listed.

Thus, we can tentatively conclude that community size was important for innovation in this study because it connoted a summary of factors that included motivation, obstacles, and resources in a highly conducive combination. Neither community size, farm size, size of health department, nor size of firm should be accepted hastily as an accurate predictor of innovation. Size itself is not related to innovativeness by logical necessity; it becomes significant only when it implies or indicates the conceptual variables that are important in themselves.

Motivation, obstacles, and especially resources account substantially for differences in the number of innovative programs operated by agencies of different size. It is now desirable to ascertain whether larger health departments put greater relative emphasis on innovative services than smaller ones, or if they merely adopted many more programs. A new dependent variable was constructed to investigate this question – the proportion of total increases in resources devoted to initiating and expanding non-traditional services during the period 1960–64, or, put another way, the ratio of progressive programming to increases in all programs, new and existing, traditional and non-traditional. For brevity, let us call this variable 'proportional innovation'. The correlation between health department expenditures and innovation so defined is $r = 0.04$. This result is surprising, but unequivocal; health department size and, presumably, the resources available as a consequence of size, had on the average almost no impact upon proportional innovation during this period of time.

It would be incorrect to infer that the resources bound up with organizational size (or even only with local health department size) are invariably unrelated to proportional innovation. It may be, for example, that had this same study been carried out ten years earlier, the correlation between health department expenditures and proportional innovation would have proved substantially higher. It is possible that at that time very few small departments had adopted any non-traditional programs, whereas the large departments no doubt already had. In that case, the correlation between expenditures and proportional innovation would almost certainly have been greater ten years ago than 0·04, although the total amount of innovation in all health departments at that time may have been quite small. The fact remains, however, that size – and therefore the resources implied by size – was not associated with greater proportional innovation in these agencies. Until contrary empirical evidence and sound theoretical justification are presented, one must at least remain skeptical of a causal relationship between organizational size and the proportion of increased resources that will be allocated to innovation.

Proportional innovation might perhaps be considered a faulty operational measure in that large departments, because of a substantially greater growth rate, may actually be more innovative than small departments when they devote approximately the same proportion of their growth to non-traditional services. Growth rates are not greater with increased size in these organizations, however, nor has such been found to be true of other kinds of organizations. It is now generally agreed that there is little or no relation between size of firm and expected percentage rate of growth. Mansfield (pp. 1034–5) finds slightly higher growth rates for small firms *that survive* than for large firms, but the differences are slight, and do not affect the general argument (Simon, 1964).[17] The correlation between health department size and growth during 1960–64 as a percentage of size is $r = 0·16$. Thus, large and small organizations are increasing at roughly the same rate.

Although it is clear that size on the average had no appreciable impact on proportional innovation, it is equally clear that large

17. See also the articles by Mansfield and by Simon and Bonini cited there.

departments did tend to adopt substantially more non-traditional programs than small ones and it is germane to ask which resources may have led to this effect. To find answers to this question, an analysis was made of the median size of the health departments adopting each non-traditional program. Each program was assigned a numerical score – the median size of the agencies that adopted it – and the highest and lowest one-third of a list of programs ranked according to this criterion were singled out for special attention. The complete analysis is too lengthy to be presented here in detail, but the major conclusions can be stated briefly. First, the need or demand for a greater variety of programs in large communities occasioned only a few of the observed differences in number of programs adopted. Services such as air pollution control, the coordination of a number of community health agencies, and occupational or industrial health were, as might be expected, more likely to be found in large urban health jurisdictions. The remaining differences suggested by the two lists may be accounted for most reasonably by differences in resources between small and large departments. The effective resources appear to be as follows:

1. Small departments reach an early limit on variety of programming because of a limitation on the number of different activities into which one person's time may be fragmented. Large departments are not so limited simply because their greater number of personnel gives them the flexibility of assigning at least one full-time or half-time employee to each of a great many services.

2. Small departments have difficulty attracting specialized personnel such as nutritionists, research scientists, social workers and medical specialists. This limitation tends to restrict their non-traditional programs to those for which traditional kinds of personnel may be employed. Large departments attract specialized personnel much more easily.

3. Small departments have little slack in funds obtained from local sources, thereby depending heavily on single-purpose grants for innovation. Large departments, on the other hand, are able to devote a substantial percentage of their local funds to non-traditional programs.

4. Small departments innovate largely in program areas for which grant funds are readily available from the state health department. Large departments are more likely to receive funds and personnel directly from the federal government, as well.

These, then, appear to be the important specific resources enabling large local health departments to adopt many more non-traditional programs than smaller ones. Note that in another setting, such as an industrial organization, the effects of size upon innovation would no doubt be due to an entirely different set of resources, and in some general cases, size may have no implications whatever for the resources available for innovation.

Because they lack the resources needed for diversification, small health departments are unable to support a great variety of non-traditional services. However, by intra-organizational transfers, state grants and other means, they were able to find the resources to place as many personnel in non-traditional programs as larger agencies in proportion to size, over the five-year period, 1960–64. Moreover, when they did acquire additional resources during this period, they put as great a proportion of the total into non-traditional programs as did their larger counterparts. These three facts lead one to suspect that, on the average, the smaller agencies devoted their increased resources to relatively fewer non-traditional programs but on a relatively greater scale. A case-by-case analysis confirmed this suspicion. On the other hand, large health departments are able to support a great variety of services and, clearly, do so. They are exercising an option, however. Why should the large departments choose to adopt a large number of programs when they could easily use the same funds to launch fewer programs on a larger scale or to expand existing innovative enterprises?

This question may be answered at least in part by the concept of 'slack' innovation introduced by Cyert and March (1963). Slack innovation in these organizations would be innovation motivated largely by a desire for prestige and professional status on the part of the health officer and other health department staff members. In general, if organizational capability remains after the most pressing problems are attended to, some or all of such capability tends to be allocated to status-motivated innovation.

Note that this outcome would probably be manifested here by a greater number of different non-traditional activities, as opposed to increased emphasis upon existing activities, which does not ordinarily confer further prestige. Thus, since variety brings the bonus of professional approval, and since large departments have the resources to support greater variety, they have a strong tendency to adopt many more innovative programs than their smaller counterparts. In the general case, when an organization possesses the resources necessary to operate more innovative programs and can thereby obtain professional approval for its members, we would expect to find that it does indeed operate more. One important contributory condition is the general absence of systematic, dependable, retrospective evaluation of decisions regarding the allocation of resources.

Thus, this discussion points to large organizational size as a *facilitator* of innovation more than as a motivator of innovation. The analysis is consistent with the hypothesis concerning slack innovation offered by Cyert and March and it also helps explain some apparent discrepancies in the relationship between size and innovation in industrial firms. For small firms, technological advances may often be examples of what Cyert and March call 'problem' innovation, since the firm may need these new techniques to bring about indispensable improvements in its market position. For this reason, relatively unsuccessful firms have been found to be leaders in the adoption of some specific, extremely important technological improvements (Adams and Dirlam, 1966). However, if one studies a broad range of innovations, the larger and more successful firms – the firms more able to undertake slack innovation – should be found to lead the field in total adoptions. Such was the finding of Mansfield (1963; see also Mansfield, 1961) in his research, and that finding has been replicated here with respect to local health organizations.

It may by no means be concluded from this discussion that either large or small departments do a more effective public health job – because of greater breadth of innovative programming on one hand, or greater depth, on the other. One can think of numerous reasons why one style or the other might lead to a more effective total program, or why style, in this sense, would be totally irrelevant. In the last analysis, the question can only be resolved by systematic evaluation of total program effectiveness.[18]

Nor should we conclude that innovation is necessarily frivolous when motivated by concern for professional status rather than organizational production or service goals. A more realistic view is simply that such innovation is often non-rational: how adequately a formal organization will serve the needs of its public, especially unexpressed needs, appears to depend largely upon the values assumed by one or more professional groups in their own struggles for social prestige and survival. It is problematic whether value choices that are good or bad for a professional group lead to action choices that are good or bad for an organization and its public. No doubt, status innovation is sometimes at the root of profound progress while at other times it is merely a waste of resources.

A multiplicative model of innovation

Support has been provided for the inference that innovation is a function of motivation, obstacles and resources. It remains to determine how these variables act in combination. In such a case, the political scientist and the sociologist frequently turn to the linear additive multiple correlation procedure, a mathematical model that suits the exigencies of survey data quite well. If the analyst were to use a multiplicative model, for example, he might well find himself in a series of awkward positions as he confronted negative values, the desirability of making changes of scale (such as standardizing), and the absence of true ratio scales, as in attitude measurement. The tools for depicting non-additive relationships mathematically are not as accessible, nor do they appear to be as versatile as additive tools.

Multiple correlations provide quite 'good' results, in terms of proportion of variance explained, when applied to the data of this study. (For example, the multiple correlation of progressive programming with expenditures, activism–ideology, per cent white collar and supervisor training in the four American states is $R = 0.73$.) However, it is not entirely reasonable to apply such

18. For an excellent methodology for evaluation of public programs, see Deniston *et al.* (1968).

a model. It is more reasonable to expect an interactive rather than an additive result.

One relationship of interest is that between the activism–ideology of the local health officer and the adoption of non-traditional programs by the department. In the group of forty-nine health departments in which the health officer interviewed was highly likely to have presided over the initiation of all the agency's non-traditional programs, it was found that these two variables were related at the level $r = 0.38$, both in the study population as a whole and in the US health departments considered separately. It may well be, however, that this relationship is contingent to some extent upon the balance of obstacles and resources prevailing in different cases. When the obstacles are relatively great and the resources small, for example, it would be predicted that even the highly liberal and active health officer might not find it possible to innovate, at least not in substantially greater measure than his counterpart with relatively low motivation. If the balance were tipped heavily in the other direction, however, health officer motivation would be expected to make a great deal of difference. The highly motivated health officer would probably be extremely innovative, while his counterpart with relatively little motivation might not introduce any changes at all in spite of the ease with which he could apparently do so.

In order to test this prediction the group of forty-nine health departments was divided into 'high' and 'low' subgroups according to the level of resources available to them, and the regression of innovation on health officer attitudes was examined within each subgroup. A relatively low regression coefficient would be expected in the group characterized by few resources, but a relatively high slope in the group with resources more favorable to innovation, where the attitudes of the health officer would be likely to have substantial effect.

In the total group of forty-nine organizations, the regression coefficient of innovation (the adoption of non-traditional programs) on the activism–ideology of the health officer is $b = 0.15$. In the twenty health departments whose expenditures in 1959 were below \$100,000, the comparable slope was found to be $b = 0.06$, whereas in the twenty-nine health departments with expenditures above \$100,000, it is $b = 0.28$. When resources are high, in other words, a unit increase in health officer motivation, as measured, has about four-and-a-half times the effect upon innovation as it does when resources are low. (In the US health departments considered separately, the comparable coefficients are $b = 0.16$, for the group as a whole, and $b = 0.07$ and $b = 0.22$ for the subgroups characterized by low and high resources, respectively.) This difference in slopes suggests that there is, in fact, an interaction in the relationship such that the two independent variables, motivation and resources, may well provide an accurate *multiplicative* prediction of innovation.

Since we are dealing here with three interval – or assumed interval – scale variables, it is possible to go somewhat beyond the recognition of a difference in slopes in testing the fit of these data to a multiplicative mathematical model. The model would state that

$$I = k \cdot M^{b_1} \cdot R^{b_2}, \qquad 1$$

where I = innovation, M = motivation, R = resources, and k is a constant of proportionality. However, we may establish a prediction equation using the transformation

$$\log I = \log k + b_1 (\log M) + b_2 (\log R) \qquad 2$$

and use standard least-squares procedures for the purpose of estimation.[19] It would then be of interest to calculate the goodness-of-fit, of this logarithmic expression of the relationship, and to compare it with the fit of an ordinary linear additive model to the same data, employing the same variables. The ordinary multiple correlation of the adoption of non-traditional services with both health officer attitudes and health department expenditures, using only this subgroup of forty-nine health departments, is $R = 0.70$. In terms of proportion of variation explained, $R^2 = 0.49$. The proportion of variation in these same innovation scores explained by the antilog of the right hand side of equation 2, above, is $r^2 = 0.53$. Thus, the multiplicative model provides at least as good a fit to the data as the additive model. When only

19. Blalock (1961), pp. 91–2. For other suggested treatments of multiplicative relationships, see Blalock (1965); Coleman (1964); Russett, *et al.* (1964); Alker, Jr (1965, 1966).

the health departments in the four American states are considered the goodness-of-fit of the additive model is $R^2 = 0.59$, whereas the multiplicative model again yields a slightly higher goodness-of-fit measure, $r^2 = 0.66$ (as a correlation, $r = 0.81$). When obstacles are considered as well,[20] the goodness-of-fit measures for the multiplicative model in the whole group and in the US only are $r^2 = 0.63$ and $r^2 = 0.72$, respectively, whereas this time for the additive model they are exactly the same, $R^2 = 0.63$ and $R^2 = 0.72$.

Thus, the empirical observations are consistent with the hypothesis that innovation is a multiplicative function of the motivation to innovate and the resources available for innovation. We were not able to obtain a highly satisfying discrimination between the two models; it is true that the multiplicative model does not provide a clearly better fit than the additive model, or vice versa. However, for two reasons noted by Blalock, fairly good additive approximations of relationships that are actually more complex are to be expected: 'In general, additive models seem to approximate reality reasonably well, given a limited range of variation and sizeable "random" fluctuation that make accurate specifications difficult' (Blalock, 1965, p. 373). As behavioral science progresses, however, we will hopefully capture a greater range of values on each variable employed, so that the nature of effects will be more clearly delineated, and we will also both improve the validity of specific measurements and consider or control more of the factors relevant to each analysis, so that random and nonrandom fluctuation will be reduced. As we approach attainment of these objectives, it is logical that the mathematical models we employ be dedicated as much as possible by theoretical considerations and as little as possible by disciplinary tradition. When two fairly simple forms of explanation are equally effective in organizing empirical events, the one that is theoretically more cogent is to be preferred.

20. The resources term in the equation becomes, in this case, an obstacles–resources term. It was calculated by adding together the expenditures and per cent white collar scores, after first weighting each with the appropriate partial slope from the regression of adoption on activism–ideology, expenditures, and per cent white collar.

It has been suggested more than once that the kind of theoretical case confronted in the present research involves a multiplicative relationship. Atkinson has proposed a general theory to account for 'motivated' behavior, or achievement-oriented behavior, in which any such behavior is a multiplicative function of motivational variables, on one hand, and 'expectancy' (the subjective probability of success), on the other.[21] Note that this latter psychological variable may easily be translated into our terms as an objective probability of success – the balance between resources and obstacles. The present results, therefore, may be seen as a specific instance of the operation of Atkinson's hypothesis. In yet another study, Palmore and Hammond (1964) have come to an identical analytical conclusion regarding closely similar independent and dependent variables. After analysing records of welfare recipients in New Haven, these investigators concluded that deviant behavior (juvenile delinquency) is a multiplicative function of what may again be viewed as indicators of motivation and resources. The motivational variables are summarized by the concept 'blockage of legitimate opportunity' and are indicated operationally by race, sex and success in school. The resource–obstacle variables are summarized by the concept 'availability of illegitimate opportunity', and are indicated by measures of both family deviance and neighborhood deviance. Blalock (1965, p. 379) in fact, has attempted to draw a direct analogy between the variables discussed by Palmore and Hammond and those discussed by Atkinson.

Taking Atkinson's proposed theory of 'motivated' behavior as a hypothesis, we note that Palmore and Hammond have used the same kind of model and what appear to be very similar conceptual predictors to explain *deviant* behavior. The present

21. Atkinson (1957). Atkinson actually uses two aspects of total inclination to act – basic psychological drive, such as the need for achievement, and incentive value attached to the object of the behavior in question. These are multiplied together and it is their product that is multiplied by the expectancy factor to obtain a prediction of behavior. The present study does not distinguish the basic drive from the incentive component of overall motivation; both are probably involved to a certain extent in motivation as measured here. Atkinson's article has most recently been reprinted (and also updated) in Atkinson and Feather (1966), see also chs 2, 20.

research has again used a multiplicative model and similar independent variables to explain *innovative* behavior. Together, these two studies provide substantial empirical support for Atkinson's more general psychological formulation. Moreover, the concepts of innovation and social deviance are closely allied. Merton (1957, pp. 131–94) has specifically designated the deviant behavior of the gangster and the juvenile delinquent as 'innovation'. In his well-known paradigm, innovation is distinguished from other modes of adaptation to cultural norms – conformity, ritualism, retreatism and rebellion – by constituting a behavioral pattern in which cultural goals are accepted but institutionalized means for achieving them are rejected. This formulation has been clarified by Harary and others (1966) so that the meaning of 'the rejection of institutionalized means' in the case of innovation is expanded to include the substitution of other means for attaining the culturally approved goal. The delinquent is an innovator, according to Merton, in that he has accepted the cultural goal of individual material success but rejected socially accepted means, and adopted non-accepted means, of attaining that objective.

Thus, it has been suggested that several related forms of behavior depend multiplicatively on the motivation to venture into a new pattern of action and the net resources available for accomplishing that purpose. The hypothesis has grown out of the analysis of empirical observations as well as from more abstract inference. Further research is now needed to elaborate upon this theoretical proposition, which would seem to have exceptionally wide application in the social sciences.

Conclusions

This research began with a concern for the responsiveness of public agencies to changes in the general problems they were designed to meet. We did not study the whole of this question but rather attacked one essential facet, the ability of such organizations to adopt and emphasize programs that depart from traditional behavior. On the other hand, our focus goes somewhat beyond the problem of responsiveness in that it is relevant to questions of organizational innovation in general, whether justified by environmental changes or prompted by any of a host of other possible stimuli.

It was initially proposed that extent of innovation is a negative function of obstacles and a positive function of the motivation to innovate and the availability of relevant resources. The data collected from ninety-three local public health organizations supported this proposition, athough, as operationalized, the relationships were weak in some cases. The variable emerging as by far the most powerful predictor of innovation was 'size', but we concluded that this relationship cannot be considered theoretically complete. Rather, size should be expected to predict innovativeness only insofar as it implies the presence of motivation, obstacles and resources. In the present case, organizational size proved to be an excellent indicator of the relevant resources available to local health departments for the adoption of a large number of non-traditional programs.

The analysis of the data yielded several additional conclusions that would seem to merit further test and elaboration:

1. In attempting to derive accurate predictions of behavior from attitudes or beliefs, such as ideologies, the belief itself should be qualified by the intensity with which it is held and one may well expect the belief–behavior relationship to be qualified by one or more contingent conditions.

2. With regard to many kinds of innovation in public organizations, the relationships among community size, organizational size and extent of innovation form a developmental sequence. Larger communities generally require larger service organizations, and it is the resources of the larger organization that lead to innovation. Thus, large organizations in small communities may be expected to adopt many innovations: small organizations in large communities will adopt few.

3. A great deal of innovation in organizations, especially large or successful ones, is 'slack' innovation. After solution of immediate problems, the quest for prestige rather than the quest for organizational effectiveness or corporate profit motivates the adoption of most new programs and technologies.

4. Once the diffusion of innovations has progressed far enough to include late adopters, organizational size and wealth will have no bearing upon the relative emphasis accorded to innovative as opposed to traditional activities.

5. Lastly, and perhaps most importantly for theoretical development, innovation is viewed as a multiplicative function of the motivation to innovate and the balance between the obstacles and resources bearing upon innovation.

References

ADAMS, W., and DIRLAM, J. B. (1966), 'Big steel, invention and innovation', *Q. J. Econs*, vol. 80, May, pp. 167–89.

ALKER, H. R., Jr (1965), *Mathematics and Politics*, Macmillan, pp. 108–11.

ALKER, H. R., Jr (1965), 'The long road to international relations theory: problems of statistical nonaddivity', *World Politics*, vol. 18, July, pp. 639–44.

American Public Health Association (1940), *Amer. J. Pub. Health*, vol. 30, pp. 1099–106.

ATKINSON, J. W. (1957), 'Motivational determinants of risk-taking behavior', *Psychol. Rev.*, vol. 64, pp. 359–72.

ATKINSON, J. W., and FEATHER, N. T. (eds.) (1966), *A Theory of Achievement Motivation*, Wiley, chs. 1, 2, 20.

BARNETT, H. G. (1953), *Innovation*, McGraw-Hill, p. 7.

BLALOCK, H. M. (1961), *Causal Inference in Non-experimental Research*, University of North Carolina Press, pp. 83–91.

BLALOCK, H. M. (1965), 'Theory building and the statistical concept of interaction', *Amer. sociol. Rev.*, vol. 30, June, pp. 374–80.

BLAU, P. M. (1963), *The Dynamics of Bureaucracy*, 2nd edn. rev., University of Chicago Press.

BURNS, T., and STALKER, G. M. (1961), *The Management of Innovation*, Tavistock Publications, pp. 85–6, 89, 121-2.

COLEMAN, J. S. (1964), *Introduction to Mathematical Sociology*, Free Press, pp. 224–35.

CYERT, R. M., and MARCH, J. G. (1963), *A Behavioral Theory of the Firm*, Prentice-Hall, pp. 278–9.

DENISTON, O. L., ROSENSTOCK, I. M., and GETTING, V. A. (1968), 'Evaluation of program effectiveness', *Pub. Health Reps*, vol. 83, April, pp. 323–35.

EISENSTADT, S. N. (1963), *The Political Systems of Empires*, Free Press, pp. 27, 33–112.

EMERSON, H. (1945), *Local Health Units for the Nation: A Report*, Commonwealth Fund, p. 2.

FLIEGEL, F. C. (1956), 'A multiple correlation analysis of factors associated with adoption of farm practices', *Rur. Sociol.*, vol. 21, pp. 288–9, 291.

GOULDNER, A. W. (1957, 1958), 'Cosmopolitans and locals: toward an analysis of latent social roles', *Admin. Sci. Q.*, vol. 2, December and March, pp. 281–306 and pp. 444–80.

GUETZKOW, H. (1965), 'The creative person in organizations', in G. A. Steiner (ed.), *The Creative Organization*, Chicago University Press, pp. 35–45.

HAEFNER, D. P., KEGELES, S. S., KIRSCHT, J. P., and ROSENSTOCK, I. M. (1967), 'Preventive actions concerning dental disease, tuberculosis and cancer', *Pub. Health Reps*, vol. 82, May, pp. 451–9.

HAGE, J., and AIKEN, M. (1967), 'Program change and organizational properties: a comparative analysis', *Amer. J. Sociol.*, vol. 72, March, pp. 516–17.

HARARY, F., *et al.* (1966), 'Merton revisited: a new classification for deviant behavior', *Amer. sociol. Rev.*, vol. 31, October, pp. 693–7.

HYNEMAN, C. S. (1950), *Bureaucracy in a Democracy*, Harper, p. 26.

LEAVITT, H. J. (1965), 'Applied organizational change in industry: structural, technical and human approaches', in J. G. March (ed.), *Handbook of Organizations*, Rand McNally, pp. 1144–70.

MANSFIELD, E. (1961), 'Technical change and the rate of imitation', *Econometrica.*, vol. 29, pp. 741–66.

MANSFIELD, E. (1963), 'The speed of response of firms to new techniques', *Q. J. Econs*, May, pp. 293–304.

MERTON, R. K. (1949, 1957), *Social Theory and Social Structure*, Free Press, pp. 387–420.

MUSTARD, H. S. (1945), *Government in Public Health*, Commonwealth Fund.

MYTINGER, R. E. (1965), 'Innovations in public health', unpublished doctoral dissertation, University of California, p. 212.

MYTINGER, R. E. (1967), 'Barriers to adoption of new programs as perceived by local health officers', *Pub. Health Reps.*, vol. 82, February, pp. 108–114.

PALMORE, E. B., and HAMMOND, P. E. (1964), 'Interacting factors in juvenile delinquency', *Amer. sociol. Rev.*, vol. 29, December, pp. 848–54.

ROGERS, E. M. (1958), 'A conceptual variable analysis of technological change', *Rur. Sociol.*, vol. 23, pp. 139–40, 143–5.

ROGERS, E. M. (1962), *Diffusion of Innovation*, Free Press.

RUSSETT, B. M., *et al.* (1964), *World Handbook of Political and Social Indicators*, Yale University Press, pp. 322–40.

SIMON, H. A. (1964), 'Comment: firm size and rate of growth', *J. polit. Econ.*, vol. 72, February, p. 81.

SIMON, H. A. (1967), 'The changing theory and changing practice of public administration', in I. de Sola Pool (ed.), *Contemporary Political Science: Toward Empirical Theory*, McGraw-Hill, pp. 86–120.

STEINER, G. A. (ed.) (1965), *The Creative Organization*, Chicago University Press, pp. 16–18.

THOMPSON, V. A. (1965), 'Bureaucracy and innovation', *Admin. Sci. Q.*, vol. 10, June, pp. 2, 12.

WILSON, J. Q. (1966), 'Innovation in organization: notes toward a theory', in J. D. Thompson (ed.), *Approaches to Organizational Design*, Pittsburgh University Press, p. 196.

WILSON, J. Q., and BANFIELD, E. C. (1964), 'Public-regardingness as a value premise in voting behavior', *Amer. polit. Sci. Rev.*, vol. 58, December, pp. 876–87.

ZALD, M. N., and DENTON, P. (1963), 'From evangelism to general service: the transformation of the YMCA', *Admin. Sci. Q.*, vol. 8, no. 2, p. 234.

Part Four Models of Growth

Models constructed to explain the size-distribution of firms have emphasized the absence of an observed correlation between size and percentage growth. The noncorrelation takes the force out of some long-standing arguments about returns to scale, but it provides no substitute hypotheses concerning the variables which do correlate with growth. 'A model of business firm growth' starts with the premise that individual firms may deviate from industry-wide patterns, and then asks how long such deviations generally last.

'Organizational metamorphosis' attempts to assess the effectiveness of metamorphosis models of organizational development. Smooth, evolutionary change accounts for 60 to 80 per cent of the nonlinear variance in output over time – leaving 20 to 40 per cent of the variance as attributable to metamorphoses, oscillations or random events. On the whole, metamorphic explanations of the nonevolutionary variance are more effective than oscillatory explanations are, but successful metamorphosis models will have to place more emphasis on forces external to the organization than existing models do.

Very seriously considered for inclusion in this section was 'Returns to scale and the optimal growth of firms' by Robert Lucas. It develops a theory of growth which is consistent both with rational economic management and with constant returns to scale. However, the paper assumes a level of mathematical expertise with which few organization theorists would feel comfortable.

6 Y. Ijiri and H. A. Simon

A Model of Business Firm Growth

Y. Ijiri and H. A. Simon, 'A model of business firm growth',
Econometrica, vol. 35, no. 2, 1967, pp. 348–55.

A number of stochastic models, embodying various forms of
Gibrat's law of proportionate effect, have been shown to generate
skew distribution functions resembling the actual size distributions of business firms (see Simon and Bonini, 1958). In a
previous paper (Ijiri and Simon, 1964) we presented some results
of the simulation of such a model permitting serial correlations
over time in the size changes of individual firms. The aim of the
present paper is to carry further the analysis of autocorrelated
growth, by proposing an economically meaningful scheme for its
analysis and applying the scheme to some data on large American
firms.

In studying business firm growth, we often encounter cases
where a firm suddenly acquires an impetus for growth. Perhaps
by innovating in production or marketing processes, or perhaps
as an effect of new management staffs or techniques, the firm
grows much more rapidly than the other firms in the industry, as
measured, say, by the ratio of the current firm size to its size in
the previous time period. Thus, we may observe that, while most
of the firms in the industry are growing at, say, 5 per cent a year,
some firms grow at 10 per cent.

Furthermore, a firm that grew 10 per cent last year is likely to
grow more rapidly than average again this year as a result of the
carry-over effects of an innovation that occurred in a previous
year on operations in subsequent periods. This carry-over
becomes more and more likely as we shorten the length of the
time period we are considering from a year to a month, week or
day. Moreover, on the average, a firm which grew rapidly in one
year subsequently retains a greater share of the industry assets –
or market share if sales are used as a measure of firm size – from

that time on than do firms that have enjoyed only the average industry growth. Therefore, not only the growth rate over and above the average growth rate, but also the period when the extra growth took place are important factors in the individual firm's growth relative to the industry growth.

In this paper, we develop a model to represent such characteristics of firms' growth, so that the process may be analysed further. In the final section we estimate the key parameter of the model for the recent growth of large American business firms.

The growth model

Let us represent by S_{it} the size of the ith firm at the end of the tth period. The size may be measured by the total assets of the firm or by its sales volume. We shall assume that there are N firms in the industry. For convenience, we shall consider a single industry, but will show later that the analysis may be applied to the economy of a given country as a whole.

Consider the relation that defines size ratios, r_{it}:

$$S_{it} = r_{it} S_{i(t-1)} \quad (t = 1, 2, \ldots, T). \qquad 1$$

Hence, the quantity r_{it} may be called the growth ratio of the ith firm in the tth period. Let us decompose r_{it} into two factors: one, a growth factor applicable to the ith firm only (the individual growth factor), ρ_{it}, and the other, a growth factor that affects equally all firms in the industry (the industry growth factor), $\bar{\rho}_t$. Then we decompose r_{it} into ρ_{it} and $\bar{\rho}_t$ by the definitional equation:

$$r_{it} = \rho_{it} \cdot \bar{\rho}_t \quad (t = 1, 2, \ldots, T). \qquad 2$$

Hence $\quad S_{it} = \rho_{it} \cdot \bar{\rho}_t S_{i(t-1)} \quad (t = 1, 2, \ldots, T). \qquad 3$

Equations 2 and 3 are merely definitions of the growth rate factors. The industry growth ratio $\bar{\rho}$, affects the size of all firms in the industry equally and the individual growth factor, ρ_{it}, is the residual of the ith firm's growth that has taken place in the tth period over and above the industry growth factor.

Equation 2 defines only the product of the industry growth factor, $\bar{\rho}_t$ and the individual growth factor, ρ_{it}; this product can be decomposed into its factors in any way that seems theoretically or statistically convenient. From the standpoint of the theoretical model, the individual growth factors should be defined so as to be statistically independent of the industry growth ratio. From a practical, statistical standpoint, however, it is satisfactory to identify the industry growth ratio with the quantity $\bar{\rho}_t = \Sigma_i S_{it}/\Sigma_i S_{i(t-1)}$, that is, with the ratio of the size of the industry in the current period to its size in the previous period. Then $\bar{\rho}_{it}$ is a measure of the change in the ith firm's share of market in the industry (using sales volume to measure size); so that if $\rho_{it} = 1$, the ith firm has grown just rapidly enough to retain its share of market. With this definition, the statistical dependence of the average growth ratio on any individual growth factor will be too slight to bias significantly the estimates of parameters of the model, provided, of course, that the number of firms is relatively large.

From 3 we have

$$S_{it} = \left(\prod_{\tau=1}^{t} \rho_{i\tau} \right) \left(\prod_{\tau=1}^{t} \bar{\rho}_\tau \right) S_{i0}. \qquad 4$$

That is,

$$\log S_{it} = \sum_{\tau=1}^{t} \log \rho_{i\tau} + \sum_{\tau=1}^{t} \log \bar{\rho}_\tau + \log S_{i0}. \qquad 5$$

By means of definitions, we have attained, in equations 4 and 5 a decomposition of the size of the ith firm into a product of factors accounting for its growth. The first set of factors in the product reflects idiosyncratic events that distinguish this firm's history from the histories of other firms in the industry. The second set of factors determines the industry's growth. The final factor is the initial size of the firm.

Suppose that S_{i0} is given and $\bar{\rho}_\tau$, the industry growth ratio is also given for all $\tau = 1, 2, \ldots, t$. Then the only remaining factor in determining S_{it} is

$$\prod_{\tau=1}^{t} \rho_{i\tau}.$$

We now assume that the quantities ρ_{it} satisfy the following hypothesis.

Hypothesis. The individual growth ratio ρ_{it} of the ith firm in the tth period is the product of some power of the growth ratio

$\rho_{i(t-1)}$ of the same firm in the $(t-1)$st period and a random factor ε_{it}, which is distributed independently and identically for every firm and for every t, i.e.

$$\rho_{it} = \varepsilon_{it}\rho_{i(t-1)}^{\alpha}, \qquad\qquad 6$$

where α is a constant, and

$$\rho_{i1} = \varepsilon_{i1}. \qquad\qquad 7$$

Notice that this hypothesis takes into account the following facts that we often observe in the analysis of firm growth.

1. The expected value of the individual growth ratio is independent of the firm's size (Gibrat's law).

2. The individual growth ratio in one period is related to the individual growth ratio in the previous period (a single-period Markov process).

3. The individual growth ratio of a firm is determined independently from that of other firms. That is, factors that affect more than one firm are considered to be absorbed in the industry growth ratio $\bar{\rho}_t$.

4. With α in the range $0 \leqslant \alpha < 1$, an individual growth ratio in one period will have decaying effects on the ratios in subsequent periods. That is, a firm that grew more than (or less than) the industry growth rate in the previous period, namely $\rho_{i(t-1)} > 1$ (or $\rho_{i(t-1)} < 1$), on the average tends to grow more than (or less than) the industry growth rate in the current period but at a rate closer, on the average, to the industry growth rate than in the previous period, namely $|\rho_{it}-1| < |\rho_{i(t-1)}-1|$.

Under our hypothesis we can develop the model as below. From 6 and 7, we have

$$\log \rho_{it} = \log \varepsilon_{it} + \alpha \log \rho_{i(t-1)} \qquad\qquad 8$$

$$= \sum_{\tau=1}^{t} \alpha^{(t-\tau)} \log \varepsilon_{i\tau}.$$

Hence
$$\sum_{t=1}^{T} \log \rho_{it} = \sum_{t=1}^{T} \sum_{\tau=1}^{T} a^{(t-\tau)} \log \varepsilon_{it} \qquad \textbf{9}$$
$$= (1+a+a^2+ \ldots +a^{T-1}) \log \varepsilon_{i1} +$$
$$+ (1+a+\ldots+a^{T-2}) \log \varepsilon_{i2} + \ldots +$$
$$+ (1+a+\ldots+a^{T-k}) \log \varepsilon_{ik} + \ldots + \log \varepsilon_{iT}$$
$$= \sum_{t=1}^{T} \frac{1-a^{T-t+1}}{1-a} \log \varepsilon_{it}.$$

Thus, from 5 and 9,
$$\log S_{it} = \sum_{\tau=1}^{t} \frac{1-a^{(t-\tau+1)}}{1-a} \log \varepsilon_{i\tau} + \sum_{\tau=1}^{t} \log \bar{\rho}_\tau + \log S_{i0}. \qquad \textbf{10}$$

We may remark that in the special case where $\log \varepsilon_i$ is normally distributed with mean zero and variance σ^2, ε_i has a log normal distribution with mean 1. Let

$$x_{it} = \sum_{\tau=1}^{t} \frac{1-a^{(t-\tau+1)}}{1-a} \log \varepsilon_{i\tau}. \qquad \textbf{11}$$

Clearly, x_{it} is normally distributed, since it is a weighted sum of independent random variables, each of which is normally distributed. In what follows, however, we assume independence of the $\log \varepsilon_{it}$'s, but we do not assume normality. Since the mean of $\log \varepsilon_i$ is zero, the mean of x_{it}, denoted by Ex_{it}, is also zero, for

$$Ex_{it} = E\left(\sum_{\tau=1}^{t} \frac{1-a^{(t-\tau+1)}}{1-a} \log \varepsilon_{i\tau} \right) \qquad \textbf{12}$$
$$= \sum_{\tau=1}^{t} \frac{1-a^{(t-\tau+1)}}{1-a} E \log \varepsilon_{i\tau} = 0.$$

On the other hand, the variance of x_{it}, denoted by Dx_{it}, is given by

$$Dx_{it} = D\left(\sum_{\tau=1}^{t} \frac{1-a^{(t-\tau+1)}}{1-a} \log \varepsilon_{i\tau} \right) \qquad \textbf{13}$$
$$= \sum_{\tau=1}^{t} \left(\frac{1-a^{(t-\tau+1)}}{1-a} \right)^2 D \log \varepsilon_{i\tau}$$
$$= \frac{\sigma^2}{(1-a)^2} \sum_{\tau=1}^{t} [1-2a^{(t-\tau+1)}+a^{2(t-\tau+1)}]$$
$$= \frac{\sigma^2}{(1-a)^2} \left(t - 2a\frac{1-a^t}{1-a} + a^2\frac{1-a^{2t}}{1-a^2} \right).$$

Note that $\operatorname*{Lim}_{t \to \infty} Dx_{it} = \infty$

and that for $0 \leqslant a < 1$

$$Dx_{it} > D\left(\sum_{\tau=1}^{t} \log \varepsilon_{i\tau}\right)$$ 15

with the equality sign holding if and only if $a = 0$ or $t = 1$, since

$$\frac{1 - a^{(t-\tau+1)}}{1-a} > 1 \quad \text{for all} \quad 1 \leqslant \tau < t, 0 < a < 1, t > 1.$$ 16

Now let us return to equation 10 for $\log S_{it}$. If the second and the third terms in the right-hand side of the equality are assumed to be determinate, the distribution function of $\log S_{it}$ is completely determined by the distribution function of x_{it}, except the position of the mean. Therefore, as t increases the probability density function for $\log S_{it}$ becomes flatter and flatter, the distribution function approaching asymptotically:

$$F(x) = \tfrac{1}{2}.$$ 17

On the other hand, we have

$$\begin{aligned} D(\log \rho_{it}) &= D(\log \varepsilon_{it} + a \log \varepsilon_{i(t-1)} + \ldots + a^{t-1} \log \varepsilon_{i1}) \quad 18 \\ &= D \log \varepsilon_{it} + a^2 D \log \varepsilon_{i(t-1)} + \ldots a^{2t-2} D \log \varepsilon_{i1} \\ &= (1 + a^2 + \ldots a^{2t-2})\sigma^2. \end{aligned}$$

Thus $\operatorname*{Lim}_{t \to \infty} D(\log \rho_{it}) = \dfrac{\sigma^2}{(1-a^2)}.$ 19

The multiplier

We can compare the limit of the variance of $\log \rho_{it}$ just derived with the variance of the unweighted average, over time, of the ε's. Let us call the latter average y_{it}, defined by:

$$y_{it} = \frac{1}{t} \sum_{\tau=1}^{t} \log \varepsilon_{i\tau}.$$ 20

Because of the independence of the ε_{it}, we have immediately:

$$Dy_{it} = \sigma^2.$$ 21

Thus α operates as a multiplier on the $\log \varepsilon_{it}$, increasing the resulting variance in the growth ratios from σ^2 to $\sigma^2/(1-\alpha^2)$.

The empirical meaning of α may be seen in the following manner. For simplicity, assume that

$$\log \bar{\rho}_\tau = c \quad \text{for all} \quad \tau = 1, 2, \ldots, t-1, t, t+1, \ldots \qquad 22$$

where c is a constant and

$$\log \varepsilon_{i\tau} = 0 \quad \text{for all} \quad \tau = 1, 2, \ldots, t-1. \qquad 23$$

Then $\log S_{i\tau}$ is given by

$$\log S_{i\tau} = c\tau + \log S_{i0} \quad \text{for} \quad \tau = 1, 2, \ldots, t-1. \qquad 24$$

Suppose that $\log \varepsilon_{it} \neq 0$, while $\log \varepsilon_{i\tau} = 0$ for $\tau = 1, \ldots, t-1$, and that α is equal to zero. Then the effect of $\log \rho_{it}$ is to make a parallel shift of the time path for $\log S_{i\tau}$ by the quantity $\log \varepsilon_{it}$ (see Figure 1).

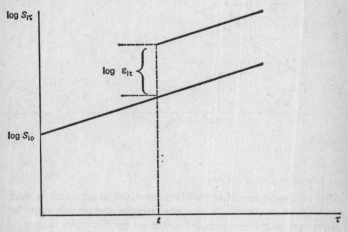

Figure 1

When $\alpha = 0$, there is no carry-over effect on the growth in the subsequent periods, hence the line after the shift will be parallel to the original one if the subsequent terms $\log \varepsilon_{i\tau}$ for $\tau > t$, are all zero.

Next consider the case where $0 < a < 1$ and $\log \varepsilon_{i\tau} = 0$ for all τ except $\tau = t$. Then the time path of $\log S_{it}$ is shifted by the quantity $\log \varepsilon_{it}$ at the period t. It is shifted again in the period $t+1$ by the quantity $a \log \varepsilon_{it}$; in the period $t+2$ by the quantity $a^2 \log \varepsilon_{it}$, and so on. The actual growth curve, then, approaches asymptotically (Figure 2):

$$\log S_{it} = c\tau + \log S_{i0} + \frac{1}{1-a} \log \varepsilon_{it}. \qquad \mathbf{25}$$

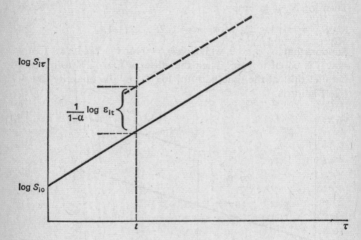

Figure 2

A two-level generalization

The stochastic model is readily generalized to admit more than two causes of change in size. For example, the growth ratio for each firm might be expressed as the product of three factors: a ratio for the economy as a whole, a factor describing the growth of the firm's industry relative to the economy as a whole, and a factor expressing the growth of the individual firm relative to its industry. Then equation **2** would be replaced by:

$$r_{ijt} = \rho_{ijt} \cdot \rho_{jt} \cdot \bar{\rho}_t \quad (t = 1, 2, \ldots, T), \qquad \mathbf{2'}$$

where $\bar{\rho}_t$ is the average rate for the economy, ρ_{jt} the growth factor associated with the jth industry, and ρ_{ijt} the factor associated with the ith firm in the jth industry.

Alternatively, we can combine the first two factors in 2′, arriving again at a product of two factors, the first of which reflects the joint effect of the idiosyncratic growth of the firm's industry relative to the economy and of the individual firm relative to the industry. In the next section we shall use this latter interpretation, formally identical with the original model of equation 2, to analyse some growth rates in the American economy.

Growth of large American firms

To illustrate the application of the model, we have estimated α for the recent growth of large American firms. The data are the sales of the ninety-six largest American firms, obtained from the *Fortune* tabulation,[1] for the years 1954, 1958, and 1962. A four-year time interval was used so that the middle-run growth trends of individual firms would not be swamped by short-run business cycle fluctuations. Defining, as above, $\bar{\rho}_t = \Sigma_i S_{it}/\Sigma_i S_{i(t-1)}$, the economy growth ratio was found to be 1·27 both for the four-year period 1954–8 and for the four-year period 1958–62. (This corresponds to a growth rate of about 6 per cent per annum.) These quantities, inserted in equation 3, provided estimates for the ρ_{it} for the same two time intervals (call them ρ_{i1} and ρ_{i2}, respectively). Inserting the logarithms of these growth factors in equation 8, the method of least squares was used to estimate α. The regression equation is:

$$\log \rho_{i2} = 0{\cdot}35 \log \rho_{i1} - 0{\cdot}00034, \quad \text{or} \quad \alpha = 0{\cdot}35. \qquad 26$$

Thus α, the factor measuring the degree of persistence of sudden growth, was slightly greater than one-third for large American firms over a four-year period. A firm that experienced an unusually rapid growth in the first four-year period could expect a

1. Data for four of the 100 largest firms in 1962 were not usable, because the data were not available for all three years, or because large-scale mergers had made the data entirely non-comparable. The smaller non-comparabilities from year to year that undoubtedly exist for some of the remaining firms were simply ignored.

greater than average growth in the second four-year period. But the logarithm of the ratio measuring the excess would be, on the average, only one-third as large during the second period as during the first. Thus, a firm that doubled its share of market (i.e. of the total economy) in the first four years ($\rho_{i1} = 2$), could be expected, on the average, to increase its share of market by about 28 per cent in the second four-year period [for log ($1 \cdot 28$) $\sim$ $0 \cdot 105 = 0 \cdot 35$ (log 2)]. Rapidly growing firms 'regress' relatively rapidly to the average growth rate of the economy.

The same point may also be stated using equation 25. Since for these data, $1/(1-a) = 1 \cdot 54$, a firm that experienced a 'windfall' growth of magnitude log ε_{it} during the first four-year period could expect a total effect of this 'windfall' upon log S_{it} of $1 \cdot 54$ log ε_{it} before its growth rate returned again to the average for the economy.

Since our data provide only two time intervals for comparison, they do not allow us to test the assumption that the log ε_{it} are distributed independently for all time periods.

Conclusion

In this paper we have proposed a model of business firm growth that decomposes the growth of a firm into an industry-wide component and a component peculiar to that firm. We have developed a Markov-process model for the individual component of growth, and have shown how to estimate the key parameter of the model, a parameter measuring the persistence of spurts in growth.

References

IJIRI, Y., and SIMON, H. A. (1964), 'Business firm growth and size', *Amer. econ. Rev.,* vol. 54, March, pp. 77–89.

SIMON, H. A., and BONINI, C. P. (1958), 'The size distribution of business firms', *Amer. econ. Rev.*, vol. 48, September, pp. 607–17.

7 W. H. Starbuck

Organizational Metamorphosis

William H. Starbuck, 'Organizational metamorphosis', in R. W. Millman and M. P. Hottenstein (eds.), *Promising Research Directions*, Academy of Management, 1968, pp. 113–22.

The problem

Structural metamorphosis has been a recurrent theme in writings on organizational growth and development. The basic proposition advanced is that change in organizational structure is occasionally punctuated by abrupt, major transformations which sharply distinguish one period of organizational history from another.

This paper reports briefly on an attempt to give operational definition to the notion of organizational metamorphosis.[1] An analytic procedure is outlined, and then time series data about ten business firms are analysed to assess the explanatory efficacy of metamorphoses for the firms' histories. Each firm's history is analysed separately as if it were a single case study, but all ten firms are treated analogously as if the case study had been replicated ten times.

What metamorphosis models say

Metamorphosis models focus on structural changes which the model-builder judges to be dominant and critical. The history of an organization is divided into stages. Structural changes which occur within a given stage are de-emphasized as having lesser importance; structural changes which take place between two consecutive stages are emphasized as having greater importance. Consequently, the historical development within a single stage is cast as a relatively smooth and continuous process, but the overall development pattern is marked by sharp and discrete transitions from one stage to the next.

1. The research reported was supported by a grant from the McKinsey Foundation for Management Research.

Models proposed by Moore and Whyte illustrate the nature of such characterizations.[2] Moore wrote:

The evolution of strategies in a particular business proceeds in more or less well-defined stages. The first stage is the creation of the business activity itself .. someone or some small group of individuals possesses, develops, or stumbles on potential assets or resources which, when combined with certain other assets, provide the conditions favorable to the development of a business. . . .

The creative strategy of a business is frequently undeveloped and unbalanced in its initial form. It tends to emphasize the special interests, talents, possessions, behavior, and general orientation of the founding father. If the business is to survive in a competitive world, the original strategy must be consolidated. . . . If the first stage of a business requires a Promoter or Activity Generator, the next stage requires a Businessman or Consolidator. This is the stage when the business develops 'sound business practices'.

As the business grows and problems of adjustment increase, a new stage is reached – that of organization . . . the organization itself as a rationalization of means to ends becomes a strategic device for insuring an advantageous position in the socio-economic environment. This is the stage of the Manager, or Administrator (1959, pp. 220–22).

Whyte (1948) identified five stages in the expansion of a restaurant. In the first stage, the restaurant is small and informally organized. There is little division of labor, and relations among the owner, employees and customers are direct and personal. The second stage begins with the advent of work specialization, the owner assuming a supervisory role. Stage three is reached when the organization becomes a three-level hierarchy, with one supervisory level interposed between the owner and the first-line employees, and stage four is associated with the existence of a four-level hierarchy. The owner's relations with employees and customers become increasingly formal in the third and fourth stages, and his success depends upon his ability to manage through other managers. In the fifth stage, the single restaurant becomes a chain of restaurants, and the owner's efforts are aimed at standardizing prices, food and service across branches of the chain.

2. The models discussed in this section are reviewed somewhat more thoroughly in Starbuck (1965) [Reading 1 of this selection].

Other metamorphosis models have been proposed by Fayol (1949), Newman and Logan (1955), Marshall (1920), Perrow (1961), Herbst (1957), Starbuck (1966) [Reading 2 of this selection], Filley (1963) and Tsouderos (1955). A few of these models seem little more than heuristic classification schemes. But all of the models argue that an organization's history can be factored into nonarbitrary segments, just as a flight of stairs can be factored into separate steps.

Consider a flight of stairs. The treads define a sequence of horizontal planes which are separated by vertical planes, the risers. A point moving across the surface of a tread passes through a series of positions having the same height. Suddenly the point's height changes a great deal when it traverses a riser. Then a new tread is reached, and a new series of constant heights begins. There is no doubt the point's motion is exactly the kind of dynamic process which metamorphosis models are designed to represent. Motion across a tread generates a period of stable height; motion across a riser generates a dramatic change in height.

Observation of the moving point produces a time-series of heights, and a normal first step in time-series analyses is the elimination of long-run trend. Suppose the flight of stairs is transformed to eliminate trend. The bottom step is lifted to the height of the top step, and any general curvature is removed. Now neither treads nor risers appear either horizontal or vertical; they look like saw-tooth corrugations. The moving point falls gradually, rises gradually, falls gradually, rises gradually, falls, rises, falls. . . . The point's path is unquestionably an oscillation.

Thus, what one observer might call metamorphosis, another observer might call oscillation.[3] The two notions are not entirely separable. In the behavior of an oscillating system, periods of type A alternate with periods of type B; in the behavior of a

3. Tsouderos (1955) found that membership was the leading variable in the expansion and contraction of voluntary organizations. Income, expense and property followed time-paths like that of membership, but there was a time-lag between changes in membership and the corresponding changes in financial variables. Tsouderos observed that during the interval when membership had begun to decline and the financial variables were still increasing, the latter rose cyclically.

metamorphosing system, periods of relative stability alternate with periods of fast-change. Yet metamorphosis must be separated from oscillation. The rationales behind the two kinds of models are almost antithetical.

An oscillatory model argues that behavior is consistent and repetitious. Cycles which occur once are expected to occur more than once, and each manifestation of a cycle is expected to conform to the common pattern. The basic explanatory focus is on processes which mold behavior into persistent forms. Metamorphosis models, on the other hand, argue that behavior is irregular and nonrepetitive. Each developmental stage is expected to be unique, and metamorphoses are expected to occur at varying intervals. Causal explanation must alternate between processes which prevent change and processes which disrupt stability.

The fundamental characteristics of oscillatory and metamorphic models suggest some guidelines for classifying observed time-series. A time-series described as oscillatory should include several cycles, and each cycle should strongly resemble the rest. A time-series classified as metamorphic should divide into just a few, clearly defined stages, and the stages should be sufficiently unlike each other to testify to significant changes during metamorphosis. In terms of the analogy to a flight of stairs, an oscillatory model will be most efficient and plausible when the flight is composed of many small and identical steps; a metamorphosis model will be most efficient and plausible when the flight is composed of a few large steps each of which has its own shape.

The next section presents one strategy we have pursued in determining whether an organization's history looks like a flight of stairs, and whether the steps are more metamorphic than oscillatory.

An analytic technique

Because the notion of metamorphosis is a broad one, the first question to answer is: what kinds of metamorphoses are worth looking for? All kinds of variables could undergo rapid and drastic transitions. But most of these variables are not central to the interests of organization theorists, and to demonstrate that irrelevant variables change rapidly on occasion would evoke no interest at all.

In the present study, the available data concern manufacturing firms. The firms perform a variety of social functions, but nearly all of these social functions are related in a direct, monotonic fashion to the production of physical products. As a first approximation, it makes sense to treat the production of physical output as the firms' most basic social function, and to measure the importance of metamorphoses in terms of their effects on output. Metamorphoses which do not change output will be ignored, and metamorphoses which do change output will be attended to. It must also be decided how to describe organizational structures. The raw data, which were collected by Mason Haire, are very complete and detailed. People are identified by their hierarchical ranks and by the kinds of work they do. Each organization could be described in terms of a large number of variables.

The author resolved this dilemma by specifying six descriptive variables, each of which states the number of employees of a given type. The first five variables constitute a mutually exclusive partitioning of all employees in the firm. *Production* employees are defined as the workers on the shop floor and their foremen. *Sales* employees are defined as those who communicate with customers or potential custmers in a way which might influence purchase decisions. *Control* employees are those specializing in performance evaluation, e.g. general managers, industrial engineers and accountants. *Research* employees include those engaged in product or market research. All remaining personnel are classified as *service* employees. The sixth employment category is *management*; it overlaps all of the other five categories, intersecting most weakly with service and most strongly with control.

Table 1 gives rough descriptions of the ten firms studied, the number of successive observations of each firm, and the average proportions of employees in each of the six categories.

The focus of study has now become a relation of the form

$$Q = \pi(x_1, x_2, x_3, x_4, x_5, x_6, t) \qquad\qquad 1$$

where Q represents output, x_1 to x_6 represent the numbers of employees in the six categories, and t is time. The function π is a kind of production function. It shows the output produced with alternative combinations of inputs, but the only inputs considered

Table 1 The Firms Studied

Code name of firm	Product	Market area on last data date	Firm's age on		Total employment on		Number of employment observations	Proportion of total employment classified as					
			First data date	Last data date	First data date	Last data date		Production	Sales	Control	Research	Service	Management
Addie	Various forms of one staple food	National	30	69	30	240	40	0·32	0·41	0·12	0·00	0·15	0·11
Beata	Newspapers and books	Regional	17	59	55	178	43	0·66	0·13	0·08	0·00	0·13	0·10
Carla	Prepared foods	Regional	1	45	1	395	38	0·66	0·20	0·02	0·00	0·12	0·07
Daisy	Industrial capital goods	National	1	38	3	177	38	0·52	0·17	0·13	0·02	0·17	0·19
Edith	Decorating materials	National	0·5	31·5	8	217	29	0·53	0·06	0·09	0·13	0·19	0·14
Faith	Women's clothing	Regional	1	19	14	963	19	0·81	0·10	0·04	0·01	0·04	0·04
Gilda	Electronic equipment	National	1	15	20	2653	27	0·46	0·11	0·22	0·09	0·12	0·24
Hazel	Aircraft	National	1	14·5	18	1000·5	15	0·36	0·08	0·26	0·22	0·08	0·12
Irene	Electrical building materials	National	0·5	13	8	288	18	0·76	0·08	0·08	0·01	0·07	0·08
Janet	Structural products of metal and plastic	National	1	12	4	383	17	0·53	0·10	0·20	0·05	0·07	0·08
							Means:	0·56	0·14	0·12	0·05	0·12	0·12

are the different numbers of employees. Raw materials and physical plant and equipment are not explicitly included.

Equation 1 is too general to be of any use. Previous analyses of data from these firms successfully employed production functions which were linear in the logarithms of the variables (Starbuck, 1965). Therefore, equation 1 is stated in a form appropriate to logarithmic variables:

$$\frac{1}{Q}\frac{dQ}{dt} = \frac{1}{Q}\frac{\partial Q}{\partial t} + w_1\frac{1}{x_1}\frac{dx_1}{dt} + w_2\frac{1}{x_2}\frac{dx_2}{dt} + \ldots + w_6\frac{1}{x_6}\frac{dx_6}{dt} \qquad 2$$

where $w_i = \frac{x_i}{Q}\frac{\partial Q}{\partial x_i}$.

We take equation 2 as a basic description of the relation between organization structure and output, and we analyse the changes in this relation over the life of the firm.

Somewhat idealistically perhaps, we attempt to separate all changes into one of four categories:

1. Changes consistent with a long-run pattern of development that ignores structural shifts.

2. Changes resembling cyclical deviations from the long-run pattern.

3. Changes resembling metamorphic deviations from the long-run pattern.

4. Changes resembling random deviations from the long-run pattern – due to errors in the measurement of variables, unanticipated exogenous shocks, short-run trial-and-error learning, and the like.

The long-run pattern is defined on the basis of equation 2. Actual changes are divided into the portion consistent with the long-run pattern and the portion which is deviant. Then the autocorrelations within the deviant portion are examined for evidence of randomness or cyclic nonrandomness.

This analytic process is directly analogous to the flight of stairs example discussed in the preceding section, and the decomposition of change into long-run and short-run patterns is analogous to transformation of the stairs to eliminate trend. The flight of stairs was transformed by lifting every step to the same height, without altering the relative sizes or shapes of the individual steps. In the case of organizations, the long-run pattern of development must be defined in a way which puts high output levels into correspondence with low output levels, without altering the relative sizes or shapes of deviations from the trend. The flight of stairs transformation was ripple-free in the sense that the trend cut smoothly through all of the steps, and the organizational transformation must be ripple-free in the sense that the long-run pattern cuts smoothly through all of the shifts in organizational structure.

What do these requirements imply in the context of equation 2? There are seven things to look at – the six w's and the term $\frac{1}{Q}\frac{\partial Q}{\partial t}$ – and structural change could be associated with any of the seven. Suppose, however, that all seven are constant over time:

$$\frac{1}{Q}\frac{\partial Q}{\partial t} = K_{01} \quad \text{and} \quad w_i = K_i.$$

Equation 2 becomes:

$$\frac{1}{Q^*}\frac{dQ^*}{dt} = K_{01}+K_1\frac{1}{x_1}\frac{dx_1}{dt}+K_2\frac{1}{x_2}\frac{dx_2}{dt}+\ldots+K_6\frac{1}{x_6}\frac{dx_6}{dt}, \qquad 3$$

and integration with respect to t gives:

$$\log Q^* = K_{00}+K_{01}\,t+K_1\log x_1+K_2\log x_2+\ldots+K_6\log x_6 \qquad 4$$

where K_{00} is an undefined constant.

Q^* is a long-run pattern of the sort needed. Consider the right-hand side of equation 4 as the sum of a function of t and a function of the x's:

$$\log Q^* = \log Q^*_t+\log Q^*_x$$
$$\log Q^*_t = K_{00}+K_{01}t$$
$$\log Q^*_x = K_1\log x_1+K_2\log x_2+\ldots+K_6\log x_6.$$

Q^*_t represents the output obtained over time from a set of 'equivalent' organizational structures, and Q^*_x defines the equivalence class to which a particular organizational structure belongs. All structures having the same value of Q^*_x are grouped together on the premise that they fall on the same long-run trend curve, just as, say, all points of transition from a riser to a tread would be grouped together in describing the trend of a flight of stairs. And all of the trend curves are assumed to be parallel straight lines in log Q, just as, say, the trend line through the riser-tread transitions would be parallel to the trend line through the tread-riser transitions. That is,

$$\log Q^* = \text{constant} + K_{01}t$$

where K_{01} has the same value for every equivalence class and the constant is unique to each equivalence class.

Confronted with actual time-series data on one of the ten firms, the initial step is to estimate the K's. Then Q^* is computed and compared with the observed Q. The question is whether the deviations ($\log Q - \log Q^*$) represent (a) cyclical deviations, (b) random deviations, or (c) metamorphic deviations.

As much as anything else, the question is answered by looking at a graph of the deviations over time and speculating about its properties. However, there is a second graph which can be used to augment the first: a correlogram.[4] The vertical axis of the correlogram represents the estimated correlation between two deviations which are separated by a given time-lag, and the horizontal axis represents the various possible time-lags, beginning with zero and increasing as far as the data will permit. Thus, the first point on the correlogram is the estimated correlation between deviations separated by a lag of zero; since this is correlation of a variable with itself, the estimate is always unity. The second point is the estimated correlation between deviations separated by a time-lag of six months; the third point is the correlation between deviations separated by a year; the fourth point, eighteen months; and so on. The correlogram ends when the time-lag equals the overall length of the time-series, although the sample sizes become quite small long before the end is reached, and the last few correlation estimates are very unreliable.

Figure 1 gives some standards of comparison for correlograms. The graphs assume that infinitely large samples are available. Actual correlograms based on sample sizes in the hundreds

4. See also Wold (1954 and 1965).

usually differ erratically from the prototypes. The time-series in this study are very short indeed; the longest includes only forty-three observations. So there is every reason to expect ambiguity.

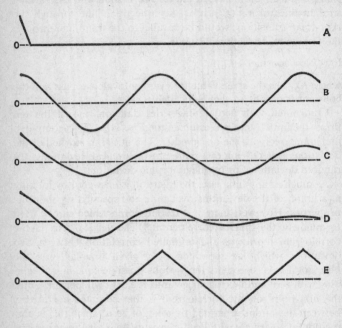

A. A purely random series
B. A purely sinusoidal series
C. A sinusoidal series in which the oscillations account for about half of the variance
D. A sinusoidal series in which the oscillation is produced by imperfect feedback
E. A pure saw-tooth series

Figure 1 Correlogram patterns associated with random and oscillatory series – assuming infinite sample sizes

Development in ten firms

Does one need the notion of metamorphosis at all? Possibly Q^* is such an accurate approximation to Q that elaborate analyses of the deviations between Q^* and Q would add little information. Table 2 gives the correlations between Q^* and Q.

Table 2 The Correlations between Log Q^* and Log Q

Firm	Correlation subject to the usual null hypothesis that log Q is constant over time	Correlation subject to the null hypothesis that log Q changes linearly with time	Sample size
Addie	0·985	0·896	40
Beata	0·989	0·777	43
Carla	0·993	0·853	38
Daisy	0·986	0·769	38
Edith	0·994	0·795	29
Faith	0·999	0·996	19
Gilda	0·996	0·832	27
Hazel	0·997	0·973	15
Irene	0·999	0·990	18
Janet	0·997	0·951	17

At first glance, it would appear that there is indeed some reason to doubt the need for a more elaborate theory than equation 4. The smallest correlation between log Q and log Q^* is 0·985, a figure which leaves only 3 per cent of the variance in log Q 'unexplained'. However, the usual correlation coefficient is more than a little misleading. It assumes the null hypothesis 'log Q constant'. Not in our most fanciful state of mind would we conjecture that the output of a firm is constant over time.

At the very least, log Q should change linearly with time. Correlations based on the null hypothesis of linear temporal change are also given in Table 2, and they suggest that there is room for improvement. High correlations occur only where the sample size is small – for example, the data on firm Hazel allow just seven degrees of freedom.

Figures 2 through 11 show the nature of the deviations between Q^* and Q for the ten firms. The top graph in each figure gives the actual output (solid line) and corresponding hypothetical output (dashed line). The middle graph shows the deviation log $Q-$ log Q^*. The bottom graph shows the correlogram. In most cases, interviews with members of the organizations have turned up dates which they consider to be prominent events in the organizations' histories; these are noted at the bottom of each figure.

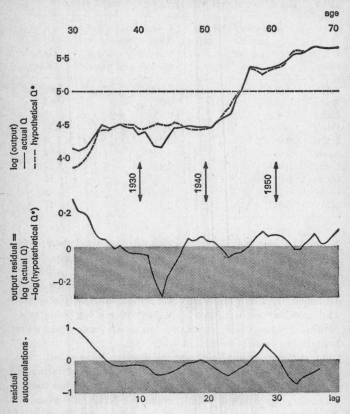

Figure 2 Addie

Within the span of history covered by these data, there have been three events of overwhelming historical significance: the First World War, the Depression, and the Second World War. It is both encouraging and reassuring to observe that the deviation patterns display plausible responses to these events. The data on three firms – Addie, Beata and Carla – span the First World War. All three firms were 'over-producing' during the war, actual output exceeding hypothetical output. Presumably

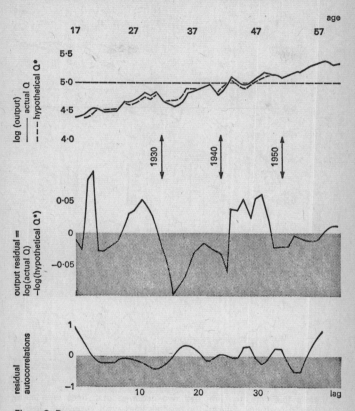

Figure 3 Beata

more workers were working overtime and their motivation was higher in the war years.

The data on five firms – Addie through Edith – span the Depression and the Second World War. All five firms were 'underproducing' during the Depression, hypothetical output exceeding actual output. Apparently workers were put on short hours or short wages, but relatively few employees were actually laid off. The only firm which reacted promptly and forcefully to the

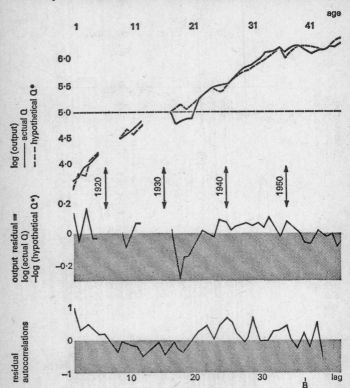

B. Before this date, the firm had two major product lines with many products in each line. One of the product lines was dropped at time B. Production employment decreased 26 per cent, but the other five employment categories remained near their former values.

Figure 4 Carla

Depression was Daisy, and the author cannot help wondering if Daisy's responsiveness is a consequence of the firm being a capital goods producer. Four of the five firms were 'over-producing' during the Second World War. The exception was Addie, which over-produced during 1941 and 1942, but then started under-producing.

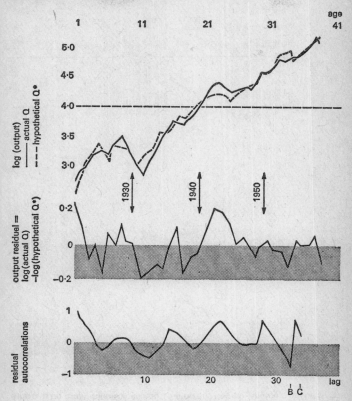

B. Incorporation date; operated as a partnership prior to this date.
C. Sold to another corporation and operated as a wholly-owned subsidiary after this date.

Figure 5 Daisy

Haire's interviewers identified various dates as being significant ones in the firm's histories. Unfortunately, these data were not collected systematically – interviews were not designed to elicit

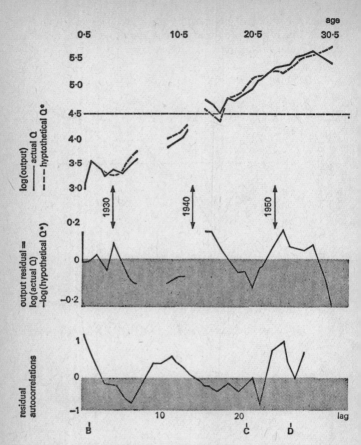

B. Became a wholly-owned subsidiary of a major retailing firm on this date. During the first twenty-one years, the retailer purchased 70 to 90 per cent of Edith's output, but Edith was autonomously managed by the founder.

C. The founder retired on this date, and was replaced by the former general manager, who had been with the firm for twenty years. Intensive efforts were begun to obtain orders from new customers, and the retailer's portion of Edith's output was reduced to about 50 per cent.

D. The president (former general manager) retired on this date, and was replaced by a man who had been a production supervisor for three years and then the general manager for two years.

Figure 6 Edith

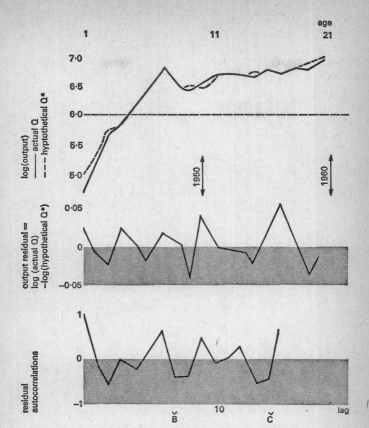

B. A period of major retrenchment in which dollar volume decreased 30 per cent and total employment decreased 47 per cent. There were numerous reassignments of personnel among the various departments.

C. A period of major organizational redesign during which the number of formally designated departments doubled.

Figure 7 Faith

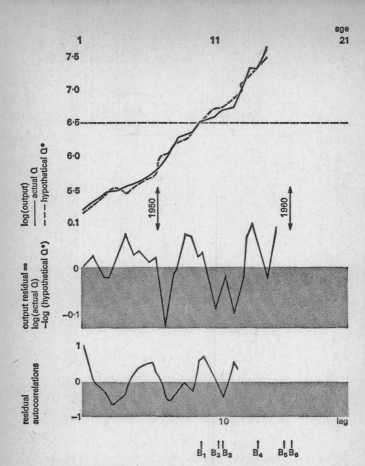

B. On date B_2, the firm initiated a series of organizational changes which shifted its structure from functional decentralization to product decentralization. B_1 is a reference date before the reorganization began; B_2 to B_6 are the dates of reorganization.

Structure after date	Number of functional divisions	Number of product divisions	Number of subsidiaries
B_1	7	0	1
B_2	2	2	0
B_3	4	2	0
B_4	4	2	2
B_5	4	3	2
B_6	2	5	0

Figure 8 Gilda

them and the interviewers did not generally write them down. However, we can compare these dates with the residuals graphs to see whether they seem to correspond with shifts in productivity.

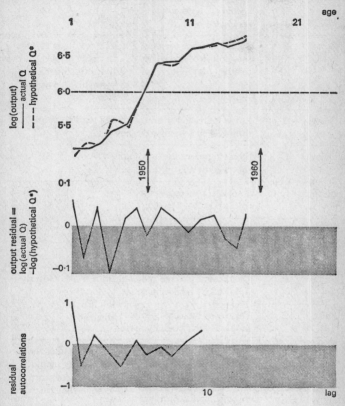

Figure 9 Hazel

The comparison is given in Table 3. Of the ten instances, seven or eight appear to have produced changes in productivity, but the evidence is far from conclusive. We have no way of tracing the causal relationships between the noted events and the presumed consequences, and we have no way of knowing what other events

Table 3 Possible Relations between Productivity Shifts and Significant Historical Dates

Firm	Date	Associated productivity changes (see graph of residuals)	Remarks
Carla	B	Small decrease for one year followed by a relatively large increase	The residuals include so many erratic shifts that it is difficult to view this one as significant
Daisy	B	Large increase for one year followed by a small increase	See remark above
Daisy	C	Small increases for two years followed by a large decrease	
Edith	C	Consistent increases for four years	
Edith	D	Insignificant shifts for two years followed by a large decrease	
Faith	B	Decreases for three years followed by a large increase	Both B and C were undertaken to make the firm more efficient
Faith	C	Decreases for three years followed by a small increase	
Gilda	B_2, B_3	Moderate increase, moderate decrease, then three successive increases	Gilda's management philosophy includes periodic reorganization to keep the structure flexible
Gilda	B_4	Two decreases followed by an increase	
Janet	B	One large decrease followed by several small shifts	

occurred but were not noted. All we can say is that we cannot reject the notion that causal relations were at work.

Looking at the residuals graphs *per se* leads one to conclude

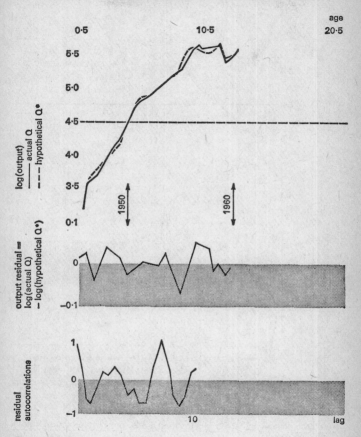

Figure 10 Irene

that the deviations are not random. Only Hazel's residuals can easily be cast as random events. However, Carla's and Janet's residuals include large non-systematic components, and Faith's residuals are so small and erratic that there is little advantage in trying to explain them.

The clearest instances of oscillatory behavior are Gilda and

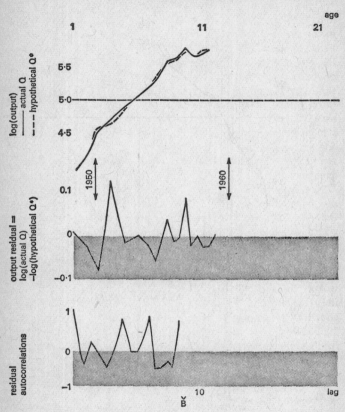

B. A large drop in military orders instigated a 26 per cent reduction in total employment.

Figure 11 Janet

Daisy. Gilda appears to initiate an efficiency drive every four years, producing rising efficiency for about two years and then falling efficiency for about two years. Interviews with the firm's managers confirm that the efficiency drive is basic in their philosophy, but they perceive each drive as an event with unique characteristics.

Daisy operates in a highly variable environment, and fundamental economic changes explain at least some of the variations in the residual series. However, the economic forces acting on Daisy are qualitatively equivalent to the forces acting on Addie, Beata, Carla and Edith. If exogenous effects were the only causes of change the periodicities of the five correlograms should be the same. Addie and Beata show periods of nine to ten years, Carla thirty years, Edith twelve years, and Daisy seven years. The significance of exogenous events is evidently moderated by the structural propensities of the firms themselves. Carla appears comparatively indifferent to exogeneous events, and Daisy appears to add cyclic variability to the variability inherent in its environment.

Not even in the cases of Gilda and Daisy, however, does an oscillatory theory offer clear advantages over a metamorphic theory. Gilda acknowledges its tendency to manage by feedback – efforts to increase efficiency when a state of under-production is diagnosed and relaxed management as a result of over-production – but the actors inside the firm perceive each cycle as distinct from the next, and the graphical similarity of successive cycles is weak. The most serious liability of an oscillatory theory is illustrated in the behavior of Addie. Addie's residuals graph shows two comparatively noise-free cycles between 1933 and 1955. The cycles could have been generated by a slowly-reacting feedback control system. But can we accept the implication that Addie's productivity in the 1950s was partly determined by the great Depression?

A tentative conclusion

On the basis of the analyses reported here, it appears that metamorphic theories are both meaningful and useful. A significant portion of the variation in structural–functional relationships cannot be explained in terms of smooth evolution, and the deviations of actual from evolutionary are clearly nonrandom in nine of the ten firms studied. An oscillatory explanation for the deviations accounts for a comparatively small portion of them, and it raises problematic issues about the persistent consequences of events which occurred in the distant past.

In contrast to most existing metamorphic theories, however, these data imply that forces external to the organization itself instigate and moderate many of the dominant structural changes. The history of a firm which went through the First World War, the Depression, and the Second World War cannot be understood if one is not conscious of the impact of these events on the firm's performance. The structural–functional changes which are significant in the histories of these ten firms appear to be the resultants of both the managerial strategies pursued and the externally determined problems to be solved.

References

FAYOL, H. (1949), *General and Industrial Management*, Pitman.

FILLEY, A. C. (1963), 'A Theory of Business Growth', unpublished manuscript, School of Commerce, University of Wisconsin.

HERBST, P. G. (1957), 'Measurement of behaviour structures by means of input–output data', *Hum. Relat.*, vol. 10, pp. 335–46.

MARSHALL, A. (1920), *Principles of Economics*, 8th edn, Macmillan.

MOORE, D. G. (1959), 'Managerial strategies', in W. L. Warner and N. H. Martin (eds.), *Industrial Man*, Harper, pp. 219–26.

NEWMAN, W. H., and LOGAN, J. P. (1955), *Management of Expanding Enterprises*, Columbia University Press.

PERROW, C. (1961), 'The analysis of goals in complex organizations', *Amer. sociol. Rev.*, vol. 26, pp. 854–66.

STARBUCK, W. H. (1965), 'Organizational growth and development', in J. G. March (ed.), *Handbook of Organizations*, Rand McNally, pp. 451–533 [see Reading 1 of this selection].

STARBUCK, W. H. (1966), 'The efficiency of British and American retail employees', *Admin. Sci. Q.*, vol. 11, pp. 345–85 [see Reading 2 of this selection].

TSOUDEROS, J. E. (1955), 'Organizational change in terms of a series of selected variables', *Amer. sociol. Rev.*, vol. 20, pp. 206–10.

WHYTE, W. F. (1948), *Human Relations in the Restaurant Industry*, McGraw-Hill.

WOLD, H. O. A. (1954), *A Study in the Analysis of Stationary Time Series*, Almqvist & Wiksell.

WOLD, H. O. A. (1965), 'A graphic introduction to stochastic processes', in H. O. A. Wold (ed.), *Bibliography on Time Series and Stochastic Processes*, Oliver & Boyd, pp. 7–76.

Part Five
Administrative Structure and Growth

'Effects of size, complexity, and ownership on administrative intensity' is a significant paper for at least two reasons. First, previous studies of administrative structure have tended to adopt the mechanistic view that structure results from technological rationality. Louis Pondy argues that structure is only partially determined by technology, and is also partially determined by managerial discretion; his analysis suggests that managerial motives have significant effects. Second, organization theorists have tended to base their statistical analyses on standardized nonparametric or linear models without attempting to show that the assumptions underlying these models are appropriate to the phenomena being studied, and they have tended to ignore the biases accompanying the use of surrogate variables. Pondy derives his analytic model from explicit and plausible assumptions, and he estimates the biases produced by using plant-size data in place of organization-size data.

'The context of organization structures' is one of an important series of related studies conducted by Derek Pugh, David Hickson, C. R. Hinings and their associates. The first article in the series, 'Dimensions of organization structure', showed that two-thirds of the observed variation among sixty-four structural variables could be summarized with three composite variables (factors). 'The context of organization structures' relates these three composite variables to contextual variables such as size, location and dependence upon a parent organization. A third article in the series, 'An empirical taxonomy of structures of work organizations', develops a classification scheme for organizational structures. And a fourth article, 'Operations technology and organization structure', traces relationships between organization structure and the technology on which the organization depends. Were there space, this fourth article would be reprinted here, for it shows that technological effects on structure are more pervasive in small organizations than in large ones.

8 L. R. Pondy

Effects of Size, Complexity and Ownership on
Administrative Intensity[1]

L. R. Pondy, 'Effects of size, complexity and ownership on
administrative intensity', *Administrative Science Quarterly*, vol. 14,
no. 1, 1969, pp. 47–61.

For a sample of forty-five manufacturing industries, the number
of administrative personnel per 100 production workers varies
from 8·7 for the logging industry to 131·1 for the drug industry,
with a mean of 37·7 and a standard deviation of 28·8. This is a
wide variation in an important structural characteristic of formal
organizations. A theory of organization structure ought to explain
why the relative size of the administrative component varies so
widely across organizations in different industries, and should
also have something to say about the *optimum* administrative
intensity for a given industry or organization, i.e. optimum in
terms of maximum efficiency or profit for a given level of operation. The purpose of this paper is to present such a theory as
applied to manufacturing firms and to report the results of testing
it against available census data.

Managerial discretion versus technological determinism

The central idea of the theory is that the number of administrative personnel employed in an organization is *chosen* so as to
maximize the achievement of goals of the dominant management
coalition. For example, for the classical owner-managed firm, it

1. A number of persons provided helpful comments and criticisms on an
early draft of this paper. The author wishes to express his thanks to John
O. Blackburn, Peter Clark, David G. Davies, Louis D. Volpp, and especially
to Louis DeAlessi, William H. Starbuck and Oliver E. Williamson.
Starbuck's comments were particularly helpful in treating the problem of
bias in estimates resulting from using data on plant size, and Williamson's
comments were most helpful in understanding the factors related to
variations in the $1-(U_2/U_1)$ variable. The author, of course, accepts final
responsibility for any errors.

is assumed that the size of the administrative component is increased as long as the marginal return exceeds the marginal cost of additional administrative personnel. (The decision rule is slightly more complex for the firm managed by nonowners, who do not have a direct stake in the profitability of the firm.) Thus the relative size of the administrative component of an organization is treated as a variable *subject to managerial discretion* (Williamson, 1964).

This treatment is in contrast to most analyses, which assume administrative intensity to be *technologically* determined by the task of the organization or by other situational or structural characteristics. For example, it has been argued that:

1. Task complexity and division of labor create problems of coordination, which in turn require administrative personnel to perform coordination functions (Blau and Scott, 1962, p. 227).

2. With spatial dispersion of organization members, and multiple departments in an organization, coordination is more difficult and requires more administrators than with spatially concentrated members (Anderson and Warkov, 1961).

3. Variability and heterogeneity of the task environment require large numbers of administrators to standardize, stabilize, and regulate input and output transactions, so that the core technology of the organization can operate in an environment of technical rationality (Thompson, 1967).

Hypotheses deriving from these arguments have been subjected to a large amount of more or less rigorous empirical testing. Data from numerous studies consistently support the first argument (Anderson and Warkov, 1961; Bell, 1967; Campbell and Akers, 1968; Chester, 1961; Heydebrand 1967; Lindsay, 1968; Pugh *et al.*, 1968; Raphael, 1967; Woodward, 1965). As Starbuck (1965) warns, however, one should be wary of accepting the consistency of these results too eagerly, because of the great variations across studies in defining and measuring both complexity and administrative intensity. This comment, of course, applies to the other two hypotheses as well.

The second argument is weakly supported by data on tax-supported colleges and universities (Hawley *et al.*, 1965) and by data on public schools, provided size is controlled (Lindenfeld, 1961). However, data collected by Raphael (1967) on local labor unions strongly contradict the hypothesis.

The third argument is generally consistent with Chandler's (1962, esp. ch. 7) longitudinal and cross-sectional analysis of the administrative structure of American corporations. Recent research by Harvey (1968) and by Lawrence and Lorsch (1967, pp. 17–18), however, suggests that administrative intensity is *lower* i.e. larger span of control, fewer hierarchical levels, in those organizations or organizational subunits facing changeable or unpredictable environments and technologies (e.g. basic and applied research divisions) than in those facing relatively stable or predictable environments and technologies (e.g. sales and production divisions).

The implicit assumption common to all of these assertions, hypotheses and empirical studies is that the task, design and environment of the organization *determine* an administrative component of uniquely appropriate size. However, the deterministic approach fails to consider the contribution of administrative personnel to the goals of management; and it fails to take account of the costs (or other consequences) of under-coordination or over-coordination. In doing so, it ignores the developments of the last two decades in the theory of organizational decision making (Cyert and March, 1963; Feldman and Kanter, 1965). Empirical studies of administrative structure, lacking the integrating principle of rational, goal-seeking behavior, have too often consisted of a search for empirical regularities with no consistent theoretical basis. And hypotheses have amounted to little more than *ad hoc* statements about empirical regularities, rather than being shown to be isomorphic to propositions rigorously derived from more fundamental postulates.

The relationship between administrative intensity and organization size provides an example. Graicunas (1933) argued that administrative intensity would increase with the size (number of members) of an organization because the number of relationships to be coordinated increases faster than the number of persons being coordinated. Some research workers have since conjectured that if the complexity of the relationships among people, i.e. 'interconnectedness', were controlled, the positive correlation between administrative intensity and organization size might disappear or even become negative; see, e.g. Blau and Scott (1962), pp. 227. In fact, as is indicated in the results section of this paper, some empirical evidence bears out this conjecture. However, no one has explained why it might be *rational* – relative to the goals of the organization – for administrative intensity to decrease with organization size. The usual explanation (Rushing, 1967, p. 288–9) is that as an organization grows without increasing in complexity – i.e. by merely adding activities of a type that already exist – administrators perform essentially the same analyses but merely transmit them to more people. Thus, it is argued, the administrative component may grow, but at a slower rate than the rest of the organization. But this explanation, besides not being derived from the more fundamental postulate of rational goal-seeking, does not and cannot predict how the rate of decrease of administrative intensity with size might itself vary with complexity or other factors.

One of the objectives of the theory to be presented is to provide this missing rational basis for explaining empirical regularities associated with variations in administrative intensity.

Proposed model

In the present formulation, administrative personnel are treated as one of the factors of production, along with the more traditional input factors of labor and capital. As with labor and capital, the marginal productivity of administrative personnel is assumed to be positive but decreasing. For a manufacturing organization, the total physical output of the organization is assumed to be given by the following production function, which is merely an expansion of the well-known Cobb–Douglas production function (Douglas, 1948)[2]:

2. It is assumed that this production function is descriptive only of organizations large enough to realize the principal economies that size affords. It is further assumed that it is descriptive of the actual production function in the relevant range, though perhaps not for all ranges of the variables.

$$Q = \Theta A^{\alpha} K^{\beta} X^{\gamma}, \quad 0 < \alpha, \beta, \gamma < 1 \qquad\qquad 1$$

where Q = total output in number of physical units,
$\quad\quad\;\; A$ = number of administrative personnel,
$\quad\quad\;\; K$ = total productive capital of the organization,
$\quad\quad\;\; X$ = number of production personnel
$\quad\quad\;\; \Theta$ = productivity scale factor,
$\quad \alpha, \beta, \gamma$ = marginal relative productivities of administration, capital and labor, respectively.

If there are constant returns to scale, then the production function is homogeneous and of the first order and

$$\alpha + \beta + \gamma = 1. \qquad\qquad 2$$

However, Tullock (1965), Williamson (1967) and Downs (1967, pp 112–43) argue that there are increasing cumulative control losses across hierarchical levels, which result in decreasing returns to scale, in which case it would be expected that

$$\alpha + \beta + \gamma = 1 - \lambda, \quad 0 < \lambda < 1, \qquad\qquad 3$$

where λ is the control-loss parameter. Furthermore, if

$k = K/X$ = capital intensity per worker,
A/X = administrative intensity per worker,
then the production function can be written

$$Q = \Theta (A/X)^{\alpha} k^{\beta} X^{1-\lambda}. \qquad\qquad 4$$

Finally, it is assumed that productivity is directly related to the degree of occupational specialization; that is,

$$\Theta = \Theta_0 S^{\sigma}, \quad 0 < \sigma < 1, \qquad\qquad 5$$

where S = number of distinct occupational specialties represented in the labor force of the organization,
$\quad\;\; \sigma$ = marginal relative productivity of specialization,
$\quad\;\; \Theta_0$ = productivity scale factor.

This merely asserts that a worker's productivity increases as he becomes more specialized. The variable S is used both as a measure of worker specialization and as a measure of the functional complexity of the organization, i.e. number of distinct occupational specialties represented in the labor force. The requirement that $0 < \sigma < 1$ means simply that there are positive but decreasing returns to specialization. Doubling the number of occupational specialties for a given organization task will increase productivity, but is not likely to increase it by as much as a factor of two. Thus, the final form of the production function is given by

$$Q = \Theta_0 S^\sigma (A/X)^\alpha k^\beta X^{1-\lambda}. \qquad 6$$

Suppose now that a profit-maximizing motive is imputed to the management of the organization. The device of motivating management is the means by which the model is made *discretionary* rather than deterministic. Profit and cost are given by

profit = revenue — cost,
  cost = variable nonwage costs + labor costs + administrative
        costs + fixed costs

therefore

$$\pi = pQ - rQ - W_0 X - W_1 A - FC, \qquad 7$$

where π = profit,
        p = market price of product per unit,
        r = variable nonwage product costs per unit,
        W_0 = average wage per production worker,
        W_1 = average salary per administrative worker,
        FC = fixed costs.

Assuming now that the organization has already made its decisions regarding capital intensity, degree of specialization, and number of production workers, it is further assumed that it will set the administrative intensity to maximize profits. To find this point equation 7 is differentiated with respect to A/X and the derivative is set equal to zero; that is,

$$\frac{d\pi}{d(A/X)} = \alpha\Theta_0 (p-r)(A/X)^{\alpha-1} k^\beta S^\sigma X^{1-\lambda} - W_1 X = 0. \qquad 8$$

Solving for the optimum administrative intensity gives

$$(A/X)^* = [\alpha\Theta_0 (p-r)/W_1]^{1/(1-\alpha)} \times k^{\beta/(1-\alpha)} S^{\sigma/(1-\alpha)} X^{-\lambda/(1-\alpha)}, \qquad 9$$

where the asterisk denotes an optimum. That is, if it is assumed that organizations choose an administrative intensity to maximize profits, then the model predicts that administrative intensity should be positively correlated with the ratio of net price to administrative salary, with capital intensity, and with degree of specialization (functional complexity), and negatively correlated with organization size, as measured by the number of production personnel. Note that the negative relationship between administrative intensity and organization size is due to the existence of control losses across hierarchical levels. This is discussed further in the section on size effects in the Discussion on pp. 318–25 (see especially equations 27, 28 and 29).

Utility-maximizing version of the model

With the separation of ownership and management, management's motivations may not be strictly oriented toward profit maximization. Management may be motivated to increase administrative personnel beyond the optimum profit point. After all, nonowner managers do not share directly in increased profits, although they may share more directly by spending those profits on subordinate administrative personnel to enhance their prestige, to make their jobs easier, and so on; that is, they value hierarchical expense *per se*, as well as profitability. Or management may attach a *negative* 'expense preference' to administrative personnel (Williamson, 1964). Owner-managers, for example, may not wish to weaken control of the organization by bringing into the administrative structure persons outside of their families. They may even be willing to accept a lower profit as a result of being underadministered, in exchange for maintaining close personal or family control of the organization. The dominant managers' utility function is defined to include both profit and hierarchical expense (following Williamson, 1964, 1967); that is,

$$U = U(\pi_0 - H, H), \qquad 10$$

where U = utility function of dominant management coalition,
π_0 = profit exclusive of administrative costs,
$H = W_1 A$ = hierarchical expense (administrative costs).

Since both π_0 and H can be expressed in terms of number of administrative personnel, A, then it is only necessary to differentiate U with respect to A, set the derivative equal to zero, and solve for that administrative intensity which maximizes managerial utility; that is,

$$\frac{dU}{dA} = U_1\left(\frac{d\pi_0}{dA} - \frac{dH}{dA}\right) + U_2\frac{dH}{dA} = 0, \qquad 11$$

where U_1 and U_2 are the partial derivatives of U with respect to the first and second arguments. But

$$\frac{d\pi_0}{dA} = \frac{dR}{dA} = \text{marginal net revenue,} \qquad 12$$

where R = net revenue = $(p-r)Q$.

Since A does not enter either labor costs or fixed costs, and since

$dH/dA = W_1$ = marginal cost of one additional administrative worker, 13

the maximum condition can be restated as,

$$\frac{dR}{dA} = W_1\left(1 - \frac{U_2}{U_1}\right). \qquad 14$$

That is, if the management of the organization values administrative overhead *per se* (i.e. $U_2 > 0$), administrative intensity will be expanded even beyond the point where marginal revenue equals marginal cost. We would expect this condition to increase as ownership and management became more and more separated. Alternatively, if administrative overhead is *negatively* valued (i.e. $U_2 < 0$), administrative intensity will be maintained below the point of maximum profit. The optimum administrative intensity for maximum utility is given by

$$(A/X)^* = [\alpha\Theta_0(p-r)/W_1]^{1/(1-\alpha)} \times k^{\beta/(1-\alpha)} S^{\sigma/(1-\alpha)} X^{-\lambda/(1-\alpha)} \times \\ \times [1 - (U_2/U_1)]^{-1/(1-\alpha)}, \quad 15$$

which differs from the maximum profit optimum only by the presence of the $[1 - (U_2/U_1)]^{-1/(1-\alpha)}$ term. If the manager does not value administrative overhead, then $U_2 = 0$, and equation 15 reduces to that given by the profit-maximizing model in equation 9.

Under what conditions might U_2/U_1 be exected to increase or decrease? It has already been argued that as the manager's *personal* stake in the profitability of the organization decreases his relative preference for hierarchical expenses *per se* will increase. This is likely to be the case when ownership and management are separated, i.e. when the active top management of the organization is made up of professional, nonowner managers. Stock-option and other incentive plans for upper management are, of course, intended to make managers' utility functions more nearly coincident with the profit-oriented goals of the stockholders. Such incentive schemes are likely to produce a depressing effect on U_2/U_1. Even in the absence of such incentives, managers cannot afford to ignore profit goals altogether, lest they be dismissed or lose their promotions and salary increases. The extent to which the stockholders can effectively enforce their goals on management is a function primarily of how closely or widely the stock is held and whether the board of directors is an inside board made up of active members of management, or an outside board made up of elected representatives of the stockholders not within the organization. Like incentive schemes, closely held stock and an outside board are likely to depress U_2/U_1.

The U_2/U_1 preference ratio may also be affected by the opportunity set; that is, the more profit an organization is *already* making, the less its managers will value *additional* profit. Thus, U_1, the marginal utility of profit, will decrease as total profit increases, and, *ceteris paribus*, U_2/U_1 will increase. This is likely to be the case when large profits accrue to organizations as a result of monopolistic or oligopolistic market structure, barriers to entry, patent protection, and the like. Thus, in large organizations, the downward pressure on administrative intensity resulting from control losses may be offset by the upward pressure of larger profits made possible by its ability to control its market and technological environment. As U_2/U_1 increases, $[1-(U_2/U_1)]^{-1/(1-\alpha)}$ also increases, and the model predicts a positive correlation between administrative intensity and those factors which exert upward pressure on U_2/U_1 (e.g. ownership–management separation, and conditions favorable to excess profits). An empirical test of the ownership aspect of this prediction, together with the earlier predictions, follows.

Empirical test of the model

The equation to be tested is of the form,

$$A/X = a_0[(p-r)/W_1]^{a_1}k^{a_2}S^{a_3}X^{a_4} \times [1-(U_2/U_1)]^{a_5}, \qquad \textbf{16}$$

a_0, a_1, a_2, a_3, a_4 and a_5 are parameters to be estimated from the data, and are assumed to be constant across organizations. It has been predicted that $a_1 > 0$, $a_2 > 0$, $a_3 > 0$, $a_4 < 0$, $a_5 < 0$.

In order to transform this model into a form suitable for using techniques of linear regression analysis to estimate the parameters, it is necessary to take natural logarithms of both sides of the equation, with the result that

$$\ln(A/X) = \ln a_0 + a_1 \ln[(p-r)/W_1] + a_2 \ln k + a_3 \ln S + \\ + a_4 \ln X + a_5 \ln[1-(U_2/U_1)]. \qquad \textbf{17}$$

Data

This model has been tested using census data from a sample of forty-five manufacturing industries (Bureau of the Census, 1958, 1960). Of sixty-two manufacturing industries for which data are available in the *Occupation by Industry* census, seventeen were eliminated because they represented miscellaneous or heterogeneous categories. This is a similar sample to that used by Rushing (1967) in a recent study, except that it includes five industries not included by Rushing, and excludes one industry that he included. Rushing included data from the 'miscellaneous plastic products' category because it is the only industry classification for plastics. In this analysis this industry as well as the other sixteen miscellaneous groups were excluded. Rushing also eliminated data from five industries in which 'one or more of the three administrative categories are typically involved in production operations'. While this justification applies more or less to two of the industries eliminated – drugs and newspaper publishing – it is less convincing for the other three, paints, aircraft, and printing. All five of these industries are included here and only the seventeen 'miscellaneous' and 'not specified' industry classifications are excluded. Rushing excluded some of the most interesting data points from his sample in the five included in this analysis. (The statistical analysis is not markedly changed when the drug and newspaper publishing industries are removed from the sample.)

Although it would have been desirable to test this model on data by *organization*, this type of information is not available in the published census data. Therefore industry averages have had to be used to represent the 'typical' organization in each industry. Since industry averages are weighted by size of organization, the data represent primarily characteristics of large organizations in each industry. Furthermore, because size and the other variables covary across industries, data on industry averages create more multicollinearity problems than would occur with raw data. Efforts are being made to secure other data by organization, in order to subject the model to a more rigorous test.

There is one further problem with the census data, though only a minor one. Data on the total number of personnel and the occupational breakdown are drawn from the *Occupation by Industry* subject report (Bureau of the Census, 1960), and data on the other variables are drawn from the *Census of Manufactures* (Bureau of the Census, 1958). The *Occupation by Industry* subject report uses an industrial classification system that is not the same as the Standard Industrial Classification (SIC) used in the *Census of Manufactures*; however, it provides the SIC codes for industries listed that correspond to the industries in the *Census of Manufactures*.

Measures

A description of the measure used for each of the variables follows.

Administrative intensity. This is the number of administrative personnel per 100 production workers in a given industry. 'Administrative personnel' is defined to include all those in the standard occupational census categories of 'managerial', 'professional', and 'clerical' personnel. 'Production workers' comprise all those in the 'craftsman', 'operative', and 'laborer' categories. This definition is identical to that used by Rushing (1967) and Stinchcombe (1959). Defined in this way, 'administrative personnel' includes those employed by the central headquarters staff as well as those located at operating plants.

Market price net of variable nonwage costs, $p-r$. This is roughly equivalent to value added per unit of output. The census defines 'value added' as the dollar value of shipments, plus receipts for services rendered, plus value added by merchandising operations, plus net change in finished goods and work-in-process inventories, minus cost of materials, supplies, containers, fuel, purchased electrical energy, and contract work (Bureau of the Census, 1958, p. 13). Since the definition of a unit of output is arbitrary, an attempt has been made to obtain a standardized measure of $p-r$ by dividing the total value added for an industry by the total number of production workers.

Average administrative salary. This is total administrative payroll expenses divided by the total number of administrative personnel.

Capital intensity. This is the total undepreciated fixed assets per production worker.

Functional complexity. This is closely related to Rushing's measure, 'division of labor'. If all occupational specialties in an industry are equally populated, then only the number of occupational specialties need be counted to get a measure of functional complexity. However, the effective number of occupational specialties will be somewhat less than this, if the workers are concentrated in a few of the categories. Rushing's measure of division of labor for a specific industry is given by

$$D = 1-[\Sigma\, X_i^2/(\Sigma\, X_i)^2],$$

where X_i is the number of workers in the ith occupational grouping. This reduces to $D = 1-(1/N)$, when all groupings are equally populated, where N is the total actual number of specialties. Calculating D as Rushing did, $S = 1/(1-D)$ is defined to be the *effective* number of occupational specialties, or functional complexity.

Number of production personnel per organization. Ideally, to determine the average size of an organization in a given industry, one need only divide the total number of production personnel in the industry by the number of organizations in the industry. Unfortunately manufacturing census data are collected by 'establishment' (roughly equivalent to a plant), not by organizations, partly to conceal the identity of large organizations. The number of organizations in an industry is given in only ten out of the forty-five cases. The rank order correlation between average organization size and average plant size is $+0.988$ for these ten cases, so that average size of plant has been used instead of average size of organization. However, this procedure will tend to bias estimates of the regression coefficients. Another procedure might be to use data only from the ten industries for which information on the average size of organizations is available. But with only four degrees of freedom, estimates of regression coefficients are likely to be statistically insignificant. This problem is discussed in more detail in the section on results.

Separation of ownership and management. As already discussed, the U_2/U_1 ratio may vary because of market structure, availability of stock option plans, etc., as well as because active managers are not also owners. In this paper, only the ownership aspects of variations in U_2/U_1 are investigated; the effects of market structure, etc., are left to future research. The ratio U_2/U_1 reflects the degree to which the management of a firm is willing to trade profit for administrative expense. The percentage of managers in the industry who are owner–managers is used as a very rough measurement of $1-(U_2/U_1)$ for a given industry. As the percentage of owner–managers increases, one would expect the aggregate managerial preference for administration expense to decrease and $1-(U_2/U_1)$ to increase. Another possible substitute measure of owner–management separation is the percentage of establishments in an industry that belong to corporations, as opposed to proprietorships or partnerships. This measure was also used in the regression analyses, and the results were qualitatively the same, although slightly less significant than those with the owner–manager measure. This is the least satisfactory measure of the six variables. In particular, there is some concern whether any variations in the percentage of owner–managers would remain, once small organizations were omitted from the sample. If differences were to remain the same results might not be obtained. At this stage of the research, this problem has not been resolved. More work simply needs to be done.

Results of regression analysis

The coefficients of the relevant variables were estimated using equation 17 as the regression model. All coefficients except that for capital intensity were in the expected direction and statistically significant. The coefficient of determination, adjusted for degrees of freedom, was $R^2 = 0.57$; that is, it explained 57 per cent of the variance in administrative intensity. This appears to be especially satisfactory for the very rough type of data being used. The inter-correlations among the variables are shown in Table 1, the results for the utility-maximizing model in Table 2, and those for the profit-maximizing model in Table 3.

Table 1 Means, Standard Deviations and
Log-Log Inter-Correlations for all Variables

Variables	$(p-r)/W_1$	k	S	X	$1-(U_2/U_1)$	A/X
k	0·62					
S	0·23	0·27				
X	−0·07	0·31	0·20			
$1-(U_2/U_1)$	−0·32	−0·56	−0·24	−0·74		
A/X	0·61	0·46	0·48	0·03	−0·45	—
Mean	2·07	11·4*	5·36	128·2	0·177†	37·7‡
Standard deviation	0·99	10·8	3·08	234·0	0·145	28·8

* Thousands of dollars.
† Proportion of managers self-employed.
‡ Number of administrators per 100 workers.

The finding that administrative intensity is negatively correlated with organization size is consistent with those of others (Anderson and Warkov, 1961; Bendix, 1956; Blau *et al.*, 1966; Campbell and Akers, 1968; Chester, 1961; Haas *et al.*, 1963; Hawley *et al.*, 1965; Heydebrand, 1967; Indik, 1964; Lindenfeld, 1961; Lindsay, 1968; and Melman, 1951). The finding by Blau *et al.* on small bureaucracies is particularly interesting in view of Starbuck's (1965, pp. 499–501) suggestion that administrative intensity is probably an increasing function of organization size for organizations of fewer than 100 employees. However, a few other studies have produced positive correlations, between size and administrative intensity (Haire, 1959; Raphael, 1967; Tsouderos 1955).

As Raphael demonstrates in her study, one must exercise extreme caution in interpreting zero first-order correlations between size and administrative intensity. The positive correla-

Table 2 Results of Regression Analysis of Administrative Intensity for 45 Manufacturing Industries Based on Utility-Maximizing Model

Model: $(A/X)^* = a_0(p-r/w_1)^{a_1} k^{a_2} S^{a_3} X^{a_4}(1-U_2/U_1)^{a_5}$

$R^2 = 0.57$, $F = 12.5$, $df = (5, 39)$, $p < 0.0005$

Variables	Parameter	Estimate of parameter	Standard error of coefficient	t	Level of significance
Constant	a_0	15·3	—	—	—
Net price/salary	a_1	0·462	0·201	2·304	<0·025
Capital intensity	a_2	−0·047	0·111	−0·425	n.s.
Functional complexity	a_3	0·437	0·130	3·372	<0·005
Organization size	a_4	−0·266	0·093	−2·731	<0·005
Proportion of owner–managers	a_5	−0·453	0·129	−3·505	<0·005

Table 3 Results of Regression Analysis of Administrative Intensity for 45 Manufacturing Industries Based on Profit-Maximizing Model

Model: $(A/X)^* = a_0(p-r/W_1)^{a_1} k^{a_2} S^{a_3} X^{a_4}$

$R^2 = 0.44$, $F = 9.76$, $df = (4, 40)$, $p < 0.0005$

Variables	Parameter	Estimate of parameter	Standard error of coefficient	t	Level of significance
Constant	a_0	9·8	—	—	—
Net price/salary	a_1	0·678	0·127	3·315	<0·005
Capital intensity	a_2	0·047	0·122	0·385	n.s.
Functional complexity	a_3	0·433	0·147	2·952	<0·005
Organization size	a_4	−0·012	0·074	−0·159	n.s.

tion appeared in her case only when a third variable, spatial dispersion of members, was controlled. It is important to note that, for the sample in this study, the *first-order* log correlation is 0·03 – essentially zero. It is only *when a measure of ownership–management separation is introduced that the partial regression coefficient of size becomes significantly negative*. When the percentage of owner–managers is omitted from the regression, i.e.

when the profit-maximizing model is used, the value of R^2 drops significantly, and the regression coefficient of the size variable becomes insignificant (see Tables 2 and 3). The coefficient associated with functional complexity is surprisingly stable (0·437 versus 0·433), but that associated with net price to salary ratio changes markedly (from 0·462 to 0·678). The instability of coefficient estimates is due in large part to the multicollinearity associated with the owner–manager variable. (The first-order log correlations of the percentage of owner-managers with net price to salary ratio and organization size are $-0·32$ and $-0·74$, respectively. This is roughly analogous in experimental design to having variables confounded, so that their effects cannot be separated. The major effect of multicollinearity among the independent variables is that regression estimates are biased, and explanatory power tends to be arbitrarily allocated among the independent variables. With Farrar and Glaubner's (1967) 'diagnostics', the owner–manager variable has been demonstrated to be the dominant source of multicollinearity in the analysis. This, of course, does not solve the problems associated with multicollinearity. As suggested earlier, changing the data base from industry averages to data on individual organizations may help somewhat.

There are two possible explanations for the lack of significance of the coefficient of capital intensity. First, the capital stock measure – undepreciated fixed assets – may be inappropriate. It appears now that a measure more closely related to *productive* capital, e.g. depreciated plant and equipment, might have yielded the expected result, but this was not tried. Second, if productive capital takes the form of mechanized or automated equipment, some of the coordinative functions may be performed by the machinery itself. This would tend to reduce the requirements for administrative personnel and counteract the marginal return to administration resulting from higher capital intensity (Blau and Scott, 1962, pp. 176–83).

Bias resulting from use of plant-size data

As suggested earlier, the use of data on average *plant* size rather than average *organization* size tends to bias *all* of the regression coefficient estimates. This can be illustrated as follows. Suppose *plant* size, X, is a function of *organization* size, Y, as well as the other independent variables; then

$$\ln X = b_0 + b_1 \ln[(p-r)/W_1] + b_2 \ln k + b_3 \ln S + \\ + b_4 \ln Y + b_5 \ln[1-(U_2/U_1)]. \quad \textbf{18}$$

Substituting this expression for $\ln X$ in equation **17**, gives

$$\ln(A/X) = a_0 + b_0 a_4 + (a_1 + b_1 a_4) \ln[(p-r)/W_1] + \\ + (a_2 + b_2 a_4) \ln k + (a_3 + b_3 a_4) \ln S + b_4 a_4 \ln Y + \\ + (a_5 + b_5 a_4) \times \ln[1-(U_2/U_1)]. \quad \textbf{19}$$

The estimates in equation **19** thus include bias corrections in *all* coefficients as a result of the use of plant-size data. The parameters in equation **18** were estimated using data on the subsample of ten industries for which organization data were available, with the following results:

$$\ln X = 0.845 - 0.525 \ln[(p-r)/W_1] - 0.012 \ln k + 0.004 \ln S + \\ (0.101) \qquad\qquad (0.040) \qquad (0.039) \\ + 0.713 \ln Y - 0.315 \times \ln[1-(U_2/U_1)], \quad R^2 = 0.999. \quad \textbf{20} \\ (0.028) \qquad (0.046)$$

The standard errors of the coefficients are given in the parentheses below each coefficient. Thus, by using plant-size data, relatively little bias was introduced into estimates of the coefficients of the capital-intensity and functional-complexity variables, but the results given in Table 2 tend to *understate* the magnitude of the effect of 'net price to salary' ratio, and *overstate* the effects of size and ownership. If the estimates in equation **20** are assumed to be descriptive of the entire forty-five-industry sample, the corrected estimates for the administrative intensity expression would be

$$\ln(A/X) = 12.4 + 0.602 \ln[(p-r)/W_1] - 0.044 \ln k + \\ + 0.436 \ln S - 0.190 \ln Y - 0.369 \ln[1-(U_2/U_1)], \quad \textbf{21}$$

where Y denotes *organization* size rather than plant size. These estimates should be compared with those in Table 2.

To illustrate the effects of bias further, the coefficients in equations **17** and **19** were estimated directly from data on the subsample of ten industries. Because of the small sample size, the standard errors of the coefficients are large, and none of the estimates is statistically significant. However, the adjusted R^2 is still 0·57 in both cases, as for the full sample. The results, using average plant size are:

$$\ln A/X = 17\cdot2 + 0\cdot806 \ln [(p-r)/W_1] + 0\cdot139 \ln k + 0\cdot345 \ln S - \\ (1\cdot280) \qquad\qquad (0\cdot426) \qquad (0\cdot364) \\ -0\cdot535 \ln X - 0\cdot689 \times \ln [1-(U_2/U_1)]. \quad \textbf{22} \\ (0\cdot534) \qquad (0\cdot619)$$

Using average organization size they are:

$$\ln (A/X) = 10\cdot8 + 1\cdot081 \ln [(p-r)/W_1] + 0\cdot147 \ln k + \\ (1\cdot108) \qquad\qquad (0\cdot428) \\ +0\cdot342 \ln S - 0\cdot382 \ln Y - 0\cdot533 \times \ln [1-(U_2/U_1)]. \quad \textbf{23} \\ (0\cdot364) \qquad (0\cdot301) \qquad (0\cdot507)$$

The direction of bias, as shown in equations **22** and **23**, is consistent with the earlier analysis of the tendencies toward overstatement or understatement. The estimates in equation **22** are, of course, slightly different from those in Table 2, because the characteristics of the industries in the ten-industry subsample are somewhat different from those in the full sample. The industries in the subsample, relative to those in the full sample, are higher on the measures of administrative intensity, net price to salary ratio, capital intensity, and average plant size, and lower on functional complexity and proportion of owner–managers.

These difficulties point up again the need to test the model using organization-by-organization data rather than just industry averages.

Discussion

Despite the statistical difficulties, it is possible to have confidence in the finding that administrative intensity is positively related to functional complexity. This finding is consistent with the prediction and interpretation of the technological determinists; that is, that functional complexity leads to coordination problems, which require more administrative personnel. However, this finding is interpreted differently here: as functional complexity increases, the marginal productivity of administrative personnel also increases, and it therefore becomes *more profitable* at the margin to employ administrators. From equation **6**,

$$Q = \Theta_0 S^\sigma A^\beta k^\beta X^{1-\lambda-\alpha}.\qquad 24$$

Marginal productivity of administration is given by

$$\partial Q / \partial A = \alpha \Theta_0 S^\sigma A^{\alpha-1} k^\beta X^{1-\lambda-\alpha}\qquad 25$$

and $\quad \dfrac{\partial}{\partial S}\left(\dfrac{\partial Q}{\partial A}\right) > 0;\qquad 26$

that is, marginal productivity of administration, and thus the optimal number of administrators, increases with functional complexity.

One can also be confident that if type of ownership is held constant, administrative intensity will decrease with increasing size of organization. (It is important to note that this is a statement about cross-sectional effects, not longitudinal ones!) This is consistent with the common allegation that there are administrative economies of scale; that is, if the size of the labor force increases by some percentage y, then the number of administrative personnel *needs* to increase only by some percentage $z < y$. This again is an argument following from technological determinism. However, the present managerial discretion model suggests an entirely different interpretation, as a result of the phenomenon of control loss. If the parameter λ equals zero, i.e. if there are no labor diseconomies of scale resulting from control loss, then the model implies that administrative intensity should be constant with respect to organization size (see equation 9). However, if $\lambda > 0$, as seems likely, and a given administrative intensity is maintained, then the marginal productivity of administration *decreases* with size. Technological requirements aside, it simply is not *profitable* to maintain or increase administrative intensity as the size of the organization increases. This can be seen by rearranging the term on the right-hand side of equation 25, giving

$$\partial Q / \partial A = \alpha \Theta_0 S^\sigma (A/X)^{\alpha-1} k^\beta X^{-\lambda};\qquad 27$$

then $\quad \dfrac{\partial}{\partial X}\left(\dfrac{\partial Q}{\partial A}\right) < 0, \quad \text{for } A/X = \text{constant.}\qquad 28$

This effect can be explained solely with reference to the phenomenon of control loss across hierarchical levels. One of the implications of this result is that one would expect a weaker negative correlation between size and administrative intensity among those organizations that have minimized control losses. Such organizations might be those with highly developed bureaucratic controls, those with a high level of goal similarity among members, etc. Under such conditions, the marginal productivity of administration would not decrease as markedly with organization size.

However, the preceding analysis assumes that functional complexity S, and capital intensity, k, are constant and do not vary with size, but as can be seen from Table 1, both S and k are positively correlated with size for the sample studied. If variations in S and k with size are taken into account, then it can be shown that, for constant A/X

$$\frac{d}{dX}\left(\frac{\partial Q}{\partial A}\right) = \left(\frac{\partial Q}{\partial A}\right)\left[\frac{\sigma}{S}\left(\frac{dS}{dX}\right)+\frac{\beta}{k}\left(\frac{dk}{dX}\right)-\frac{\lambda}{X}\right]. \qquad 29$$

That is, assuming $dS/dX > 0$ and $dk/dX > 0$, if X is sufficiently large and S and k are sufficiently small, then it is possible that $d/dX(\partial Q/\partial A) > 0$. Under these conditions, the marginal productivity of administration and therefore administrative intensity would *increase* with size of organization! At least relative to manufacturing organizations, labor unions might be expected to have a lower functional complexity and a lower capital intensity. It is interesting, therefore, that Raphael's (1967) study of labor unions is one of the few that show a positive partial correlation between size of organization and relative size of the administrative component. The same result might be expected in other large, relatively unspecialized, labor-intensive organizations, such as church hierarchies, government agencies, and professional associations. Thus Parkinson's famous dictum – that administrative staff increases faster than the rest of the organization – may be true only for a certain class of organizations. Furthermore, because of the indirect effects of size on complexity and capital intensity, it may be that for some organizations, a more than proportional increase in administrative staff may very well be rational, relative to organizational criteria of efficiency.

The most important finding of this research is the negative relationship between administrative intensity and the proportion of owner–managers, or conversely, the positive relationship between size of administration and ownership–management separation. As already indicated, the same relationship holds although somewhat less strongly, for percentage of corporations in an industry – as opposed to proprietorships or partnerships – as a measure of ownership–management separation. It is argued here that this is because professional managers have a stronger preference for hierarchical expense *per se* than owner–managers, but there are three other explanations for this finding:

1. Professional administrative personnel are more efficient than owner–managers and their families; their marginal productivity is higher; therefore it is profitable to employ more of them. However, their salaries tend to be higher, so that this partly counteracts their higher productivity.

2. Owner–managers and employed relatives are willing to work longer hours than professionals; therefore fewer are needed to get the administrative work done. Analysis of the *components* of administration makes this explanation questionable. The *managerial* component is essentially not correlated with measures of ownership–management separation. The positive correlation between administrative intensity and ownership–management separation is due almost solely to the professional–technical and clerical components.

3. Owner–managers are unwilling to dilute their personal power and control over the organization by adding professional, nonfamily personnel, even if it means accepting a lower profit. This is the most convincing of the alternative explanations. It is also not inconsistent with the basic notion that variability in administrative intensity is partly due to differing utility functions of top management.

To illustrate the effect of different utility functions more explicitly, equation 7 is treated, following Williamson (1964), as a 'possibility curve' that relates administrative intensity to profitability for a given level of operation. This is shown in Figure 1 as a curve which rises as long as the marginal return to administration exceeds W_1, the marginal cost of administration, and falls when the marginal return is less than W_1. Also shown in

Figure 1 are several indifference curves for the classical owner-manager who values only profitability. The point of tangency. indicates the administrative ratio that yields maximum profit.

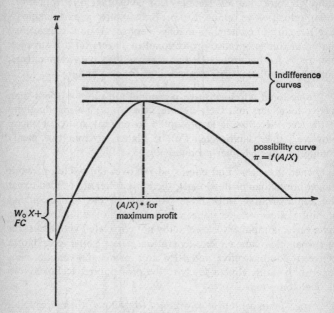

Figure 1 Possibility curve and indifference map for classical owner-manager

Figure 2 shows the same possibility curve, but a new set of indifference curves appropriate for professional, nonowner managers who value hierarchical expense *per se*, as well as profitability. In the extreme, the professional manager's indifference curves would all be vertical, and he would expand the administrative component until the organization reached the point at which profitability equalled the minimum profit acceptable to the stockholders. The 'excess' administrative expense over that appropriate for maximum profit would be a measure of the organizational slack absorbed by management (Cyert and March, 1963).

As suggested, the owner–manager may actually attach a negative preference to administrative staff, thus sacrificing some profitability in return for avoiding dilution of control. In this

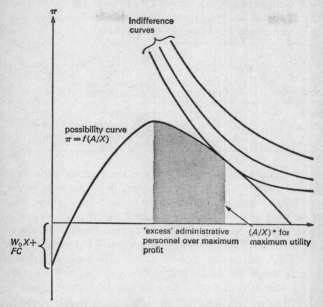

Figure 2 Possibility curve and indifference map for professional, non-owner-manager

case, his indifference curves would slant upwards from left to right, in the opposite direction from those shown in Figure 2, and his maximum utility point for administrative intensity would occur to the left of that appropriate for maximum profit. In such a case, one would expect the profit–maximizing version of the model to provide a poor fit to such organizations, but the utility-maximizing version to provide a good fit.

As a rough test of this idea, the full sample of forty-five industries was divided into three subsamples: one with a low, one with a medium, and one with a high percentage of incorporation of establishments. Both the profit-maximizing and utility-maximizing models were tested on data from each subsample. The results are shown in Table 4.

Table 4 Comparative Goodness of Fit of the Profit-Maximizing and Utility-maximizing Models for Industries with High, Medium and Low Degree of Incorporation

Degree of incorporations	Per cent of plants incorporated	n	R^2 (adjusted) Profit model	R^2 (adjusted) Utility model
High	77–100%	15	0·80	0·88
Medium	61–74	16	0·44	0·40
Low	4–58	14	0·09	0·85

As can be seen, data from the owner–managed industries (low degree of incorporation) provide a singularly poor fit to the profit model, but an excellent fit to the utility model. At the other extreme, data on professionally managed industries (high degree of incorporation) fit the profit model extremely well, and the fit is improved only slightly by including $1-(U_2/U_1)$ term, i.e. the utility-maximizing model. For industries with a medium degree of incorporation, the adjusted R^2 actually drops from the profit model to the utility model – because one additional degree of freedom is used up without any improvement in fit. Although this analysis is highly tentative, one might wish to draw the inference that proprietorships and partnerships tend to be underadministered relative to a profit criterion. Furthermore, industries with a high degree of incorporation appear to have an administrative intensity consistent with profit-maximizing motives, with possibly only a moderate amount of 'excess' administration. The data seem to suggest that 'expense preference' (Williamson, 1964) for administrative staff shifts from a negative to a positive preference as one moves from owner–managed to professionally managed organizations.

In conclusion, it is argued that administrative intensity in organizations is a function of both economic and technological variables, but is also strongly influenced by managerial motivations and patterns of ownership. If the analysis of the data has not 'proved' the theory, it has at least given it plausibility. Furthermore, formalizing the theory as a mathematical model has made it possible to derive testable conjectures which were neither obvious in the present data nor yet systematically investigated by others.

References

ANDERSON, T., and WARKOV, S. (1961), 'Organization size and functional complexity: a study of administration in hospitals', *Amer. sociol. Rev.*, vol. 26, pp. 23–8.

BELL, G. D. (1967), 'Determinants of span of control', *Amer. J. Sociol.*, vol. 73, pp. 100–109.

BENDIX, R. (1956), *Work and Authority in Industry*, Wiley.

BLAU, P. M., HEYDEBRAND, W. V., and STAUFFER, R. E. (1966), 'The structure of small bureaucracies', *Amer. sociol. Rev.*, vol. 31, pp. 179–91.

BLAU, P. M., and SCOTT, W. R. (1962), *Formal Organizations*, Chandler.

BUREAU OF THE CENSUS (1958), *Census of Manufactures, Summary Statistics*, US Dept of Commerce.

BUREAU OF THE CENSUS (1960), 'Occupation by industry', Subject Report 7C, US Population Census, US Dept of Commerce.

CAMPBELL, F. L., and AKERS, R. L. (1968), 'Organizational growth and structural changes in occupational associations', unpublished paper presented at annual meeting of Amer. Sociol. Assoc.

CHANDLER, A. D. (1962), *Strategy and Structure: Chapters in the History of Industrial Enterprise*, MIT Press.

CHESTER, T. E. (1961), *A Study of Post-War Growth in Management Organizations*, project 347, European Productivity Agency.

CYERT, R. M., and MARCH, J. G. (1963), *A Behavioral Theory of the Firm*, Prentice-Hall.

DOUGLAS, P. H. (1948), 'Are there laws of production?', *Amer. econ. Rev.*, vol. 38, pp. 1–41.

DOWNS, A. (1967), *Inside Bureaucracy*, Little, Brown and Co.

FARRAR, D. E., and GLAUBNER, R. R. (1967), 'Multi-collinearity in regression analysis: the problem revisited', *Rev. Econs Stats.*, vol. 49, pp. 92–107.

FELDMAN, J., and KANTER, H. E. (1965), 'Organizational decision making', in J. G. March (ed.), *Handbook of Organizations*, Rand McNally, pp. 614–49.

GRAICUNAS, V. A. (1933), 'Relationship in organization', *Bull. Internat. Manag. Instit.*, vol. 7, pp. 39–42.

HAAS, E., HALL, R. H., and JOHNSON, N. J. (1963), 'The size of the supportive component in organizations: a multi-organizational analysis', *Soc. Forces*, vol. 43, pp. 9–17.

HAIRE, M. (1959), 'Biological models and empirical histories of the growth of organizations', in M. Haire (ed.) *Modern Organization Theory*, Wiley, pp. 272–306.

HARVEY, E. (1968), 'Technology and the structure of organizations', *Amer. Sociol. Rev.*, vol. 33, pp. 247–59.

HAWLEY, A. W., BOLAND, W., and BOLAND, M. (1965), 'Population size and administration in institutions of higher education', *Amer. sociol. Rev.*, vol. 30, pp. 252–5.

HEYDEBRAND, W. V. (1967), 'Division of labor and coordination in organizations: a comparative study', unpublished manuscript, Dept Sociology, University of Chicago.

INDIK, B. P. (1964), 'The relationship between organization size and supervision ratio', *Admin. Sci. Q.*, vol. 9, pp. 301–12.

LAWRENCE, P. R., and LORSCH, J. W. (1967), 'Differentiation and integration in complex organization', *Admin. Sci. Q.*, vol. 12, pp. 1–47.

LINDENFELD, F. (1961), 'Does administrative staff grow as fast as organization?', *School Life*, vol. 43, pp. 20–23.

LINDSAY, P. D. (1968), 'Administrative staff size in national labor unions', unpublished manuscript, Grad. Sch. of Bus., University of Pittsburgh.

MELMAN, S. (1951), 'The rise of administrative overhead in the manufacturing industries of the United States: 1899–1947', *Oxford Economic Papers*, vol. 3, pp. 61–112.

PUGH, D. S., HICKSON, D. J., HININGS, C. R., and TURNER, C. (1968), 'Dimensions of organization structure', *Admin. Sci. Q.*, vol. 13, pp. 65–105.

RAPHAEL, E. E. (1967), 'The Anderson–Warkov hypothesis in local unions: a comparative study', *Amer. sociol. Rev.*, vol. 32, pp. 768–76.

RUSHING, W. A. (1967), 'The effects of industry size and division of labor on administration', *Admin. Sci. Q.*, vol. 12, pp. 273–95.

STARBUCK, W. H. (1965), 'Organizational growth and development', in J. G. March (ed.), *Handbook of Organizations*, pp. 451–533, Rand McNally [see Reading 1 of this selection].

STINCHCOMBE, A. L. (1959), 'Bureaucratic and craft administration of production: a comparative study', *Admin. Sci. Q.*, vol. 4, pp. 168–87.

THOMPSON, J. D. (1967), *Organizations in Action*. McGraw-Hill.

TSOUDEROS, J. E. (1955), 'Organization change in terms of a series of selected variables', *Amer. sociol. Rev.*, vol. 20, pp. 206–10.

TULLOCK, G. (1965), *The Politics of Bureaucracy*, Public Affairs Press.

WILLIAMSON, O. E. (1964), *The Economics of Discretionary Behavior: Managerial Objectives in a Theory of the Firm*, Prentice-Hall.

WILLIAMSON, O. E. (1967), 'Hierarchical control and optimum firm size', *J. polit. Econ.*, vol. 75, pp. 123–38.

WOODWARD, J. (1965), *Industrial Organization: Theory and Practice*, Oxford University Press.

9 D. S. Pugh, D. J. Hickson, C. R. Hinings and C. Turner

The Context of Organization Structures[1]

D. S. Pugh, D. J. Hickson, C. R. Hinings and C. Turner,
'The context of organization structures', *Administrative Science Quarterly*,
vol. 14, no. 1, 1969, pp. 91–114.

The structure of an organization is closely related to the context within which it functions, and much of the variation in organization structures might be explained by contextual factors. Many such factors, including size, technology, organizational charter or social function, and interdependence with other organizations, have been suggested as being of primary importance in influencing the structure and functioning of an organization.

There have been few attempts, however, to relate these factors in a comparative systematic way to the characteristic aspects of structure, for such studies would require a multivariate factorial approach in both context and structure. The limitations of a unitary approach to organizational structure have been elaborated elsewhere (Hinings *et al.* 1967), but its deficiencies in the study of contextual factors are no less clear. Theorists in this area seem to have proceeded on the assumption that one particular contextual feature is the major determinant of structure, with the implication that they considered the others less important. Many writers from Weber onwards have mentioned size as being one of the most important causes of differences between structures, and large size has even been considered as characteristic of bureaucratic structure (Presthus, 1958). Others argue for the pre-emptive importance of the technology of production or service in determining structure and functioning (Dubin, 1958; Perrow, 1967; Woodward, 1965; Trist *et al.*, 1963). Parsons (1956) and Selznick (1949) have attempted to show in some detail that the structure and

1. This work was conducted when the authors were members of the Industrial Administration Research Unit, the University of Aston in Birmingham, England. Research conducted by that Unit is jointly supported by the Social Science Research Council and the University.

functioning of the organization follow from its social function, goals, or 'charter'. Eisenstadt (1959) emphasized the importance of the dependence of the organization on its social setting, particularly its dependence on external resources and power, in

Table 1 Conceptual Scheme for Empirical Study of Work Organizations

Contextual variables	*Structural variables*†
Origin and history	*Structuring of activities*
Ownership and control	Functional specialization
Size	Role specialization
Charter	Standardization (overall)
Technology	Formalization (overall)
Location	
Resources	*Concentration of authority*
Dependence	Centralization of decision making
	Autonomy of the organization
*Activity variables**	Standardization of procedures for
Identification	selection and advancement
(charter, image)	
Perpetuation	*Line control of workflow*
(thoughtways,	Subordinate ratio
finance,	Formalization of role performance
personnel services)	recording
Workflow	Percentage of workflow
(production,	superordinates
distribution)	
Control	*Relative size of supportive component*
(direction,	Percentage of clerks
motivation,	Percentage of nonworkflow
evaluation,	personnel
communication)	Vertical span (height)
Homeostasis	
(fusion,	*Performance variables*
leadership,	Efficiency
problem solving,	(profitability,
legitimization)	productivity,
	market standing)
	Adaptability
	Morale

* Bakke (1959).
† Pugh *et al.* (1968).

influencing structural characteristics and activities. Clearly all of these contextual factors, as well as others, are relevant; but without a multivariate approach, it is not possible to assess their relative importance.

A previous paper described the conceptual framework upon which the present multivariate analysis is based (Pugh *et al.*, 1963), and a subsequent paper its empirical development (Pugh *et al.*, 1968). It is not a model of organization in an environment, but a separation of variables of structure and of organizational performance from other variables commonly hypothesized to be related to them, which are called 'contextual' in the sense that they can be regarded as a setting within which structure is developed. Table 1 summarizes the framework and also includes a classification of activities useful in the analysis of organization functioning (Bakke, 1959).

The design of the study reported in the present paper treats the contextual variables as independent and the structural variables as dependent. The structural variables are, firstly, *structuring of activities*; that is, the degree to which the intended behavior of employees is overtly defined by task specialization, standard routines, and formal paper work; secondly, *concentration of authority*; that is, the degree to which authority for decisions rests in controlling units outside the organization and is centralized at the higher hierarchical levels within it; and thirdly, *line control of workflow*; that is, the degree to which control is exercised by line personnel instead of through impersonal procedures. The eight contextual variables were translated into operational definitions and scales were constructed for each of them. These were then used in a multivariate regression analysis to predict the structural dimensions found.

This factorial study using cross-sectional data does not in itself test hypotheses about *processes*, e.g. how changes in size interact with variations in structuring of activities, but it affords a basis for generating such hypotheses.

Sample and methods

Data were collected on fifty-two work organizations, forty-six of which were a random sample stratified by size and product or purpose. The sample and methods have been described in detail in a previous paper (Pugh *et al.*, 1968). For scaling purposes, data on the whole group were used, but for correlational analyses relating scales to each other, and for prediction analyses relating contextual variables to structural ones, only data on the sample of forty-six organizations were used. None of the data was attitudinal.

The data were analyzed under the heading of the conceptual scheme. To define the variables operationally, scales were constructed that measured the degree of a particular characteristic. The scales varied widely. Inkson *et al.* (1967) discussed the variety of scaling procedures used. Some were simple dichotomies (such as impersonality of origin) or counts (such as number of operating sites); some were ordered category scales, locating an organization at one point along a postulated dimension (such as closeness of link with customers or clients). Some were stable, ordered scales established by linking together a large number or items exhibiting the characteristic on the basis of cumulative scaling procedures, such as workflow rigidity, an aspect of technology. Some were summary scales extracted by principal-components analysis to summarize a whole dimension, such as operating variability, an aspect of charter. In this way, forty primary scales of context were constructed and then reduced to fourteen empirically distinct elements, which are listed in Table 2 together with their correlations with the main structural variables as defined in Table 1. Table 3 gives their intercorrelations. The methodological implications of this analysis are discussed in Levy and Pugh (1969).

The study of contextual aspects of organizations will inevitably produce a much more heterogeneous set of scales than the comparable study of the structural aspects; for the scales are selected, not from a common conceptual base, but for their postulated links with structure. One of the objectives of using the multivariate approach described here would be to test the relationship between disparate aspects of context, and to attempt a conceptual clarification of those aspects demonstrated to be salient in relation to organizational structure.

It was not possible to investigate the variable 'resources' adequately. For human and ideational resources, the wide-ranging interviews within a comparatively short time span made it impossible to obtain adequate data. Material and capital resources were found to reduce to aspects of size, and the relative disposition of these resources, e.g. capital versus labor, was found to be better regarded as an aspect of technology.

Table 2 Elements of Organization Context

Elements of context	Product-moment correlation with structural factors		
	Structuring of activities	Concentration of authority	Line control of workflow
*Origin and history (3)**			
Impersonality of origin	−0·04	0·64	0·36
Age	0·09	−0·38	−0·02
Historical changes	0·17	−0·45	−0·03
Ownership and control (7)			
Public accountability	−0·10	0·63	0·47
Concentration of ownership with control	−0·15	−0·29	−0·21
Size (3)			
Size of organization†	0·69	−0·10	−0·15
Size of parent organization†	0·39	0·39	−0·07
Charter (7)			
Operating variability	0·15	−0·22	−0·57
Operating diversity	0·26	−0·30	−0·04
Technology (6)			
Workflow integration	0·34	−0·30	−0·46
Labor costs	−0·25	0·43	0·32
Location (1)			
Number of operating sites	−0·26	0·39	0·39
Dependence (10)			
Dependence	−0·05	0·66	0·13
Recognition of trade unions	0·51	0·08	−0·35

* Numbers in parentheses indicate number of primary scales.
† Logarithm of number of employees.

Table 3 Intercorrelations of Contextual Variables (Product-moment Coefficients, N = 46)

Scale title	Impersonality of origin	Age	Historical changes	Public accountability	Concentration of ownership with control*	Size of organization†	Size of parent organization†	Operating variability	Operating diversity	Workflow integration	Labor costs	No. of operating sites	Dependence	Trade unions
Impersonality of origin	—													
Age	−0·20	—												
Historical changes	−0·34	0·51	—											
Public accountability	0·66	0·00	−0·25	—										
Concentration of ownership with control*	−0·40	−0·03	−0·02	−0·21	—									
Size of organization†	0·07	0·16	0·29	0·01	−0·55	—								
Size of parent organization†	0·45	−0·12	−0·10	0·51	0·29	0·43	—							
Operating variability	−0·26	−0·24	−0·16	−0·35	0·00	−0·24	−0·19	—						
Operating diversity	−0·23	0·00	0·13	−0·14	0·10	0·26	−0·10	0·02	—					
Workflow integration	−0·25	0·07	0·05	−0·35	0·00	0·08	−0·09	0·57	0·33	—				
Labor costs	0·41	−0·24	−0·31	0·34	−0·09	−0·28	0·08	−0·27	0·01	−0·50	—			
No. of operating sites	0·14	−0·07	−0·08	0·34	−0·20	−0·14	0·16	−0·56	−0·05	−0·58	0·16	—		
Dependence	0·53	−0·32	−0·38	0·53	−0·50	−0·17	0·63	0·05	−0·19	−0·05	0·26	0·05	—	
Recognition of trade unions	0·04	−0·04	−0·11	0·17	−0·21	0·36	0·37	0·19	0·01	0·21	−0·15	−0·12	0·22	—

* N = 42 for all correlations with this variable.
† Logarithm of number of employees.

Contextual variables

Origin and history

An organization may have grown from a oneman business over a long period of time, or it may have been set up as a branch of an already existing organization and so develop rapidly. During its development it may have undergone many or few radical changes in purpose, ownership, and other contextual aspects. An adequate study of the impact of these factors on organizational structure must be conducted on a comparative longitudinal basis (Chandler, 1962); but even in a cross-sectional study such as this, it is possible to define and make operational three aspects of this concept.

Impersonality of origin. This variable distinguishes between entrepreneurial organizations, personally founded, and bureaucratic ones founded by an existing organization. Impersonally founded organizations might be expected to have a higher level of structuring of activities, whereas personally founded organizations would have a higher degree of concentration of authority. The data on the present sample, however, show no relationship between impersonality of origin and structuring of activities ($r = -0.04$), but a strong relationship between impersonality of origin and concentration of authority ($r = 0.64$). (With $N = 46$, all correlations 0.29 and above are at or beyond the 95 per cent level of confidence.) To a considerable extent this relationship is due to the fact that government-owned, and therefore impersonally founded, organizations tend to be highly centralized. Such organizations tend to be line controlled in their workflow, thus contributing to the relationship ($r = 0.36$) between impersonality of origin and line control of workflow. The lack of relationship with structuring of activities, which is common to all three scales of this dimension, underlines the need to examine present contextual aspects in relation to this factor rather than historical ones.

Age. The age of the organization was taken from the time at which the field work was carried out. The range in the sample varied from an established metal goods manufacturing organization, founded over 170 years previously, in 1794, to a government inspection department, which began activities in the area as a separate operating unit twenty-nine years previously. No clear relationship was found between age and impersonality of origin ($r = -0.20$). Stinchcombe (1965) has argued that no relationship should be expected between the age of an organization and its structure but rather between the structure of an organization and the date that its industry was founded. The present data support this conclusion in that no relationship is found between age and structuring of activities ($r = 0.09$) or line control of workflow ($r = 0.02$). Age was related to concentration of authority ($r = -0.38$), older organizations having a tendency to be more decentralized and to have more autonomy.

Historical changes. The organizations in this sample did not have adequate historical information on the extent of contextual changes for use in a cross-sectional investigation; but it was possible to obtain limited information as to whether particular changes had occurred, and thus to develop a scale for the *types* of contextual changes that had occurred, namely whether at least one change had occurred in the location of the organization, in the product or service range offered, and in the pattern of ownership. Item analysis carried out using the Brogden–Clemens coefficient (Brogden, 1949) gave a mean item-analysis value of 0.85, suggesting that it was possible to produce a scale of historical changes by summing the items. The organizations were distributed along the scale from no changes to all three types of changes. As expected, there was a strong correlation of this scale with age ($r = 0.51$), older organizations tending to have experienced more types of change. There was also a strong relationship, perhaps mediated by age, between historical changes and concentration of authority ($r = -0.45$), such changes being associated with dispersion of authority.

Ownership and control

The differences in structure between a department of the government and a private business will be due to some extent to the different ownership and control patterns. Two aspects of this concept, public accountability and the relationship of the ownership to the management of the organization were investigated. For wholly owned subsidiary companies, branch factories, local government departments, etc., this form of analysis had to be applied to the parent institution exercising owning rights, in some cases through more than one intermediate institution, e.g. committees of the corporation, area boards, parent operating companies, which were themselves owned by holding companies, etc. The ultimate owning unit is referred to as the 'parent organization'.

Public accountability. This was a three-point category scale concerned with the degree to which the parent organization – which could, of course, be the organizational unit itself, as it was in eight cases – was subject to public scrutiny in the conduct of its affairs. Least publicly accountable would be a company not quoted on the stock exchange; next, organizations that raised money publicly by having equity capital quoted on the stock exchange, also public cooperative societies; and most publicly accountable were the departments of the local and central government. On the basis of the classical literature on bureaucracy as a societal phenomenon, it might be hypothesized that organizations with the greatest exposure to public accountability would have a higher degree of structuring of activities, and a greater concentration of authority. The data on the present sample show relationships more complicated than this, however.

First, it must be emphasized that although this sample included eight government departments, all the organizations had a nonadministrative purpose, which could be identified as a workflow (Pugh, *et al.*, 1968, Table 1). This is not surprising in this provincial sample, since purely administrative units of the requisite size, i.e. employing more than 250 people, are few outside the capital. The relationships between public accountability and structure must be interpreted in the light of this particular sample.

No relationship was found between public accountability and structuring of activities ($r = -0.10$). This structuring factor applies to the workflow as well as administrative activities of the organization, and it appears that government organizations with a workflow are not differentiated from nongovernment organizations on this basis. On the other hand there was a positive relationship between public accountability and concentration of authority ($r = 0.63$), standardization of procedures for selection and advancement ($r = 0.56$) and line control of workflow ($r = 0.47$). These all point to centralized but line-controlled government workflow organizations (Pugh *et al.*, 1969). The scale of standardization was a bipolar one, and a high score meant that the organization standardized its procedures for personnel selection and advancement, and also that it did *not* standardize its procedures for workflow. The relationship between public accountability and this standardization scale suggests that the government workflow organizations standardize their personnel procedures, but rely on professional line superordinates for workflow control.

Relationship of ownership to management. The concepts of Sargent Florence (1961) were found most fruitful in studying this aspect of ownership and control, but the method used was the selection of variables for a correlational approach, rather than classification on the basis of percentages. Florence studies the relationships of shareholders, directors, and executives. Where these groups were completely separate there was full separation of ownership, control, and management; where they were the same, then ownership, control and management coalesced. Between these two extremes, the scales were designed in the present study to measure the degree of separation. Company records and public records were examined and five scales developed for the patterns of shareholding and the relationships between the ownership and the management of the organization. For the four foreign-owned organizations in the sample, this information was not available in England; the analysis was therefore based on $n = 42$ (Table 4). A sixth scale was developed for interlocking directorships; that is, the percentage of directors who held other directorships outside the owning group. The intercorrelation matrix of these six variables suggested that factor analysis would be helpful in summarizing an extensive analysis of ownership (Table 5). A principal-components analysis was thus applied to the matrix and a large first factor accounting for 56 per cent of the variance was extracted, which was heavily loaded on all variables except interlocking directorships and was therefore termed 'concentration of ownership with control'.

As would be expected, there was a negative relationship between public accountability and concentration of ownership with control ($r = -0.51$); the more publicly accountable the owner-

Table 4 Ownership and Control (N = 42)

Scale number and title		Range %	Mean	SD
12.01	Concentration of voteholdings (percentage of equity owned by top twenty shareholders)	0–100	38·47	32·37
12.03	Voteholdings of individuals (percentage of individuals among top twenty shareholders)	0–100	17·19	26·89
12.04	Directors among top twenty voteholders (percentage of directors among top twenty shareholders)	0–100	20·69	29·39
12.05	Directors' voteholdings (percentage of equity owned by all directors combined)	0–99·9	9·40	19·61
12.06	Percentage of directors who are executives	0–100	46·11	32·73
12.09	Interlocking directorships (percentage of directors with other directorships beyond owning organization)	0–100	45·22	33·73

ship, the less concentrated it was, with central and local government ownership epitomizing diffuse ownership by the voting public.

Table 5 Ownership and Control: Intercorrelation Matrix (Product-Moment Coefficients, N = 42)

	Concentration of voteholdings	Voteholdings of individuals	Directors among top twenty voteholders	Directors' voteholdings	Percentage of directors who are executives	Interlocking directorships
Concentration of voteholdings	—					
Voteholdings of individuals	0·62	—				
Directors among top twenty voteholders	0·54	0·87	—			
Directors' voteholdings	0·55	0·90	0·78	—		
Percentage of directors who are executives	0·26	0·30	0·37	0·20	—	
Interlocking directorships	0·32	0·03	0·04	0·09	0·33	—

The discussion about the effects of differing patterns of personal ownership on organizations and society originated with Marx, and has since polarized into what Dahrendorf (1959) has called the 'radical' and 'conservative' positions. It is generally agreed that there has been a progressive dispersion of share ownership following the rise of the corporation, but there is little agreement, or systematic evidence, on the effects of this. The radicals (Burnham, 1962; Berle and Means, 1937) argue that present ownership patterns have produced a shift in control away from the entrepreneur to managers, who become important because of their control over the means of production and the organization of men, materials and equipment. The result then of dispersion of ownership is likely to be dispersion of authority. However, the conservatives (Mills, 1956; Aaronovitch, 1961) argue that the dispersion of capital ownership makes possible the concentration of economic power in fewer hands, because of the inability of the mass of shareholders to act, resulting in a concentration of authority.

The results obtained with this sample support neither of these positions. The correlation given in Table 2 of concentration of ownership with control with concentration of authority ($r = -0.29$) might suggest that concentration of ownership is associated with dispersion of authority; but it must be remembered that this correlation is obtained for the whole sample, which includes government-owned organizations, whereas the discussion of the effects of ownership patterns has been concerned entirely with private ownership. When the government organizations were extracted from the sample, the correlation disappeared ($r = -0.08$ for $N = 34$). No relationships were found between the structure of an organization and the ownership pattern of its parent organization. This lack of relationship is quite striking, particularly in view of the extent of the correlation found with other contextual variables. Since ownership and control seemed to have its impact through the degree of public accountability, and the other variables did not have an additional effect, there seemed to be grounds for not proceeding with them in a multivariate analysis.

Size

There has been much work relating size to group and individual variables, such as morale and job satisfaction, with not very consistent results (Porter and Lawler, 1965). With few exceptions, empirical studies relating size to variables of organization structure have confined themselves to those broad aspects of the role structure which are here termed 'configuration' (Starbuck, 1965). Hall and Tittle (1966), using a Guttman scale of the overall degree of perceived bureaucratization obtained by combining scores on six dimensions of Weberian characteristics of bureaucracy in a study of twenty-five different work organizations, found a small relation between their measurement of perceived bureaucratization and organization size ($\tau = 0.252$ at the 6 per cent level of confidence).

In this study the aspects of size studied were number of employees, net assets utilized, and number of employees in the parent organizations.

Number of employees and net assets. It was intended that the sample be taken from the population of work organizations in the region employing more than 250 people, but the sample ranges from an insurance company employing 241 people to a vehicle manufacturing company employing 25,052 (mean 3370; standard deviation 5313). In view of this distribution, it was felt that a better estimate of the correlation between size and other variables would be obtained by taking the logarithm of the number of employees (mean 3.12; standard deviation 0.57).

'Net assets employed by the organization' was also used, because financial size might expose some interesting relationships with organization structure that would not appear when only personnel size was considered. The sample ranged from under £100,000 – an estimate for the government inspection agency whose equipment was provided by its clients – to a confectionery manufacturing firm with £38 million. The attempt to differentiate between these two aspects of size proved unsuccessful, however, as the high correlation between them ($r = 0.78$) shows. Taking the logarithm of the two variables raised the correlation ($r = 0.81$). For this sample, therefore, a large organization was big both in number of employees and in financial assets. The logarithm of the number of employees was therefore taken to represent both these aspects of size.

The correlation between the logarithm of size and structuring of activities ($r = 0.69$) lends strong support to descriptive studies of the effects of size on bureaucratization. (This correlation may be compared with that between actual size and structuring of activities, $r = 0.56$, to demonstrate the effects of the logarithmic transformation.) Larger organizations tend to have more specialization, more standardization and more formalization than smaller organizations. The *lack* of relationship between size and the remaining structural dimensions, i.e. concentration of authority ($r = -0.10$) and line control of workflow ($r = -0.15$) was equally striking. This clear differential relationship of organization size to the various structural dimensions underlines the necessity of a multivariate approach to context and structure if oversimplifications are to be avoided.

Indeed, closer examination of the relationship of size to the main structural variables underlying the dimension of concentration of authority (Pugh *et al.*, 1968, Table 4) points up a limitation in the present approach, which seeks to establish basic dimensions by means of factor analysis. As was explained in that paper, the structural factors represent an attempt to summarize a large amount of data on a large number of variables to make possible empirically based comparisons. But the cost is that the factor may obscure particular relationships with the source variables which it summarizes. For some purposes, therefore, it may be interesting to examine particular relationships. The lack of relationship between size and concentration of authority, for example, summarizes (and therefore conceals) two small but distinct relationships with two of the component variables. There is no relationship between size and autonomy ($r = 0.09$), but there is a negative relationship between size and centralization ($r = -0.39$), and a positive one between size and standardization of procedures for selection and advancement ($r = 0.31$). The relationship with centralization has clear implications for the concept of bureaucracy. Centralization correlates *negatively* with all scales of structuring of activities except one: the more specialized, standardized and formalized the organization, the *less* it is centralized. Therefore on the basis of these scales, there can be no unitary bureaucracy, for an organization that develops specialist offices and associated routines is decentralized. Perhaps when the responsibilities of specialized roles are narrowly defined, and activities are regulated by standardized procedures and are formalized in records, then authority can safely be decentralized. Pugh *et al.* (1969) discuss the interrelationship of the structural variables in particular types of organization.

Size of parent organization. This is the number of employees of any larger organization to which the unit belongs. The literature on bureaucracy often implies that it is the size of the larger parent organization that influences the structure of the sub-unit. The important factor about a small government agency may not be its own size, but that of the large ministry of state of which it is a part. Similarly, the structure of a subsidiary company may be more related to the size of its holding company. The number of employees in the parent organizations ranged from 460 to 358,000 employees. The size of the parent organization correlated positively, after logarithmic transformation, with structuring ($r = 0.39$) and concentration of authority ($r = 0.39$) but not with line control of workflow ($r = -0.07$). The classical concept of bureaucracy would lead to the hypothesis that the size of the parent organization would be highly correlated with structuring of activities and concentration of authority, therefore the support from this sample was relatively modest. The correlation with structuring ($r = 0.39$) is much lower than the correlation of *organization* size and structuring ($r = 0.69$). The impact of the size of an organization is thus considerably greater than the size of the parent organization on specialization, standardization, formalization, etc. But a relationship with concentration of authority is not found with organization size ($r = -0.10$). Thus large groups have a small but definite tendency to have more centralized subunits with less autonomy. This relationship would be partly due to the government-owned organizations, inevitably part of large groups, which were at the concentrated end of this factor.

Charter

Scales. Institutional analysts have demonstrated the importance of the charter of an organization, that is, its social function, goals, ideology and value systems in influencing structure and functioning (Parsons, 1956; Selznick, 1949). To transform concepts which had been treated only descriptively into a quantitative form that would make them comparable to other contextual aspects, seven ordered category scales were devised. Four of them characterized the purpose or goal of the organization in terms of its 'output', the term being taken as equally applicable to products or services:

1. Multiplicity of outputs – ranging from a single standard output to two or more outputs.

2. Type of output – a manufacturing-service dichotomy.

3. Consumer or producer outputs or a mixture of both.

4. Customer orientation of outputs – ranging from completely standard outputs to outputs designed entirely to customer or client specification.

Three scales were devised for ideological aspects of charter:

5. Self-image – whether the ideology of the organization as indicated by slogans used and image sought emphasized the qualities of its outputs.

6. Policy on multiple outputs – whether the policy was to expand, maintain or contract its range of outputs.

7. Client selection – whether any, some, or no selectivity was shown in the range of customers or clients served by the organization.

Table 6 gives the details of the seven scales and Table 7 the intercorrelation matrix between them. This suggested that factor analysis would be helpful in summarizing the data, and a principal components analysis applied to the matrix gave the results shown in Table 8.

Operating variability. This factor, accounting for 30 per cent of the variance, was highly loaded on the variables, consumer or producer outputs, customer orientation of outputs, and type of output. It was therefore conceptualized as being concerned with manufacturing nonstandard producer goods as against providing standard consumer service. The manufacturing producer end of the scale was linked with an organizational emphasis on self-image, whereas the consumer service end emphasized outputs. The scale was therefore constructed by a weighted summing of

Table 6 Charter

Distribution N = 46	Score	Scale number and title
		Scale no. 14·02 *Multiplicity of outputs*
19	1	Single output with standard variations
8	2	Single output with variations to customer specification
19	3	Two or more outputs
		Scale no. 14·03 *Type of output*
14	1	Service (nonmanufacturing)
32	2	Manufacturing (new physical outputs in solid, liquid or gaseous form)
		Scale no. 14·04 *Type of output*
16	1	Consumer (outputs disposed of to the general public or individuals)
7	2	Consumer and producer
23	3	Producer (outputs disposed of to other organizations which use them for, or as part of, other outputs)
		Scale no. 14·06 *Customer orientation*
11	1	Standard output(s)
7	2	Standard output(s) with standard modifications
6	3	Standard output(s) with modification to customer specification
22	4	Output to customer specification
		Scale no. 14·07 *Self-image*
24	1	Image emphasizes qualities of the *organization itself*
6	2	Image emphasizes both the organization and the output
16	3	Image emphasizes qualities of the *output* of the organization
		Scale no. 14·08 *Policy on outputs multiplicity*
5	1	Contracting the range of outputs
26	2	Maintaining the range
15	3	Expanding the range
		Scale no. 14·09 *Ideology: client selection*
28	1	No selection, any clients supplied
14	2	Some selection of clients
4	3	Clients specified by parent organization

the scores on all these variables – the weighting being necessary to equate the standard deviations – and then standardizing the

Table 7 Intercorrelation Matrix (Product-Moment Coefficients, N = 46)

	Multiplicity of outputs	Service–manufacturing	Consumer–producer	Customer orientation	Self-image	Client selection	Expansion–contraction of range
Multiplicity of outputs	—						
Service manufacturing	0·15						
Consumer–producer	0·05	0·37	—				
Customer orientation	0·38	0·18	0·59	—			
Self-image	−0·05	−0·17	−0·33	−0·13	—		
Client selection	−0·14	−0·02	0·28	−0·04	−0·18	—	
Expansion–contraction of range	0·07	−0·14	−0·09	0·07	0·10	−0·09	—

sums to a mean of fifty and a standard deviation of fifteen. This produced the range of scores on the scale given in Table 9. The

Table 8 Charter: Principal-Components Analysis

	Factor loading	
Scales	Operating variability*	Operating diversity†
Consumer–producer output	0·85	0·16
Customer orientation of outputs	0·74	−0·41
Type of output (service manufacturing)	0·57	0·00
Self-image	−0·52	−0·34
Multiplicity of outputs	0·37	−0·66
Client selection	0·23	0·66
Expansion–contraction of range	−0·15	−0·48

* Percentage of variance = 30 per cent.
† Percentage of variance = 20 per cent.

lower scores distinguished organizations giving only a standard service, e.g. teaching, transport, retailing, from organizations (with high scores) producing nonstandard producer outputs to customer specification, (metal goods firm, engineering repair unit, packaging manufacturer, etc.), with those organizations having a standard output range in the middle.

Table 9 Operating Variability

Number of organizations N = 46	Score	Type of organization
1	48	Component manufacturer
6	45	Two metal goods manufacturers Component manufacturer Abrasives manufacturer Packaging manufacturer Glass manufacturer
2	43	Printer Repairs for government department
4	42	Two component manufacturers Motor component manufacturer Metal motor component manufacturer
2	41	Vehicle manufacturer Engineering tool manufacturer
1	40	Component manufacturer
3	37	Civil engineering firm Carriage manufacturer Metal goods manufacturer
3	36	Vehicle manufacturer Confectionery manufacturer Local authority water department
2	35	Motor-tire manufacturer Commercial vehicle manufacturer
4	34	Motor component manufacturer Non-ferrous metal manufacturer Research division Food manufacturer
3	33	Engineering component manufacturer Domestic appliances manufacturer Local authority civil engineering department
1	32	Component manufacturer
2	31	Government inspection department Toy manufacturer
3	30	Brewery Insurance company Food manufacturer
1	27	Local authority transport department
6	25	Local authority baths department Co-operative chain of retail stores Chain of retail stores Savings bank Chain of shoe repair stores Department store
1	23	Omnibus company
1	21	Local authority education department

Operating diversity. This factor of charter, accounting for 20 per cent of the variance, emphasized multiplicity of outputs, policy on whether to expand the range of kinds of outputs, client selection and self-image. The more diversely operating organizations were a glass manufacturer, a metal manufacturer and a brewery; the more restricted were a motor component manufacturer, a domestic appliance manufacturer and a scientific inspection agency.

Eisenstadt (1959), Parsons (1956), Selznick (1949, 1957), Wilson (1962), and Clark (1956) have discussed the effects of the goals of an organization on its structure, but there has been almost no detailed empirical work on the actual relationship between goals and structure. Selznick (1949) showed how the goal of democracy led to decentralization in the TVA, and also suggested that the role structure of an organization is the instittional embodiment of its purpose. Wilson (1962) suggested a relationship between goals and methods of recruitment and means of selection. Clark (1956) as well as Thompson and Bates (1957) emphasized both the marginality and the degree of concreteness of the goal as a determinant of the direction of organizational adaptation. Blau and Scott (1962) made one of the few attempts to classify organizations by their goals, suggesting that internal democracy goes with mutual benefit goals, efficiency with business goals, a professional structure with service goals and bureaucratic structure with commonweal goals.

Scales of organizational charter were related to structure, and operating variability was shown to be strongly associated with line control of workflow ($r = -0.57$). Thus the more an organization is concerned with manufacturing nonstandard producer goods, the more it relies upon impersonal control of workflow; the more it is providing a standard consumer service, the more it uses line control of its workflow through the supervisory hierarchy. Organizations showing operating diversity, however, tended to be more structured in activities ($r = 0.26$) and more dispersed in authority ($r = -0.30$).

Technology

Scales. Technology has come to be considered increasingly important as a determinant of organizational structure and functioning, although comparative empirical studies of its effects on structure are few, mainly case studies on the effects on the operator's job and attitudes (Walker, 1962). Thompson and Bates (1957), however, compared a hospital, a university, a manufacturing organization and a mine for the effects of their technologies on the setting of objectives, the management of resources and the execution of policy. The main work on the classification of technology in relation to organization structure has been that of Woodward (1965). She related mainly 'configuration' aspects of the structure of manufacturing organization, e.g. number of levels of authority, width of spans of control, to a classification of their production systems according to the 'controlability and predictability' of the process.

In the present study the need to develop suitable measurements of overall organizational technology made the level of generality achieved by the Woodward classification desirable; but the need to develop concepts of technology that applied to all the organizations in the sample precluded the direct adoption of that scale. A full account of the development of scales of technology and their relationship to organization structure is given in Hickson, *et al.* (1969). Only the scales included in the present analysis are described here.

Technology is here defined as the sequence of physical techniques used upon the workflow of the organization, even if the physical techniques involve only pen, ink and paper. The concept covers both the pattern of operations and the equipment used, and all the scales developed are applicable to service as well as to manufacturing organizations. Five scales of related aspects of technology were developed.

Thompson and Bates (1957) defined the 'adaptability' of the technology as 'the extent to which the appropriate mechanics, knowledge, skills and raw materials can be used for other products' and, it may be added, services. An attempt to operationalize some aspects of this definition is given in Table 10, which shows a scale of *workflow rigidity*. This consists of eight biserial items concerned with the adaptability in the patterns of operations; for example, whether the equipment was predominantly multi-purpose or single-purpose, whether rerouting of work was possible, etc. Since this was a scale of composite items, item analysis was used to test the scaleability. The mean item analysis value of 0·84 indicates that it is legitimate to add the scores on these items to form a workflow rigidity score for an organization.

Table 10 Scale of Workflow Rigidity

Item	Number of organizations (N = 52)†	Item analysis value*
No waiting time possible (versus waiting time)	8	0·82
Single-purpose equipment (versus multi-purpose)	13	0·78
Production or service line (versus no set line)	42	1·00
No buffer stocks and no delays possible (versus buffer stocks and delays)	9	0·71
Single-source input (versus multisource input)	12	0·67
No rerouting of work possible (versus rerouting possible)	15	0·80
Breakdown stops all workflow immediately (versus not all workflow stops)	6	0·97
Breakdown stops some or all workflow immediately (versus no workflow stops)	35	0·95

* Mean item analysis value = 0·84.
† Since this is a test of internal consistency and scaleability, the whole group of fifty-two organizations was used (Pugh *et al.*, 1968).

Two other scales of technology utilized the concepts outlined by Amber and Amber (1962). They postulated that 'the more human attributes performed by a machine, the higher its automaticity' and compiled a scale of automaticity together with clear operational definitions, which could be applied to any piece of equipment from a pencil to a computer, and which categorized each into one of six classes. The two scales based on these concepts were: the *automaticity mode*, i.e. the level of automaticity of the bulk of the equipment of the organization; and the *automaticity range*; i.e. the highest-scoring piece of equipment an organization used, since every organization also scored the lowest possible by using hand tools and manual machines.

The fourth scale, *interdependence of workflow segments*, was a scale of the degree of linkage between the segments of an organization; a segment being defined as those parts into which the workflow hierarchy was divided at the first point of division beneath the chief executive. The three points on the scale were: segments duplicated in different locations, all having the same final outputs; segments having different final outputs, which are not inputs of other segments; and segments having outputs which become inputs of other segments. The final scale, *specificity of criteria of quality evaluation*, was a first attempt to classify the precision with which the output was compared to an acceptable standard. The three points on the scale were: personal evaluation only; partial measurements of some aspect(s) of the output(s); measurements used over virtually the whole output, to compare against specification (the 'blueprint' concept).

Correlations. As expected, these measures tend to be highly intercorrelated. A principal components analysis extracted a large first factor accounting for 58 per cent of the variance, with loadings of over 0.6 on all scales, and of over 0.8 on three of them. A scale of *workflow integration* was therefore constructed by summing the scores on the component scales. Among organizations scoring high, with very integrated, automated and rather rigid technologies, were an automobile factory, a food manufacturer and a swimming baths department. Among those scoring low, with diverse, nonautomated, flexible technologies, were retail stores, an education department and a building firm.

There were no clear relationships between workflow integration and the variables of size, origin and history, or concentration of ownership with control and negative relationship with public accountability ($r = -0.35$), largely because the government-owned organizations in the sample were predominantly service and therefore at the diverse end of the workflow integration scale. The correlations between workflow integration and operating variability ($r = 0.57$) and diversity ($r = 0.33$) reflect the close relationship between the ends of the organization and the means it employs to attain them.

Workflow integration showed modest but distinct correlations with all the three structural factors, the only contextual variable to do so, as can be seen from Table 2. The relationships of technology are therefore much more general than is the case with size, for example, which has a greater but more specific effect. The positive correlation between workflow integration and structuring of activities ($r = 0.34$) would be expected since highly integrated and therefore more rigid technologies would be associated with a greater structuring of activities and procedures. Similarly, the correlation with concentration of authority ($r = -0.30$) suggests that because of the increasing control resulting directly from the workflow itself in an integrated technology decisions tend to become more routine and can be decentralized. But the fact that the correlations are not higher than this emphasizes that structuring may be related to other contextual factors, such as size. The relationship of technology to line control of workflow, however, was very clear ($r = -0.46$); the more integrated the technology, the more the reliance on impersonal control. It must be emphasized, however, that these relationships were found on the whole sample of manufacturing and service organizations. When manufacturing organizations only were considered, some of the relationships showed considerable change (Hickson *et al.*, 1969).

Labor costs. This is a second related, but conceptually distinct, aspect of the technology of the workflow and is expressed as a percentage of total costs. The range in the sample was from 5 to 70 per cent, with engineering organizations scoring low and public services high. The scale correlated with workflow integration ($r = -0.50$), high integration being associated with reduced labor costs. Its correlations with the structural factors are comparable with those for technology, after adjusting the signs.

Location

The geographical, cultural and community setting can influence the organization markedly (Blau and Scott, 1962). This study controls for some of these effects in a gross way, for all organizations of the sample were located in the same large industrial conurbation, and the community and its influence on the organizations located there were taken as given (Duncan *et al.*, 1963). Compared with the national distribution, the sample was overrepresented in the engineering and metal industries, and unrepresented in mining, shipbuilding, oil refining and other industries. Because of the location, however, regional cultural differences of the sort found by Thomas (1959) as to role conceptions, were avoided.

One aspect of location which discriminated between organizations in the sample, was *number of operating sites*. The range formed a Poisson distribution, with 47 per cent of the sample having one site; but six organizations had over a hundred sites, and two over a thousand. This distribution did not appear to be a function of size ($r = 0.14$) but of the operating variability aspect of charter ($r = -0.56$). Manufacturing organizations were concentrated in a small number of sites (the largest number being nine), whereas services range across the scale. The number of operating sites was therefore correlated with the workflow integration scale of technology ($r = -0.58$), and with public accountability ($r = 0.34$), this last correlation reflecting the predominantly service function of the group of government-owned organizations.

This pattern of inter-relationships among the contextual variables led to the expectation of relationships between number of operating sites and the structural dimensions which would be congruent with those of operating variability and workflow integration. The correlations of number of operating sites with structuring of activities ($r = -0.26$), concentration of authority ($r = 0.39$) and line control of workflow ($r = 0.39$) confirm the relationships with charter and technology, and suggest a *charter–technology–location* nexus of interrelated contextual variables having a combined effect on structure.

Dependence

The dependence of an organization reflects its relationships with other organizations in its social environment, such as suppliers, customers, competitors, labor unions, management organizations and political and social organizations.

Dependence on parent organization. The most important relationship would be the dependence of the organization on its parent organization. The *relative size* of the organization in relation to the parent organization was calculated as a percentage of the number of employees. This ranged from under 1 per cent in two cases – a branch factory of the central government, and a small subsidiary company of one of the largest British private corporations in the country – to 100 per cent in eight independent organizations. The distribution was Poisson in form with a mean and standard deviation of 37 per cent. The next scale was a four-point category scale concerned with the *status* of the organization in relation to the parent organization:

1. Principal units (eight organizations) where the organization was independent of any larger group although it might itself have had subsidiaries or branches.

2. Subsidiary units (eighteen organizations) which, although part of a larger group, had their own legal identity with, for example, their own boards of directors.

3. Head branch units (four organizations) which did not have separate legal identity although they were the major operating components of the parent organization and the head office of the parent organization was on the same site.

4. Branch units (sixteen organizations) operating parts of a parent organization which did not satisfy the preceding criteria.

The third aspect of the relation between the organization and the parent organization was given by the degree of *organizational representation on policy-making bodies*. This three-point scale ranged from the organization being represented on the policy-making body of the parent organization, e.g. board of directors, city council, through the organization being represented on an intermediate policy-making body, e.g. board of directors of an operating company but not of the ultimate owning holding company, committee of the city council, to the organization having no representative on any policy-making body of the parent organization. As would be expected, these three variables were highly correlated (Tables 11, 12).

A related variable was the number of *specializations contracted out* by the organization. In many cases these would be available as services of the parent organization to the organization, although account as also taken of the various specialist services, e.g. consultants, used outside the parent organization. The specializations were as defined in the structural scale of functional specialization (Pugh *et al.*, 1968, Appendix A), and ranged from one specialization contracted out – two engineering works, a printer and a builder – to no less than fifteen of the sixteen specializations contracted out – an abrasives manufacturer and a packaging manufacturer – with a mean 7·2 and standard deviation 4·0.

Dependence on other organizations. The suppliers and customers or clients of the organization must also be considered. The operating function of the organization can be regarded as being the processing of inputs and outputs between supplier and client, and the degree to which the organization is integrated into the processual chain by links at either end can be measured. Five category scales were developed to elucidate this concept (with details given in Table 11). They were concerned with the integration with suppliers and clients, and response in the output volume to client influence, etc. To establish a single dimension measuring the degree to which the organization was integrated into this system, the five scales were transformed into biserial form. Item analysis was carried out on the eighteen-item scale generated and yielded a mean item analysis value of 0·70, which seemed to justify the addition of the items into a total scale, *vertical integration.* At one extreme was a confectionery manufacturer and an engineering components firm supplying goods from stock with a large number of customers after obtaining their supplies from a large variety of sources; at the other extreme were organizations – vehicle components, civil engineering, scientific research – obtaining their resources from a small number of suppliers and supplying their product or service to a small number of clients, often the owning group only, who had a marked effect upon their workflow scheduling.

For *trade unions* a scale of five ordered categories was developed of the extent to which unions were accepted as relevant to the activities of the organization. The scale was: no recognition

Table 11 Dependence

Distribution N = 46	Score	Scale number and title
		Scale no. 18.07 *Relative size** Range = 0–100 Mean = 37·4 SD = 37·3
		Scale no. 12.10 *Status of organization unit*
16	1	Branch
4	2	Head branch (headquarters on same location)
18	3	Subsidiary (legal identity)
8	4	Principal unit
		Scale no. 12.11 *Organizatinal representation on policy-making bodies†*
19	1	Organization not represented on top policy-making body
		Organization represented on local policy-making body
4	2	but not on top policy-making body
23	3	Organization represented on policy-making body
		Scale no. 18.06 *Number of specializations contracted out‡* Range = 1–16 Mean = 7·2 SD = 4·0
		Scale no. 18.17 *Vertical integrations§* Range = 1–16 Mean = 7·7 SD = 3·5
		Scale no. 18.03 *Integration with suppliers*
4	1	No ownership ties and single orders
7	2	No ownership and single contracts or tenders
8	3	No ownership and short-term contracts, schedule and call-off
6	4	No ownership and yearly contracts, standing orders
7	5	Ownership and contractual ties
14	6	Ownership and tied supply
		Scale no. 18.05 *Response in outputs volume to customer influence*
12	1	Outputs for stock
5	2	Outputs for stock and to customer order
21	3	Outputs to customer order
2	4	Outputs to customer order and to schedule and call-off
6	5	Outputs to schedule and call-off
		Scale no. 18.08 *Integration with customers: type of link with customers*
24	1	Single orders
9	2	Regular contracts
10	3	Long-term contracts (over two years)
3	4	Ownership

Distribution N = 46	Score	Scale number and title
		Scale no. 18.09 *Integration with customers: dependence of organization on its largest customer*
30	1	Minor outlet (less than 10% of output)
10	2	Medium outlet (over 10% of output)
3	3	Major outlet (over 50% of output)
3	4	Sole outlet
		Scale no. 18.10 *Integration with customers: dependence of largest customer on organization*
11	1	Minor supplier (less than 10% of particular item)
5	2	Medium supplier (over 10% of particular item)
21	3	Major supplier (over 50% of particular item)
9	4	Sole supplier with exclusive franchise

* Size of unit as a percentage of size of parent organization.
† Internal and parent organizations.
‡ The specializations are those of functional specialization (Pugh *et al.*, 1968, Appendix A). Scores are out of a possible sixteen.
§ This scale is formed by the total of the scores on the eighteen items representing the following five scales: 18.03, 18.05, 18.08, 18.09, 18.10.

given, only partial recognition given (i.e. discussions for certain purposes, but not negotiations); full recognition given to negotiate on wages and conditions of service on behalf of their members; full recognition given plus facilities for union meetings to

Table 12 Dependence: Intercorrelation Matrix (Product-Moment Coefficient ($N = 46$))

	Relative size	Status of organization unit	Organizational representation on policy-making body	Specializations contracted out	Vertical integration	Trade unions
Relative size	—					
Status of organization unit	0·68	—				
Organizational representation on policy-making body	0·50	0·65	—			
Specializations contracted out	−0·60	−0·51	−0·52	—		
Vertical integrations	−0·40	−0·34	−0·36	0·45	—	
Trade unions	−0·09	−0·16	−0·25	0·19	0·28	—

be held regularly on the time and premises of the organization; as in the preceding plus the recognition of a works convenor to act on behalf of all unions with members in the organization.

Organizations in the sample were located in all the categories, with the modal position being full recognition; but five organizations did not recognize unions, and eleven gave the maximum recognition including a works convenor.

Examination of the intercorrelations between these six variables of dependence (Table 12) and of their correlations with other important aspects of context (Table 13) shows considerably higher correlations with size of parent organization than with size of organization, and considerably higher correlations with concentration of ownership with control (a variable applied to the parent organization) than with operating variability or workflow integration (variables applied to the operations of the individual organizations themselves). This pattern lends support to the view that these measures are tapping aspects of the dependence of the organization, particularly its dependence on external resources and power as in Eisenstadt's (1959) formulation. The one exception was the variable of recognition of trade unions, which had its largest contextual correlation with organization size, and is therefore concerned with a different aspect of interdependence. Impersonality of origin (from origin and history) and public accountability (from ownership and control) show the same pattern of higher correlation with the parent organization than with the unit, indicating that impersonally founded organizations are likely to be more dependent on their founding organizations; and that more publicly accountable organizations are more likely to be dependent on outside power with government-owned organizations being the extreme case.

These relationships suggested the application of factor analysis to a correlation matrix containing the seven variables. A principal-components analysis applied to the matrix produced a large first factor *dependence*[2] accounting for 55 per cent of the variance, which was heavily loaded on all seven scales (on six of the seven, the loadings were above 0·7; the remaining loading on vertical integration was 0·58). The scores for dependence were obtained by an algebraic weighted sum of the scores on the four most highly loaded component scales, the weightings being obtained

2. We are grateful to our colleague Diana C. Pheysey for suggesting this formulation and for much valuable critical comment on an earlier draft of this paper.

by a multiple regression analysis of the component scales on the factor. A high score characterized organizations with a high degree of dependence, which tended to be impersonally founded, publicly accountable, vertically integrated, with a large number of specializations contracted out, small in size relative to their parent organization, low in status, and not represented at the policy-making level in the parent organization, e.g. branch units in packaging civil engineering, and food manufacture, a central government repair department, and a local government baths department. Organizations with low dependence were independent organizations characterized by personal foundation, low public accountability, little vertical integration, few specializations contracted out, and where the parent organization was the organization itself, e.g. a printing firm, the very old metal goods firm, a chain of shoe repair stores, and an engineering component manufacturer.

The correlation of dependence with the structural factors was focused largely on concentration of authority ($r = 0.66$), in every case, for dependence and its component scales the correlation being much greater than with the other factors, as Table 13 shows. Indeed, apart from the correlations with impersonality of origin and public accountability, none of the other correlations reached the 5 per cent level of confidence. Dependent organizations have a more centralized authority structure and less autonomy in decision making; independent organizations have more autonomy and decentralize decisions down the hierarchy.

The relationships between dependence and the component scales of concentration of authority vary. Centralization, as defined and measured in this study, is concerned only with the level in the organization which has the necessary authority to take particular decisions (Pugh *et al.*, 1968, p. 76); the higher the necessary level, the greater the centralization. No account was taken of the degree of participation or consultation in decision-making as in Hage and Aiken's (1967) formulation of the concept. These were regarded as aspects for study at the group level of analysis. Neither is it possible for such a statement as the following to hold: 'The decisions were centralized on the foreman since neither the superintendent nor the departmental manager had the necessary experience.' In the present formulation this would be

Table 13 Dependence

	Concentration of ownership with control	Size of parent organization†	Operating variablity	Workflow integration	Size of organization	Structuring of activities	Concentration of authority	Line control of workflow
Status of organization unit	0·45	−0·27	0·01	0·05	0·17	0·13	−0·63	−0·07
Organizational representation on policy-making bodies	0·41	−0·19	−0·01	0·19	0·20	0·14	−0·63	−0·18
Number of specializations contracted out	−0·32	0·40	0·11	0·09	0·01	0·18	0·53	0·00
Relative Size	0·47	−0·38	−0·08	−0·03	0·16	0·03	−0·40	−0·13
Vertical integration	−0·15	0·39	0·21	−0·12	−0·06	0·06	0·29	−0·04
Trade unions*	−0·21	0·25	0·19	0·21	0·36	0·51	0·08	−0·35
Impersonality of origin	−0·40	0·36	−0·26	−0·25	0·07	−0·04	0·64	0·36

Public accountability of parent organization	−0·51	0·45	−0·35	−0·35	0·01	−0·10	0·63	0·47
Dependence	−0·50	0·37	0·05	−0·05	−0·17	−0·05	0·66	0·13

* This variable was not included in the scale of dependence.

† In this table, the size of the parent organization was not logarithmically transformed.

regarded as relative decentralization. Autonomy was measured by the proportion of decisions that could be taken within the organization as distinct from those which had to be taken at the level above it. Thus independent organizations of necessity had more autonomy since there was no level above the chief executive, and the correlation between dependence and this component of concentration of authority was $r = -0.72$. The relation of centralization (which is concerned with the whole range of levels in the hierarchy) with dependence is less, but still high ($r = 0.57$). Dependent organizations also have a distinct tendency to standardize the procedures for selection and advancement ($r = 0.40$), a major component of concentration of authority. So dependent units have the apparatus of recruitment routines, selection panels, formal establishment figures, etc., of their parent organizations.

Relation between structure and context

In this investigation of the relationship of organization structure to aspects of the context in which the organization functions, the use of scaling and factor analytic techniques has made possible the condensation of data and reorganization of concepts and has

Table 14 Salient Elements of Context (Product-Moment Correlations with Structural Factors)*

Elements of context	Structuring of activities	Concentration of authority	Line control of workflow
Age	—	−0·38	—
Size of organization†	0·69	—	—
Size of parent organization†	0·39	0·39	—
Operating variability	—	—	−0·57
Operating diversity	—	−0·30	—
Workflow integration	0·34	−0·30	−0·46
Number of operating sites	—	0·39	0·39
Dependence	—	0·66	—

* With $N = 46$, correlations of 0·29 are at the 5 per cent level of confidence, and correlations of 0·38 are at the 1 per cent level of confidence.
† Logarithm of number of employees.

established eight distinctive scales of elements of context. These scales, shown in Table 14 together with their correlations with the structural dimensions, denote the variables that are salient among those which have been thought to affect structure. Relationships between structure and age, size, charter (operating variability, operating diversity), technology (workflow integration), location (number of operating sites) and dependence on other organizations are exposed by the correlations. At the same time the correlations raise questions about the relationship between ownership pattern and administrative structure.

The multivariate prediction of structure from context

From inspection of Table 14 and of the intercorrelation matrix in Table 3, certain elements of context can now be identified. The variables in Table 14 are now used as independent variables in a prediction analysis of the structural dimensions. The pattern of these correlations, that is, that where they are high they are specific, and where they are low, they are diffused, indicates that the predictions should be attempted on a multivariate basis. In this case consideration had to be given to choosing not only predictors with high correlations with the criterion, but also having low intercorrelations among themselves. If high intercorrelations among the predictors were allowed, then, since the high correlations with the criterion would be aspects of the same relationship, the multiple correlation would not be increased to any extent. If the intercorrelations between the predictors were low, then each would make its distinct contribution to the multiple correlation.

These problems can be illustrated from the attempt to obtain a multiple prediction of structuring of activities from the three contextual variables correlated with it (Table 14). Size is clearly the first predictor, with a correlation of $r = 0.69$, and the question is whether taking account of size of parent organization and workflow integration will increase predictive accuracy. In spite of its greater correlation with the criterion, the size of the parent organization would be expected to make a smaller contribution to the prediction than workflow integration, since it has a strong correlation with the first predictor ($r = 0.43$); whereas the technology measure is not correlated with organization size ($r = 0.08$). This is in fact the case as shown in the first section of Table 15, which gives the multiple prediction analyses for the three structural factors.

Table 15 shows for each predictor variable, the single correlation with the criterion, the multiple correlation obtained by adding this predictor to the preceding ones, the F ratio corresponding to the increase obtained on the addition of this predictor, the degrees of freedom corresponding to the F ratio when $N = 46$,

Table 15 Multiple Prediction Analysis of Structural Factors

Contextual predictors of structural factors	Single correlation	Multiple correlation	F ratio	Degrees of freedom	Level of confidence
Structuring of activities					
Size	0·69	0·69	39·6	1:44	> 99%
Workflow integration	0·34	0·75	8·2	1:43	> 99%
Size of parent organization	0·39	0·76	1·9	1:42	NS
Concentration of authority					
Dependence	0·66	0·66	34·2	1:44	> 99%
Location (number of operating sites)	0·39	0·75	12·5	1:43	> 99%
Age of organization	−0·38	0·77	2·5	1:42	NS
Operating diversity	−0·30	0·78	3·0	1:41	NS
Workflow integration	−0·30	0·78	0·0	1:40	NS
Size of parent organization	0·39	0·79	0·4	1:39	NS
Line control of workflow					
Operating variability	−0·57	0·57	20·7	1:44	> 99%
Workflow integration	−0·46	0·59	1·7	1:43	NS
Number of sites	0·39	0·59	0·1	1:42	NS

and the level of confidence at which the increase due to this predictor can be quoted. It will be seen from the first section of Table 15 that the correlation 0·69, between size and structuring of activities, is increased to a multiple correlation of 0·75 when workflow integration is added as a predictor. But the multiple correlation shows no noticeable increase when size of parent organization is added as a third predictor; that is, its predictive power has already been tapped by the two previous variables.

It must be emphasized that this procedure assesses only the predictive power of the contextual variables, not their relative importance in any more general sense. It cannot be concluded that the relationship of size of parent organization to structuring of activities is less important than that of workflow integration, because it adds less to the multiple correlation. Indeed the original higher correlation shows that this is not the case. Because of the interaction of the variables, the effects of organizational size and size of parent organization are confounded, in this study, as the correlation between them shows. A full examination of their relative effects would require a sample in which they were not correlated, as is the case with the technology measure.

The same argument applies to the multiple prediction of concentration of authority (Table 15). Here again there is a clear first predictor, dependence, with a correlation of 0·66 but then a choice of intercorrelated variables. The selection was made in order to get as high a multiple correlation as possible with as few predictors as possible, but the fact that the later predictors add nothing to the multiple correlation does not mean that they have no impact, only that predictive power has been exhausted by previous related variables. The existence of the charter–technology–location nexus referred to above is supported by the fact that when any one of these variables is used as a predictor, the remaining two do not add to the multiple correlation. Table 15 shows the multiple correlation of 0·75 obtained by using the location measure together with dependence as predictors. When the technology scale of workflow integration is substituted as the second predictor, the multiple correlation is 0·71; when the operating diversity scale of charter is used, the multiple correlation is 0·70.

The prediction of line control of workflow shows this same phenomenon, where the addition of predictors, because of their interrelationships, does not improve on the original single correlation of operating variability with the criterion.

The size of the multiple correlations obtained with the first two factors, each 0·75 with two predictors, together with the small number of predictors needed, strongly supports the view that in relation to organization structure as defined and measured in this study, salient elements of context have been identified. Thus a knowledge of the score of an organization on a small number of contextual variables makes it possible to predict, within relatively close limits, its structural profile. Given information about how many employees an organization has, and an outline of its technology in terms of how integrated and automated the work process is, its structuring of activities can be estimated within fairly close limits. Since in turn the score of the organization on structuring of activities summarizes an extensive description of broad aspects of bureaucratization, the organization is thereby concisely portrayed in terms of this and similar concepts. Likewise, knowing the dependence of an organization on other organizations and its geographical dispersion over sites tells a great deal about the likely concentration of authority in its structure. *Size, technology, dependence and location* (number of sites) are critical in the prediction of the two major dimensions (structuring of activities, concentration of authority) of the structures of work organizations.

Multiple predictions of the order of magnitude obtained are as high as can be expected with this level of analysis. Higher values would imply that there were no important deviant cases, and that differences as to policies and procedures among the members of an organization have no effect on its structure. And this is obviously not so. The multiple predictions discussed here are applicable only to this sample. When the regression equations obtained are applied to another similar sample for prediction purposes, there is likely to be a reduction in the multiple correlations. The extent of this reduction can be strictly gauged only by investigating another similar sample of organizations. This cross-validation study is at present being undertaken, but a first attempt to estimate the likely amount of reduction was made by splitting the sample into two subsamples of twenty-three organizations, each stratified in the same way as the whole sample. Table 16 gives the multiple regressions on structuring of activities and concentration of authority for the whole sample and for the two subsamples separately. The multiple correlations and the weightings are of the same order of magnitude. A 'robust' prediction on the basis of simple weightings was also calculated. These correlations should be less subject to shrinkage. The stability of the correlation of 0·57 between operating variability and line control of workflow is indicated by correlations on the two subsamples of 0·50 and 0·65.

Summary and discussion

This study has demonstrated the possibilities of a multivariate approach to the analysis of the relationships between the structure of an organization and the context in which it functions. Starting from a framework as outlined in the conceptual scheme summarized in Table 1, aspects of the context and structure of the organization were sampled in order to establish scales which discriminated among organizations in a large number of aspects. From this sampling 103 primary scales of structure and context were developed as a basis for the analysis of the interrelationships among them.

Table 16 Multiple Regression on Structural Factors

Structural factors	Whole sample	Subsamples		'Robust' weightings
		1	2	
Structuring of activities				
Weightings of predictors				
Size	0·67	0·72	0·60	2
Workflow integration	0·29	0·14	0·43	1
Multiple correlation	0·75	0·73	0·79	0·74
Concentration of authority				
Weightings of predictors				
Dependence	0·64	0·50	0·77	2
Location	0·36	0·40	0·33	1
Multiple correlation	0·75	0·66	0·84	0·75

By scaling and factor analytic techniques, these were then summarized to form three basic dimensions of structure and eight salient elements of context (Table 14). The analogy with the psychological-test constructor who samples behavior in order to establish dimensions of personality is clear, and the same limitations apply. Thus while a claim can be made for the internal consistency and scaleability of these measures, no claim can be made as to the comprehensiveness with which they cover the field. This is particularly clear in the attempt to elucidate aspects of context, a concept which, although in some respects narrower than that of environment, is still very wide. Emphasis was therefore placed on those aspects of context that had been held to be relevant to structure on the basis of previous writings. The size of the multiple correlations obtained indicates that at least some of the salient aspects of context were tapped.

The predictability of the structural dimensions from contextual elements serves as external validating evidence for the structural concepts themselves. It has now been shown that besides being internally consistent and scaleable, as previously demonstrated, they can also be related in a meaningful way to external referents. Indeed the size of the correlations inevitably raises the question of causal implications. It is tempting to argue that these clear relationships are causal – in particular, that *size, dependence, and the charter–technology–location nexus largely determine structure.*

It can be hypothesized that size causes structuring through its effect on intervening variables such as the frequency of decisions and social control. An increased scale of operation increases the frequency of recurrent events and the repetition of decisions, which are then standardized and formalized (Haas and Collen, 1963). Once the number of positions and people grows beyond control by personal interaction, the organization must be more explicitly structured. In so far as structuring includes the concept of bureaucracy, Weber's observation that 'the increasing bureaucratic organization of all genuine mass parties offers the most striking example of the role of sheer quantity as a leverage for the bureaucratization of a social structure' is pertinent (Gerth and Mills, 1948).

Dependence causes concentration of authority at the apex of publicly owned organizations because pressure for public accountability requires the approval of central committees for many decisions. The similar position of small units in large privately owned groups is demonstrated by the effect that a merger may have upon authority. After a merger, a manager of the smaller unit 'may no longer be able to take a certain decision and act upon it independently. He may have to refer matters to people who were complete strangers to him a few months earlier' (Stewart *et al.*, 1963).

Integrated technology may be hypothesized to cause an organization to move towards the impersonal control end of the line-control dimension. Line control is adequate in shops or in municipal schools or building maintenance gangs, where the technology of the tasks is not mechanized and each line supervisor and primary work group is independent of all the others. But as workflow integration reaches the production line or automated stages, where large numbers of tasks are interdependent, more control is needed than can be exercised by the line of command alone. Udy (1965) summarizes this in his proposition, 'The more complex the technology . . . , the greater the emphasis on administration.'

The causal argument need not run only one way. It can be suggested that a policy of specializing roles and standardizing procedures, that is, of structuring, would require more people, that is, growth in size. Concentration of decisions in the hands of an owning group is likely to result in more economic integration among the subsidiaries concerned, that is, more dependence; while the production control, inspection and work-study procedures of staff control might raise the level of workflow integration in the technology.

But a cross-sectional study such as this can only establish relationships. Causes should be inferred from a theory that generates a dynamic model about changes over time. The contribution of the present study is to establish a framework of operationally defined and empirically validated concepts, which will enable processual and dynamic studies to be carried out on a much more rigorous and comparative basis than has been done previously. The framework is also seen as a means of controlling for organizational factors when individual and group level variables are being studied. Such studies must now be conducted with reference not only to differences in size, but also in dependence, operating function, workflow integration, etc., and with reference to the demonstrated relationship between these aspects of context and organization structure.

References

AARONOVITCH, S. (1961), *The Ruling Class*, Lawrence & Wishart.

AMBER, G. H., and AMBER, P. S. (1962), *Anatomy of Automation*, Prentice-Hall.

BAKKE, E. W. (1959), 'Concept of the social organization', in M. Haire (ed.), *Modern Organization Theory*, Wiley, pp. 16–75.

BERLE, A. A., and MEANS, G. (1937), *The Modern Corporation and Private Property*, Macmillan.

BLAU, P., and SCOTT, W. R. (1962), *Formal Organizations*, Chandler.

BROGDEN, H. E. (1949), A new coefficient: application to biserial correlation and to estimation of selective efficiency', *Psychometrika*, vol. 14, pp. 169–82.

BURNHAM, J. (1962), *The Managerial Revolution*, Penguin.

CHANDLER, A. D. (1962), *Strategy and Structure*, MIT Press.

CLARK, B. R. (1956), 'Organizational adaptation and precarious values', *Amer. sociol. Rev.*, vol. 21, pp. 327–36.

DAHRENDORF, R. (1959), *Class and Conflict in Industrial Society*, Stanford University Press.

DUBIN, R. (1958), *The World of Work*, Prentice-Hall.

DUNCAN, O. D., SCOTT, W. R., LIEBERSON, S., DUNCAN, B., and WINSBOROUGH, H. (1963), *Metropolis and Region*, Johns Hopkins University Press.

EISENSTADT, S. N. (1959), 'Bureaucracy, bureaucratization and de-bureaucratization', *Admin. Sci. Q.*, vol. 4, pp. 302–20.

FLORENCE, P. S. (1961), *Ownership, Control and Success of Large Companies*, Sweet and Maxwell.

GERTH, H. H., and MILLS, C. W. (eds.) (1948), *From Max Weber: Essays in Sociology*, Routledge & Kegan Paul.

HAAS, E., and COLLEN, L. (1963), 'Administrative practices in university departments', *Admin. Sci. Q.*, vol. 8, pp. 44–60.

HAGE, J., and AIKEN, M. (1967), 'Relationship of centralization to other structural properties', *Admin. Sci. Q.*, vol. 12, pp. 72–92.

HALL, R. H., and TITTLE, C. R. (1966), 'A note on bureaucracy and its correlates', *Amer. J. Sociol.*, vol. 72, pp. 267–72.

HICKSON, D. J., PUGH, D. S., and PHEYSEY, D. C. (1969), 'Operations technology and formal organization: an empirical reappraisal', *Admin. Sci. Q.*, vol. 14, no. 3, pp. 378–97.

HININGS, C. R., PUGH, D. S., HICKSON, D. J., and TURNER, C. (1967), 'An approach to the study of bureaucracy', *Sociology*, vol. 1, January, pp. 62–72.

INKSON, J. H., PAYNE, R. L., and PUGH, D. S. (1967), 'Extending the occupational environment: the measurement of organizations', *Occup. Psychol.*, vol. 41, pp. 33–47.

LEVY, P., and PUGH, D. S. (1969), 'Scaling and multivariate analysis in the study of organizational variables', *Sociology*, vol. 3, no. 2, pp. 193–213.

MILLS, C. W. (1956), *The Power Elite*, Oxford University Press.

PARSONS, T. (1956), 'Suggestions for a sociological approach to the theory of organizations, 1 and 2', *Admin. Sci. Q.*, vol. 1, June and September, pp. 63–85, 225–39.

PERROW, C. (1967), 'A framework for the comparative analysis of organizations', *Amer. sociol. Rev.*, vol. 32, April, pp. 194–208.

PORTER, L. W., and LAWLER E. E. III, (1965), 'Properties of organization structure in relation to job attitudes and job behavior', *Psychol. Bull.*, vol. 64, pp. 25–51.

PRESTHUS, R. V. (1958), 'Towards a theory of organizational behavior' *Admin. Sci. Q.*, vol. 3, pp. 48–72.

PUGH, D. S., HICKSON, D. J., and HININGS, C. R. (1969), 'An empirical taxonomy of structures of work organizations', *Admin. Sci. Q.*, vol. 14, no. 1, pp. 115–26.

PUGH, D. S., HICKSON, D. J., HININGS, C. R., MACDONALD, K. M., TURNER, C., and LUPTON, T. (1963), 'A conceptual scheme for organizational analysis', *Admin. Sci. Q.*, vol. 8, pp. 289–315.

PUGH, D. S., HICKSON, D. J., HININGS, C. R., and TURNER, C. (1968), 'Dimensions of organization structure', *Admin. Sci. Q.*, vol. 13, pp. 65–105.

SELZNICK, P. (1949), *TVA and the Grass Roots*, University of California Press.

SELZNICK, P. (1957), *Leadership in Administration*, Row, Peterson.

STARBUCK, W. H. (1965), 'Organizational growth and development', in J. G. March (ed.), *Handbook of Organizations*, Rand McNally [see Reading 1 of this selection].

STEWART, R., WINGATE, P., and SMITH, R. (1963), *Mergers: The Impact on Managers*, Acton Society Trust.

STINCHCOMBE, A. L. (1965), 'Social structure and organization', in J. G. March (ed.), *Handbook of Organizations*, Rand McNally, pp. 142–93.

THOMAS, E. J. (1959), 'Role conceptions and organizational size', *Amer. sociol. Rev.*, vol. 24, pp. 30–37.

THOMPSON, J. D., and BATES, F. L. (1957), 'Technology, organization and administration', *Admin. Sci. Q.*, vol. 2, pp. 323–43.

TRIST, E. L., HIGGIN, G. W., MURRAY, H., and POLLOCK, A. B. (1963), *Organizational Choice*, Tavistock.

UDY, S. H. (1965), 'The comparative analysis of organizations', in J. G. March (ed.), *Handbook of Organizations*, Rand McNally.

WALKER, C. R. (1962), *Modern Technology and Civilization*, McGraw-Hill.

WILSON, B. R. (1962), 'Analytical studies of social institutions', in A. T. Welford *et al.*, *Society: Problems and Methods of Study*, Routledge & Kegan Paul.

WOODWARD, J. (1965), *Industrial Organization, Theory and Practice*, Oxford University Press.

Further Reading

Books

M. Crozier, *The Bureaucratic Phenomenon*, Chicago University Press, 1964.

G. E. Delehanty, *Nonproduction Workers in US Manufacturing*, North-Holland, 1968.

J. Steindl, *Random Processes and the Growth of Firms*, Hafner, and Charles Griffin, 1965.

J. D. Thompson, *Organizations in Action*, McGraw-Hill, 1967.

J. Woodward, *Industrial Organization*, Oxford University Press, 1965.

Papers

M. Aiken and J. Hage, 'Organizational interdependence and intra-organizational structure', *Amer. sociol. Rev.*, vol. 33, no. 6, 1968, pp. 912–30.

H. Albach, 'Simulation models of firm growth', *German econ. Rev.*, vol. 5, no. 1, 1967, pp. 1–26.

S. W. Becker and F. Stafford, 'Some determinants of organizational success' *J. Bus.*, vol. 40, no. 4, 1967, pp. 511–18.

G. D. Bell, 'Determinants of span of control', *Amer. J. Sociol.*, vol. 73, no. 1, 1967, pp. 100–109.

V. Blankenship and R. E. Miles, 'Organizational structure and managerial decision behavior', *Admin. Sci., Q.*, vol. 13, no. 1, 1968, pp. 106–20.

P. M. Blau, 'The hierarchy of authority in organizations', *Amer. J. Sociol.*, vol. 73, no. 1, 1968, pp. 453–67.

P. M. Blau, W. V. Heydebrand and R. E. Stauffer, 'The structure of small bureaucracies', *Amer. sociol. Rev.*, vol. 31, no. 2, 1966, pp. 179–91.

E. H. Burack, 'Industrial management in advanced production systems: some theoretical concepts and preliminary findings', *Admin. Sci. Q.*, vol. 12, no. 3, 1967, pp. 479–500.

V. E. Cangelosi and W. R. Dill, 'Organizational learning: observations toward a theory', *Admin. Sci. Q.*, vol. 10, no. 2, 1965, pp. 175–203.

G. Carlson, 'Change, growth and irreversibility', *Amer. J. Sociol.*, vol. 73, no. 6, 1968, pp. 706–14.

W. S. Comanor and T. A. Wilson, 'Advertising, market structure and performance', *Rev. Econs Stat.*, vol. 49, no. 4, 1967, pp. 423–40.

M. Crozier, 'Le problème de l'innovation des organisations economiques' *Sociologie du Travail*, vol. 10, no. 1, 1968, pp. 1–12.

W. R. Dill, D. P. Gaver and W. L. Weber, 'Models and modelling for manpower planning', *Manag. Sci.*, vol. 13, no. 4, 1966, B: pp. 142–67.

T. R. Dyckman and H. O. Stekler, 'Firm size and variability', *J. indust. Econs*, vol. 13, no. 1, 1965, pp. 214–18.

P. K. Else, 'The incidence of advertising in manufacturing industries', *Oxf. econ. Paps*, vol. 18, no. 1, 1966, pp. 88–110.

L. E. Fouraker and J. M. Stopford, 'Organizational structure and the multinational strategy', *Admin. Sci. Q.*, vol. 13, no. 1, 1968, pp. 47–64.

H. M. Gitelman, 'The labor force at Waltham Watch during the Civil War era', *J. econ. Hist.*, vol. 25, no. 2, 1965, pp. 214–43.

J. Hage and M. Aiken, 'Program change and organizational properties', *Amer. J. Sociol.*, vol. 72, no. 5, 1967, pp. 503–19.

J. Haldi and D. Whitcomb, 'Economies of scale in industrial plants', *J. polit. Econ.*, vol. 75, no. 4, 1967, pp. 373–85.

M. Hall, 'Sales revenue maximization: an empirical examination', *J. indust. Econs*, vol. 15, no. 2, 1967, pp. 143–56.

M. Hall and L. Weiss, 'Firm size and profitability', *Rev. Econs Stat.*, vol. 49, no. 3, 1967, pp. 319–31.

R. H. Hall, J. E. Haas and N. J. Johnson, 'Organizational size, complexity and formalization', *Amer. sociol. Rev.*, vol. 32, no. 6, 1967, pp. 903–12.

R. H. Hall and C. R. Tittle, 'A note on bureaucracy and its correlates', *Amer. J. Sociol.*, vol. 72, no. 3, 1966, pp. 267–72.

D. J. Hickson, D. S. Pugh and D. C. Pheysey, 'Operations technology and organization structure: an empirical reappraisal', *Admin. Sci. Q.*, vol. 14, no. 3, 1969, pp. 378–97.

H. H. Jenny, 'Pricing and optimum size in a non-profit institution: the university', *Amer. econ. Rev.*, vol. 58, no. 2, 1968, pp. 270–83.

R. F. Jewett, 'A minimum task manpower schedule technique', *Manag. Sci.*, vol. 13, no. 10, 1967, B: pp. 578–92.

E. E. Kaczka and R. V. Kirk, 'Managerial climate, work groups and organizational performance', *Admin. Sci. Q.*, vol. 12, no. 2, 1967, pp. 253–72.

D. R. Kamerschen, 'The influence of ownership and control on profit rates', *Amer. econ. Rev.*, vol. 58, no. 3, 1968, pp. 432–47.

R. J. Larner, 'Ownership and control in the 200 largest nonfinancial corporations, 1929 and 1963', *Amer. econ. Rev.*, vol. 54, no. 4, 1966, pp. 777–87.

P. R. Lawrence and J. W. Lorsch, 'Differentiation and integration in complex organizations', *Admin. Sci. Q.*, vol. 12, no. 1, 1967, pp. 1–47.

R. K. Leik and M. Matthews, 'A scale for developmental processes', *Amer. sociol. Rev.*, vol. 33, no. 1, 1968, pp. 62–75.

R. E. Lucas, Jr, 'Returns to scale and the optimal growth of firms', working paper, Grad. Sch. Indust. Admin., Carnegie-Mellon University, 1965.

W. H. McWhinney, 'On the geometry of organizations', *Admin. Sci. Q.*, vol. 10, no. 3, 1965, pp. 347–63.

J. Maniha and C. Perrow, 'The reluctant organization and the aggressive environment', *Admin. Sci. Q.*, vol. 10, no. 2, 1965, pp. 238–57.

H. M. Mann, 'Seller concentration, barriers to entry, and rates of return in thirty industries, 1950–60'. *Rev. Econ. Stat.*, vol. 48, no. 3, 1966, pp. 296–307.

H. M. Mann, J. A. Henning and J. W. Meehan, Jr., 'Advertising and concentration: an empirical investigation', *J. indust. Econs*, vol. 16, no. 1, 1967, pp. 34–45.

J. K. Mann and D. E. Yett, 'The analysis of hospital costs: a review article', *J. Bus.*, vol. 41, no. 2, 1968, pp. 191–202.

M. Marcus, 'Firms' exit rates and their determinants', *J. indust. Econs*, vol. 16, no. 1, 1967, pp. 10–22.

J. R. Mayer, 'An experiment in the measurement of business motivation', *Rev. Econs Stat.*, vol. 49, no. 3, 1967, pp. 304–18.

A. E. Mills, 'Environment and size of firm', *J. Manag. Studs*, vol. 1, no. 1, 1964, pp. 1–25.

R. J. Monsen, J. S. Chiu and D. E. Cooley, 'The effect of separation of ownership and control on the performance of the large firm'. *J. Econs*, vol. 82, no. 3, 1968, pp. 435–51.

D. C. Mueller, 'The firm decision process: an econometric investigation', *Q. J. Econs*, vol. 81, no. 1, 1967, pp. 58–87.

C. Perrow, 'Hospitals: technology, structure and goals,', in J. D. March (ed.), *Handbook of Organizations*, Rand McNally, 1965, pp. 910–71.

D. S. Pugh, D. J. Hickson and C. R. Hinings, 'An empirical taxonomy of structures of work organizations', *Admin. Sci. Q.*, vol. 14, no. 1, 1969, pp. 115–26.

D. S. Pugh, D. J. Hickson, C. R. Hinings and C. Turner, 'Dimensions of organizational structure', *Admin. Sci. Q.*, vol. 13, no. 1, 1968, pp. 65–105.

S. J. Pullara and L. R. Walker, 'The evaluation of capital expenditure proposals', *J. Bus.*, vol. 38, no. 4, 1965, pp. 403–8.

R. E. Quandt, 'On the size distribution of firms', *Amer. econ. Rev.*, vol. 56, no. 3, 1966, pp. 416–32.

E. E. Raphael, 'Power structure and membership dispersion in unions', *Amer. J. Sociol.*, vol. 71, no. 3, 1965, pp. 274–83.

E. E. Raphael, 'The Anderson–Warkov hypothesis in local unions: a comparative study', *Amer. sociol. Rev.*, vol. 32, no. 5, 1967, pp. 768–76.

J. Riew, 'Economies of scale in high school education', *Rev. Econs Stat.*, vol. 48, no. 3, 1966, pp. 280–87.

W. R. Rosengren, 'Structure, policy and style: strategies of organizational control', *Admin. Sci. Q.*, vol. 12, no. 1, 1967, pp. 140–64.

W. A. Rushing, 'The effects of industry size and division of labour on administration', *Admin. Sci. Q.*, vol. 12, no. 2, 1967, pp. 273–95.

W. A. Rushing, 'Hardness of material as related to division of labour in manufacturing industries', *Admin. Sci. Q.*, vol. 13, no. 2, 1968, pp. 229–45.

S. Saltzman, 'An econometric model of a firm', *Rev. Econs Stat.*, vol. 49, no. 3, 1967, pp. 332–42.

J. M. Samuels and D. J. Smyth, 'Profits, variability of profits and firm size', *Economica*, vol. 35, no. 138, 1968, pp. 127–39.

F. M. Scherer, 'Firm size, market structure, opportunity and the output of patented inventions', *Amer. econ. Rev.*, vol. 55, no. 5, 1965, pp. 1097–1125.

E. Schwartz, 'Note on a theory of firm growth', *J. Bus.*, vol. 38, no. 1, 1965, pp. 29–33.

S. E. Seashore and E. Yuchtman, 'Factorial analysis of organizational performance', *Admin. Sci. Q.*, vol. 12, no. 3, 1967, pp. 377–95.

J. P. Shelton, 'Allocative efficiency vs. "X-efficiency": comment', *Amer. econ. Rev.*, vol. 57, no. 5, 1967, pp. 1252–8.

T. Y. Shen, 'Economies of scale, expansion path and growth of plants', *Rev. Econs Stat.*, vol. 47, no. 4, 1965, pp. 420–28.

T. Y. Shen, 'Cyclical behaviour of manufacturing plants', *J. indust. Econs*, vol. 16, no. 2, 1968, pp. 106–25.

T. Y. Shen, 'Competition, technology and market shares', *Rev. Econs Stat.*, vol. 50, no. 1, 1968, pp. 96–102.

C. G. Smith, 'A comparative analysis of some conditions and consequences of intra-organizational conflict', *Admin. Sci. Q.*, vol. 10, no. 4, 1966, pp. 504–29.

L. W. Stern and W. M. Morgenroth, 'Concentration, mutually recognized interdependence and the allocation of marketing resources', *J. Bus.*, vol. 41, no. 1, 1968, pp. 56–67.

A. L. Stinchcombe, 'Social structure and organizations', in J. D. March (ed.), *Handbook of Organizations*, Rand McNally, 1965, pp. 142–93.

S. Terreberry, 'The evolution of organizational environments', *Admin. Sci. Q.*, vol. 12, no. 4, 1968, pp. 590–613.

A. Touraine, V. Ahtik, S. Ostrowetsky-Zygel, and M. Castells, 'Mobilité des entreprises et structures urbaines', *Sociologie du Travail*, vol. 9, no. 4, 1967, pp. 369–405.

J. G. Udell, 'An empirical test of hypotheses relating to span of control', *Admin. Sci. Q.*, vol. 12, no. 3, 1967, pp. 420–39.

E. C. Venables, 'Success in technical college courses according to size of firm', *Occup. Psychol.*, vol. 39, no. 2, 1965, pp. 123–34.

W. K. Warner and A. E. Havens, 'Goal displacement and the intangibility of organizational goals', *Admin. Sci. Q.*, vol. 12, no. 4, 1968, pp. 539–55.

P. B. Warr, M. W. Bird and R. W. Hadfield, 'A study of supervisors in the iron and steel industry', *Occup. Psychol.*, vol. 39, no. 4, 1965, pp. 235–45.

L. W. Weiss, 'An evaluation of mergers in six industries', *Rev. Econs Stat.*, vol. 47, no. 2, 1965, pp. 172–81.

T. L. Whistler, H. Meyer, B. H. Baum and P. R. Sorensen, Jr, 'Centralization of organizational control: an empirical study of its meaning and measurement', *J. Bus.*, vol. 40, no. 1, 1967, pp. 10–26.

H. C. White, 'Control and evolution of aggregate personnel: flows of men and jobs', *Admin. Sci. Q.*, vol. 14, no. 1, 1969, pp. 4–11.

J. Williamson, 'Profit growth and sales maximization', *Economica*, vol. 33, no. 129, 1966, pp. 1–16.

O. E. Williamson, 'Hierarchical control and optimum firm size', *J. polit. Econs*, vol. 75, no. 2, 1967, pp. 123–38.

E. Yuchtman and S. E. Seashore, 'A system resource approach to organizational effectiveness', *Amer. sociol. Rev.*, vol. 32, no. 6, 1967, pp. 891–903.

Acknowledgements

Permission to reproduce the Readings in this volume is
acknowledged from the following sources:

1 Rand McNally and Company and (for individual passages
   within this article) American Sociological Association,
   McGraw-Hill Book Company, Houghton Mifflin Company,
   John Murray Publishers Ltd., Prentice-Hall Inc., Routledge &
   Kegan Paul Ltd, The University of North Carolina Press, The
   Macmillan Company, Massachusetts Institute of Technology
   Press, Harvard University Press, Controller of Her Majesty's
   Stationery Office, University of Washington, J. McGuire,
   C. P. Bonini, National Society for the Study of Communication,
   American Economic Association, D. G. Moore, John Wiley and
   Sons Inc., University of Chicago Press, Clarendon Press, *Harvard
   Business Review*, University of Michigan Institute for Social
   Research, *Behavioural Science*, R. M. Cyert, E. A. Feigenbaum,
   J. G. March, Plenum Publishing Company Ltd. and Organization
   for Economic Co-operation and Development
2 *Administrative Science Quarterly* and W. H. Starbuck
3 *Administrative Science Quarterly*, F. Friedlander and H. Pickle
4 University of Chicago Press, N. J. Demerath III and V. Thiessen
5 American Political Science Association and L. B. Mohr
6 Econometric Society
7 *Academy of Management Journal*
8 *Administrative Science Quarterly* and L. Pondy
9 *Administrative Science Quarterly*, D. S. Pugh, D. Hickson,
   C. R. Hinings and C. Turner

Author Index

Subject Index